Unmeasured Information and the Methodology of Social Scientific Inquiry

Unmeasured Information and the Methodology of Social Scientific Inquiry

by

Donald W. Katzner
University of Massachusetts

KLUWER ACADEMIC PUBLISHERS
Boston / Dordrecht / London

Distributors for North, Central and South America:
Kluwer Academic Publishers
101 Philip Drive
Assinippi Park
Norwell, Massachusetts 02061 USA
Telephone (781) 871-6600
Fax (781) 871-6528
E-Mail <kluwer@wkap.com>

Distributors for all other countries:
Kluwer Academic Publishers Group
Distribution Centre
Post Office Box 322
3300 AH Dordrecht, THE NETHERLANDS
Telephone 31 78 6392 392
Fax 31 78 6546 474
E-Mail <services@wkap.nl>

Electronic Services <http://www.wkap.nl>

Library of Congress Cataloging-in-Publication Data

Katzner, Donald W.
Unmeasured information and the methodology of social scientific inquiry / Donald W. Katzner
p. cm.
Includes bibliographical references and index.
ISBN 0-7923-7336-7 (alk. paper)
Social sciences--Methodology
H61 .K29 2001
300/.7/2--dc21 01-029937

Printed on acid-free paper.

Printed in the United States of America

Contents

Preface vii

1. Introduction: Science, Social Science, and Measurement 1

PART 1: Methodology

2. Our Mad Rush to Measure: How Did We Get into this Mess? 27

3. In Defense of Formalization in Economics 47

4. On Not Quantifying the Non-Quantifiable 61
   Reply to Brennan 77
   Letter to the Editor 81

5. Notions of Closeness in a Non-Quantifiable Setting 83

6. The Role of Formalism in Economic Thought, with Illustration Drawn from the Analysis of Social Interaction in the Firm 113

7. Institutionally Determined Parameters in Economic Equations 157

8. The Misuse of Measurement in Economics 175

9. Analysis with Ordinal Measurement 197

PART II: Applications

10. Effort and Efficiency in the Neoclassical Firm 219

11. The Efficiency of Organizational Forms 231

12. Attitudes, Rationality, and Consumer Demand 253

13. Political Structure and System and the Notion of Logical Completeness 275

14. The Formal Structure of Argument in Professor Apter's *Choice and the Politics of Allocation* 281

Index 299

Preface

I have three reasons for bringing out the ensuing collection of essays. First, since analysis without measurement (this is generally not the same thing as what is commonly referred to as "qualitative methods" or "qualitative research" in the social science literature) is a relatively new scholarly endeavor, I am striving to enhance its visibility by attracting a wider audience than what would normally be possible with single, narrowly-focused essays published in scattered journals. Second, several of these essays may, in the minds of potential readers, appear to have been published in places that, if not obscure, are at least inconvenient to locate. Collecting them in a single anthology, then, will help to increase their accessibility. Third, I am trying to suggest, as strongly as I can, that analysis without measurement is a viable intellectual enterprise that ought to be taken seriously in social science. This last point will clearly be enhanced if the whole that follows turns out, as I hope and suspect it does, to be greater than the sum of its parts. All the same, each reader will have to judge for himself or herself the extent to which I have, through the present collection, successfully made the case for taking up analysis without measurement.

The partitioning of these essays into two groups is somewhat, though by no means completely arbitrary. The organizational intention was that Part I should focus on the methodology of analyzing phenomena that are, at least to a significant extent, incapable of measurement, and Part II should show how that methodology can be applied in specific cases. However, although Part II contains only applications, Part I incudes more than what a narrow characterization of methodology would normally entail. For example, Essays 5 and 6 incorporate applications that are intended to enhance and illustrate specific aspects of the methodology, and Essays 8 and 9 suggest the kinds of things that can go wrong when the lack-of-measurement problem that the methodology attempts to address is ignored and the phenomenon under investigation is improperly taken to be quantified. With two main exceptions, the essays of Part I are arranged roughly in order of "decreasing" generality. That is, the more philosophical and methodological tends to precede the theoretical and more concrete. The two main exceptions are the summaries of the essays presented in the second half of the introductory essay, and the historical survey of Essay 2. The applications in Part II are all theoretical in nature. (That of Essay 5 mentioned above is empirical. A more substantial empirical application appeared as *Choice and the Quality of Life* (Beverly Hills: SAGE, 1979) and is not republished here). All essays in both parts are self contained and can be read in any order. Thus, for example, a reader primarily interested in the analytical particulars of the methodology and its operationality might start with Essay 4 and then immediately skip to any one of the essays of Part II.

In preparing this anthology, I have attempted to correct all typographical and other errors that I could find in the original publications. I have also made minor changes to enhance the consistency of the argument and the unity of the vision that I am trying to present. Where papers have been revised from what was originally published, the names of persons who contributed to those revisions have been added to the original footnotes that acknowledged assistance received. I am most grateful for the help given me on both the original publications and their subsequent revisions. The individual who is most frequently recognized in these footnotes is Douglas Vickers. Beyond his role in developing numerous specific essays as affirmed in the footnotes, I would like, in addition, to express my thanks here for his general encouragement and support over many, many years.

It should also be stated that I have not made any attempt to eliminate the relatively small amount of overlap both between these essays and the material already published in *Analysis without Measurement* (Cambridge University Press, 1983), and among several of the essays themselves. This is because I believe that the first and third goals described above are more likely to be achieved if the anthology as a unit, as well as each of the essays it contains, stand on their own. Regardless, the few places where the reader may encounter something previously read in the anthology that follows are mostly identified in the introduction and, in all cases, are easily skipped.

1
Introduction: Science, Social Science, and Measurement[1]

Science, as practiced by physicists, chemists, biologists, and other physical scientists, is, no doubt, one of our most successful and respected intellectual enterprises. Clearly, in the case of science, success and respect have been intertwined with each other. On the one hand, science is looked up to because of its ability to explain and predict, and because, as a result, it is the primary reason for an enormous extension of, and improvement in, the quality of life that many human beings lead. Medical and biological sciences have provided cures for numerous diseases and adequate food for expanding populations. Other segments of physical science (together with the technological developments they have spawned) have given us central heating, refrigeration, the automobile, plastics, television, the computer, and much, much more. Thus success has bred respect. On the other hand, respect has brought increased funding into science along with the resources those funds provide, and it has encouraged many individuals to take up science as a career. Respect has therefore resulted in the expansion of scientific activity which, in turn, has brought forth more success. So pervasive and penetrating has been the combination of suc-

[1] Thanks are due to Andy B. Anderson, Jonathan Barrett, Peter Haas, Randall G. Stokes, and Douglas Vickers for their generous help in preparing this essay.

cess and respect that it has led, in some quarters, to the glorification of science. Both those who practice it and scientific work itself are frequently held in the highest esteem. It is no wonder, then, that social science has often attempted to cloak itself in the mantle of science.

But is social science really science? That, of course, depends on what is meant by the term "science". Unfortunately, however, several centuries of philosophical argument have failed to provide an exhaustive, universal prescription that fully characterizes science. Indeed, with the abandonment in the middle of the twentieth century of such comprehensive schemes as positivism and falsificationism, meaning by the latter that science is concerned virtually exclusively with the disproof of hypotheses, some philosophers seem to have become content to limit their discussions to describing the properties of "good" science. In this vein, Kincaid [13], for example, while retaining a place for the testing and potential falsification of hypotheses, takes a broader view. Science, he claims [13, p. 21], is an activity that generally "... promotes ... knowledge and truth." For him, good science not only contains falsifiable statements, but it also fits data accurately, its scope is wide, it coheres within itself and with established knowledge from outside its purview, it is successful in obtaining useful information, and it is objective in so far as human beings are capable of objectivity. Good science also is subjected to tests. These tests must be capable of testing specific, isolated hypotheses, of ruling out competing hypotheses, and of making sure that it is the data that lead to the acceptance or rejection of the hypotheses and not the background assumptions, or the conditions of the environment in which the test is conducted. Finally, the explanations of good science are either causal in nature or show how diverse phenomena fit into common patterns.[2] Kincaid's purpose is to defend the social sciences, and the thrust of his argument is that, pressed against these standards, social science can be, and often is, good science.

Yet, even if one accepts the still-controversial proposition that social science can be good science, it is nevertheless necessary to admit that there are numerous differences between social science and the clearly more successful and more highly respected physical sciences. (A few of the successes of the latter were mentioned at the outset.) The significance of some of these differences is more contentious than that of others. In the case of social science, the objects of study are human activities and relations among human beings rather than actions of, and relations among, non-sentient and unmotivated physical entities. This means that the ontological status of humanity necessarily pervades social science inquiry. Now, generally speaking, there are two different interpretations of human existence. On the one hand, individuals may be per-

[2] Kincaid [13, pp. 50-55].

ceived as being totally constituted by the material pieces (e.g., neurons and other cells, molecules, atoms, etc.) of which they are made up. From this vantage point, which may be referred to as philosophical materialism, if enough were known about the properties of these material pieces (including the ways in which they interact with other material pieces both within and outside of the individual), then a person's behavior in any situation could be determined with a high degree of accuracy from a careful examination of his material characteristics and his environment. A parallel assertion could be made with respect to the behavior of an institution which is, from the perspective of philosophical materialism, fully comprised of the people who form it.

On the other hand, it may be thought that human beings have cognitive capacities that go beyond, and are not solely determined by, their material parts. That is, knowing all of the material facts about a person is not sufficient to explain his behavior. This implies that, in relation to the world in which human beings live and act, only the experiencing of things and events can directly interact with those extra-material cognitive capacities, since the material pieces cannot go that far. Of course, due to the individual's continually changing knowledge and circumstances, the interactions with respect to things and events can happen in any particular way only once, only when the individual makes intellectual contact with them, and only in the order in which those contacts actually occur. All mental processes, regardless of whether they relate to material or non-material elements, together with whatever knowledge has been accumulated, necessarily contribute to the making of an individual's decisions. It follows that experience and its orderly interaction with the extra-material capacities become of major significance in the generation of human behavior.

This latter view of the ontological status of mankind has many immediate consequences, five of which may be noted here: First is the fact that time cannot always be conceived in terms of the idea of "logical" time that physical science has generally assumed to be appropriate for investigating the physical world.[3] That is, the relevant notion of time in social science is often "historical" time, or that which is actually experienced by human beings, in which each moment in history is unique, and in which time reversals (such as the restarting of a differential equation) are not possible.[4] A second consequence

---

[3] Logical time orders events in sequence of occurrence without regard to the manner in which these events are experienced in reality as past events, present events, and future events. For a more complete discussion of the differences between this and the notion of historical time introduced next, see Katzner [11, pp. 5-8].

Of course, in some areas of physical science, for example in geology and in the dating of fossils, the passing of historical time bears importantly on analysis and conclusions.

[4] To expand, in part, on the uniqueness idea, Vickers [20, p. 7] has characterized the human

is that change in the world of human beings has a different flavor, including far less foreseeable regularity, than change in the physical world. Here the deliberative actions and reactions of sentient individuals taking place amid the uncertainties created by change are of paramount importance. And this becomes all the more significant when it is recognized that, given existing knowledge, change may not necessarily be even remotely predictable and may be produced instead by unanticipated irregularities and shocks. Third, because the objects of study in social science relate to human activities and relations, the less-than-perfect knowledge possessed, that is, the considerable ignorance of the individuals in question, along with the meanings and interpretations they hold, have to be taken into account. Fourth, for the same reason, motivations such as rationality, or the drive to achieve the best result based on the contemplation of imagined possible outcomes in the absence of full knowledge, become an important part of explanation in social science. And fifth, to the extent that physically identical persons have distinct experiences, interpretations of them, and hence knowledge, their motivations and behavior in identical situations can differ markedly. Thus, where one individual may be propelled by the desire to be rational, another might be directed by religious codes or cultural traditions. Of course, the middle three consequences on this list also have relevance when the individual is regarded as the sum of his material parts alone. But clearly, the interpretation of human behavior in these respects depends on the commitment or otherwise to philosophical materialism. Regardless, in the physical as distinct from social sciences, neither knowledge, ignorance, meanings and interpretations, nor motivations driving actions exist in relation to the objects of study.

At least two additional distinctions between the physical and social sciences arise less directly from, though not completely independently of, the humanity, or absence thereof, that is present in the objects of study. Both have significance regardless of whether the individual is taken to have a cognitive capacity that is independent of his material parts. One is that social scientists do not have nearly as much control as do physical scientists of the things that need to be held fixed in "laboratory experiments". All experimentation, indeed, more generally, all attempts at corroboration with observed phenomena in all endeavor that strives to be scientific, rest on *ceteris paribus* requirements. And many of these are extremely difficult, if not impossible, to enforce in social science. Finally, it is often easier to measure the elements of physical phenom-

condition in historical time as one with (a) a discontinuous epistemological status, in that what the individual knows at each moment is unique (it depends on all that he has experienced before), and (b) a continuous ontological status because there is no modification, even across historical time, of his personhood.

ena than those relating to social phenomena. More often than not, appropriate scales on which to measure salient and potentially decisive social science variables do not even seem to exist. Issues and problems associated with this last matter will be addressed at length in this and in subsequent essays.

Differences like these have opened the door to specific philosophical debates. One perspective from which to enter such discussions, and one that will be seen to bear in various ways on the significance of the essays of this volume, is to ask about the extent to which epistemological parity obtains between the physical and the social sciences. Now epistemology is concerned with such things as the origins of, the processes of creation of, the nature of, the limits of, and the validity and usefulness of knowledge. That is, it has to do with the source, the meaning, and the force of explanation. Explanation, in turn, has two parts: the thing being explained and the explanation of it. The former consists of the objects of inquiry; the latter is derived in terms of relations between those objects. Questions relating to the presence or absence of epistemological parity between two discourses, then, would necessarily focus on comparisons of the properties taken to exist in their respective objects of inquiry, and also on comparisons of the general character of the relations employed in their explanation.

Thus, to investigate whether social science attains epistemological parity with physical science, it is necessary to examine questions like (i) What is the origin and the method of formation of hypotheses about the objects of inquiry and relations among them in the social sciences? (ii) What is the quality of, and the meaning of, the knowledge obtained upon subjecting those hypotheses to empirical tests? (iii) What is the potential usefulness of that knowledge in explaining and predicting the behavior of human beings and groups of human beings? And (iv), to what extent, if at all, is investigation in social science more vulnerable to the intrusion of the values of the investigator than in physical science? In spite of the fact that the objects of inquiry in social science are sentient beings, while those in physical science are not, epistemological parity between the two would still be established if it could be demonstrated, among other things, that hypotheses in social science are provoked by universes of observation with the same characteristics as those in the physical sciences, that the testing of those hypotheses permits the construction of meaningful explanations of past events, and that the definitions of objects of inquiry in social science, and the analytical structures created to examine them, are sufficiently stable over time that conclusions formed on the basis of testing can be extrapolated into the future. In addition, it would need to be shown that human values do not interfere in the construction of explanation in social science any more than in physical science.

Now, it has already been suggested that, to date, social science has not been nearly as successful in contributing to human betterment as physical science, nor (probably as a consequence) has it been viewed with even remotely similar respect. This could be attributed to the relative infancy of the subject as a systematic intellectual discipline or, accepting the view that human beings are more than the sum of their material parts, it could be accounted for by citing the possibility that while the actual laws governing the physical universe (though known only in part to mankind) are immutable, those directing human behavior are always subject to change. But it might also, in part, have something to do with an absence, in certain regards, of epistemological parity of social science with physical science which may or may not be potentially correctable. Were that to be the case, once the reasons for the lack of parity are investigated and exposed, it might become possible, by removing some of the obstacles that are capable of elimination, to push social science epistemologically closer to physical science. To the extent that this could be accomplished, social science might then produce better explanation and more useful results. It would therefore become a more successful endeavor and, under those circumstances, the respect accorded to it might be considerably enhanced.

Not surprisingly, the question of epistemological parity between the physical and social sciences, like the question of whether social science is science, is unresolved and controversial. In covering themselves and their work with the aura of science, many practitioners of social science have suggested or implied complete epistemological parity. For example, it may easily be inferred from Lundberg [14, pp. 24,25], a sociologist, that sociology has no choice but to "follow the rough road" that the physical sciences have pursued. A similar inference for political science may be drawn from Deutsch [4, pp. 7,8]. And according to Hutchison [6, p. 38], some economists have suggested an epistemological parity between economics and physics that would "... render the methodological analysis, prescriptions, strategy or tactics, derived from one ... entirely appropriate, almost without qualification or reservation, to the other ...." But many other social scientists have dissented.[5] Moreover, both support for, and opposition to, this view can be found among philosophers in their discussions, for example, about the role of meanings, interpretations, and mo-

[5] See, for example, Andreski [2, pp. 20-23], a representative of sociology, Ricci [16, pp. 286, 294-298] in political science, and Hutchison [7, p. 141] in economics. Campbell [3] and Toulmin [19, pp. 504-508] suggest alternative approaches to epistemology itself that, if accepted, would place the question of epistemological parity between physical and social science in a different light.

tivations (rationality) in social science analysis.[6]

To give some idea of how the existence of epistemological parity of social science with physical science can be considered further and possibly refuted, three examples among many of the issues that could be raised are considered below. These are, in turn, the status of laws, the corroboration of statements, and the problem of measurement.[7] It should be emphasized, however, that numerous social scientists and philosophers do not accept the position on the status of laws set out below, where emphasis is given to the role of historical time in social science inquiry. This historical-time perspective on laws, although it provides a reasonable basis for the essays that follow, is included here primarily for illustrative purposes to clarify the notion of epistemological parity. Indeed, the essays that follow, though set in a logical time context, are largely independent of the attitude taken towards time, and their analytical significance does not turn exclusively on the conception of time that may be assumed to be relevant.

In physical science, a law is a universal statement that, while it establishes a cause and effect relation and provides a basis for explanation and prediction, is independent of any specific object to which it applies, and is also independent of time and place. It is generally accepted that, for example, the law of gravity in physics meets these requirements. But, with regard to social science, and from the perspective that the individual has a cognitive capacity that goes beyond the sum of his material parts, it has been argued by Shackle [17], [18, Ch. 7], Vickers [20], and others, that the historical time environment in which human beings (both the objects of study as well as the investigator himself) live rules out the possibility of ever having knowledge of future human behavior. Only activities that have occurred in the past or are currently unfolding can (however imperfectly) be known. The actions of individuals, groups, and institutions that are yet to come cannot. And not only is the future unknown to humans; it is also unknowable. This absence of knowledge of the future, their argument goes on, precludes the specification of all probabilities of future events, subjective or otherwise, that relate to human behavior. On this view, an individual, for example, being a unique person and with unique knowledge at each moment of time, cannot say today what action he will take tomorrow because he does not know (even probabilistically) the conditions that will exist when tomorrow arrives, nor does he know how he himself will change in the interim. More generally, it is not possible to know in advance if any structure

[6] See, for example, the essays in Parts III and IV of the anthology put together by Martin and McIntyre [15].

[7] Further discussion relating to laws and corroboration may be found in, respectively, Martin and McIntyre [15, Pt. II], and Kincaid [13, Ch. 3].

in place one day will still exist in the same form, or even exist at all, the next. For decisions and activities that are taken today create the structures, unknown today, that will stand tomorrow. Thus, for example, before the collapse of the Soviet Union, an astute observer might have been able to determine that that country was in serious trouble. He might even have been able to spin various scenarios depicting possible paths that the Soviet Union might have followed. But he would not have been able to predict, in the usual scientific sense of the term, its demise. In general, then, with such pervasive uncertainty about the future, prediction is neither tenable nor possible. Its untenability and impossibility arise from the general instability of structures over time and from the fact that actions in the present necessarily create an unknowable future. Indeed, structures that might form the basis of such predictions have been likened to the images in a kaleidoscope in their ability to dissolve "at a touch".[8]

Accepting such an outlook in the conduct of inquiry, laws in the social sciences, unlike those in the physical sciences, cannot be projected into the future. Of course, one of the main reasons for establishing laws in the physical sciences is to achieve a degree of explanation that permits prediction. But in the social sciences, explanation to the same degree and prediction of the same kind cannot be achieved. Laws in social science only apply to, and are relevant, for the past and present. They are not, therefore, independent of time, and the quality of the knowledge they entail is insufficient for them to be used predictively as in physical science. It follows that, at least in this one respect, social science does not achieve epistemological parity with the physical sciences.[9]

Consider, next, the issue of corroboration. Laboratory experimentation is usually the primary method of corroborating statements in the physical sciences. Such experiments, as pointed out above, are always conducted under appropriate *ceteris paribus* conditions. That is, standard experimental procedures invariably involve the holding of a specified number of variables fixed while the explanatory competence of other variables is investigated. Of course, the *ceteris paribus* can never be complete even in physical science. And this means that any unexplained variance may be due to the omission of explanatory variables which have not be impounded in the *ceteris paribus*. Even so, without the ability to hold enough of the necessary variables fixed, laboratory corroboration would break down. But in the social sciences, it is often diffi-

[8] Shackle [18, p. 42].

[9] The argument could also be made that, because individuals from different cultures can be motivated differently, the laws of social science are also not independent of place (Katzner [12]). This would provide a further reason, were the argument accepted, for a lack of epistemological parity between social and physical science.

cult to meet this standard and even to ensure that the most significant of the requisite *ceteris paribus* conditions are actually enforced. For example, suppose the behavior of an individual is thought to be rationally determined by his preferences. To corroborate this hypothesis, the characteristics of that person's behavior as revealed in repeated observations of it need to fit certain patterns. But since each observation is taken at a different moment in time, and since the individual's preferences exist only in his mind and are not, given the present state of social science, known to the investigator, any observation that contradicts the required pattern can always be explained away as a consequence of preferences that have changed through time. That is, the impossibility of knowing, as a practical matter, if the *ceteris paribus* restriction of fixed preferences is in play while observations are taken precludes the drawing, with any degree of certainty, of inferences relating to the individual's motivations from observations of his behavior. This particular problem has to do with the possible lack of homogeneity of a certain variable (in the present case, preferences) across time, and it arises from the sentientness of the object of inquiry. It is also independent of the approach taken (the two possibilities have been described earlier) with respect to the ontological status of humanity. Alternatively, when dealing with data collected by government agencies, it is hard to determine exactly what remained constant, if anything at all, during the data-gathering process. This means that the quality of knowledge provided by the testing of social science laws derived from past observations is not the same as that furnished by tested physical science laws. That is, there is more uncertainty attached to social science laws, and they are less reliable as elements of explanation. Corroboration, then, is a second area in which the social sciences seem to lack epistemological parity with the physical sciences.

Finally, there is the problem of measurement. Numerous yardsticks developed over many centuries such as rulers, balances, columns of mercury, etc., provide the means for at least cardinally (or intervally) measuring a broad variety of variables in the physical sciences. These measures are, by and large, generally accepted and widely used. They are also meaningful both in terms of the logical structure upon which measurement generally rests and in terms of the use to which the numbers that represent measurements are normally put. There can be little doubt that the ability to measure precisely at the cardinal or ratio level has played a major role in the successes enjoyed by the physical sciences.

But as has been remarked previously, measures like these are simply not available in many areas of social science. There are no generally accepted and appropriate yardsticks available for calibrating such abstract variables as freedom, honesty, culture, and enterprise. And, at present, in most cases there do not seem to be any good ideas of how to proceed in constructing scales on which they can be meaningfully and at least cardinally measured.[10] Indeed, and without ignoring the many empirical techniques that have been developed to handle unquantified variables (such as, for example, tests for association, the use of dummy variables in regression analysis, and the so-called logit model[11]), the lack of ability to measure is so endemic in the social sciences that numerous unquantified elements thought to be important are either represented by dubious but scalable "proxies,"[12] or excluded from analyses altogether. And numerous analyses themselves are not even undertaken because they involve the unmeasurable in decisive ways. These measurement difficulties point to a seemingly further departure from epistemological parity of social science with physical science in at least two respects: First, the use of proxy variables can only, at best, reduce what might have been hoped for as the accuracy and relevance of the explanation produced by the analysis in question. At worst, it can render that analysis completely devoid of explanatory importance. For the use of a proxy implies the assumption of a stable relation between the thing that is desired to be measured and the proxy (see Essay 8 below). And this assumption, which introduces knowledge where none formerly existed, is often not justified in reality. Second, rephrasing questions to avoid unquantified variables, or ignoring such questions and variables entirely, leads to the creation of a less significant, less distinguished, and less useful body of knowledge than would otherwise be the case. In either circumstance, the quality of knowledge produced by social science apparently cannot measure up to the quality of knowledge fashioned by physical science and, as is the result in the other instances of failure to achieve epistemological parity with physical science described above, the efficacy and success of social science does not seem

---

[10] In the earlier stages of the development of economics, it was thought that "utility" provided a cardinal measure of individual pleasure and pain. This derived from the well-known pleasure-pain calculus of Bentham's utilitarianism, and was endorsed by Jevons [8, Ch. 3] in 1871. In due course, however, economists came to the realization that utility actually measured pleasure and pain only ordinally.

To cite another illustration, while political scientists more or less agree on some of the structures or properties that cardinal measures of, say, political power should have (see, for example, Alker [1, pp. 197-206]), there is no general consensus on the particular measures that ought to be employed.

[11] These and a few others are described in Analysis without Measurement [10, Chs. 12,13]. See also Essay 4 in this volume.

[12] Measures (or exact measures) are numbers that are generally accepted as calibrating exactly what they are intended to calibrate. Proxies are inexact measures that everyone agrees do not gauge exactly what is supposed to be gauged, but are used as "approximations" or representations anyway because exact measures are not available.

to be able to match that of physical science.

The apparent lack of epistemological parity arising from the inability to measure in the social sciences is an especially serious matter, and it is that issue that is submitted to intensive investigation in the essays of this volume. For in the twentieth century, mankind has become more fixated on numbers and measures than at any time in the past. Society at large seems to have accepted the idea that for purposes of public discussion, knowledge requires measurement. To repeat one popular refrain, "We simply have to be able to measure in order to know were we stand and if we are making progress." Academics, too, have fallen into line, measuring success by numbers of publications and numerical student evaluations of classroom performance. Indeed, matters have progressed to the point at which, according to Eberstadt [5, p. 1], "... mankind lives under a tyranny of numbers" that is both injurious and enslaving, and likely to become worse.

The second (i.e., the next) essay in the present collection ("Our Mad Rush to Measure: How Did We Get into this Mess?") traces back to antiquity the emergence of today's emphasis on measurement. That essay argues, however, that the first major turn in a direction favoring quantification did not come until the work of Galileo during the seventeenth century which emphasized, largely for the first time, relations among variables, experimentation, and measurement. The movement toward measurement continued apace at the rate to which it was brought by Galileo until the great acceleration of the twentieth century when it became dominant in public discourse. That dominance was brought about by the creation of a myth, namely, that objective science and measurement were synonymous, and also by the enormous growth of scientific activity itself and the accompanying far-reaching spread of quantitative scientific knowledge into the popular culture. Regardless, as a consequence of the current fixation on numbers and measures, social science, with its inability to measure so many of its fundamental variables, looks even worse to its practitioners and to the public. The apparent failure to achieve epistemological parity in this respect is often regarded as a black eye that is a major obstacle to success and respect in social science.

None of this discussion of the measurement issue is meant to belittle the significance of the status of laws and the difficulty of corroboration in social science as barriers to the achievement of epistemological parity with physical science. But the ability, or potential ability, to overcome the impediments that lead to failure, and thereby increase the success and respect accorded to social science, is considerably different in each of the three cases. First, accepting the relevance and pervasiveness of historical time and ignorance of the future, and assuming the consequent inability to project the structures of social science analysis beyond the present, epistemological parity of social science with physical science in terms of the status of laws is clearly impossible. That is so because the laws of physical science are independent of time, while those of social science are not. Whether such a conclusion means that social science will forever remain less successful (and less respected) than physical science is an open question that will not be addressed here.[13]

Second, a parallel and forever-unavoidable breakdown of epistemological parity cannot be claimed in reference to the *ceteris paribus* difficulty that arises with corroboration in social science. For it is not inconceivable that future generations will find better ways of circumventing this obstruction than are presently known. Part of that development, for example, may be similar to currently available devices that make use of the notion of the stability of average values of variables describing economic and social classes as distinct from those non-average variables relating to the individuals within such classes. Should that happen, this aspect of the current absence of epistemological parity between the physical and social sciences will have been surmounted to some extent and the likelihood of success in the latter will have been increased.

Third, with regard to the measurement problem, and to summarize the principal conclusion to be drawn from the essays of this anthology, the ostensible failure of social science to reach epistemological parity with physical science, in the sense that an inability to measure properly seems to produce inferior knowledge, is more apparent than real. For the means to overcome the difficulty are already available. These were set out in *Analysis without Measurement* (Cambridge: Cambridge University Press) in 1983. Rather than concentrating on the construction of cardinal (interval) or ratio measures of hard-to-scale variables, that book focused on the question of how phenomena involving the unmeasured and unmeasurable can be investigated and understood in the absence of numerical gauges to represent them. This was accomplished by developing a methodology of static and dynamic modeling that is capable of handling unquantified variables. The techniques obtained, some examples of which will be referred to subsequently, were then illustrated by applying them in several social science fields. The book also reviewed and illustrated standard tools (a few of these have already been mentioned above) for empirical corroboration of hypotheses and propositions that contain uncalibrated vari-

[13] One of the implications that may be drawn from Katzner [11] is that even though laws in social science cannot be projected into the future, at least in the ease of economies, significant explanation is still possible. Hence, ignoring other reasons for a possible lack of epistemological parity, success is also attainable but with respect to a notion of success that eschews prediction of future events.

ables.

It should be pointed out (see Essay 9 below) that in the absence of cardinal or ratio measurement, many mathematical concepts and methods available for organizing and manipulating numerical magnitudes and variables are no longer available. This includes all arithmetic operations along with the rules and formulas, such as matrix operations, differentiation of functions, and analysis of variance, that depend on them. Also included on the list of forbidden techniques are the use of non-zero Jacobian determinants as a component of the sufficient conditions for solving systems of simultaneous equations, Lagrange multipliers for locating constrained maximum and minimum values, and evaluations of the signs of the real parts of eigenvalues to uncover the stability properties of certain dynamic equations. Clearly, the development of a methodology to overcome these losses and deal effectively with the unquantified world is not a trivial matter. Analytical constructions and manipulative techniques that can be, and are, put to good use in this regard include the notion of function, and the operations of function composition and inversion.

A simplified and intuitive summary of the methodology developed in *Analysis without Measurement* is presented in Essay 4 of this anthology, "On Not Quantifying the Non-Quantifiable." In employing that investigative apparatus, attention focuses on elements, like countries or their cultures, which, while they are not necessarily quantifiable, are understood in every case to be well defined and distinct. Paralleling standard techniques of analysis in the quantified world, systems of simultaneous functional relations having unquantified elements in both their domains as well as their ranges may be constructed and solved uniquely (assuming unique solutions of the constructed relations exist) to obtain outcomes determined by the system. To uniquely solve such a system means, as it does when every variable is at least cardinally quantified, that all but one of the vectors of variable values satisfying one or more relation are eliminated as possible outcomes because they are inconsistent with at least one of the remaining relations. (This is the same thing that happens when two independent numerical equations whose graphs are intersecting lines in the Euclidean plane are solved to discover the coordinates of their intersection point.) Conditions under which a system of two functional relations involving two unmeasured variables and an unmeasured parameter can be solved to express the former as functions of the latter are given in Essay 4. (More general conditions for more than two functions and variables are provided in *Analysis without Measurement*, Chapter 5.) Examples of the manner in which relations among non-numerical variables can be employed in this way to produce meaningful explanations at both individual and more aggregative levels include the determination of possible qualities of life an individual might lead from interrelated personally perceived characteristics and more objective situational characteristics in *Choice and the Quality of Life* [9] (not reprinted here), and also appear in Essays 7, 13, and 14 below.

General ordering relations among distinct, unquantified elements arise in much the same way, and with the same significance, as when the elements in question appear in the guise of cardinally or ratio measured vectors. And under well-known conditions, certain kinds of these orderings can be represented, even in the unquantified case, by a single-valued numerical function. In this regard, it should be noted that a function representing an ordering of unquantified elements assigns to each element a number that indicates its relative position in the ordering: the "higher up" in the ordering, the larger the number. Such a function, of course, has a unique maximum if the number assigned to one of the unquantified elements, called the unique maximizing element, is larger than those assigned to all others. Clearly, the unique maximizing element, if it exists, is that element highest up in the underlying ordering. Thus the idea of maximization carries over to the non-quantified world, and this, in turn, points to the possibility of constructing explanations of behavior in terms of decision-making or choice that rests on it. Although not discussed in Essay 4 (see *Analysis without Measurement*, Section 5.4), maximization is employed in several non-numerical contexts of choice in the applications of Essays 6, 10, and 11.

One of the traditional methods of modeling change in a quantified environment is to think of the current values of variables as related to past values of the same variables. Without modification, an identical conceptualization also works when numerical scales on which to cardinally or ratio measure variables are not available. Systems of these latter kinds of relations, referred to below as periodic functional relations, can generate, from initial conditions, both (unquantified) stationary and (unquantified) non-stationary time paths. Such dynamic relations provide the basis for understanding institutional modification across time in Essay 7. Stationary time paths, that is, time paths along which no change in any variable value occurs, emerge as solutions, in the sense described above, of simultaneous functional relations derived from their associated periodic counterparts. In addition it is possible to think of non-stationary time paths as, say, converging or diverging from stationary paths. But to be able to talk about such concepts as convergence and divergence in the absence of measurement requires a way of characterizing the notion of "closeness" between non-numerical entities. All of this is described in Essay 4 in reference to a single periodic functional relation with one unscaled variable modifying over time and one unscaled and unchanging parameter. In that essay, sufficient conditions for stability or convergence of non-stationary time paths are suggested, though neither with precision nor in detail, and the closeness of two unquantified elements is expressed with respect to the number of properties or characteristics that they have in common.

Finally, Essay 4 suggests a few elementary means of empirically checking statements involving non-quantified variables. It turns out that there is considerable literature on this subject already available, and the essay merely cites a few of the possibilities.

The overall point of Essay 4, and that of *Analysis without Measurement* itself, is that an absence of an ability to measure is no barrier to the conduct of rigorous and scientific inquiry in social science or even, for that matter, in physical science. Methodologically speaking, just about everything that can be done with measures present can also be done when they are not. And, subject to any qualifications arising from such issues in social science as the status of laws and corroboration with observed phenomena described above, the quality and meaning of the knowledge so obtained is on a par with that secured through application of standard methods and procedures in physical science. The only difference in the case of much of social science is that the power and convenience furnished by (cardinally- or ratio-) measured numbers cannot be employed because, obviously, the numbers themselves are not available. In these respects, then, an inability to measure cannot, by itself, be a cause of a failure of social science to achieve epistemological parity with physical science. Any such failure, to the extent that it exists, would therefore need to be established on other grounds, such as those discussed earlier.

It is worth digressing for a moment to identify the source and meaning of the previously-alluded-to added power present in analyses with at least cardinal measurement. That power is derived from the ability to write an explicit functional equation such as $y = x^2$ which can be said to hold for all x without having to identify the exact relationship between each value of x and the corresponding value of y. That is, it is not necessary to list all pairs (x, y), like (1,1), (2,4), (3,9), ..., that satisfy the equation in order to define it. On the other hand, the only way to define a functional equation with two non-quantified variables is to enumerate all pairs that exist in that relation.[14] Thus, although it is possible to conceive of infinite sets of unmeasured variable values and imagine relations among them,[15] complete characterizations of such rela-

[14] When x and y are ordinally measured, the equation $y = x^2$ can still be written down for all numerical values of x, but its meaning and usefulness is, in general, severely limited. See Essays 8 and 9 below.

[15] See *Analysis without Measurement* [10, Sect. 7.2].

tions cannot be given. It follows that the power to encompass a wider domain is necessarily lost in the propositions and conclusions obtained with the less-fully-specified relations that involve unmeasured variables because the latter cannot be said to apply as extensively. But the extra power contained in results with cardinally measured variables does not come without cost. For the explicit designation of a quantified functional relation, admitting as it does a greater extent of specification than would be possible if the variables under consideration were unquantified or unquantifiable, involves increased assumption content. It assumes, that is, that the relation is explicitly characterized at more points. And given that, in our limited world, only a finite number of pairs of any relation, measured or otherwise, can ever be observed, the possibility of invoking relations that are overly extensive and assert too much is more likely when quantified variables are in use.

Since the publication of *Analysis without Measurement*, a number of clarifications, extensions, and advances have been made in the methodology of dealing with non-quantifiable phenomena, as well as in the application of the methodology to various substantive problems in the social sciences at both theoretical and empirical levels. Moreover, some work in this vein was actually published before *Analysis without Measurement* but, for various reasons, was not included in it. The remaining essays in the present anthology assemble these efforts in one place. Their main purpose here is to elucidate, enhance, and apply the methodology of analysis without measurement. Taken as a totality, they may be thought of, in part, as addressing in some detail two central questions: What can analysis without measurement do, and how can it do it? The answers that emerge add flesh to the stark proposition asserted above that, except for the convenience and power that numbers provide, analysis without measurement can achieve the same level of investigative discourse as traditional inquiry into the cardinally- or ratio-quantified world.

As pointed out in the Preface, the essays themselves are grouped into two categories. Those that pertain in some way to the methodology of analysis without measurement, or methodological issues that are approached from the perspective of analysis without measurement, are presented first (Part I) and are followed by those that are substantive applications of analysis without measurement to specific fields of social science (Part II). Each essay is now summarized in turn.

The main point of Essay 2, which begins Part I and has already been summarized above, is to trace the development, in the Western world, of the historic rush to measure that has led intellectual inquiry and society into significant errors of both analysis and omission. These errors, some of which are detailed in Essays 8 and 9, strongly suggest the need for methods for dealing with phenomena that appear, at least at present, to be incapable of measurement.

The third essay of the anthology, "In Defense of Formalization in Economics," although purportedly directed only at economics, can be more broadly construed as a universal argument in favor of employing formalization throughout social science. Indeed, it implies that formalization as such is a necessary part of scholarly endeavor in general. Although this conclusion is beyond reproach, the ability to meaningfully quantify the elements of the analytical structures to which formalization has made its indispensable contribution is often called into question. But Essay 3 suggests that analysis without measurement enables formalized relations to be established between unquantified causal forces with the same competence and effectiveness as between the numerically measured variables of fully quantified experience. Thus, the effect of this essay is to support the application of analysis without measurement in all areas of social science. The specific argument of the essay may be summarized as follows: Formalization consists of the development and analysis of relations among variables that can be said to constitute a model. (The process of extracting formalizations from what will be called "dialectical" reality is described in Essay 6.) Essay 3 argues that such constructions must be relevant to the reality under consideration, that their primary purpose is to explain, and that they may be thought of as analogies or metaphors. Many valid justifications for the employment of formalizations of this kind have been given and are summarized in the essay. But when their relevance is suspect, when the questions they are intended to answer are of dubious merit, or when they are undertaken more for their own sake rather than to address particular issues, the employment of such formalizations becomes inappropriate. In the latter cases, the problem is not with formalization *per se* but, rather, with the use to which formalization has been put.

The reply and letter following the fourth essay — the latter essay was summarized earlier — concern embellishments of certain methodological points and need no further comment here. Before turning to the fifth essay, it should first be recalled that when analyzing the periodic functional relations described in reference to Essay 4, one of the issues that arises concerns the possible convergence of typical non-stationary time paths to a stationary time path (assuming that the latter exists). And to talk about convergence, it is necessary to have some idea of what it means for the values of unquantified variables to become close to each other. Although considerable attention was devoted to this problem in Chapter 3 of *Analysis without Measurement*, a highly condensed version of which appears in Essay 4, that discussion was rather limited in that it focused on only one possible concept of closeness. The purpose of the fifth essay, "Notions of Closeness in a Non-Quantifiable Setting," is to rectify that omission. The essay defines, analyzes, and compares five notions of closeness that do not require cardinal scales for calibrating the objects whose closeness is being considered. (One of these notions is the original concept of Essay 4 and *Analysis without Measurement.*) When the objects are orderings, the number of identically ordered pairs and a construction similar to a distance function characterized by Kemeny and Snell arise as special cases. All notions studied are based on equivalence classes derived from relations on the set of all objects. The argument includes a discussion contrasting these notions of closeness with those derived from the idea of a metric, along with an examination of the role of equivalence classes in defining closeness in general. The essay concludes with an application of the same notions of closeness to the calculation of closeness among countries using data collected by Adelman and Morris. Clearly, even in the absence of cardinal or ratio quantification, closeness, either independently construed or in reference to the stability properties of periodic relations, is a significant part of analytical endeavor. Its usefulness as an independent idea is exhibited in Essay 5. And that latter exhibition points to wider application.

With the general issues and methodological techniques of the first four essays of Part I (i.e., Essays 2-5) out of the way, attention turns to the actual use of formalism in analytical endeavor.[16] The sixth essay of the anthology, "The Role of Formalism in Economic Thought, ...," like Essay 3 and the remaining essays of Part I that have yet to be described here, although written specifically for economists, applies more generally to a broad array of fields in social science. Its purpose is to explore the function, scope, and usefulness of formalism in analytical thought. (Formalism, as described in Essay 3, is a particular kind of formalization.) In this regard, it extends the argument of Essay 3 in support of the utilization of formalism in all areas of social science and especially for those investigations in which appropriate measures of the relevant properties and forces are not available. The specific questions it addresses include: where did formalism come from, what does it do, how does it do it, and what are its prerequisites, limitations, power, and potential. The answers to many of these questions are illustrated by the actual "doing" of an analysis, namely, that of the social interaction among employees through the rules they issue for others and the activities in which they engage in the firm. Since the

[16] Roughly speaking, the terms "formalization" (employed earlier) and "formalism" (used here) are synonyms. Of course, the precise meaning of each depends on the context in which it appears.

variables in this analysis are, for the most part, non-numerical, the essay serves to provide an example of a complete application of analysis without measurement to a static, theoretical topic. That is, it depicts the process of proceeding from dialectical reality, through abstraction, to the construction of an "arithmomorphic" model[17] employing unmeasured variables and, finally, to some theoretical results.[18] A more primitive version of the model itself appeared as Chapter 11 in *Analysis without Measurement.*

The uses to which the methodology of analysis without measurement might conceivably be put are quite extensive and varied. One non-obvious potentiality is the provision of an explanation of how static and dynamic, non-numerical forces can give rise to dynamic quantified change. The seventh essay, "Institutionally Determined Parameters in Economic Equations," illustrates this possibility. In so doing, it provides an example of an analysis that employs a fully-quantified dynamic equation, along with both periodic and static simultaneous relations involving unquantified variables, in its structure. The point of the essay is to explore what it means to say that a parameter in an equation is "institutionally determined." The argument begins with a cardinally- or ratio-quantified, single-equation model of the trade cycle in which short-term cycles are superimposed on long-term cycles. The short-term cyclical motion at issue derives from the forces present in the quantitative, internal dynamic of the equation itself, while the long-term cyclical motion is the result of regular, institutionally determined shifts in values of certain of the equation's parameters. The latter parameter values, though numerical in character, are a consequence of an unquantified institutional configuration that changes over time according to its own periodic dynamic. The general conclusion is that relegating a parameter to the realm of the institutionally determined amounts to covering up a whole host of complexities (in this case, unquantified) which may have important bearing on the problem at hand.

An unfortunate aspect of current practice in social science is to take variables that are (i) unmeasurable or, as of yet, unmeasured, or (ii) only ordinally measured, and either treat them as if they were at least cardinally quantified, or use, as mentioned earlier, proxy variables that are at least cardinally quantified in their place. This is especially common in economics, but it also extends into other areas of social science as well. The eighth essay, entitled "The Misuse of Measurement in Economics," examines the kinds of things that can go wrong when these practices are invoked. That is, it points out, as was indi-

---

[17] An arithmorphic model is one that is built up from variables whose values are all distinct and discrete.

[18] Of course, the same process applies when appropriate measures of the variables in question are available.

cated above, some of the errors to which this approach can lead and, thereby, enhances the importance and significance of the methodology of analysis without measurement presented and explored in the present volume. In particular, various examples are used to show how, when cardinal scales are inappropriately assumed or substituted for what is less-than-cardinally scaled, the logical structure of models can fall apart, and any relation to the phenomenon in reality that is the focus of analysis or the object of explanation can disappear. The main conclusion is that, in many important cases if not most, the practices result in constructions and analyses that are without meaning and significance. And this is so even when prediction is the only goal. Thus, it would seem that when at least cardinal measures of the relevant variables are not available, scholars often have little choice but to engage in analysis without measurement.

But, it might be asked, suppose "a little bit" of measurement is available. That is, if variables are not cardinally quantified, it might still be possible to measure them ordinally. In that case, can some of the efficacy and convenience of having numerical cardinal measures be restored? The ninth essay, "Analysis with Ordinal Measurement" answers this question with the phrase "generally no!" and thus reinforces the importance and significance of the methodology of analysis without measurement established by Essay 8. Although, it turns out, there are a few mathematical properties that are independent of the choice of scale, it is still true that results obtained with many of the standard mathematical techniques administered to ordinally measured variables depend critically on the particular scales on which those variables are calibrated. For applying a legitimate increasing transformation to any of the ordinal scales employed, which, logically, has no impact on the information content of the numbers measured on that scale, can, and frequently does, alter the results. Such results, then, because they are scale-dependent, can have, as in the previously summarized essay, neither meaning nor significance. Similar reasoning implies that ordinal-variable models containing systems of static and periodic equations are typically not viable tools for understanding simultaneous behavior, dynamic or otherwise. Nor is rational behavior a meaningful assumption when it requires maximization with respect to one or more ordinally gauged variables.[19] Thus the general conclusion follows that analysis with ordinal variables cannot usually be expected to produce significant results. Analysis without measurement again seems to be the only recourse.

The remaining essays in the present collection (i.e., those of Part II) may

---

[19] A similar point is made in Essay 8. It should be noted, however, that ordinality in the range of the function being maximized causes no difficulties.

all be viewed as theoretical applications of the methodology of analysis without measurement to specific areas of social science. These essays not only provide illustration beyond those given in Essays 6 and 7 of how the methodology can be employed, but they also exhibit its breadth and potential as well. In particular, they examine, respectively, the role that effort, an unquantified variable whose values are chosen by the firm's employees, plays in the operation of the firm; how social interaction among employees, expressed in terms of unquantified rules imposed on them and the unquantified activities in which the engage, affects the form of organization of the firm; how unquantified attitudes encroach on an individual's selection of quantified commodity baskets and thereby influence his demand behavior; how the distinction between political structure and system can be made with considerable precision in the context of unmeasurable societal and political characteristics; and, finally, how the logical structure of an existing verbally-described model containing only unquantified variables can be examined.

More specifically, "Effort and Efficiency in the Neoclassical Firm," the tenth essay, demonstrates that the production function assumed in typical, neoclassical, microeconomic analyses is rather specialized: when worker effort (taken to be unquantified) is variable this production function will obtain only under certain idealized, institutional conditions such as those associated with bureaucracies and clans. If the latter conditions are not met, then the firm need not be technically efficient and the allocation of effort within it is not necessarily "internally" Pareto optimal in production.

The eleventh essay, "The Efficiency of Organizational Forms," is concerned with the general efficiency properties of the bureaucratic, clan, military, and market forms of firm organization. The model upon which the analysis is based focuses on the (unquantified) activities in which employees engage and on the constraints imposed on those activities by persons higher up in the hierarchical structure of the firm. Efficiency notions expressed in terms of both the cost of administration and Pareto optimality are explored, and idealized versions of the four organizational forms considered are shown both to eliminate the former cost and to achieve the latter efficiency. This essay overlaps with the one that precedes it, in part in its use of the notion of bureaucracy and clan. In addition, the model it employs is similar to that developed in Essay 6 ("The Role of Formalism in Economic Thought, ...") to illustrate the doing of an analysis without measurement in general.

The twelfth essay, "Attitudes, Rationality and Consumer Demand," examines the role that attitudes might play in determining demand behavior. This is accomplished by inserting an attitude parameter into the individual's utility function and following it as it emerges as a parameter in the individual's demand functions derived from constrained utility maximization. In particular, certain attitude characteristics expressed in the utility function are identified, and the manner in which they manifest themselves as properties of the demand functions are explored. (The essay is concerned neither with the intertemporal stability of these kinds of demand functions in general, nor with that of their specific functional forms.) Circumstances in which attitudes are first taken to be unquantified and then assumed, for comparative purposes, to be cardinally quantified, are considered.

The thirteenth essay, "Political Structure and System and the Notion of Logical Completeness," is an early, more narrowly focused version of Chapter 8 of *Analysis without Measurement*. Since it was originally published before the methodology that justifies the technique it employs, no reference to that methodology appears. The purpose of the essay is to show how the distinction between political structure and political system can be construed as a distinction between, respectively, a system of simultaneous relations involving unquantified political variables and that system's solution. Many of the variables and relations themselves are taken from a book by Apter. The essay also discusses tests for determining when models of the sort presented are logically complete. Another of Apter's books forms the basis of the fourteenth essay, "The Formal Structure of Argument in Professor Apter's *Choice and the Politics of Allocation*." This essay attempts to translate Apter's general verbal theorizing in the book cited in its title into a formal analysis that captures the essence of a good part of his argument. The model of simultaneous periodic relations among unquantified variables that emerges can be thought to be implicit in his work, and presenting his argument in terms of that model both enhances its clarity and helps to identify some of its weaknesses. In addition, expression in terms of the model also allows assumptions and conclusions to be stated with greater precision, and it has the potential of suggesting directions in which extensions might be both possible and fruitful.

Although published separately and not reproduced here, *Choice and the Quality of Life* [9] is worth brief mention at this point since it furnishes an extensive empirical application of the methodology of analysis without measurement. That short volume first presents a model within which the quality of life an individual leads can be defined in terms of abstract and unquantified characteristics like security, freedom, and self esteem. Through the administration of questionnaires to two small samples of subjects, it then empirically examines the potential consistency of the model with individual thought processes. That is, it tests the possibility that people might actually be able to employ, if they do not already do so in rough approximation, such a model as the basis for thinking about, and evaluating, their own qualities of life. The main results were shortened and summarized in Chapter 14 of *Analysis without Measurement*.

The last six essays described above (the essays of Part II plus *Choice and the Quality of Life*) clearly demonstrate that analysis without measurement in the context of social science is more than just a sterile mental exercise. Models and analyses that explain real social science phenomena, and in which one or all of the variables involved are unmeasured, can be constructed and subjected to rigorous empirical examination. In so doing, variables that are only ordinally measured can always, if necessary, be treated as if they were not measured at all and, as is argued in what follows, more reliable results can be achieved and some hitherto unrecognized errors can be avoided.

Generally speaking, analysis without measurement is a potentially productive method of inquiry which is capable of asserting meaningful hypotheses and producing significant conclusions. The absence of an ability to measure, then, does not, by itself, obstruct the social scientist's ability to do, with the same force of meaning and importance, what the physical scientist does. There is no need for the social scientist to be embarrassed by a measurement "problem" because that problem does not, in point of fact, exist. Epistemological parity of social science with physical science cannot be denied on the grounds that measurement of key social science variables is not possible.

References

1. Alker, H. R., *Rediscoveries and Reformulations* (Cambridge: Cambridge University Press, 1996).
2. Andreski, S., *Social Sciences as Sorcery* (London: Deutsch, 1972).
3. Campbell, D. T., "Evolutionary Epistemology," in *Methodology and Epistemology for Social Science* (Chicago: University of Chicago Press, 1988), pp. 393-434.
4. Deutsch, K. W., *The Nerves of Government* (New York: Free Press, 1996).
5. Eberstadt, N., *The Tyranny of Numbers* (Washington: AEI Press, 1995).
6. Hutchison, T.W., *Knowledge and Ignorance in Economics* (Oxford: Blackwell, 1977).
7. ________, "On the Relations between Philosophy and Economics, Part II: To What Kinds of Philosophical Problems Should Economists Address Themselves?" *Journal of Economic Methodology* 4 (1997), pp. 127-151.

8. Jevons, W. S., *The Theory of Political Economy*, 5th ed. (New York: Kelley, 1965).
9. Katzner, D. W., *Choice and the Quality of Life* (Beverly Hills: SAGE, 1979).
10. ________, *Analysis without Measurement* (Cambridge: Cambridge University Press, 1983).
11. ________, *Time, Ignorance, and Uncertainty in Economic Models* (Ann Arbor: University of Michigan Press, 1998).
12. ________, "Economics and the Principal of Uniformity," *Economia Politica* 17 (2000), pp. 237-252.
13. Kincaid, H., *Philosophical Foundations of the Social Sciences* (Cambridge: Cambridge University Press, 1996).
14. Lundberg, G. A., *Can Science Save Us*? (New York: Longmans-Green, 1947).
15. Martin, M., and L. C. McIntyre, *Readings in the Philosophy of Social Science* (Cambridge: MIT Press, 1994).
16. Ricci, D. M., *The Tragedy of Political Science* (New Haven: Yale University Press, 1984).
17. Shackle, G. L. S., *Decision, Order and Time in Human Affairs*, 2nd ed. (Cambridge: Cambridge University Press, 1969).
18. ________, *Epistemics and Economics* (Cambridge: Cambridge University Press, 1972).
19. Toulmin, S., *Human Understanding*, v. 1 (London: Oxford University Press, 1972).
20. Vickers, D., *Economics and the Antagonism of Time* (Ann Arbor: University of Michigan Press, 1994).

PART I

Methodology

2
Our Mad Rush to Measure: How Did We Get into this Mess?[1]

In our quest to describe, analyze, understand, know, and make decisions, we moderns, it seems, attempt to measure everything. The pages of our popular newspapers and magazines are full of measures. So are our scholarly journals. We measure the physical world. We measure our society, our economy, our polity, our culture, and ourselves. Give us a problem and our impulse — almost reflex — is to measure all we can think of that relates to it. We evaluate performance by measurement. We attempt to understand our quality of life in terms of measurement. We analyze and define government policy in the context of measurement. What is not measurable we strive to render measurable, and when we cannot, we dismiss it from our thoughts and justify our neglect by assigning it the status of the "less important." Lord Kelvin's dictum [56, p. 80] appears to reign supreme: "... when you can measure what you are speaking about and express it in numbers you know something about it;

---

[1] Methodus 3, no. 2 (December, 1991), pp. 18-26. © International Network for Economic Method. Reprinted with permission.

The author acknowledges, with gratitude, the help of Andy B. Anderson, Carol E. Heim, Andrew M. Kamarck, Larry Owens, Theodore M. Porter, John W. Servos, Robert C. Sleigh, jr., Douglas Vickers, and Robert P. Wolff, and absolves them of any responsibility for the final result.

but when you cannot measure it, when you cannot express it in numbers, your knowledge is of a meagre and unsatisfactory kind: it may be the beginning of knowledge, but you have scarcely, in your thoughts, advanced to the stage of *science*, whatever the matter may be."

A moment's reflection, however, is all that is needed to realize that measurement and thought-forms based only on what is measured cannot possibly do everything we expect them to do. One aspect of the problem is expressed in St. Augustine's complaint: "For so it is, oh Lord my God, I measure it; but what it is that I measure I do not know."[2] Clearly, without having the means for knowing what should be measured, and without knowing the relationship between what is actually measured and what is intended to be measured (uncertainties which, more often than not, seem to be present), meaning and significance cannot be imputed to the numbers, even if only "approximations," that result from measurement. These issues arise most frequently when dealing with such things as, for example, the quality of life. But quite apart from the meaning and significance of measurements is the fact that by omitting from our considerations what cannot be measured, or what we do not know how to measure, often leads to irrelevance and even error. In the quality-of-life example, how is it possible to conceive of this concept in any general way without thinking about such hard-to-scale components as security, freedom, self esteem, the presence of challenge, etc.?[3] To ignore such (currently) non-quantifiable elements is to divorce one's thoughts from any general notion of what the quality of life might be. Thus the blind pursuit of numbers has misled those who have purported to "measure" the quality of life into a questionable exercise.[4] Likewise, bargaining situations cannot be completely understood without explicitly accounting for the many also-difficult-to-calibrate political, social, and psychological pressures under which negotiators operate. If only muddled thinking by a few persons was at stake, the matter would be of lesser consequence. But when a state secretly sterilizes individuals only because their "measured intelligence" on a flawed intelligence test is too low,[5] then bitterly dashed hopes and human suffering become the issue. And when a society and its leaders begin to think of war in terms of measurements of troops sent, bombs dropped, body counts, villages pacified, and so on, and when decisions about war are based only on those measurements to the exclusion of non-quantifiable elements like

---

2 St. Augustine's *Confessions*, Bk. 11, Ch. 26. Translation of this passage provided by Andrew M. Kamarck.

3 Katzner [23, Chs. 1,4-7].

4 *Ibid.*, Sect. 2.2.

5 The State of Virginia engaged in this practice from 1924 to 1972. The legal basis for it was upheld by the U.S. Supreme Court in 1927. See Gould [18, pp. 335,336].

"fighting spirit,"[6] then national honor can be disgraced and lives can be unnecessarily lost. Thus lessons abound, some more painful than others, that point to the importance of the non-quantifiable.

Yet, in spite of these lessons, our enchantment with measurement persists. We continue our excesses, perhaps with a little more discomfort than before. Measurement is relatively easy and convenient. It has become natural for us. It makes us feel good because it imparts the (frequently illusory) impression that we know something.[7] And it is also not difficult, and even tempting, to ignore what cannot be measured. We seem to be caught up in a culture of measurement which we are unable to let go. The purpose of the present paper is to attempt a very broad and tentative description of the long evolving process of how this came to be so.

I

It is well to begin with some preliminary definitions and facts. Subsequent discussion generally focuses on the development of knowledge through analysis. For present purposes, analysis may be taken to consist of the definition of variables and relations (or, sometimes, laws) among them, along with the determination of the conclusions that can be inferred from the assumed or observed properties of such constructions. Of course, the definition of variables is based on the identification of categories and concepts, and relations can be specified verbally in words and sentences, or expressed as mathematical equations. Analysis is abstract. It can be theoretical or empirical (or both); but in any event, analysis, even theoretical analysis, is tied in some appropriate way to reality. Collections of relations of an analysis are sometimes referred to as models.

A quantitative, quantified, or numerical variable is one whose values are all numbers. A measured variable is a quantified variable whose numerical values are thought of as measurements of a particular property on a specific ordinal, interval (cardinal), or ratio scale. Thus, by these definitions, so-called

---

[6] See, for example, Smith [52, pp. 285,286] and Tolstoy [57, p. 1148].

[7] In this regard, McClosky [35, p. 484n] relates the story of Frank H. Knight, the economist who, upon observing a paraphrase of Kelvins dictum (cited above) inscribed on the front of the Social Science Building at the University of Chicago, is said to have remarked: "Yes, and when you *can* express it in numbers your knowledge is of a meagre and unsatisfactory kind." Moreover, the first part of the dictum is clearly misleading, if not patently wrong. As Standen [55. p. 85] points out, scientists once measured the ratio of the elasticity of ether (a substance that was believed to fill all space but could not be seen, tasted, felt, or weighed) to its density. Then in 1887 Michelson and Morley showed that ether could not exist.

"dummy" variables are numerical, non-measured variables. A qualitative or non-quantified variable is a variable whose values are not numbers. Variable values in this case have to be distinct, non-overlapping, verbal descriptions. For example, the variable "country" may range over the countries of the world, each identified by a name or a collection of sentences. Since it is always possible to assign a unique, but arbitrary, number to each (distinct) verbal variable value (this is sometimes referred to as nominal measurement), any qualitative variable can always be represented as a quantitative variable, albeit one that is non-measured.

Similarly, a relation among variables is quantitative, measured, or qualitative according as all of its variables are, respectively, quantitative, measured, or qualitative. A relation is called mixed when at least one of its variables is not in the same quantitative-measured-qualitative category as the others. Quantitative relations often appear as mathematical equations that employ the operations of arithmetic. Although arithmetic operations cannot be applied when using qualitative variables, qualitative relations may nevertheless be expressed in mathematical form by indicating which values of the dependent variables are to be associated with specific values of the independent variables. Thus the relation that maps the countries of the world into the continents on which they are found may be described as a mathematical function.

In parallel to the above categorization of relations, an analysis is quantitative (quantified or numerical), measured, or qualitative (non-quantified) as all of its relations are quantitative, measured, or qualitative, respectively. An analysis is mixed if either at least one of its relations is mixed or any two of its relations fall in separate quantitative-measured-qualitative categories. Examples of quantified analyses are well-known. They include efforts that involve only theorizing or only the collecting and summarizing of numerical data as well as the more full-blown combinations of theoretical and statistical work. Examples of non-quantified and mixed analyses are given below. Techniques for constructing and dealing with qualitative variables and relations in non-quantified and mixed analyses have been discussed elsewhere.[8] As a rule the phrase "analysis with measurement" will henceforth refer to measured analyses whereas the phrase "analysis without measurement" will signify qualitative analyses. It is attempts to analyze with measurement (i.e., to conduct measured analyses) that, to a considerable extent, underlie and motivate the "mad rush" to measure described earlier. That many such efforts have been quite useful (such as the gathering of economic data to measure unemployment, economic growth and inflation) and even spectacularly successful (for example, those

[8] Katzner [24]. See also Essay 4 in this volume.

that have allowed the placement of men on the moon) is not at issue. There can be little doubt about the significant role that measurement has played in the development of knowledge. Present concern, rather, is with the tendency to direct attention, exclusively and independently of the competency of the measures invoked, to measured analyses at the expense of everything else.

It is an interesting fact that analyses with measurement or, allowing for earlier times, analyses involving numbers that might not represent measurements, co-exist side-by-side throughout history with analyses that make no direct use of either measures or numbers. This phenomenon dates to antiquity and, in spite of the current overemphasis on measurement, persists today. Thus, on the one hand, the ancient Greeks were concerned with the description and analysis of natural shapes. They were primarily philosophers and geometers, and were decidedly less interested in numerical details that might have practical application.[9] To the Pythagoreans of southern Italy, on the other hand, all was number.[10] The essence of natural phenomena was to be found in number and numerical relations. Such was also the case, for example, with music in which numerical proportions were discovered to underlie harmony.[11] Even human characteristics and interactions were understood in terms of numerical properties. Among other things, the number 7 was identified with health, 4 with justice, and 5 with marriage. As time progressed, this juxtaposition of qualitative and quantitative analyses evolved into a contiguity of analyses with and without measurement. Indeed, Galileo's measured law of uniform acceleration, Newton's measured law of gravitation, and Einstein's measured law of the interchange of mass and energy, to name but a few, keep company with the likes of the qualitative law of chemistry that acids react with alkalis to form salts, Darwin's qualitative theory of evolution, the qualitative structural models of elementary particle physics and classical genetics, and Weber's [59],[60] qualitative relation between religious beliefs and economic activity. Even statistical analysis has been applied to qualitative as well as quantitative data.[12]

A second fact worthy of note is the existence, also throughout history, of the fear of, or skepticism and criticism concerning, the use of numbers and measures. Taboos against and superstitions about counting and measuring are common across the world and over the ages.[13] St. Augustine's concern has al-

---

[9] Kline [26, pp. 34,35].

[10] *Ibid.*, pp. 76,77, and Heath [21, p. 37].

[11] Guthrie [20, pp. 24-28].

[12] For a general discussion of the application of statistical analysis to the qualitative world see Goodman [17]. An interesting illustration is the Mosteller and Wallace [38] determination of the authorship of the unsigned *Federalist* papers.

[13] Gaster [15, p. 483] and Kula [31, pp. 13-17].

ready been cited. Much later, in the early years of the twentieth century, Pearl [42, p.75] confessed to having doubts in spite of devoting 15 years to the application of statistical methods to biological problems. Burtt [8, pp. 302-305] argued that our understanding of the physical world was, at the same time, both enriched and impoverished by the seventeenth century scientific revolution which, among other things, brought measured analysis to the forefront of physical science. Still more recently, a small number of social scientists have spoken out against real and potential excesses in the employment of measures. To illustrate, Sorokin [53] objected to what he called "quantophrenia," or the rampant misuse and abuse of numerical procedures arising from a mania for precise, quantitative research. And Keynes [25, p. 156] accused Tinbergen, an econometrician, of "alchemy" and "black magic."

In light of these facts, the central question raised in this paper can be focused more sharply: How did it happen that, in spite of the availability of alternatives (at least through examples), and in spite of the criticisms directed against it over the years, analysis with measurement so completely triumphed over analysis without measurement that today's analytical emphasis overwhelmingly, if in many cases improperly, focuses exclusively on it?

II

Crombie [10, p. 15] dates the intellectual need to quantify, at least in medieval physics, to the early twelfth century. Its roots go back even further to ancient times. The Babylonians and Egyptians required measures for a variety of practical purposes, including the construction of canals, dams, and pyramids.[14] And even though he was not interested in quantification *per se*, Socrates still foreshadowed Kelvin when (according to Plato) he said in another context, "And the arts of measuring and numbering and weighing come to the rescue of the human understanding ... and the apparent greater or less, or more or heavier, no longer have the mastery over us, but give way before calculation and measure and weight?"[15] However, throughout the middle ages, natural philosophers were mostly concerned with clarifying and understanding cosmogony, cosmology, and the system of natural philosophy that they inherited from the ancients. Although the need to quantify arose in response to these ends, quantification itself was always considered to be of secondary importance. When quantification was discussed, it was examined mostly in

[14] Kline [28, pp. 11,21,22].

[15] Plato [44, p. 431].

theoretical terms and usually divorced from considerations of actual scientific measurement.[16] The only exceptions that arose came about due to a strong practical demand for the solution of a pressing problem.[17] Thus the measurement of time was explored because of the necessity to develop an accurate calendar and a way of telling the time of day at different latitudes and at different seasons. The measurement of space was taken up because of its importance to surveying, navigation, and cartography. And the measurement of weight was investigated as a result of the needs of metallurgists. Moreover, it was not until about 1500 A.D., when the institutionalization of our present system of numeral notation (taken from the Hindus) was completed, that ordinary Europeans began to develop the technical competence to deal with quantities of any size in a relatively simple and abstract way.[18]

According to Crombie [10, pp. 29,30], the balance began to tip in favor of measurement in the seventeenth century when a complete dialogue, that had not previously existed except in a very rudimentary and fragmentary way, developed between quantified theory and quantified theoretical and experimental procedures. As it gathered steam, the necessity of measurement began to be felt much more urgently both as an internal, intellectual need and as a response to external, practical pressures. In conjunction with this development, Kepler, in the early part of the century construed the old distinction between primary and secondary qualities (that is, qualities of the world that describe or reveal reality as opposed to those that do not) as a contrast of qualities that could be numerically measured against those for which such quantification was not possible.[19] Thus knowledge of the real world became knowledge of measured characteristics. Galileo extended the idea by taking the notion of primary quality to refer to something that, in addition to being quantitative, was also absolute, objective, and immutable. That which emerged as merely relative, subjective, fluctuating, and qualitative (i.e., which reflected secondary qualities) fell in the realm of opinion and illusion.[20]

But these refinements in the concepts of primary and secondary quality were only the beginning. For the publication of Galileo's *Discourses and*

[16] Such was the case, for example, with the 14th century "Oxford calculators" of Merton College. See Grant [19, pp. 55-59].

[17] Crombie [10, p. 29].

[18] Prior medieval practice did not employ written numbers in making arithmetic calculations. Numbers were usually written as Roman numerals and calculations were performed separately on a counting board. The introduction of the present numeral notation system gradually ended this rather awkward custom and written numbers came to be used for calculation. Menninger [37, pp. 191,192,287,294,424,440-445].

[19] Burtt [8, pp. 56,57].

[20] Burtt [8, pp. 73-76].

Mathematical Demonstrations Concerning Two New Sciences in 1638 marks a watershed in the transition from qualitative to measured analysis quite apart from its rejection of anything except the quantitative as a source of knowledge. Before Galileo, one would consider, say, a stone falling to the ground and attempt to explain why it fell, and why it fell to the earth. The Aristotelians gave answers to these questions that survived through the middle ages: The stone fell because it had weight. Furthermore, since all objects in the universe, if left unrestrained, would move to their "natural places," and since the natural place of objects with weight was on the earth (i.e., at the center of the universe), the stone had to fall to the earth.[21] Galileo proposed to replace such superficial explanation by measured analysis. But in so altering the focus and questions of explanation, his proposal implied nothing less than a change in the meaning of explanation itself.[22] For instead of asking *why* the stone fell, Galileo would ask about the *characteristics of the stone as* it fell. Specifically, he would (i) express the most fundamental properties of the falling stone in terms of measures and use these measures to define quantitative variables, and (ii) analyze the falling stone by constructing relations among the variables that are built up deductively from axiomatic or observed principles.[23] Out of this procedure emerged, among other things, Galileo's measured law of uniform acceleration referred to earlier, namely, $d = kt^2$, where d is measured distance fallen after t units of measured time, and k is a numerical constant.

Although Galileo's law was originally expressed (with full mathematical precision!) only in words, it was not long before it came to be represented in the symbolic, equation form above.[24] Descartes, of course, was responsible for perceiving the general correspondence between numerical, algebraic formulae and geometric, spatial relations.[25] Such a correspondence would apply, in particular, to those spatial relations, like Galileo's, describing motion. Moreover, his comparison of the universe of physical bodies to a vast machine that had been set in motion at the Creation was the first comprehensive attempt to picture the cosmos in material and mechanical instead of spiritual and teleological terms.[26] This set the stage for the Boyle-Locke-Leibniz vision of the world as

[21] Kline [27, p. 172].

[22] From the perspective of the argument of this paragraph, the fact that the Aristotelian explanation happens to he qualitative is of no consequence. The important point is the substantive change in the nature of explanation proposed by Galileo.

[23] Kline [26, pp. 185-188]. It does not matter whether Galileo's epistemology is understood in terms of rationalism (Koyré [29, p. 38]) or empiricism (Drake [12, p. 107]). His proposal carries the same significance under either interpretation.

[24] Kline [28, p. 338].

[25] Burtt [8, p. 97].

[26] Burtt [8, pp. 103,105].

"... a big clock once wound up by the Creator, and since kept in orderly motion by nothing more than his 'general concourse'."[27] As they developed, then, the laws of mechanics, indeed the concept of mechanism itself, were closely allied with algebraic quantification. And it was in such quantitative, algebraic form that much of quantitative science developed afterwards.

But, as indicated earlier, non-quantified laws cannot be described as simply as the mere specification of a numerically algebraic rule. Rather, it is necessary to explicitly link the values of certain variables with those of certain other variables, and to do this formally requires a sufficiently abstract notion of function. Kline [28, pp. 338-340,403-406,949,950] traces the history of the development of the function concept from its origins to the 1837 definition give by Dirichlet that is still in common use today: "... y is a function of x when to each value of x in a given interval there corresponds a unique value of y." Although Dirichlet's definition is (and has been) easily generalized by permitting x and y to vary over abstract sets rather than intervals of numbers, Kline's discussion suggests that through the nineteenth century mathematicians primarily thought of functions in quantitative terms.[28] It was probably not until the start of the twentieth century, after Cantor had begun his work on the theory of sets, that mathematicians started to seriously consider the idea of a function without reference to quantity.[29] Thus the revolution wrought by Galileo placed analysis without measurement at a distinct disadvantage. Not only did it project the Pythagorean stress on number into the center of science, but it also brought about the translation of quantitative analysis into a simple, usable, and relatively accessible form. And, in spite of the fact that the Galilean revolution implied the same change in focus for analyses in general, both with and without measurement, except that in the latter case numbers would be replaced by verbal descriptions (this, of course, was not recognized until much later), a corresponding simplicity, usability, and accessibility did not become available to non-quantified analyses for quite some time until the use of not-necessarily-numerical functions became commonplace. The Greek emphasis on the qualitative was down but not yet out.

The blows that finally did qualitative analysis in were not served up until the end of the nineteenth century. Before describing them, however, there are some other matters that require attention. Consider, first, the role of measurement in quantitative analysis, in particular, in physical science, after Galileo.

---

27 Burtt [8, p. 105].

28 One exception was Boole [4, pp. 70,71] whose 1854 notion of function, though essentially characterized over a qualitative domain, was rather restrictive and highly specialized in its application to only certain kinds of algebraic expressions in the context of symbolic reasoning.

29 See, for example, Russell [47, p. 263], the first edition of which was published in 1903.

The popular belief is that measurement has two functions, namely, to provide the means by which theories (including laws or relations) are "confirmed" or "rejected," and to be a source for the inference of new theories. But Kuhn [30] argues that this is not so. What scientists actually do is to seek "reasonable agreement" between "relevant" measurements on the one hand and theories on the other.[30] In seeking reasonable agreement scientists tend to push the numbers to conform to the theory. Indeed, they often cannot obtain confirmation until they know what the theory says the numbers should look like. Hence theories are not really "tested" against measurements. Obversely, measurements taken "without some knowledge of the regularity to be expected almost never speak for themselves."[31] In other words, with a few notable exceptions (e.g., Boyle's Law relating the pressure of a gas to its volume, and Hooke's Law linking spring distortion to applied force), the inference of new theories from measurements does not take place. (And even in the exceptional cases when it did, the scientists involved knew everything in advance but the particular form of the quantitative relation for which they were looking.[32])

The actual functions of measurement, according to Kuhn, are two-fold: Science develops through a process of infrequent theoretical breakthroughs (which may or may not be of sufficient consequence to constitute a paradigm change) and complex and consuming consolidations of those breakthroughs. Most scientific work is necessarily involved with consolidation, and it is this consolidation that paves the way for the next breakthrough. One function of measurement, then, is to engage in the search for reasonable agreement between theory and measurements, since the latter search constitutes a large portion of the consolidation effort. The second function is to aid in the discovery of unreconcilable anomalies. Such discoveries tell the scientist when and where to look for new theories.

Kuhn also points out that qualitative formulation, both theoretical and empirical, is normally a prerequisite to quantitative results. Indeed, in the absence of the requisite qualitative formulation, the danger is that measurement may be undertaken for the sake of measurement alone.[33] But this does not mean that the only way to make progress is to move from the qualitative to the quantitative. For, as suggested above, Galileo's entire program of exploration, including the search for reasonable agreement and the discovery of unreconcilable

30 Recently, scholars have also considered the social, political, cultural, and other forces that impinge on this process. See, for example, Shapin and Schaffer [49], Wise [61] and, in the field of psychology, Danziger [11].

31 Kuhn [30, p. 45].

32 *Ibid.*

33 Shryock [50, p. 91].

anomalies can take place in the context of analysis without measurement. All that is required is to replace numerical measurements by data consisting of verbally described variable values. Reasonable agreement between such data and a theory is reached when the observed variable values and the theory "conform."[34] If they cannot be made to conform, the presence of "unreconcilable anomalies" is revealed.

Of course, in its quantified and general form, Galileo's program of replacing superficial explanation by measured analysis was extraordinarily successful. In addition to many new discoveries, it also led to the resolution of controversies in the quantitative realm that were still up in the air. These successes were, no doubt, at least partly behind Kant's [22, p. 6] identification of science with quantification: "... in every special doctrine of nature only so much science proper can be found as there is [quantitative] mathematics in it." They are also one of the main reasons why Galileo's program spilled over beyond the bounds of physical science. Cohen [9, p. 44] cites a second possibility: "Quantification ... creates a sense of [certainty], uniformity and finitude .... [It] can be a powerful method of analysis and a powerful explanatory tool. In the turbulent and disorderly years of the seventeenth century, quantification must have seemed an alluring way to impose order on a world in flux." A third is suggested by Porter [46, pp. ix,xi]: "... reliance on number and quantitative manipulation minimizes the need for intimate knowledge and personal trust." It helps in securing results that are independent of the people who produce them. In the political and bureaucratic realm, "... the drive to supplant personal judgment by quantitative rules reflects weakness and vulnerability ... [associated with] the absence of a secure and autonomous community."

Clearly, there are constraints that limit the spillover effect in any given field at any particular moment. These include the nature of the problems under investigation in that field, the state of outside quantitative techniques that may be imported into the field, the extent of the acquaintance of the scholars of that field with quantitative methods, the *Weltanschauung* of the field, and the availability of relevant numerical data.[35] The last of these elements is critical because in many areas outside the physical sciences numerical data cannot be constructed through laboratory experimentation. But during the seventeenth century, the growth of nationalism and commerce and the increasing tendency to identify the welfare of society with that of the state, forced governments to begin to collect numerical data to assess the status of society.[36] A bureau of

34 For an illustration see Katzner's [23, Chs. 5,6] experiments to confirm the existence of a "quality-of-life technology."

35 Spengler [54, p. 131].

36 Shryock [50, p. 95].

statistics was established as early as 1602 in Paris, and by the end of the century a number of impressive data-collection efforts had been completed. One of these was undertaken in England by William Petty who directed his energies to the analysis of government policy. Petty [43, p. 244] called his approach "political arithmetic" and in 1690 explained it as follows: "The Method I take to do this, is not yet very usual; for instead of using only comparative and superlative Words, and intellectual Arguments, I have taken the course ... to express my self in Terms of Number, Weight, or Measure; to use only Arguments of Sense, and to consider only such Causes, as have visible Foundations in Nature; leaving those that depend upon the mutable Minds, Opinions, Appetites, and Passions of particular Men, to the Consideration of others." As the state became increasingly involved in economic, social and other affairs, the necessity for more and better measures grew. These events helped to focus the interest of investigators on quantified analysis and were eventually responsible for starting the spread of the gospel of quantification beyond the confines of purely intellectual pursuits. In any case, by the end of the eighteenth century the ascendancy of quantitative analysis was well underway in just about every general area of analytical endeavor.

III

The end of the nineteenth century witnessed a dramatic surge in the use of quantified analyses in the non-physical sciences.[37] Psychologists such as Binet and Pavlov began to quantify characteristics of the mind, and sociologists like Durkheim started to demonstrate that private behavior could be studied by quantifying their public distributions. Pearson launched his life-long pursuit of the scientific solution of societal problems through the application of statistical methods. And in the hands of Jevons, Walras, and Fisher, etc., the quantitative mathematization of economic theory and the integration of abstract models and statistical analysis in economics took off.[38] Suddenly, all facets of humanity seemed to be opened up to measured scientific inquiry.

Within the milieu fashioned by this explosion in quantification, two developments occurred that sealed the fate of qualitative analysis.[39] The first of these was the creation of the myth of the synonymity of objective science

[37] Lerner [33, pp. 12,13]. A detailed description of many aspects of this surge may be found, for example, in Porter [45].

[38] Spengler [54, pp. 139,140].

[39] The way in which these developments played out in terms of the spread of applications of probability and statisitics has been described by Gigerenzer, *et al* [16].

and measurement. Now it had been clear for a long time that, to contribute to knowledge, analysis had to be "objective." Ever since the acceptance of Galileo's statement of the distinction between primary and secondary qualities, the idea had become so commonplace that it had hardly been noticed by the physical scientists. But in the non-physical sciences, where subjectivity could sneak in through any number of back doors and at any moment, investigators were always more conscious of the problem. This is evident at least as far back as Petty's 1690 attempt, cited earlier, to avoid the things that come from "mutable Minds, Opinions, Appetites, and Passions." It is more obvious in LePlay [32, pp. 137,139,146,147] who, writing in 1877, claimed that by applying the same principles to human societies that he had employed in studying plants and minerals, he was able to shed his prejudices and create a scientific approach. Although his critics, so he said, were entrapped by their preconceived ideas and were unable to accept factual evidence that was contrary to their political or religious beliefs, "Nevertheless, I have confidence in the scientific method that bases true science on the observation of social facts ...." In the mid 1890s, Durkheim [14, pp. 34,44] flatly asserted that one must deal only with objective facts and employ a method of analysis that permits them to be studied objectively. And the cover of its 1959 paperback edition, initially published in 1924, jubilantly proclaims Watson's *Behaviorism* [58] as, "The book that initiated a revolution in its attempt to make psychology an objective science."

Of course, it is impossible to completely divorce oneself from one's values and biases. Opinion, prejudice, and egoism always intrude upon and influence scientific belief.[40] The real issue, then, given the nature of measured and unmeasured analysis as defined, is in what sense, if any, can either (or both) be regarded as objective? However, this question, as interesting and significant as it is, is irrelevant to the present story.[41] Suffice it to say that by the turn of the twentieth century, the necessity for some kind of objectivity had been universally recognized throughout non-physical science.

And what could be more objective than a measurement, a number? Quantification seemed to mean the substitution of objective standards for subjective judgement. It would limit the possibility of error. It was clean, unambiguous, and powerful, and it appeared to remove human values and private biases from interfering with logical thought. This myth, that objective science (or analysis) is synonymous with measurement, seems to have crystallized among many of

---

40 Boring [7, p. 535].

41 An answer for measured analysis is given, for example, by Ackermann [2, pp. 128,129]. See also Myrdal [40] and Porter [46].

the practitioners of measured analysis in non-physical science by the year 1900 as a natural justification of the activity in which they were engaged. Although not all of the non-physical scientists were taken in by it, the myth is nevertheless implicit in much of the attention devoted to the construction of measures in the twentieth century and in the frequent refusal to consider those elements that do not appear to be capable of measurement. Lundberg [34, p.41] made it explicit: "... an honest description of the technique by which any understanding or insight is achieved will either involve quantitative procedures ... or be of no general scientific import." But clearly, the myth of synonymity is only a myth and nothing more. Subjective elements can enter into the selection of the measures to employ, the construction and interpretation of those measures, and in the taking of the measurements themselves. Indeed, Gould [18, p. 27] has argued in general, and shown in the particular case of measuring intelligence, that "... quantitative data are as subject to cultural constraint as any other aspect of science ..." and that *a priori* prejudice has led scientists both to invalid conclusions from adequate numerical data and, in the process of gathering it, to the distorting of the numerical data itself.

Nevertheless, the myth of synonymity of objective analysis and measurement spread. As the twentieth century progressed, quantity quickly achieved supremacy over the full spectrum of human knowledge, and quality was left to the "humanists-in-retreat."[42] Along with it, "... a whole series of ethical distinctions, based upon the notion of pure and absolute qualities without relation to their amounts, [was] instinctively discarded by a considerable part of mankind...."[43] The questionable measures of the quality of life mentioned at the outset illustrate one of the consequences of this effect.

But the story does not end here. For, as indicated above, there was a second development that contributed to the demise of respectability of unmeasured analysis. This development, which was also responsible for the acceptance of the myth of synonymity by the general public, was the considerable growth in scientific activity (including the numbers of individuals engaged in it) and the spread of scientific knowledge in the public arena, and the consequent reinforcing interaction between the scientific community and society. Now the growth of scientific activity and the spread of scientific knowledge since 1850 has been well documented. The former, largely inspired by the demands of war, was aided by the formal establishment of roles and careers for scientists in society [51, pp. 96,97]; the latter by the broadening of the educational system to achieve universal participation [1, pp. 61,62]. Moreover, interaction

---

42 Lerner [33, p. 14].
43 Mumford [39, p. 328].

between the scientific community and society has always been present. As early as 1722, less than 100 years after the publication of Galileo's *Discourses* signaled the shift towards quantification, the cult of measured analysis entered the literary world. For, as Schorer [48, p. xiii] argues, in *Moll Flanders* Defoe revealed the mercantile mind for whom morality was based on "amounts" of virtue as measured by quantities of worldly goods.

In general, science is an activity involving human beings who live and communicate, not only in the world of science, but also in the wider societies in which they are members.[44] When entering the scientific world, the practitioners of science do not leave behind the knowledge, experience, attitudes, values, and biases they have taken from the outside world. Nor, upon leaving, do they forget about their scientific work. This is one facet of the continual interaction between science and society, and the more people that are involved in scientific ventures, the greater its effect. Another facet is the education of individuals with respect to the progress of science through teachers, publications, and public discussions, and the ensuing requests by society that scientists attempt to solve certain, often pressing, problems. (The latter scientific work, of course, is frequently financed by appropriate government agencies, foundations, and businesses.) A third facet is the transmission of scientific knowledge to industry (and agriculture) both in the form of technology to be applied in production,[45] and in the form of means to understand and manage workers and economic and social situations related to production.[46] A fourth facet, and one that has appeared only recently, is the frequent and unwarranted transfer of intellectual and moral authority by society at large to those who have participated in successful scientific inquiry. That is, individuals who have achieved scientific success are often called upon to make public judgments, or are accorded the prerogative of doing so, on matters well outside their areas of scientific expertise. Because they are held in such esteem, society eagerly awaits their pronouncements on subjects about which they may know very little, or which rely mainly on their own personal values and biases, in the hope that their demonstrated scientific ingenuity will enable them to penetrate where other attempts have failed. The combined impact of these effects is to make science a part of the popular culture shared by everyone. This is what happened, according to Boorstin [5, Ch. 9], to the invention of the clock. The clock became an integral component of Western life because it was transformed into a public machine. Clocks were placed on church steeples and in town belfries to sig-

---

44 Mendelsohn [36, pp. 3,4].

45 See, for example, Dupree [13] and Noble [41].

46 See, for example, Baritz [3].

nal the time for prayers and other events. Gradually the use of the clock spread as it filled more and more needs. Thus, for example, clocks were eventually placed in factories as a means of keeping track of hours worked. By contrast, in China, where for many years the clock was hidden in secrecy, it never (until recently) was integrated into Chinese life.

The translation of Boorstin's argument into the present context provides an explanation of the widespread acceptance by the public of the myth of synonymity between objective science and measurement. Quantified analysis became a part of the popular culture because beginning around 1900 it increasingly crossed over into the public domain through the interactive effects described above, in particular through the publication of a large variety of statistics (which had already begun in the previous decade[47]) and the ensuing public debates and analyses based on them, and also through public description and dissemination of the quantitative aspects of scientific discovery. With respect to public description and dissemination, it is clear that the quantitative pieces of science are the more spectacular. They are easier to communicate and understand, and easier for lay individuals to adapt in solving problems that are encountered in their own private lives. By contrast, because they are not as striking, and because they are more difficult to explain, understand, and adapt,[48] non-quantified analyses remained in the secret closets of science. Thus the success of quantitative analysis and the myth of synonymity were transmitted into the public domain without the accompaniment of significant alternatives and objections. It is not surprising, then, that the myth has met with little public resistance and persists in the popular culture today. And having been accepted by the public, it reinforces, through the interactive mechanisms identified above, the perpetuation of the same myth in the scientific community.

Ironically, due to relatively recent experiments in the world of physics, the arena in which the first movements toward quantification and away from qualitative analysis were taken, theoretical physicists of today, though still aiming for numerical results in the end, are returning to the non-quantifiable to gain a better handle on what they have observed. The retreat began in earnest more than a half a century ago with the discovery of the Heisenberg uncertainty prin-

---

47 For example, parts of Booth's survey of London [6] were published as early as 1889.

48 In terms of quantitative analysis, it is not hard, for example, to identify discomfort with air temperatures that measure too high or too low, or to recognize that traveling at a higher velocity for the same amount of time allows one to cover a greater distance. But it is considerably more difficult to understand as precisely the qualitative relation between security and freedom in human life situations, and the significance that such a relation might have in determining one's quality of life. (A discussion of the latter may be found in Katzner [23, Sect. 4.1]).

ciple that measurements of the exact positions of small particles are generally not possible, and the so-called theory of strings is one of its latest outcomes. Perhaps this effect will eventually work its way into the non-physical sciences and the public domain, finally bringing our mad rush to measure under more reasoned control.

References

1. *Academic American Encyclopedia*, v. 7 (Danbury: Grolier, 1986).
2. Ackermann, R. J., *Data, Instruments, and Theory* (Princeton: Princeton University Press, 1985).
3. Baritz, L., *The Servants of Power* (Middletown: Wesleyan University Press, 1960).
4. Boole, G., *An Investigation of the Laws of Thought* (New York: Dover, 1958).
5. Boorstin, D. J., *The Discoverers* (New York: Vintage, 1983).
6. Booth, C., *Life and Labour of the People in London* (London: Macmillan, 1902).
7. Boring, E. G., "The Validation of Scientific Belief," *Proceedings of the American Philosophical Society* 96 (1952), pp. 535-539.
8. Burtt, E. A., *The Metaphysical Foundations of Modern Physical Science*, 2nd ed. (London: Routledge and Kegan Paul, 1932).
9. Cohen, P. C., *A Calculating People: The Spread of Numeracy in Early America* (Chicago: University of Chicago Press, 1982).
10. Crombie, A. C., "Quantification in Medieval Physics," in *Quantification*, H. Woolf, ed. (Indianapolis: Bobbs-Merrill, 1961), pp. 13-30.
11. Danziger, K. *Constructing the Subject* (Cambridge: Cambridge University Press, 1990).
12. Drake, S., *Galileo at Work* (Chicago: University of Chicago Press, 1978).
13. Dupree, A. H., ed., *Science and the Emergence of Modern America, 1865-1916* (Chicago: Rand McNally, 1963).
14. Durkheim, E., *The Rules of Sociological Method*, S. A. Solovay and J. H. Mueller, trans. (Glencoe: Free Press, 1938).
15. Gaster, T. H., *Myth, Legend and Custom in the Old Testament* (New York: Harper & Row, 1969).
16. Gigerenzer, G., *et al*, *The Empire of Chance* (Cambridge: Cambridge University Press, 1989)

17. Goodman, L. A., *Analyzing Qualitative/Categorical Data* (Cambridge: Abt Books, 1978).
18. Gould, S. J., *The Mismeasure of Man* (New York: Norton, 1981).
19. Grant, E., *Physical Science in the Middle Ages* (New York: Wiley, 1971).
20. Guthrie, K. S., *The Pythagorean Sourcebook and Library*, D. R. Fideler, ed. (Grand Rapids: Phane Press, 1987).
21. Heath, Sir T. L., *A Manual of Greek Mathematics* (New York: Dover, 1963).
22. Kant, I., "Metaphysical Foundations of Natural Science," in *Philosophy of Material Nature*, J. W. Ellington, trans. (Indianapolis: Hackett, 1985).
23. Katzner, D. W., *Choice and the Quality of Life* (Beverly Hills: SAGE, 1979).
24. ________, *Analysis without Measurement* (Cambridge: Cambridge University Press, 1983).
25. Keynes J. M., Comment on "On a Method of Statistical Business-Cycle Research. A Reply," by J. Tinbergen, *Economic Journal* 50 (1940), pp. 154-156.
26. Kline, M., *Mathematics in Western Culture* (New York: Oxford University Press, 1953).
27. ________, *Mathematics and the Physical World* (London: Murray, 1959).
28. ________, *Mathematical Thought from Ancient to Modern Times* (New York: Oxford University Press, 1972).
29. Koyré, A., "Galileo and Plato," in *Metaphysics and Measurement* (London: Chapman & Hall, 1968), pp. 16-43.
30. Kuhn, T. S., "The Function of Measurement in Modern Physical Science," in *Quantification*, H. Woolf, ed. (Indianapolis: Bobbs-Merrill, 1961), pp. 31-63.
31. Kula, W., *Measures and Men*, R. Szreter, trans. (Princeton: Princeton University Press, 1986).
32. LePlay, F., *On Family, Work, and Social Change*, C. B. Silver, trans. (Chicago: University of Chicago Press, 1982).
33. Lerner, D., "On Quantity and Quality," in *Quantity and Quality*, D. Lerner, ed. (New York: Free Press, 1961), pp. 11-34.
34. Lundberg, G. A., "Quantitative Methods in Social Psychology," *American Sociological Review* 1 (1936), pp. 38-60.
35. McClosky, D. N., "The Rhetoric of Economics," *Journal of Economic Literature* 21 (1983), pp.481-517.
36. Mendelsohn, E., "The Social Construction of Scientific Knowledge,"

in *The Social Production of Scientific Knowledge*, E. Mendelsohn, P. Weingart, and R. Whitley, eds. (Dordrecht: Reidel, 1977), pp. 3-26.
37. Menninger, K., *Number Words and Number Symbols* (Cambridge: MIT Press, 1969).
38. Mosteller, F., and D. L. Wallace, *Inference and Disputed Authorship: The Federalist* (Reading: Addison-Wesley, 1964).
39. Mumford, L., *Technics and Civilization* (New York: Harcourt Brace, 1934).
40. Myrdal, G., *Objectivity in Social Research* (New York: Pantheon, 1969).
41. Noble, D. F., *America by Design* (New York: Knopf, 1979).
42. Pearl, R., *Modes of Research in Genetics* (New York: Macmillan, 1915).
43. Petty, Sir W., "Political Arithmetick," in *The Economic Writings of Sir William Petty*, v. 1, C. H. Hull, ed. (Cambridge University Press, 1899), pp. 233-313.
44. Plato, *The Dialogues*, B. Jowett, trans., *Great Books of the Western World*, v. 7 (Chicago: Encyclopedia Britannica, 1952).
45. Porter, T. M., *The Rise of Statistical Thinking* 1820-1900 (Princeton: Princeton University Press, 1986).
46. ________, *Trust in Numbers* (Princeton: Princeton University Press, 1995).
47. Russell, B., *The Principles of Mathematics*, 2nd ed. (New York: Norton, 1937).
48. Schorer, M., Introduction to *Moll Flanders* by D. Defoe (New York: Random House, 1950).
49. Shapin, S., and S. Schaffer, *Leviathan and the Air-Pump* (Princeton: Princeton University Press, 1985).
50. Shryock, R. H., "The History of Quantification in Medical Science," in *Quantification*, H. Woolf, ed. (Indianapolis: Bobbs-Merrill, 1961), pp. 85-107.
51. Sills, D. L., ed., *International Encyclopedia of the Social Sciences*, v. 14 (New York: Macmillan, 1968).
52. Smith, A. (pseud. G. J. W. Goodman), *Supermoney* (New York: Random House, 1972).
53. Sorokin, P. A., *Fads and Foibles in Modern Sociology and Related Sciences* (Chicago: Henry Regnery, 1956).
54. Spengler, J. J., "On the Progress of Quantification in Economics," in *Quantification*, H. Woolf, ed. (Indianapolis: Bobbs-Merrill, 1961), pp. 128-146.

55. Standen, A., *Science Is a Sacred Cow* (New York: Dutton, 1950).
56. Thomson, Sir W. (Baron Kelvin), "Electrical Units of Measurement," in Popular Lectures and Addresses, v. 1 (London: Macmillan, 1891), pp. 80-143.
57. Tolstoy, L., *War and Peace*, L. Maude and A. Maude, trans. (New York: Simon and Schuster, 1942).
58. Watson, J. B., *Behaviorism* (Chicago: University of Chicago Press, 1924).
59. Weber, M., *The Protestant Ethic and the Spirit of Capitalism*, T. Parsons, trans. (New York: Scribner, 1956).
60. ________, *The Sociology of Religion*, E. Fischoff, trans. (Boston: Beacon Press, 1963).
61. Wise, M. N., "Work and Waste: Political Economy and Natural Philosophy in Nineteenth Century Britain, Parts I, II, and III," *History of Science* 27 (1989), pp. 263-301, 391-449, and 28 (1990), pp. 221-261.

3
In Defense of Formalization in Economics[1]

These days, it seems, a lot of people are dissatisfied with a lot of economic analysis. Numerous articles and books have been written detailing complaints.[2] Numerous sessions at conventions take up the issue. One often sees and hears words such as "malaise," "disarray," and "crisis" applied to describe the current state of affairs. In perhaps the strongest rebuke of received economic theory yet, one of its founding fathers, none other than J.R. Hicks [8, p. 365], repudiated his own work by altering his identity: "Clearly I need to change my name," he wrote in 1975. "Let it be understood that *Value and Capital* (1939) was the work of J. R. Hicks, a 'neoclassical' economist now deceased; *Capital and Time* (1973) — and *A Theory of Economic History* (1969) — are the works of John Hicks, a non-neoclassic who is quite disrespectful toward his 'uncle'." Much of Hicks' subsequently published work appears under the newly-assumed name of its author.

---

[1] *Methodus* 3, no. 1 (June, 1991), pp. 17-24. © International Network for Economic Method. Reprinted with permission. (Originally presented at a joint session of the International Network for Economic Method and the American Economic Association, Washington D. C., December, 1990.)

The author would like to thank Randall Bausor, Philip Mirowski, Stephen A. Resnick, and Douglas Vickers for their help.

[2] For example, Katouzian [14], Klammer and McCloskey [20], McCloskey [23], [24], Ward [32], Woo [36], and the collections of essays edited by Bell and Kristol [1] and Wiles and Routh [35].

On the list of objectionable facets of economic analysis singled out for special complaint, the formalization of economic reasoning is often at or near the top.[3] Witness, for example, Prest's advice [28, p. 131] to the aspiring graduate student of economics: "The suggested Ph.D. thesis title 'n solutions to n - 1 problems' is a very promising theme for an academic career devoted to High Theory. Nowadays this is the super-highway to eminence and professional acclaim. And you will very quickly discover that your standing and stature will rise in geometrical proportion to the irrelevance and obscurity of what you say and write. Abraham Lincoln was wrong here: you can fool all of the people all of the time — without much effort, either." I want to argue in this paper, however, that formalization *per se* is not the problem, and that the real difficulty lies in the nature of the questions that economists tend to ask and in the assumption content of the analyses constructed to provide the answers. Indeed, formalization is, for many of us, a powerful and appropriate means of analytical expression whose avoidance would only weaken our incisiveness and create more problems than its non-use would resolve.[4] Even the argument of Prest's advice relies on a formalization that relates "standing and stature" proportionally to spoken or written "irrelevance and obscurity."

It should be noted at the outset that although it certainly has contact points with both areas, subsequent discussion is not primarily concerned with either methodology or epistemology as such. There are a variety of methodologies and epistemologies in economics and most make room for formalization in analysis, using and interpreting their analytical structures in a variety of ways.[5] However, the present discussion accepts the dominant methodology and epistemology in economics today which is based on a separation or dichotomy between reality and thoughts about reality and which, at least epistemologically, results in rationalism or empiricism or some combination thereof. Also accepted are the currently existing standards of scholarly discourse that have emerged from this background. Thus the issues considered here have not so much to do with the general implications of methodology and epistemology for formalization and vise versa, but are concerned, rather, with certain kinds of things that can be said of formalization given the methodology and episte-

[3] Complaints about formalization and responses to those complaints are not new. A notable collection of papers, one attacking, and the others defending the use of mathematics (a special kind of formalization) in economics appeared in 1954 in the *Review of Economics and Statistics* (36, pp. 357-386). For a history of how mathematics and formalization entered economics and how their use became so widespread, see Mirowski [25].

[4] This is not to say that there are not other means of analytical expression that are equally powerful and appropriate. But given current professional standards and our backgrounds, formalization is often the mode of choice.

[5] See, for example, Katzner [16].

mology employed.

I

Let me begin by defining the concept of formalization and discussing its properties, its purpose, and what it does.

The aim of analysis is to explain or clarify worldly phenomena.[6] Analysis proceeds by organizing and exploring the thoughts one has about those phenomena. The explanations that are achieved may or may not carry with them an ability to predict. In economics there are a number of routes such organizations and explorations may take. To analyze by example requires the examination of highly detailed specific instances or case studies to illustrate the phenomena under consideration. Another form of analysis, storytelling, is the giving of a narrative account of the phenomena in which "... fact, theory, and values are all mixed together in the telling."[7] But the most common method of analysis in economics involves the creation and study of models. A model of something — call the thing T — is a construct having enough in common with the observable facets of T that insight into T can be obtained by studying the model. Albert Einstein and Leopold Infeld [5, p. 33] gave the following illustration for physical models: Imagine you are presented with a watch and asked to explain how it works, but are not allowed to remove its cover. One way to proceed is to obtain appropriate springs, gears, and what not,[8] and build a "model" of the watch whose behavior duplicates the observed behavior of the original. You could then give an explanation of how your model behaves, and say that the original watch works analogously to, or as if it were, your model. Clearly, there are many different models, and hence explanations, that could be built. But all explanations function by identifying something in the model (here, the movement of the model's "hands") with what is observed (the movement of the hands on the original watch). In economics, of course, models are usually not physical things. Rather they are mental constructs based on assumptions,

6 See Caldwell [2, pp. 179,180].

7 e.g., Ward [32, p. 180]. It is possible to think of storytelling as encompassing both description (including analysis by example) and formalization (including model building). For example, one might tell a story as description that incorporates "stylized" or hypothetical facts. Alternatively, a story might make use of formalized elements as defined below, or employ both description and formalization in its telling. But in all cases, the distinctive feature of storytelling is narrative. It is in this sense that storytelling is taken here to be distinct from and independent of analysis by example and formalization.

8 Why you might choose specific gears, for example, or even why you might choose gears at all does not matter for present purposes.

abstract concepts, and relations among variables. But they function in much the same way as in the Einstein-Infeld example. Thus, in economics, model building is different from description and from analysis by example in that it essays to provide an explanation of the thing being scrutinized; it is different from storytelling in that it focuses on relations among variables rather than on narrative. Note, however, that particular economic analyses may combine examples, storytelling, and model building, as well as other forms of argument in their structures.

With these ideas in mind, formalization in economics may be defined as the development and analysis of relations among variables that constitute part (or all) of an economic model.[9] The relations themselves may be, to a greater or lesser degree, "appropriate" or "relevant," and may or may not identify or be associated with directions of causality thought to be inherent in the phenomena under investigation. Thus the purpose of formalization in economic analysis is to explain — some would add predict — observable economic phenomena. Formalization, like model building with which it is closely related, is neither description nor analysis by example or storytelling. The term "formalization" is also used, on occasion, to denote the end result of the process of formalization just described, i.e., to indicate the relations themselves. The name "formalism" is given to the special case of formalization in which the properties of the relations, as well as the implications of these properties, are fully spelled out.

Four observations concerning this notion of formalization should be noted. First, it is implicit in the definition of formalization given above that there should exist, in formalizations that are meaningfully relevant to the economic reality under examination, acceptable accordances between the model of which the formalization is a part and the observed facets of the phenomena being explained.[10] Although I will not attempt here to describe what constitutes "acceptable accordances" between a model and reality, most assuredly each economist has some idea of that which is acceptable to him, if not the acceptability standards of the economics profession at large. Furthermore, these accordances are crucial to the acceptability of both the model proposed as well as the formalizations it contains. Without such accordances, any analysis based on the model or any of its individual formalizations would be regarded as having little significance and relevance for the phenomena under investigation.

Second, formalization does not require that the variables under consider-

---

[9] It is not necessary that these relations be expressed in mathematical form.

[10] See, for example, Keynes [18, p. 296].

ation be capable of measurement.[11] In the absence of measurement, a variable's values can be specified as distinct and discrete verbal descriptions. The variable itself is the thing that can take on as values any description in the appropriate collection of verbal descriptions. Relations among such unmeasured variables can be defined in set-theoretic terms and used in model building in much the same way (except, of course, that numbers are not available) as relations among measured variables. Thus, without measurement, systems of simultaneous functional relations can be constructed and, under certain conditions, their solutions expressed as functions of parameter values. And in the same context, systems of dynamic, periodic, functional relations can be analyzed for their stability properties. A lack of ability to measure, then, is no barrier to the pursuit of formalization in economics.

Third, all formalizations that make a meaningful attempt to throw explanatory light on economic actuality are constructed through a process of abstraction. Reality is sufficiently complex that it cannot all be included in the specification of a formalization. Things have to be left out. This is so in defining variables, quantitative or not, as well as in characterizing relations.[12] Thus the contents of, or the results derived from, formalization are, at best, approximations of real or observed phenomena that are relevant only under "certain conditions" and cannot have universal applicability.[13] Exceptions necessarily arise. To handle each significant exception requires either a separate formalization addressed specifically to the exception itself, or a generalization of the original formalization that gave birth to the exception. The former leads to "localism" in analysis; the latter to formalizations that assert less and less about the real-world phenomena in question.[14]

Fourth, formalizations, like models, are analogies or metaphors. The distinction between analogy and metaphor is subtle; the following statement of their divergence will serve for present purposes. When modeling the observed behavior of a firm, for example, to say that the model is an analogy is to think of the firm as behaving "something like" that described in the model. But to take the position that the model is a metaphor means that the firm's behavior is thought of as being described or captured, with a high degree of literalness, by the model's behavior.[15] The difference is that in the first case the model itself

11 Katzner [15]. See also Essay 4 in this volume.

12 A discussion of the kinds of things that are omitted appears in Katzner [17 (this volume, Essay 6)].

13 Katouzian [14, pp. 157,158].

14 See Woo [36, pp. 29-31,69,70].

15 In economics, metaphors are sometimes established implicitly through the use of the phrase "as if." Thus, for example, under appropriate conditions a particular consumer's observed be-

(apart from its variables and relations) is an approximate similarity or likeness; in the second it is an "exact" replication.[16] But in either case, the formalizations involved liken observed reality to mental constructions in which reality is conceived of in terms of the constructions. In this way formalizations serve as both instruments of thought and as devices for communicating in an intelligible manner.[17] Their force lies in that they focus thoughts in precise ways, in that they provide standards for judging real-world behaviors, and in that they transfer the sense of one person's vision to another.

As an example of formalization in economics, consider the often-criticized, general-equilibrium model.[18] This model focuses on the notion of equilibrium and, in the tradition of methodological individualism, is built up by making assumptions about the preferences, technologies, and behaviors of fictitious, individual agents. Its purpose is to explain and clarify the observed, simultaneous, interacting behavior of real agents in an economy. Having accepted the questions this model addresses, and having accepted the equilibrium approach and the assumptions upon which the answers provided by the model are to be based, the economist has no choice but to pursue the relevant formalizations and inquire into the existence, uniqueness, and stability of equilibrium in the model.[19] An easy way to see why this must be so is to focus attention on a single, real-world market in isolation. Imagine that one were to observe the market during a particular period of time. In that case, one could see that so much of the commodity was traded at such-and-such a price or, in other words, one would observe a single point in commodity-price space. Subsequent observation in the following period would yield a second point with, say, a higher price and a larger quantity. In building a model to explain how these points came to be seen, the economist could assume (1) that there exist two distinct market demand curves each passing through one, but not the

havior may be explained as if he were a constrained utility maximizer.

[16] This is not to exclude the approximateness that comes about in the variables and the relations from the abstraction process described above.

[17] McCloskey [23].

[18] To provide but one illustration of the criticism it has received, note the following comment of Kaldor's [13, p. 13]: "... since Walras first wrote down his system of equations over 100 years ago, progress has definitely been backwards not forwards in the sense that the present set of axioms are far more restrictive than those of the original Walrasian model. The ship is no nearer to the shore, but considerably farther off, though in a logical, mathematical sense, the present system of derived tautologies is enormously superior to Walras' original effort."

[19] There seems to be some misunderstanding in the literature on this point. McCloskey [24, p. 67], for example, incorrectly states, "The problem is that ... [general theorems on existence of equilibrium do] ... not relate to anything an economist would actually want to know." Subsequent discussion addresses the issue.

same, observed point, and (2) that there exists only one market supply curve passing through them both.[20] Then, since each observed point is identified as a market equilibrium point in the model,[21] each could be explained as analogous to, or as if it were, the outcome of the interaction of supply and demand. The economist could also assert that the movement from the first point to the second occurred because of a "shift" in demand. Clearly, equilibrium must exist in the model for this explanation to work. If, moreover, the equilibrium in the model were not unique, then the explanation would be incomplete; it would allow the observed point to be identified with many equilibria, each with its own properties, and thus the reason for the movement between the two points would become clouded. Finally, when the observed point changes from the old to the new, the equilibrium in the model would have to adjust accordingly. But if the latter equilibrium were not stable, then whatever dynamics there were in the model could prevent the new equilibrium from being reached and, in that circumstance, the explanation given for the observed movement from the one point to the other would break down. An alternative interpretation of reality would be to locate observed points along time-paths that converge to equilibria in the model rather than to identify them specifically as equilibria. But in either case the questions of existence, uniqueness, and stability have to be explored because that is the only way to be sure that the model can be linked to the real world.

A similar argument applies to the full general-equilibrium model with many goods and many agents. And in spite of the fact that considerable resources and energy have already been devoted to the investigation of the existence, uniqueness, and stability questions in this context, satisfactory answers are available only in the case of existence. The problem is that, although sufficient conditions for uniqueness and stability are known, these conditions, contrary to the tenets of methodological individualism, are expressed as restrictions on aggregated, that is market, excess demand functions. Furthermore, it is not clear if it will ever be possible to give uniqueness and stability conditions that are stated with respect to the preferences or behavior of the individual agents.[22] Therefore, if methodological individualism is to be maintained, even more resources

---

[20] The assumption of a single supply curve is sufficient but not necessary for the construction of the model.

[21] Note that demand curves, supply curves, and equilibrium points cannot exist in reality. They can only be present in models. Similarly, to prove that equilibrium exists and is unique and stable in a model can never imply that unique and stable equilibria exist in the real world. The error of thinking that such elements are a part of reality has been referred to by Machlup [21, p. 12] as the "fallacy of misplaced concreteness."

[22] See Kirman [19].

and energy will have to be diverted to the mathematical analyses of general-equilibrium models. And if this quest fails, then without even questioning the realism of their assumptions or the relevance of the conclusions derived from them, general-equilibrium models will have to be discarded because they are unable to provide viable explanations of that which can be observed.

II

Justifications for the use of formalization in general, and mathematics in particular, by economists (and others) go back quite some time. Cournot [3, pp. 2-5] and Jevons [12, pp. xxi-xxv, 3-5] believed that certain forms of reasoning in economics are mathematical in character. Walras [31, pp. 47,48] thought that to be scientific is, in part, to be mathematical. More recently, Suppes [30] provides seven reasons why formalization is desirable: It aids in the clarification of conceptual problems and the building of logical foundations, in the bringing out of explicit meanings of concepts, in standardizing terminology and methods, in permitting the development of a general vision without obstruction by inessential details, in allowing the attainment of a greater degree of objectivity, in setting out the precise conditions required for the analysis to be considered, and in obtaining the minimal assumptions necessary for statement of the analysis. Debreu [4, p. 275] cites linguistic convenience and the ability to obtain deeper understanding and analytical extensions that might not otherwise be possible. Mathematical reasoning, according to Gorman [6, p. 273], is important in economics because it helps in determining "... what implies what. It is from the solid basis of such knowledge that one can make imaginative leaps into the unknown." For Solow [29, p. 33], mathematical reasoning is preferred because, *ceteris paribus* it is more exposed: "... what you see is what you get." And Weintraub [33, pp. 178,179] argues that, since we comprehend our economic world by creating mental structure, and since doing mathematics is creating mental structure in its "purest form," mathematics is naturally important and relevant in economic analysis.

All of the benefits of formalization contained in and implied by these justifications can be observed in the example of general-equilibrium analysis described in the previous section. Indeed, the general-equilibrium analogy or metaphor created through formalization is powerful, elegant, and appealing, and has led to what are considered by many to be significant results. In addition, formalization in this case can be seen as no less than the means by which the logical implications of the general-equilibrium model are worked out far enough so that its viability and usefulness can eventually be appraised. Because of its immense complexity, such a goal is probably not attainable for the subject-matter of general-equilibrium analysis without the introduction of formalization and its development to a very high degree.

What, then, is the problem? Why is there so much dissatisfaction? My contention is that the unhappiness arises from two main difficulties with current economic analysis in general. The first has been characterized by Hutchison [10, p. 88] as a "crisis of abstraction" brought about by oversimplification and the consequent irrelevance with respect to reality.[23] Hutchison traces the crisis back to that classical model builder, David Ricardo. To build a model, as pointed out earlier, Ricardo (like everyone else since) had to abstract from reality and introduce simplifying assumptions. And the most significant of these was his postulate of complete and perfect knowledge. Throughout our history, says Hutchison [10, p. 79], "This postulate has probably been the most important and pervasive single simplification, bearing more logical weight than any other, in the whole range of economic theorizing, analysis, or model-building." It is also the main source of the crisis of abstraction. "The most criticizable and unrealistic feature of '... Economic Man,' ..." to use Hutchison's words again [11, pp. 2,3], "... is not his materialism, or selfishness ... [but rather] his omniscience," and this has nothing to do with the expression of that omniscience in terms of formalizations. Thus the thing that is causing discontent here is the assumption content of the analysis and not the employment of formalization as a method of explanation.

The second difficulty that causes unease emerges from the kinds of questions that economists tend to ask. There is bound to be dissatisfaction with the application of formalization to answer what are considered to be the wrong questions. But then the problem is not really with the use of formalization. Of course, questions are set by context,[24] and the context most common today is based on the notion of equilibrium. In other words, by postulating an equilibrium framework (this is not necessarily to employ a general-equilibrium model), economists commit themselves to certain kinds of questions, far broader than mere existence, uniqueness, and stability of equilibria. But it is even more significant that when an equilibrium framework is invoked, vast areas of reality are closed off from analysis. Most notable, perhaps, is the exclusion of historical time, the frame of reference for real time, as opposed to the logical or clock time in a mechanistic model. One is reminded of Marshall's comment [22, p. 461] that:

[23] Note that this irrelevance for reality arises for a different reason than the potential irrelevance, described at the end of the previous section, of the general equilibrium model due to the possible lack of uniqueness and stability of equilibria within it.

[24] The epistemological issue of how context is determined is not discussed here.

> The theory of stable equilibrium ... helps indeed to give definiteness to our ideas; and in its elementary stages it does not diverge from the actual facts of life, so far as to prevent its giving a fairly trustworthy picture of the chief methods of action of the strongest and most persistent group of economic forces. But when pushed to its more remote and intricate logical consequences, it slips away from the conditions of real life .... [E]conomic problems are imperfectly presented when they are treated as problems of ... equilibrium, and not of organic growth ....
>
> The Statical theory of equilibrium is only an introduction to economic studies .... Its limitations are so constantly overlooked, especially by those who approach it from an abstract point of view, that there is a danger in throwing it into definite form at all. But, with this caution, the risk may be taken ....

At any rate, these exorcisms have nothing to do with the presence or absence of formalization as such but they are, it seems to me, the second reason for so much discontent.

The two difficulties or sources of dissatisfaction with economic analysis just described are, in part, transcended by what may be called the "angle of vision" that any scholar brings to his work. Angles of vision emerge from pre-analytical persuasions arising out of backgrounds and experiences, and they influence, in turn, the nature of the questions asked and the assumption content of the analyses put forward to answer them. In this way, and in a very broad sense, all scholarly enterprise is inescapably contaminated by ideology, politics, culture, and values.[25] Thus, not only are many attacks on formalization more properly understood as attacks on the questions being asked and on the assumptions being made, but also may explicitly or implicitly be raising issues concerning the rightness or wrongness of the angle of vision upon which these elements, as well as the formalizations themselves, are based.

There remains, nevertheless, the issue of whether formalization in economics has gone too far. Have we arrived at the point where economic analysis has become, to use Hick's phrase [9, p. viii], a "good game" in which the pursuit of mathematical "fun" takes priority over the shedding of light on economic phenomena? Were this so, then the fear of Katouzian [14, p. 168] that mathematical form and technique might come to determine the substance and content of economic knowledge, would be upon us. However, illustrating his thesis with respect to the development of general-equilibrium stability analysis, Weintraub [34, p. 96] takes the position that this has not yet hap-

[25] See Myrdal [27, pp. vii,viii].

pened. There exists, instead, a symbiotic relation in which both economic conceptualizations select the mathematical tools and the mathematical tools select the economic conceptualizations. Reassuring as this might be, it does not address Morishima's belief [26, p. 64] that the marginal productivity of using mathematical argument has declined, "... not from the increase in the absolute quantity of mathematics at our disposal, but from the ever greater injection of mathematics into a fixed quantity of material." Nor does it preclude the notion that formalization goes too far when improper uses are made of it. That is, economic analysis becomes a good game when, for example, excessive formalization results in the arguing out the logical implications of alternative formalized assumptions that can have no analogical or metaphorical relation to the phenomena under investigation. In such a situation the acceptable accordances between the formalizations being manipulated and reality have broken down, and further exploration of these formalizations (which actually cease to be formalizations in the sense defined earlier) is irrelevant to explanation and clarification.

In the end, the issue of whether formalization in economics has gone too far in either of these last two connotations is a judgement call. And if it has, the reason may have more to do with the sociology and psychology of our profession than with formalization itself.[26] For if a scholar chooses to tackle a problem through the use of formalization as opposed to, say, analysis by example or storytelling, it may be all or in part because of the necessities and advantages, described above, that the employment of formalization entails. But in many cases it may also be because, as Prest's advice suggests, that is where the rewards of publication, recognition, support money, promotion, and tenure are. The scholar's angle of vision notwithstanding, even the selection of the problem to work on is subject to the same reward pressures. And the structure of these rewards tends to be set by the established standards of what constitutes relevant and significant questions, and what makes up the appropriate assumption content of analyses which purport to provide answers. Clearly the existence of established standards provides a powerful rationalization for the continued use of formalization. I maintain that formalization for the sake of formalization alone has never been, and will never be, knowingly acceptable or confessed to by most economists. But this is not to say that we are immune to being fooled by the questions we ask and misled by our assumptions.

In another sense, formalization in economics cannot go too far. For as I have argued above, as soon as one commits oneself to the pursuit of the questions

---

[26] A model of the sociology of an academic profession such as economics has been proposed by Katouzian [14, pp. 119-123].

and assumptions of, say, general-equilibrium analysis, then one has no choice but to follow the accompanying formalizations to their logical ends. As the French philosopher Granger said of axiomatization [7, p. 145], which is, of course, a special kind of formalization, "If the axiomatizations proposed by ... the economist are of any use for the progress of [economic] science, it is not because they appear to ape the constructions of mathematics. It is because they offer to rational thought the sole means of escaping from the attractions of data derived from experience," and one of the few ways of extracting positive structures from the complex and confounding jumble of reality.

References

1. Bell, D., and I. Kristol, eds., *The Crisis in Economic Theory* (New York: Basic Books, 1981).
2. Caldwell, B. J., *Beyond Positivism: Economic Methodology in the Twentieth Century* (London: George Allen & Unwin, 1982).
3. Cournot, A., *Researches into the Mathematical Principles of the Theory of Wealth*, N. T. Bacon, trans. (New York: Kelley, 1960).
4. Debreu, G., "Economic Theory in the Mathematical Mode," *American Economic Review* 74 (1984), pp. 267-278.
5. Einstein, A., and L. Infeld, *The Evolution of Physics* (New York: Simon & Schuster, 1938)
6. Gorman, T., "Towards a Better Economic Methodology?" in *Economics in Disarray*, P. Wiles and G. Routh, eds. (Oxford: Basil Blackwell, 1984), pp. 260-288.
7. Granger, G. G., *Formal Thought and the Sciences of Man*, A. Rosenberg, trans. (Dordrech: Reidel, 1983).
8. Hicks, Sir J., "The Revival of Political Economy: The Old and the New," *Economic Record* 51 (1975), pp. 356-367.
9. ________, *Causality in Economics* (New York: Basic Books, 1979).
10. Hutchison, T. W., *Knowledge and Ignorance in Economics* (Chicago: University of Chicago Press, 1977).
11. ________, "Our Methodological Crisis," in *Economics in Disarray*, P. Wiles and G. Routh, eds. (Oxford: Basil Blackwell, 1984), pp. 1-21.
12. Jevons, W. S., *The Theory of Political Economy*, 5th ed. (New York: Kelley, 1965).
13. Kaldor, N., *Economics without Equilibrium* (New York: M. E. Sharpe,

1985).
14. Katouzian, H., *Ideology and Method in Economics* (New York: New York University Press, 1980).
15. Katzner, D. W., *Analysis without Measurement* (Cambridge: Cambridge University Press, 1983).
16. _______, "Alternatives to Equilibrium Analysis," *Eastern Economic Journal* 11 (1985), pp. 404-421.
17. _______, "The Role of Formalism in Economic Thought, with Illustration Drawn from the Analysis of Social Interaction in the Firm," in *The Reconstruction of Economic Theory*, P. Mirowski, ed. (Boston: Kluwer-Nijhoff, 1986), pp. 137-177. This volume, Essay 6.
18. Keynes, J. M., Letter to R. F. Harrod, July 4, 1938, in *Collected Writings* v. 14, D. Moggridge, ed. (London: Macmillan, 1973), p. 296.
19. Kirman, A., "The Intrinsic Limits of Modern Economic Theory: The Emperor Has No Clothes," *Economic Journal* 99 (Conference, 1989), pp. 126-139.
20. Klammer, A., and D. N. McCloskey, "The Rhetoric of Disagreement," *Rethinking Marxism* v. 2, no. 3 (Fall, 1989), pp. 140-161.
21. Machlup, F., "Equilibrium and Disequilibrium: Misplaced Concreteness and Disguised Politics," *Economic Journal* 68 (1958), pp. 1-24.
22. Marshall, A., *Principles of Economics*, 8th ed. (New York: Macmillan, 1948).
23. McCloskey, D. N., "The Rhetoric of Economics," *Journal of Economic Literature* 21 (1983), pp. 481-517.
24. _______, "Formalism in Economics, Rhetorically Speaking," *Ricerche Economiche* 43 (1989), pp. 57-75.
25. Mirowski, P., "The When, the How and the Why of Mathematical Expression in the History of Economic Analysis," *Journal of Economic Perspectives* 5 (1991), pp. 145-157.
26. Morishima, M., "The Good and Bad Uses of Mathematics," in *Economics in Disarray*, P. Wiles and G. Routh, eds. (Oxford: Basil Blackwell, 1984), pp. 51-73.
27. Myrdal, G., *The Political Element in the Development of Economic Theory*, P. Streeten, trans. (London: Routledge & Kegan Paul, 1953).
28. Prest, A. R., "Letter to a Young Economist," *Journal of Economic Affairs* 3 (January, 1983), pp. 130-134.
29. Solow, R. M., "Comments from Inside Economics," in *The Consequences of Economic Rhetoric*, A. Klammer, D. N. McCloskey, and R. M. Solow,

eds. (Cambridge: Cambridge University Press, 1988), pp. 31-37.

30. Suppes, P., "The Desirability of Formalization in Science," *Journal of Philosophy* 65 (1968), pp. 651-664.
31. Walras, L., *Elements of Pure Economics*, W. Jaffé, trans. (Homewood: Irwin, 1954).
32. Ward, B., *What's Wrong with Economics*? (New York: Basic Books, 1972).
33. Weintraub, E. R., *General Equilibrium Analysis: Studies in Appraisal* (Cambridge: Cambridge University Press, 1985).
34. ________, *Stabilizing Dynamics: Constructing Economic Knowledge* (Cambridge: Cambridge University Press, 1991).
35. Wiles, P., and G. Routh, eds., *Economics in Disarray* (Oxford: Basil Blackwell, 1984).
36. Woo, H. K. H., *What's Wrong with Formalization in Economics? An Epistemological Critique* (Newark: Victoria, 1986).

4

On Not Quantifying the Non-Quantifiable[1]

Ours is a world of numbers. One of the popular paradigms for scholarly work in the social sciences is a model whose fundamental concepts, at least in principle, are capable of measurement, and whose theoretical structures lead to numerically verifiable hypotheses expressed in terms of them. Ideas lacking the means of calibration are often discarded. The more quantitative the mathematical sophistication, the higher the esteem the investigation receives. This is certainly true in economics. Yet, it is quite clear that many of the urgent questions economists are called upon to answer concern phenomena which seemingly defy attempts to represent them numerically.

Examples abound. Economists have a well-developed theory of demand resting squarely on the notions of utility and maximization. But what is it about specific personalities in their relation to utility that leads them to purchase commodities in certain observed patterns? Culture, social class, and education, through utility, also have an impact on consumption patterns. How? Why do waves of "fashion" arise, and in what ways do they influence utility and hence demand? Again, it is well known how costs depend on factor prices and the latter on the demand and supply of factors themselves. But there is

---

[1] *Journal of Post Keynesian Economics* 1, no. 2 (Winter, 1978-79), pp. 113-128.

The author would like to express his appreciation to I.F Pearce for many helpful discussions and comments. Thanks are also due to Sidney Weintraub for suggesting the essay's title.

no theory to elucidate why one profession is "respectable" and another not. Nor is there much theoretical understanding of the responses of participants in labor-management disputes to the vague political, social, and psychological pressures under which they operate. Similarly, the theory of the firm describes how valuable goods are created at minimum cost and maximum profit. But there seems to be no room for the notion that the firm is also a social unit capable of generating "well-being" in addition to money income and profit. As a final illustration, the distribution of income that "ought to be" is as important to everyone as the distribution of income that actually is. Clearly this question cannot even be approached without a theory of "justice." Yet "positive" economists take pride in exorcising any such theory on the grounds that what cannot be measured is not "scientific," or that value judgments are exogenous. These last two reasons may, in fact, go very far toward explaining why the issues that are raised in all of the above examples are ignored so nonchalantly.

It may be that the apparent determination of economists to exclude non-quantifiable elements from their subject is due less to the feeling that what cannot be measured is irrelevant than to the supposition that measurability and exactness of language necessarily go together. Nevertheless, in spite of the present emphasis on statistics and lack of attention to "political economy," it is clearly not true that the only entities of interest to economists are those that can be represented on numerical scales, such as prices and the level of employment.

The purpose of the present paper is to demonstrate that exactness and measurability are not synonymous. Mathematical argument need not involve only quantifiable elements. A lack of ability to measure is no barrier to the conduct of rigorous scientific inquiry. To refuse to talk about what does not appear scalable may be one of the greatest mistakes of the current generation. Perhaps it was the particular evolution of mathematics into its present form, or the enchantment of economists with only certain aspects of it, which induced them to try to fit numbers everywhere and to turn their backs on important phenomena simply because no sensible way of attaching numbers could be found. But whatever the reason, there is little doubt that the result has contributed significantly to the narrowness of view under which economists now labor.

This paper does not present a theory nor prove a theorem. Rather, it is a plea to widen the horizons of our thought. It provides some suggestions as to how one might go about this while at the same time retaining all the exactness of mathematical expression. This is certainly not the first word on the subject of analysis without measurement — there is already considerable historical precedent for analyzing non-quantifiable phenomena in social science.[2] But it

2 Examples are provided in the works of Weber [15], [16], Parsons [11], Pareto [10], Apter [2], Goodenough [5], and Hagen [6].

is very important that the present discussion should not be the last.

Briefly, the following exposition begins with variables and relations between them. A simple simultaneous "equations" system is presented and, after a composition operation is introduced for manipulative purposes, conditions are given under which solutions exist and can be expressed as functions of parameters. Next, periodic "equations" (i.e., equations with lagged variables) are defined and explored for stationary paths and stability properties. The latter requires a digression into the idea of convergence. At this point, an analogy is drawn with the standard multiplier analysis of macroeconomic theory. Finally, some attention is directed toward the problems of empirical verification. Since general analysis and proofs can be found elsewhere (Katzner [8], [9]), the discussion below is often intuitive, motivational, and suggestive. Above all, it is designed as a simplified expositional statement to provide an appreciation of its social science applications.

Simultaneous Relations

When quantifiability is lacking, and thus arithmetic and other numerical operations are inapplicable, it is natural to begin with the notion of sets. A set, call it X, is a collection of not-necessarily-quantifiable discrete objects. Except for discreteness, no restrictions are imposed on these objects. There is nothing to prevent them from being collections of other objects or entire systems of relations (defined below). The elements (objects) of X are denoted by x. Primes, bars, asterisks, superscripts, and subscripts on x always specify particular objects of X. To illustrate one way of putting sets together, suppose agreement has been reached on a comprehensive list of n fundamental values, such as "fairness" or "honesty," that individuals may hold. Symbolize these by $\nu_1, ..., \nu_n$. Each value is assumed to be distinct and satisfactorily defined in terms of certain primitive words accepted as the basic language of discourse. Any particular individual's values would then be a sublist, say, ν_1, ν_4, ν_7, or just ν_{n-1}. Thus the set X of all possible combinations of human values consists precisely of all sublists x obtained from $\nu_1, ..., \nu_n$.

The variable "values a human being holds" may now be defined as the variable ranging over X. It is often written as x — the same symbol used to represent the elements of X. This is a perfectly valid method of characterizing variables in general: first specify the set X over which the variable runs; then define the variable as that variable which may assume as values the objects of X.

Relations between variables are also easily obtained. Let X and Y be sets whose associated variables are x and y. Then any collection of pairs (x^0, y^0), where x^0 is in X and y^0 is in Y, is said to specify a (binary) relation or relationship between x and y. For example, if X and Y are the same set of people and the relation under consideration is "sisterhood," then (x^0, y^0) is a pair in the relation if and only if x^0 and y^0 are sisters. If x denotes values human beings may hold as defined above, and y varies over personalities of candidates in an election, then the statement that individuals with certain kinds of values vote for candidates with particular personalities may be represented by a relation. The pair (x^0, y^0) is in the relation provided the values of the individual voting, x^0, and personality of the candidate, y^0, stand in the given relationship to each other.

Whenever a relation between x and y has the property that to each x^0 in X there corresponds exactly one y^0 in Y, it is called a *function* or *functional* relation. The functional requirement states that two pairs such as (x^0, y^0) and (x^0, y'), where $y^0 \neq y'$, cannot appear in the relation. Functions are often written

$$y = f(x),$$

where f is the symbolic name of the relation. Thus, the sentence, "The political personality for whom an individual votes is associated with or determined by the values of the voter," may be abbreviated as $y = f(x)$ as long as y and x are properly defined. In this case x is called the *independent* and y the *dependent* variable. If there were a second independent variable, z, and if x and z were functionally related to y, then

$$y = f(x, z),$$

that is, for every x^0 in X and z^0 in some Z, there is a unique y^0 in Y.

It is important to emphasize that neither the notion of function nor the symbolism

$$y = f(x),$$

or

$$y = f(x, z),$$

requires that the variables x, y, and z be scalable. Both are perfectly valid in non-numerical, set-theoretic contexts. Of course, quantitative methods — in particular, the calculus — are not applicable without measurement, and alternative analytical tools must be found. These are introduced shortly.

Consider first, however, the problem of formulating a conceptual structure to understand and predict an observed phenomenon. Suppose an investigator identifies two variables, x and y, and a parameter, z (a variable determined outside his realm of interest). Suppose he further hypothesizes two distinct and independent functional relations:

$$\begin{aligned} y &= f(x, z), \\ x &= g(y, z). \end{aligned} \tag{1}$$

Two questions immediately arise. In the first place, is it logically possible to conceive of f and g in force together, or are they contradictory? In other words, given a value for z, does there exist at least one pair (x^0, y^0) satisfying both relations simultaneously? This is equivalent to asking if the hypothetical structure defined by (1) is internally consistent. Second, does the structure (1) determine a unique x^0 and y^0 for each specification of the parameter z; that is, does (1) imply a functional relation between z and "solution" values of (x, y) from (1)? If so, knowledge of f, g, and z is sufficient to permit prediction of (x, y). Clearly, an affirmative answer to the second question implies an affirmative answer to the first, but not conversely. (Recall, also, the discussion of simultaneous functional relations in the introductory essay above).

These ideas may be illustrated with an analogy drawn from quantitative elementary algebra. Let z be fixed and suppose f and g represent straight lines in the real Euclidean plane pictured in Figure 1. As drawn, the simultaneous occurrence of f and g appears at a single point (x^0, y^0). In this case system (1) is internally consistent and has a unique solution; it is called *exactly determined.* If g were discarded, then f would still be an internally consistent structure, but it could not identify a unique point. The system is *underdetermined.* If a third relation were added — say, h in Figure 1 — no point could satisfy all relations simultaneously and the system would be *overdetermined.* When variables are quantifiable and relations linear, there are two conditions which, if satisfied, guarantee that (1) is exactly determinate: (a) the number of variables and relations is the same; and (b) f and g are neither parallel nor coincident lines in the plane.

When measurement is not possible, different conditions may be given which ensure that unique solutions exist and hence that (1) is internally consistent. But before these are derived, techniques for manipulating relations must be introduced. These serve to compensate, in part, for the loss of addition, subtraction, multiplication, and division in the non-quantifiable world.

Two functions, say,

$$y = r(x),$$

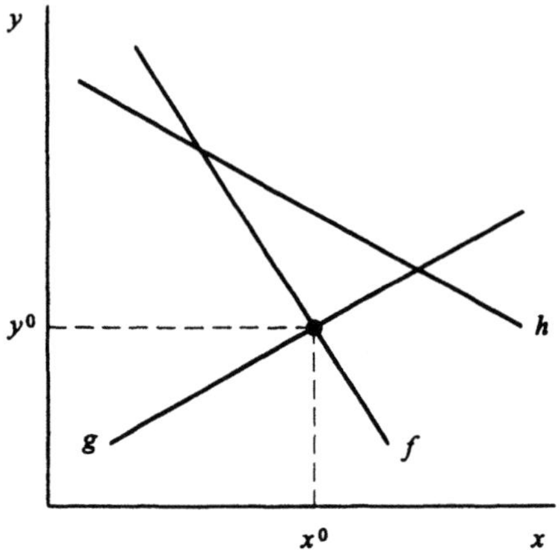

Figure 1

and

$$x = s(z),$$

can always be combined to form a third

$$y = q(z),$$

where

$$q(z) = r(s(z)).$$

That is, q is obtained by substituting $s(z)$ for x in $r(x)$. This elimination of variables procedure is often called the operation of *composition*. It is used extensively below.

To assert that the functional relation

$$y = r(x, z)$$

has an *inverse* with respect to x means that there exists a second functional relation

$$x = s(y, z),$$

such that

$$y = r(s(y, z), z).$$

Thus, given z and starting with any y^0 in Y, if one first applies s to obtain an x^0 in X and then applies r to revert to Y, one always obtains the original y^0. The inverse of r with respect to x is precisely s. Functions with inverses have very specific properties that are not pursued here.

Note that neither the combination (composition) of functions nor their inversion (i.e., the existence of their inverses) rests in any way on the presence of numerical scales. Both may be abstractly conceived in algebraic or set-theoretic terms.

Returning to (1), suppose f has an inverse with respect to z, namely,

$$z = u(x, y). \tag{2}$$

After the second relation of (1) is used to eliminate x, (2) becomes

$$z = \xi(y, z),$$

where

$$\xi(y, z) = u(g(y, z), z).$$

If ξ has an inverse, γ, with respect to y, then

$$y = \delta(z), \tag{3}$$

where

$$\delta(z) = \gamma(z, z).$$

Finally, when (3) is substituted into the second relationship of (1),

$$x = \lambda(z), \tag{4}$$

where

$$\lambda(z) = g(\delta(z), z).$$

Equations (3) and (4) express solutions of (1) as functions of the parameter z. The argument is valid whenever f and ξ have appropriate inverses. A similar conclusion could have been reached if g had had an inverse with respect to z and a function corresponding to ξ also had had the proper inverse. These ideas are easily generalized to larger systems involving any number of relations, variables, and parameters (Katzner [8], [9]).

Regardless of whether the above conditions are met, solutions of (1) may still exist. With or without solutions, "cycles" are also a possibility. Let the positive integers, denoted by the subscript t, distinguish between inputs and outputs. Think of (1), for example, as taking output $t-1$ and placing it back in the system as input $t-1$ to produce output t. Thus (1) may be rewritten in the form

$$y_t = f(x_{t-1}, z),$$
$$x_t = g(y_{t-1}, z). \tag{5}$$

Suppose the parameter z is fixed. Then, given an initial input (x^0, y^0), a sequence $(x_1, y_1), (x_2, y_2), ..., (x_t, y_t), ...,$ is generated as t moves across $1, 2, ...$ It is still required that x_t be in X and y_t be in Y for every t.

A solution of (5) is a pair $(\bar{x}, \bar{y})$ where $\bar{x}$ is in X, $\bar{y}$ is in Y, and

$$x_t = x_{t-1} = \bar{x},$$

$$y_t = y_{t-1} = \bar{y},$$

for all $t \geq 1$. In other words, start (5) at a solution and it remains there. Clearly $(\bar{x}, \bar{y})$ is a solution of (5) if and only if it is also a solution of (1). Under certain conditions, convergence (to be defined in the next section) of an arbitrary sequence (x_t, y_t) obtained from (5) implies the existence of at least one solution. A cycle is a finite sequence of pairs $(x_0, y_0), (x_1, y_1), ...,$ repeating itself over and over again in the same order. Should X and Y each contain a finite number of elements, exactly one of the following holds: every pair (x', y') with x' in X and y' in Y is (a) a solution of (5); (b) in exactly one cycle; or (c) an element of at least one sequence generated by (5) which converges to a solution. Further properties of cycles in the finite case have been explored elsewhere (Katzner [9]).

When quantification is possible, these structures are often used as a basis for organizing and understanding reality. The perfectly competitive, Walrasian model of microeconomic theory is a sophisticated illustration. It views the economic structure as a system of simultaneous relations reflecting the hypotheses that (i) all consumers are buying outputs and selling factors so as to maximize utility subject to their budget constraints; (ii) all firms are supplying outputs and hiring inputs so as to maximize profits; and (iii) supply equals demand in all markets. Economic equilibrium is a point that satisfies all relations simultaneously (see, for example, Arrow and Hahn [3]).

In the non-quantifiable world, it is possible to distinguish between political structure and political system by thinking of the former as a system of simultaneous relations and the latter as determined by it (Katzner [7 (this volume, Essay 13)]). Less formal examples may be found in Pareto [10], Parsons [11], Apter [2], and elsewhere. In principle, at least, all static phenomena involving simultaneously interacting elements can be modeled in this way. The sufficient conditions guaranteeing solutions (viz., that the number of relationships be equal to the number of variables, and that appropriate inverses exist) can be used as a basis for checking internal consistency and, of course, the same conditions could also be brought to bear were x, y, and z to be cardinally quantified in the particular application under consideration.

Change Over Time

An alternative, though related, perspective for viewing reality focuses on transformation over time. The discussion centering around (5) has already hinted at such a possibility. It is now appropriate to consider the dynamic approach more specifically. To do so, however, requires a preliminary discussion of convergence.

Consider a set X of objects and a sequence $x_1, x_2, \ldots, x_n, \ldots$ contained in it. When the elements of X can be measured, convergence is often defined in terms of ordinary Euclidean distance. That is, the sequence converges to x^* if, for every number $\varepsilon > 0$, it is possible to go far enough out in the sequence so that the distance between x^* and any remaining term is smaller than ε. Although functions with many of the properties of Euclidean distance are easily specified even in cases where quantification is absent, a more general and transparent route is followed here.

Suppose the objects of X exhibit to varying degrees a particular property α. Introduce an ordering relation, ρ_α, among them indicating the extent to which each satisfies α. Thus (x', x'') is in ρ_α if and only if x' displays property α at least as strongly as x''. To illustrate, the set of possible collections of human values discussed in the previous section could be ordered to show which combinations of values make it easier for the individual to earn the respect of others in society. Since ρ_α is taken to be reflexive and transitive, it induces an equivalence relation partitioning X into mutually exclusive and exhaustive equivalence classes. All elements within an equivalence class exhibit α to the same degree. In general, the existence of ρ_α implies neither ordinal nor interval (cardinal) measurement in the sense in which these terms are commonly used.[3]

Generally, any number of relevant properties might be identified during the course of an investigation. The collection of countable unions and finite intersections of all equivalence classes obtained from them defines a topology for

---

[3] Only for the special case in which X is countable will there be an ordinal scale (see Pfanzagl [12]). Of course, the availability of ordinal numbers still does not legitimize the use of arithmetic operations in the usual way.

X. In this context, the standard topological characterization of convergence applies: $x_1, x_2, ..., x_n, ...$ *converges* to x^* provided that for any set T containing x^* in the topology it is possible to go far enough out in the sequence for all remaining terms also to be in T. There are particular situations in which convergence means "closeness" in the sense that, as n grows, x_n and x_{n+1} become more and more alike with respect to the relative strengths of the properties they exhibit. But, as usual, exceptions to the rule are easily found.

It should be noted that the use of sets of ordering relations defined over the same class of objects is not new in social science. Riker and Ordeshook [13, pp. 308-311] begin their discussion of voting with the assumption that on every issue the voter orders the collection of all candidates according to his feelings about the candidates' positions on that issue. For each issue, then, there is one ordering of candidates per voter. By contrast, Robinson [14] shows how orderings of a collection of archaeological deposits by the frequency of appearance of artifact types (one ordering for each type) can aid in determining the overall chronological order of the deposits. Clearly, either set of orderings provides a framework within which closeness and convergence may be explored.

Returning to the problem of formulating dynamic structures, consider a simple periodic relation of the form

$$z_t = h(z_{t-1}, p). \tag{6}$$

Here z and p are, respectively, a variable and a parameter defined over some sets Z and P; the subscript t indicates time; and h is the symbolic name of the functional relation linking values of z in period $t-1$ and the parameter to values of z in period t. Again, measurement of z and p are not required for the validity of (6). Given a starting point z_0, relation (6) generates a sequence or time path of values of z:

$$z_1 = h(z_0, p),$$

$$z_2 = h(h(z0, p), p),$$

$$\vdots$$

A path through $\bar{z}$ is *stationary* whenever

$$z_t = \bar{z},$$

for all t. Starting at $\bar{z}$, relation (6) merely reproduces $\bar{z}$ over and over again.

The existence of stationary paths depends on whether or not a $\bar{z}$ can be found such that

$$\bar{z} = h(\bar{z}, p).$$

As in the previous section, if h has an inverse with respect to p, then

$$p = w(\bar{z}),$$

for an appropriate w. And if w is also invertible, $\bar{z}$ can be expressed as a function of parameter values. Therefore, under these conditions, one stationary path is associated with each value of p.

A stationary path is *globally stable* if all other time paths converge to it (in the sense defined above). Sufficient conditions ensuring convergence of individual paths can be obtained by adapting Liapunov's "second method" for analyzing stability properties of numerical differential equations. From this perspective, convergence requires the existence of a function relating z to the real numbers and having certain specific properties. The details are beyond the scope of the present discussion (Katzner [8], [9]).

These results are easily generalized to more complicated relations and systems of relations. Their use as an aid in understanding observed dynamic processes in quantitative areas of the social sciences is well known. The variety of models used to explore various aspects of economic growth provide numerous illustrations (see, for example, Allen [1]). On the non-quantifiable level, Hagen's [6] description of the emergence of innovative personalities can be reduced to a periodic relation (Katzner [9, Ch. 10]).

It is worth concluding this section with a brief reference to the multiplier analysis of quantitative macroeconomic theory. One interpretation runs as follows: Several fundamental relations (for example, the consumption function) determine an equilibrium level of income — that is, a stationary path — as a function of various parameters (autonomous investment, marginal propensity to consume, etc.). The actual time path of income emerges from a dynamic process with sufficient properties assumed to guarantee stability. Hence, at any moment the economy is on a path converging to the equilibrium or stationary path. But before evolution can progress very far, parameters change and the equilibrium income level shifts. The actual path must, in the course of time, change direction and move toward the new equilibrium. Thus, the macroeconomic world is viewed in reference to a never-ending sequence of exogenous shifts in the stable stationary path, and an actual path that is somewhat behind but always trying to catch up.

The preceding analysis suggests that such a conception of dynamic reality does not depend on the ability to measure. Stationary and actual paths can still be defined, and the, former may be assumed globally stable. Transformations in the stationary path caused by parametric variation must ultimately draw the actual path along with it. In the absence of further parameter changes, the end of the actual path, and hence its eventual direction, are known. There is no reason why non-quantifiable experience cannot be understood and policy formulated in these terms.

Empirical Verification

The formation of structure as an aid in making real phenomena intelligible is all but useless without links to the visible world. Some means for passing judgment on its empirical validity is absolutely essential. If there were no way to check its assumptions or implications against actual observation, structural development would be little more than a mental exercise. When calibration is possible, a wide variety of statistical procedures are available for the job. This concluding section will suggest the not-so-surprising fact that many of them are still applicable without it.

Informal checks of non-quantifiable assertions have been used in the past. Hagen [6], for example, compares his sequence of loss of status, retreatism, repression, and emergence of creative personalities to the historical experience of England, Japan, Colombia, and so on. He is most successful, perhaps, with Japan. The pattern of Japanese history consists of cyclical oscillations between national integration and feudal disunion. Within the turmoil created by these fluctuations, influential lords were able to defend their status; the lesser elite could not. Hagen traces the retreatism of the latter elites and the ensuing appearance of innovative persons across the years. Most recently, the Tokugawa era (1660-1867) saw the declassing of samurai, merchants, and wealthy peasants. Their descendants seem to have played a major role in the subsequent modernization of Japan.

As would be true even if numerical methods were employed, the correspondence between Hagen's theory and the historical record of Japan proves nothing. It merely provides the comfort of consistency with experience — at least for Japan. By contrast, the remarkable economic development in Pakistan between 1947 and 1960 cannot be explained as a result of loss of status of certain groups. Thus, comforting consistency and empirical refutation are the two possibilities. Statistical analysis of quantifiable phenomena, with all of its power, can do no more. On the other hand, the advantages of formal procedures are not to be denied. They furnish specific criteria for acceptance or rejection of assertions that reflect precisely the confidence one might have of their empirical viability. In reaching for this sort of exactness, Hagen tries to establish a statistical association in early twentieth-century Japan between being an economic innovator and being a descendant of one of the declassed groups. But his data are too sparse to be consequential.

A second illustration of empirical analysis of non-quantifiable phenomena appears in the efforts of Dalkey, Lewis, and Snyder [4] to obtain preliminary individual and aggregate ratings of eight career-living alternatives. Each career-living environment was described by one or two paragraphs of prose. They ranged from directing a training program in public administration at Dartmouth College to a supervisory program analyst position in Saigon. Participants were asked to evaluate and rate environments according to the extent to which they felt certain prescribed qualities (such as meaningfulness, security, newness, etc.) were present. They were also asked independently for their own personal preferences among them. The data suggested considerable variability in qualities of environments, and indicated possible ways to improve the lower scoring ones. A similar study investigated rankings of various modes of travel (also described verbally) between two points.

All formal statistical analysis rests on the theory of probability. And it is well known that the sample space (written X) over which probability is defined does not need quantification. The single tossing of a coin is a classic example. With two outcomes, heads (H) and tails (T), the sample space is

$$x = \{H, T\}.$$

In the absence of bias, both H and T are assigned probability $1/2$. The density function is uniform and if, say, H were to come before T, according to some accepted ordering, the cumulative distribution could be found.

The same ideas apply in general. A probability function may be defined on the appropriate subsets of X in the usual manner. The standard notion of random variable mapping X into a not-necessarily-quantifiable set Y also carries over without alteration. The probability function on X induces one on Y. Moreover, under certain conditions (which do not imply the existence of ordinal or interval scales), density and distribution functions may also be obtained (Katzner [9]).

Even without measurement, density functions (when they exist) can still involve parameters. Thus with $x = \{x', x''\}$ and $0 \leq \theta \leq 1$, the density

$$f(x, \theta) = \begin{cases} \frac{1}{2}(1+\theta), & \text{if } x = x', \\ \frac{1}{2}(1-\theta), & \text{if } x = x'', \end{cases}$$

depends on θ. In this context, a version of the Neyman-Pearson lemma may be proved which justifies the ordinary hypothesis-testing procedure for choosing between two values of θ. Furthermore, when it is more appropriate to determine θ by estimation, the standard procedures also apply (Katzner [9]).

Finally, there are non-parametric tests appropriate for various purposes. To test for the existence of a statistical relation between two variables, the rank or τ tests for independence may be employed. Rejection of the null hypothesis suggests a connection between them. In other contexts the test for statistical association (attempted inconclusively by Hagen) does the same thing.

Conclusion

In sum, economic inquiry does not require the introduction of proxies and pseudo-measures to accommodate phenomena that do not appear to be easily represented on numerical scales. Without losing any of the rigor of mathematical argument, it is possible to treat the not quantifiable as non-quantifiable. Internally consistent static and dynamic models can be constructed, analyzed, and subjected to empirical tests. There is no excuse, then, for setting aside important issues because it is difficult to see how the variables involved might reasonably be measured.

References

1. Allen, R. G. D., *Macro-Economic Theory* (London: Macmillan, 1970).
2. Apter, D. E., *The Politics of Modernization* (Chicago: University of Chicago Press, 1965).
3. Arrow, K. J., and F. H. Hahn, *General Competitive Analysis* (San Francisco: Holden-Day, 1971).
4. Dalkey, N. C., R. Lewis, and D. Snyder, "Measurement and Analysis of the Quality of Life," in *Studies in the Quality of Life*, N. C. Dalkey, ed. (Lexington: D. C. Heath, 1972), Ch. 4.
5. Goodenough, W. H., *Cooperation in Change* (New York: Wiley, 1966).
6. Hagen, E., *On the Theory of Social Change* (Chicago: Dorsey, 1962).
7. Katzner, D. W., "Political Structure and System and the Notion of Logical Completeness," *General Systems* 14 (1969), pp. 169-171. (This volume, Essay 13.)
8. ________, "On the Analysis of Systems Containing Non-Quantifiable

Elements," *Kybernetes* 2 (1973), pp. 147-155.
9. ________, *Analysis Without Measurement* (Cambridge: Cambridge University Press, 1983).
10. Pareto, V., *The Mind and Society*, A. Bongiorno and A. Livingston, trans. (New York: Dover, 1935).
11. Parsons, T., *The Structure of Social Action* (2 vols.), 2nd ed. (New York: Free Press, 1968).
12. Pfanzagl, J., *Theory of Measurement*, 2nd ed. (Würzburg/Vienna: Physica-Verlag, 1971).
13. Riker, W. H., and P. C. Ordeshook, *An Introduction to Positive Political Theory* (Englewood Cliffs: Prentice-Hall, 1973).
14. Robinson, W. S., "A Method for Chronologically Ordering Archaeological Deposits," *American Antiquity* 16 (1951), pp. 293-301.
15. Weber, M., *The Protestant Ethic and the Spirit of Capitalism*, T. Parsons, trans. (New York: Scribner, 1956).
16. ________, *The Sociology of Religion*, F. Fischoff, trans. (Boston: Beacon Press, 1963).

Reply to Brennan[1]

The purpose of my recent article in the *JPKE* was to present a methodological basis for incorporating into formal economic analysis (and, for that matter, political and social analysis) variables whose values do not appear to be capable of measurement. In his comment, Brennan [3] argues that my methodology has little applicability because: (1) the variable values employed in my non-quantifiable context require discrete and "exact definition ... in objective terms;" and (2) this is generally impossible for non-quantifiable variable values in social science and, in particular, cannot be done in the special case of economics. Part of statement (2) is derived from his claim that the objectivity demanded in (1) cannot be achieved. The remainder rests on a distinction made by Georgescu-Roegen between dialectical and arithmomorphic theorizing. Thus Brennan asserts that: (3) non-quantifiable variable values are dialectical in nature and cannot therefore be discrete.

My point-by-point rebuttal to Brennan can be summarized as follows: (1) non-quantifiable variable values do not require the extreme exactness and objectivity claimed by Brennan. (2) Not only is it possible to define and employ discrete non-quantifiable variable values in social science, but actually this is a very common basis for analysis. There is no reason, then, why non-quantifiable variables cannot be introduced where appropriate into economic inquiry. (3) The use of discrete non-quantifiable variable values is entirely consistent with Georgescu-Roegen's scheme and has an important role to play within it.

To begin with, as both Brennan and I have indicated, the values over which

[1] *Journal of Post Keynesian Economics* 2 (1979-80), pp. 270-273.

non-quantitative variables range must be discrete. This is necessary to permit the usual rules of Aristotelian logic to be employed, as I do, for manipulation. It does not mean, however, that complete objectivity must be realized so that everyone will agree on the definition and use of these variable values. Nor does it mean, as Brennan also suggests, that centuries-old, intractable, "ontological problems" have to be solved. There are two levels here. First, in the modeling of individual behavior, it is not important that we, the researchers, be able to perceive or describe non-quantitative variable values discretely. All that matters is that the hypothetical person who is the object of the investigation be able to do so, if only in a rough and subjective way. The "correctness" and accuracy of this individual's perceptions are not at issue. Second, for other kinds of inquiry, it is merely required that we, the investigators, subjectively agree on what constitutes relevant non-quantifiable values for a given variable, and that, again by agreement, we take these variable values, at least as an approximation, to be discrete. (When there is only one investigator, decisions on these matters are up to him. Others, of course, are free to question his judgment.) Consider, for example, the variable "security felt by an individual in his work and home environment." We might agree, for the purpose of a particular study, that the following three realizations or values of this variable are both relevant and discrete: (a) regardless of what he does, the individual feels completely at the mercy of events over which he has no control; (b) the individual feels he must work hard just to maintain his current job and life-style; any slackening of effort could be disastrous; (c) the individual feels that he is in control of his life; he has an inner peace from feeling he is able to do what he can do best in the way he wants to do it.

This is a perfectly valid and fruitful way to approach the analysis of non-quantifiable phenomena. Moreover — and here I am taking up point (2) — it appears implicitly if not explicitly throughout social science. Thus, for a political scientist to say, "different types of political systems produce different career patterns" (Apter [1, p. 163]), or for an anthropologist to write, "the established modes of action and belief, to which we refer as a people's customs, are something they have made out of experience" (Goodenough [8, p. 63]), is tantamount, in either case, to asserting a relation between two non-scalable variables. In a similar way, Fromm [5, pp. 194-197] speaks of an "inverse" relation between security and freedom. Coopersmith [4, pp. 28, 242-244] relates self esteem to success, occupation, and social status. Blau and Duncan [2, Ch. 4] study the relationship between occupation and social prestige. Katz and Lazarsfeld [9, p. 295] examine the interrelatedness of income and social participation. The list goes on and on. Further illustrations are also cited in my paper (Katzner [10, pp. 121, 124, 125 (or, respectively, pp. 68, 71, 72, 73 above)]).

The fact that non-quantitative variables have seldom been included in formal economic models is no reason that they cannot or should not be introduced. My article argues that they can no longer be ignored and suggests a way of handling them. Without taking cognizance of non-quantifiable factors when relevant, economic analysis is that much poorer.

Nothing in my article contradicts Georgescu-Roegen's distinction between dialectical (i.e., overlapping) and arithmomorphic (i.e., discrete) theorizing. On the contrary, paralleling the models of modern mathematical economics, the methodology I propose will lead to the development of arithmomorphic concepts, models, and reasoning in a non-quantitative setting. Though the ultimate aim is dialectical theory, arithmomorphic models play a crucial role. In particular, they serve to illustrate, clarify, and locate errors in their dialectical counterparts (Georgescu-Roegen [6, pp. 337-341]). For this reason, non-quantitative arithmomorphic theorizing has the potential for making the same important contribution to economic understanding as has the quantitative mathematical approach.

Finally, what may be bothering Brennan (and possibly others) is that my article presents a new method without any indication of how it can be applied. In the short space of a single article, I can hardly do justice to the presentation of the methodology, let alone the solution of real problems. New methods should always be suspect until they can be shown capable of obtaining results where none previously existed. Those who might look for a ray of hope in this direction, I would refer to my article with J. E. Russo (Katzner and Russo [13]) and book [11] on the quality of life, my article with H. Gintis (Gintis and Katzner [7]) on social interaction, profits, and Pareto optimality in the firm (a reworked version of which appears in Essay 6 of this volume), and my article [12 (this volume, Essay 14)] on the formal structure of argument in D. E. Apter's *Choice and the Politics of Allocation*.

References

1. Apter, D. E., *The Politics of Modernization* (Chicago: University of Chicago Press, 1965).
2. Blau, P. M., and O. D. Duncan, *The American Occupational Structure* (New York: Wiley, 1967).
3. Brennan, T. J., "On Not Quantifying the Nonquantifiable," *Journal of Post*

Keynesian Economics 2 (1979-80), pp. 267-270.

4. Coopersmith, S., *The Antecedents of Self-Esteem* (San Francisco: W. H. Freeman, 1967).
5. Fromm, E., *The Sane Society* (New York: Rinehart, 1955).
6. Georgescu-Roegen, N., *The Entropy Law and the Economic Process* (Cambridge: Harvard University Press, 1971).
7. Gintis, H., and D. W. Katzner, "Profits, Optimality, and the Social Division of Labor in the Firm," in *Sociological Economics*, L. Lévy-Garboua, ed. (London: SAGE, 1979), Ch. 9. Reprinted in D. W. Katzner, *Analysis without Measurement* (Cambridge: Cambridge University Press, 1983), Ch. 11.
8. Goodenough, W. H., *Cooperation in Change* (New York: Wiley, 1966).
9. Katz, E., and P. F. Lazarsfeld, *Personal Influence* (Glencoe: The Free Press, 1955).
10. Katzner, D. W., "On Not Quantifying the Nonquantifiable," *Journal of Post Keynesian Economics* 1, no. 2 (Winter 1978-79), pp. 113-128. This volume, the previous part of Essay 4.
11. ________, *Choice and the Quality of Life* (Beverly Hills: SAGE, 1979).
12. ________, "The Formal Structure of Argument in Professor Apter's *Choice and the Politics of Allocation*," *Political Methodology*, 6 (1979), pp. 217-235. This volume, Essay 14.
13. ________, and J. E. Russo, "Occupational Preferences and the Quality of Life," *Social Science Research* 6 (1977), pp. 363-378. Reprinted in D. W. Katzner, *Analysis without Measurement* (Cambridge: Cambridge University Press, 1983), Ch. 14.

Letter to the Editor[1]

Dear Dr. Mok:

The article "Surprising Results" by Levins and Warren in the recent issue of *Methodus* (4, no. 1 (June, 1992), pp. 58-64) is, in at least one respect, disappointing. The disappointment enters in the conclusion of the paper which the authors begin by saying economists should "... use mathematics when numbers are involved and leave the rest [to?] natural language" (p. 63). They then seem to claim that the "... solving of assumed equations filled with unmeasurable terms ..." is not possible (p. 64). The general suggestion is that rigorous mathematical analysis can be accomplished only when (meaningful) numerical measurements are available, and that in the absence of that kind of quantification, such analysis cannot legitimately be conducted.

This simply is not so. Indeed, it has been conclusively demonstrated that the mathematical models that economists use to understand the quantified world (such as the standard model — for example, the simple Keynesian multiplier model — in which an equilibrium exists and time paths converge to it) carry over identically, except for the fact of measurement, to a world in which none of the variables can be quantified.[2] That is, in the absence of quantified variables, one can still define and solve systems of simultaneous functional relations and simultaneous periodic equations, and express the solutions as dependent on non-quantified parameter values. Furthermore, sufficient conditions

[1] *Methodus* 4, no. 2 (December, 1992), p. 141.

[2] See D. W. Katzner, *Analysis without Measurement* (Cambridge University Press, 1983). The argument is briefly summarized in "On not Quantifiyng the Nonquantifiable," *Journal of Post Keynesian Economics* 1, no. 2 (Winter, 1978-79), pp. 113-128 (this volume, the first part of Essay 4).

can be given that ensure the existence of such solutions and, in the case of periodic equations, the existence of convergent time paths. The latter, of course, implies, in part, that it is possible to define the notion of "closeness" of variable values in a non-quantified setting.

It should also be pointed out that economists have often attempted to enrich their insights by including, sometimes analytically and sometimes with variables measured by proxies, non-quantified elements in their analyses. Examples include discussions of economic power, the quality of life, and certain resistances to economic development. It is clear, however, that even though mathematical investigations involving the non-quantifiable have not always met the highest standards, our discipline would still be all the poorer if these and other facets of what E.R. Weintraub referred to as "unmeasurable unmentionables"[3] were exorcised from its mathematical content.

[3] See his review of *Analysis without Measurement*, in the *Journal of Economic Literature* 22 (1984), p.1138.

5
Notions of Closeness in a Non-Quantifiable Setting[1]

The concept of closeness makes frequent appearances in scientific inquiry. To begin with, it is clearly present and relevant in advanced mathematical investigations involving metric spaces and/or the stability properties of differential equations. It is widely employed and studied in taxonomic biology under the heading of taxonomic resemblance,[2] and often arises in psychology as it bears upon such ideas as similarity[3] and multidimensional scaling.[4] Psychologists have also put a few of the closeness-related results derived by taxonomic biologists to their own special uses. Furthermore, some of the techniques developed in both fields have found their way into other areas. A case in point is the application of cluster analysis by Birnberg and Resnick [2, pp. 107-116] to identify colonial economies with the "most similar" characteristics.

But even at less formal and less abstract levels, where the meaning of closeness is harder to define precisely, scholars have not been shy about its use.

---

1 *Social Science Research* 17 (1988), pp. 1-28.

The author acknowledges with appreciation the assistance of Andy B. Anderson, Randall Bausor and Douglas Vickers. He also would like to thank James K. Kindahl for writing and executing the computer program that was used to calculate and analyze the values of measured closeness in Section IV.

2 See, for example, Sneath and Sokal [16].

3 See, for example, Gregson [6].

4 See, for example, Kruskal and Wish [11].

There is, to illustrate, a sizeable multi-discipline literature (e.g., Brzezinski and Huntington [3, pp. 9-14], Ellman [4], Lauterbach [13], Meyer [14], Spulber and Horowitz [18, Ch. 18], and Tinbergen [19]) addressing the issue of whether communist and capitalist countries are "converging" in the sense of becoming "closer" to each other as time progresses. This discussion has been rephrased in terms of the possible convergence of industrial societies in general by Kerr [10]. Other examples in other fields are easily found. In Economic Development, Kuznets [12, pp. 302-303] has argued that developed and less developed countries have similarly converged over time with respect to certain aspects of their economic and social structures and also with respect to particular ideological and political elements as well. An instance in Regional Economics is Hoover's [7, p. 238] reference to the convergence and divergence of regions of the U.S. with respect to their economic structures, productivities, and incomes. Outside of Economics, Spector [17, p. 347] and Zartman [20, p. 37] describe the process of successful bargaining or negotiating in the language of convergence of "interests" or of "positions."

When all relevant variables are at least cardinally quantifiable, closeness is frequently thought of in terms of Euclidean distance. One pair of points in the appropriate Euclidean space is taken to be closer together than another if the distance between the former is less than that between the latter. But in the absence of cardinal scales, or when their use is questionable, the meaning of closeness is not, as previously suggested, always clear cut and hence the problem of how to characterize and measure it arises. In those of the above less-formal studies that had to face a lack of suitable cardinal scales, either the question at issue was narrowed enough to make the available numbers "reasonably sufficient," or the meaning and measurement of the concept of closeness used in the analysis was not examined in any depth. Moreover, the interests of those exploring taxonomic resemblance, similarity and the like, have been directed more towards the practical issues arising in measuring these notions rather than towards the theoretical definition and analysis of the concept of closeness itself. The present paper attempts to get at the universal idea of closeness underlying all of these studies in as simple and direct a manner as possible. In doing so, it defines and analyzes five abstract notions, i.e., measures, of closeness that do not require the presence of cardinal scales for the variables under investigation, and applies these measures to the data on less developed countries gathered by Adelman and Morris [1] for the period 1950-1964. The primary intent is to provide a foundation for understanding and employing the idea of closeness that has, hopefully, general appeal and relevance.

One way of thinking about closeness in non-quantifiable contexts has been proposed elsewhere.[5] That approach was to order the objects whose closeness is to be studied according to various properties they possess. Each property gives rise to a single ordering of objects, and each ordering generates a unique partition of the objects into equivalence classes. The closeness of one object to another is then defined and measured ordinally as the number of common equivalence classes in which the two objects lie across all orderings. Thus the closeness of any pair of objects depends on the number of properties that the objects share, where the sharing of properties is characterized in terms of the given orderings. This measure of closeness is related to measures of taxonomic resemblance that are derived from the idea of association[6] and appears as the function m^1 in the next section. The remaining four notions of closeness introduced below (and identified as the functions m^2 through m^5) also rest on the existence of equivalence classes derived from such orderings. It turns out that the equivalence-class framework is especially useful for illuminating what measures of closeness are all about. Moreover, in the absence of such equivalence classes, the concept of closeness as usually perceived tends to break down.

Four points are worth noting at the outset. First, no distinction is made between the definition of a concept of closeness and the definition of a measure of that concept. Indeed, each notion of closeness is defined as a particular measure. This is quite natural since thoughts about closeness are usually inseparable from thoughts about the measurement of it. Second, no guidance is given for the selection of a specific concept of closeness for use in a particular investigation. The choice of measures is, to some extent, necessarily arbitrary, depending as it does on the purposes of the study as well as the on predilections of the investigator. (The same thing can be said of the measure of closeness based on Euclidean distance available in the cardinally quantifiable world. Most of us are comfortable with Euclidean distance because we have learned to appreciate its intuitive appeal. But we could just as easily have learned to appreciate something else.) Third, because no assumptions of cardinal quantifiability are made about the objects whose closeness is under scrutiny, all measures of closeness are ordinal, and not cardinal, in character. Lastly, no efforts of comprehensiveness are made. Only a few of the more simple and intuitive notions of closeness are considered.

The paper is divided into four parts. In Section I the five notions (measures) of closeness are introduced and in Section II they are analyzed and compared.

---

[5] Katzner [8, p. 63]. Katzner [8, p. 65] also considers the mathematical relationship between closeness and convergence. See also Essay 4 in this volume.

[6] Sneath and Sokal [16, pp. 129-137].

Section III examines them in relation to Euclidean distance in particular, and to metrics and pseudo-metrics in general. It also discusses the significance of the assumption that orderings and the equivalence classes they generate exist. The application of these measures to calculating closeness among countries using the Adelman and Morris data is taken up in Section IV.

I

Let X be a collection of objects and let $\{\beta_1, ..., \beta_I\}$ be a finite set of I reflexive and transitive orderings[7] of X. Then each β_i, where $i = 1, ..., I$, defines an equivalence relation on X and hence gives rise to its own collection of (mutually exclusive and exhaustive) equivalence classes partitioning X. Five notions of closeness between pairs of elements in X are considered:

First,[8] for every x' and x'' in X, define $m^1(x', x'')$ to be the function that associates to (x', x'') the number of equivalence classes that contain both x' and x'' under $\beta_1, ..., \beta_I$. The more x' and x'' are "alike" in terms of the given orderings, the higher the value of $m^1(x', x'')$, and the closer x' and x'' are said to be. Of course, for any i, either x' and x'' are assigned to the same equivalence class by the equivalence relation emerging from β_i or they are not. Hence

$$I \geq m^1(x', x'') \geq 0,$$

for all x' and x'' in X.

Now suppose the investigator has determined that some of the β_i are more important than others. Assume, in particular, that the β_i are linearly ordered in this way and refer to the ordering of the set $\{\beta_1, ..., \beta_I\}$ as the importance ranking. If β_i is higher in the importance ranking than β_j, then β_i is said to be more important than β_j. Without loss of generality, take β_I to be the most important ordering and β_1 to be the least important. Let f be the function given by

$$f(x', x'', i) = \begin{cases} 0, & \text{if } x' \text{ and } x'' \text{ are not in a common equivalence class under } \beta_i, \\ i, & \text{otherwise,} \end{cases} \tag{1}$$

[7] If X is countable, then each β_i defines its own (non-unique) ordinal measure of the elements of X. When X is uncountable, the existence of β_i is not, by itself, sufficient to determine such a measure. See Pfanzagl [15, pp. 75,79].

[8] cf., Sneath and Sokal [16, pp. 135-136].

where x' and x'' are in X, and the integer i satisfies $I \geq i \geq 1$. The second measure of closeness to be discussed here is

$$m^2(x', x'') = \frac{2}{I+1} \sum_{i=1}^{I} f(x', x'', i),$$

defined, again, for all x' and x'' in X. As before, the more equivalence classes that x' and x'' have in common, the higher the value of $m^2(x', x'')$, and a higher value for $m^2(x', x'')$ means that x' and x'' are closer together. Note that in calculating $m^2(x', x'')$, the "value" of an equivalence class shared by x' and x'' (call it 1) is weighted by the position of the ordering from which it comes in the importance ranking. Furthermore, when x' and x'' share equivalence classes under every β_i, $m^2(x', x'')$ reduces to[9]

$$\begin{aligned} m^2(x', x'') &= \frac{2}{I+1} \sum_{i=1}^{I} i, \\ &= I \end{aligned} \tag{2}$$

It follows that

$$I \geq m^2(x', x'') \geq 0,$$

for every x' and x'' in X. The relationship between m^1 and m^2 will be discussed momentarily.

The third measure of closeness continues the assumptions in the definition of m^2 concerning the importance ranking of the set $\{\beta_1, ..., \beta_I\}$. For all x' and x'' in X, define $m^3(x', x'')$ to be that integer n such that x' and x'' have common equivalence classes under each of $\beta_I, ..., \beta_{I-n+1}$, but do not share an equivalence class under β_{I-n}. Thus m^3, beginning with the most important ordering, counts the common equivalence classes across successively less important orderings until an ordering turns up for which the pair of elements in question do not share an equivalence class. If x' and x'' do not have a common equivalence class under β_I (the most important ordering), then $m^3(x', x'') = 0$ regardless of the number of equivalence classes that are shared under less im-

9 An arithmetic progression is a sequence $a_1, a_2, ..., a_n, ...$ such that $a_{n+1} = a_n + \bar{a}$, for all $n \geq 1$, where $\bar{a}$ is a fixed number. The sum of the first n terms of an arithmetic progression, S_n, is given by the formula (e.g., Feinstein and Murphy [5, p. 221]) $S_n = (n/2)(a_1 + a_n)$. This formula is used in the derivation of the second equality of equation (2).

portant orderings. As with both of the previous measures,

$$I \geq m^3(x', x'') \geq 0,$$

for all x' and x'' in X, and the higher the value of $m^3(x', x'')$, the closer x' and x''. However, in this last case, more equivalence classes in common need not raise the value of m^3, although it cannot cause the value of m^3 to fall. Observe that the notion of closeness emerging from m^3 is a "lexicographic" idea: Were x' and x'' to share equivalence classes under all but the most important ordering, they would be as close together as if they had no equivalence classes in common under any ordering.

Now let b_i represent the number of equivalence classes arising from β_i. These equivalence classes are ordered, at least partially, by an ordering induced by β_i. Assume $b_i > 1$ for each i. The last two measures of closeness to be considered are based on the supposition that each β_i actually induces a linear ordering of the b_i equivalence classes that it generates. For concreteness, denote these equivalence classes in order by

$$B_{i1}, ..., B_{ib_i},$$

where $i = 1, ..., I$, and focus attention on a fixed ordering β_i. Then for any $j = 1, ..., b_i - 1$, the equivalence classes B_{ij} and B_{ij+1} are called *adjacent* under β_i. In addition, for any integers j, k, and n such that $1 \leq j \leq j + k \leq j + n \leq b_i$, B_{ij+k} is said to lie *between* B_{ij} and B_{ij+n} under β_i. Thus if two equivalence classes under β_i are adjacent, then there is no distinct equivalence class between them.

Define the function

$$g(x', x'', i) = \begin{cases} b_i - 1, & \text{if } x' \text{ and } x'' \text{ are in the same equivalence class under } \beta_i, \\ b_i - 2, & \text{if } x' \text{ and } x'' \text{ are in adjacent equivalence classes under } \beta_i, \\ b_i - 2 - k, & \text{if there are } k \neq 0 \text{ distinct equivalence classes under } \beta_i \text{ between the equivalence class containing } x' \text{ and that containing } x'', \end{cases} \tag{3}$$

for every x' and x'' in X and every integer $i = 1, ..., I$, where $k = 1, ..., b_i - 2$. Note that when $k = b_i - 2$, the function value $g(x', x'', i) = 0$. Take

$m^4(x', x'')$, the fourth measure of closeness,[10] to be:

$$m^4(x', x'') = \sum_{i=1}^{I} \frac{1}{b_i - 1} g(x', x'', i), \tag{4}$$

for all x' and x'' in X. Thus the "nearer" x' and x'' in terms of the position in the linear ordering of the equivalence classes in which they lie under β_i, the higher the value of $m^4(x', x'')$, and the closer x' is to x''. That is, m^4 incorporates a weighting scheme, different from that of m^2, determined by the nearness of x' to x'' within an ordering. Notice the division of each image $g(x', x'', i)$ by $b_i - 1$ in (4) serves to normalize the values of m^4 so that

$$I \geq m^4(x', x'') \geq 0,$$

for all x' and x'' in X. If the assumption of an importance ranking of the orderings $\beta_1, ..., \beta_I$, is added to the picture, and if, as in the definition of m^2, the value of each pair of equivalence classes employed in the calculation of m^4, namely,

$$\frac{1}{b_i - 1} g(x', x'', i),$$

is weighted by the position of the ordering from which it comes in the importance ranking, then the last measure of closeness is obtained as

$$m^5(x', x'') = \frac{2}{I+1} \sum_{i=1}^{I} \frac{i}{b_i - 1} g(x', x'', i),$$

for all x' and x'' in X. It, too, has the property that higher values of $m^5(x', x'')$ mean that x' and x'' are closer together. Clearly, m^5 combines the weighting schemes of m^2 and m^4: Weights based on the importance ranking of the orderings are superimposed on the weights by nearness within orderings. Moreover,

$$I \geq m^5(x', x'') \geq 0,$$

for every x' and x'' in X.

Observe that in the definitions of m^4 and m^5, facts like "the equivalence classes containing x' and x'' under β_i have no distinct equivalence classes between them" have different values from but are given the same weight as "these equivalence classes have $b_i - 2$ distinct equivalence classes between them." However, in certain inquiries, it is conceivable that (depending on the

[10] cf., Sneath and Sokal [16, p. 122].

β_i) these facts might be thought to have different significance, and thus in calculating the closeness of pairs of elements in X, the investigator may want to assign them different weights. Another possibility is to introduce weights to reflect the idea that being in one equivalence class under a given ordering may have more significance than being in others. For example, the fact that x^*, say, may be nearer to x' than to x'' within an ordering could, in measuring closeness, be offset by the fact that the equivalence class in which x' appears under that ordering is of less moment that that in which x'' falls. These two weighting schemes could be imposed, singly or in combination, on any of m^1 through m^5 to produce still further measures. The complications that arise from introducing such weights, however, are not examined here.

The special circumstance in which the objects of X are themselves relations among still other objects deserves particular consideration. To be specific, let each x in X be a reflexive, transitive, and total relation (that is, an ordering in earlier terminology) defined on the same collection of S elements identified as $\{1, ..., S\}$. Then for every pair (s, t), where $s, t = 1, ..., S$, exactly one of three statements is true: (i) x places s above t, (ii) x places s and t at the same "level," and (iii) x places s below t. It follows that each pair (s, t) partitions X into three mutually exclusive and exhaustive and sets

$$E_{st} = \{x : x \text{ places } s \text{ above } t\},$$

$$F_{st} = \{x : x \text{ places } s \text{ and } t \text{ at the same level}\},$$

$$G_{st} = \{x : x \text{ places } s \text{ below } t\}.$$

Moreover, E_{st}, F_{st} and G_{st} arise as equivalence classes under the reflexive and transitive ordering β_{st} characterized, for all x' and x'' in X, by $x' \, \beta_{st} \, x''$ if and only if

(i) x' is in E_{st}, or

(ii) x' is in F_{st} and x'' is in $F_{st} \cup G_{st}$, or

(iii) x' and x'' are in G_{st}.

Note that β_{st} induces a linear ordering of these equivalence classes in which E_{st} is placed above F_{st}, and F_{st} is placed above G_{st}. Note also that the total number of pairs (s, t), and hence the total number of orderings β_{st}, is

$$I = \frac{S(S-1)}{2}.$$

With respect to previous notation, each β_{st} is a β_i for some $i = 1, ..., I$.

In this setting, the measure $\bar{m}^1(x', x'')$, where a bar has been placed over the m to indicate the specificity of the application of m^1 to pairs of relations, is the number of pairs (s, t) that are ordered in the same way by both x' and x''. Hence $\bar{m}^1(x', x'')$ can be linked to and obtained from the Kendall τ statistic.[11] To calculate $\bar{m}^4$, observe that the number of equivalence classes $b_i = 3$, for every i. Using (4), then, $\bar{m}^4(x', x'')$ is found upon halving the sum of a collection of numbers that is built up by including a 2 whenever x' and x'' order a pair (s, t) identically, a 1 whenever one of x' and x'' places s and t from a pair (s, t) at the same level and the other does not, and a 0 whenever, for a pair (s, t), one of x' and x'' place s above t and the other places s below t. Since a related function, namely,

$$2[I - \bar{m}^4(x', x'')],$$

has been studied by Kemeny and Snell [9, Ch. 2] in a different context, $\bar{m}^4$ is hereafter referred to as the *Kemeny-Snell* measure. Clearly, if neither x' nor x'' places s and t from any pair (s, t) at the same level, or if, whenever one of x' or x'' places an s at the same level as a t, so does the other, then

$$\bar{m}^1(x', x'') = \bar{m}^4(x', x'').$$

Although not done so here, m^2, m^3 and m^5 could also be analyzed with respect to similar choices of X and orderings β_{st}.

Since each of the original measures m^1 through m^5 determines a ranking of pairs of objects of X according to the notion of closeness that it defines, any of these measures could, in general, be employed to measure formally the closeness of pairs of measures. However, only m^1 and m^4 as, respectively, $\bar{m}^1$ and $\bar{m}^4$ are used in this manner in Section IV. In such cases, and with x' and x'' denoting the objects of the original X, each s and t in the above discussion would indicate a pair (x', x'') and (x^0, x^*). Furthermore, s would be placed above t by m^j (for any j) or, equivalently, (x', x'') would be placed above (x^0, x^*) by m^j if $m^j(x', x'') > m^j(x^0, x^*)$. And s and t, or (x', x'') and (x^0, x^*), would be identically ordered by, say, m^1 and m^2, provided that $m^1(x', x'') \gtreqless m^1(x^0, x*)$ according as $m^2(x', x'') \gtreqless m^2(x^0, x*)$.

II

The values of m^1 through m^5 may be compared for any pair, x' and x'', in

[11] See n. 18 on p. 109 below.

X. If x' and x'' appear in equivalence classes having $b_i - 2$ distinct equivalence classes between them for each $\beta_1, ..., \beta_I$, and hence have no equivalence classes in common, then for $j = 1, ..., 5$,

$$m^j(x', x'') = 0.$$

Similarly, if x' and x'' share equivalence classes under every $\beta_1, ..., \beta_I$, then (using (2) in the cases of m^2 and m^5)

$$m^j(x', x'') = I,$$

again for $j = 1, ..., 5$. (Observe that since x' always shares an equivalence class with itself under each β_i,

$$m^j(x', x') = I,$$

for all x' in X, and every j). To examine situations that fall between these extremes, first consider some examples. Let $I = 10$, and suppose x' and x'' share an equivalence class under 10 (the most important ordering). Suppose that under all other orderings except 1, the pairs of equivalence classes containing x' and x'' have $b_i - 2$ distinct equivalence classes between them. In the case of β_1, there are five equivalence classes and the pair of equivalence classes containing x' and x'' are adjacent. Then, from the definitions of the m^j,

$$m^1(x', x'') = m^3(x', x'') = 1,$$

$$m^2(x', x'') = \frac{20}{11}, \quad m^4(x', x'') = \frac{7}{4}, \quad m^5(x', x'') = \frac{43}{22},$$

so that

$$m^5(x', x'') > m^2(x', x'') > m^4(x', x'') > m^1(x', x'') = m^3(x', x'').$$

On the other hand, were x' and x'' to have the equivalence class under β_1 (the least important ordering) in common, were there five equivalence classes under β_2 with the ones containing x' and x'' adjacent, and were the pairs of equivalence classes containing x' and x'' under the remaining orderings all to have $b_i - 2$ distinct equivalence classes between them, then

$$m^1(x', x'') = 1, \qquad m^3(x', x'') = 0,$$

$$m^2(x', x'') = \frac{2}{11}, \quad m^4(x', x'') = \frac{7}{4}, \quad m^5(x', x'') = \frac{5}{11}.$$

Here

$$m^4(x', x'') > m^1(x', x'') > m^5(x', x'') > m^2(x', x'') > m^3(x', x'').$$

Lastly, if x' and x'' share equivalence classes under β_1 and β_{10}, and if the pairs of equivalence classes containing x' and x'' under all other orderings have $b_i - 2$ distinct equivalence classes between them, then

$$m^1(x', x'') = m^2(x', x'') = m^4(x', x'') = m^5(x', x'') = 2,$$

$$m^3(x', x'') = 1.$$

Hence in this case,

$$m^1(x', x'') = m^2(x', x'') = m^4(x', x'') = m^5(x', x'') > m^3(x', x'').$$

Returning to the general situation, consider any x' and x'' in X and suppose that x' and x'' have equivalence classes in common under k orderings, where $I > k \geq 1$. Then, of course,

$$m^1(x', x'') = k.$$

Moreover, the previous examples indicate that

$$m^1(x', x'') \gtreqless m^2(x', x''),$$

depending on the orderings under which x' and x'' share equivalence classes. It is also true, and consistent with the above examples, that

$$m^1(x', x'') \geq m^3(x', x''), \tag{5}$$

for all x' and x'' in X. The same examples further suggest that $m^2(x', x'')$ is always larger than $m^3(x', x'')$. This result is established by the following proposition:

Theorem 1. Let $I > k \geq 1$. For all x' and x'' in X such that x' and x'' share equivalence classes under exactly k orderings,

$$m^2(x', x'') > m^3(x', x'').$$

Proof:

With x' and x'' given, let k' be the number of orderings with shared equivalence classes under consecutively lower orderings beginning with β_I. Then

$$m^3(x', x'') = k' \leq k.$$

It is sufficient to show the inequality of the theorem assuming that x' and x'' have only these k' equivalence classes in common, since adding the shared equivalence classes that arise from orderings less important than $\beta_{I-k'+1}$ increases $m^2(x', x'')$ while leaving $m^3(x', x'')$ unchanged. Now the non-zero terms in the sum defining m^2 begin with $I - k' + 1$ and end with I. Hence[12]

$$
\begin{aligned}
m^2(x', x'') &= \frac{2}{I+1}\frac{k'}{2}(I - k' + 1 + I), \\
&= \frac{2}{I+1}\frac{k'}{2}(2I - k' + 1), \\
&> \frac{2}{I+1}\frac{k'}{2}(I + 1), \\
&= k' = m^3(x', x'').
\end{aligned}
$$

Q.E.D.

Clearly, if k in the hypothesis of Theorem 1 were zero, then

$$m^2(x', x'') = m^3(x', x'') = 0.$$

Turning to m^4 and m^5, let x' and x'' in X be given. Then it is obvious that

$$m^4(x', x'') \geq m^1(x', x''), \tag{6}$$

and

$$m^5(x', x'') \geq m^2(x', x''). \tag{7}$$

Furthermore, the above examples indicate that

$$m^4(x', x'') \gtreqless m^2(x', x''),$$

$$m^5(x', x'') \gtreqless m^1(x', x''),$$

$$m^4(x', x'') \gtreqless m^5(x', x''),$$

Lastly, combining (6) with (5), and (7) with Theorem 1,

$$m^4(x', x'') \geq m^3(x', x''),$$

$$m^5(x', x'') \geq m^3(x', x''),$$

[12] This derivation uses the formula in n. 9 on p. 87.

where the second inequality is strict as long as x' and x'' have an equivalence class in common under at least one ordering.

If, for any x' and x'' in X, the importance ranking of $\{\beta_1, ..., \beta_I\}$ were to modify, then of course $m^1(x', x'')$ and $m^4(x', x'')$ would not be affected. Without further assumptions, however, no conclusions concerning $m^2(x', x'')$, $m^3(x', x'')$ or $m^5(x', x'')$ can be drawn. To illustrate in the case of m^2, if an ordering having the property that x' and x'' are not contained in the same equivalence class, is placed ahead of one for which x' and x'' share an equivalence class, then since at least one of the numbers $f(x', x'', i)$ in the definition of m^2 is lower, $m^2(x', x'')$ must fall. Alternatively, interchanging two orderings in the importance ranking, each of which places x' and x'' in a common equivalence class, merely permutes two of the values of $f(x', x'', i)$ and does not alter $m^2(x', x'')$.

Likewise, altering the linear orderings of the equivalence classes under the β_i (by rearranging the order of the classes or by varying the number of them) may change $m^4(x', x'')$ and $m^5(x', x'')$, but would have no impact on $m^1(x', x'')$, $m^2(x', x'')$ and $m^3(x', x'')$.

Now suppose a new ordering is added to the set $\{\beta_1, ..., \beta_I\}$. Then $m^1(x', x'')$ and $m^4(x', x'')$ cannot fall. Only when the introduction of the new ordering increases the number of equivalence classes shared by x' and x'', will the former measure rise. The latter measure rises as long as, under the new ordering, the equivalence classes containing x' and x'' do not have the maximum number of distinct equivalence classes between them. In general, $m^3(x', x'')$ could rise, fall or remain unchanged. It would rise, for example, if the string of consecutive orderings (from the most important on down) under which x' and x'' share equivalence classes becomes longer, and it would fall if the string is interrupted by the new ordering, more important than the last of the string, and such that x' and x'' do not lie in the same equivalence class under the new ordering. The next two propositions demonstrate that, like $m^1(x', x'')$ (and also $m^4(x', x'')$), the closeness measures $m^2(x', x'')$ and $m^5(x', x'')$ necessarily rise when x' and x'' share a common equivalence class under the new ordering.

Theorem 2. Let x' and x'' be in X. Add a new ordering to $\{\beta_1, ..., \beta_I\}$ and fit it into the existing importance ranking of that set. If x' and x' are in the same equivalence class under the new ordering, then the value of $m^2(x', x'')$ rises.

Proof:

Take $f^I(x', x'', i)$ and $f^{I+1}(x', x'', i)$, respectively, to be the functions of (1) when there are, respectively, I and $I + 1$ orderings. The theorem is established by showing that

$$\frac{2}{I+1}\sum_{i=1}^{I+1} f^{I+1}(x', x'', i) > \frac{2}{I+1}\sum_{i=1}^{I} f^{I}(x', x'', i), \tag{8}$$

for all x' and x'' in X that lie in a common equivalence class under the new ordering.

Let x' and x'' in a common equivalence class under the new ordering be specified, set

$$S = \sum_{i=1}^{I} f^{I}(x', x'', i),$$

and suppose k denotes the number of non-zero elements in the sum S. If $k = 0$, then $f^{I}(x', x'', i) = 0$ for all i, and $f^{I+1}(x', x'', i) \neq 0$ for exactly one i. Thus the right-hand-side of (8) is 0 and the left-hand-side is positive. When $I \geq k \geq 1$, the smallest possible difference between S and the corresponding sum in terms of the f^{I+1} is $k + 1$. Hence the proof of (8) may be reduced to showing that

$$\frac{2}{I+1}(S + k) > \frac{2}{I+1}S. \tag{9}$$

Now, from equation (2), the largest value that S can take on is I. Hence $S < I + 1$. From this and the fact that $k \geq 1$, it follows that

$$k > \frac{S}{I+1}.$$

Therefore,

$$k(I + 1) > S.$$

By adding $IS + S$ to both sides,

$$(I + 1)(S + k) > (I + 2)S,$$

from which the required inequality (9) immediately follows.

Q.E.D.

Theorem 3. Under the hypotheses of Theorem 2, the value of $m^5(x', x'')$ rises.

Proof:

Take $g^{I}(x', x'', i)$ and $g^{I+1}(x', x'', i)$, respectively, to be the functions of (3) when there are, respectively, I and $I+1$ orderings. The theorem is established by showing that

$$\frac{2}{I+1}\sum_{i=1}^{I+1}\frac{i}{b_i-1}g^{I+1}(x',x'',i) > \frac{2}{I+1}\sum_{i=1}^{I}\frac{i}{b_i-1}g^{I}(x',x'',i), \qquad (10)$$

for all x' and x'' in X that lie in a common equivalence class under the new ordering.

Let S be the right-hand sum in (10) and let k represent the number of terms in S for which

$$\frac{i}{b_i-1}g^{I}(x',x'',i) = i.$$

If $k = 0$, then the smallest possible difference between S and the corresponding sum in terms of g^{I+1} is 1. Hence the proof of (10) follows from setting $k = 1$ in (9). When $I \geq k \geq 1$, the proof of (10) is similar to that of (8) for $I \geq k \geq 1$.

Q.E.D.

Note that the addition of a new ordering to $\{\beta_1, ..., \beta_I\}$ under which x' and x'' do not share an equivalence class cannot change $m^2(x', x'')$ as long as the new ordering is more important than the most important of the original orderings under which x' and x'' have an equivalence class in common. Otherwise, in the absence of the latter condition, that is, when β_i, say, is more important than the new ordering, and when x' and x'' share an equivalence class under β_i,

$$f^{I+1}(x',x'',i) = f^{I}(x',x'',i) + 1,$$

where f^{I+1} and f^I are the functions in the proof of Theorem 2. Hence inequality (9) with $k \geq 1$ applies and, as in the proof of Theorem 2, $m^2(x', x'')$ rises. Furthermore, Theorem 3 looses its validity upon replacing the hypothesis that x' and x'' lie in the same equivalence class under the new ordering with the weaker condition that the equivalence classes containing x' and x'' do not have the maximum number of distinct equivalence classes between them under the new ordering. To illustrate, let the new ordering be more important than $\beta_1, ..., \beta_I$, so that (using the definition of m^5)

$$m^5(x',x'') = \frac{2}{I+2}\left[S + \frac{I+1}{b_{I+1}-1}g^{I+1}(x',x'',i)\right],$$

where S and g^{I+1} are defined as in the proof of Theorem 3. Hence, if the new ordering is such that b_{I+1} is sufficiently large, then $m^5(x', x'')$ will fall.

III

It is now appropriate to consider how the previous discussion fits with the ordinary measure of closeness obtained for cardinally quantifiable variables using the Euclidean distance formula. Toward this end, reinterpret x' and x'' as the I-dimensional vectors,

$$x' = (x'_1, ..., x'_I), \qquad \text{and} \qquad x'' = (x''_1, ..., x''_I),$$

each contained in the Cartesian product X of the one-dimensional Euclidean spaces, X^i, of real numbers. That is,

$$X = X^1 \times \cdots \times X^I,$$

where the ith component of both x' and x'' is located in X^i, for $i = 1, ..., I$. The distance between x' and x'', namely $d(x', x'')$, is given by

$$d(x', x'') = \sqrt{(x'_1 - x''_1)^2 + \cdots + (x'_I - x''_I)^2},$$

for all x' and x'' in X. Note that $d(x', x'') = 0$ if and only if $x' = x''$. Typically, the smaller the value of $d(x', x'')$, the closer x' and x'' are said to be. To convert d into a measure of closeness whose scale ranges from 0 to I, where I is associated with the equality $x' = x''$, and 0 denotes the situation in which x' and x'' are as far apart as possible, assume that X is bounded and hence that d has a maximum value, D, on $X \times X$. Define the measure

$$m^d(x', x'') = \frac{D - d(x', x'')}{D} I, \tag{11}$$

on $X \times X$. Then for all x' and x'' in X,

$$I \geq m^d(x', x'') \geq 0,$$

and as x' and x'' become closer together in terms of d, $m^d(x', x'')$ rises.

The Euclidean space X^i is ordered by "$\geq$". This ordering induces an ordering, β_i, on X according to

$$x' \; \beta_i \; x'' \qquad \text{if and only if} \qquad x'_i \geq x''_i,$$

for all $x' = (x'_1, ..., x'_I)$ and $x'' = (x''_1, ..., x''_I)$ in X. The equivalence classes generated by β_i are linearly ordered by a relation obtained from β_i. Like the values of the function g in (3), the number

$$(x'_i - x''_i)^2, \tag{12}$$

is a measure of how "far apart" the equivalence classes containing x' and x'' are under β_i. (Note that (12) increases as these equivalence classes separate, while the value of g declines.) All pairs of equivalence classes and all orderings are weighted equally in the calculation of d. Hence, of all the measures of closeness discussed here, m^d is most like m^4.

Now the Euclidean distance function d is, of course, a *metric*. That is, for all x', x'', and x^* in X, d is a non-negative function having the three properties:

$$\text{(i) } d(x', x'') = 0 \qquad \text{if and only if} \qquad x' = x'',$$

$$\text{(ii) } d(x', x'') = d(x'', x'),$$

$$\text{(iii) } d(x', x'') + d(x'', x^*) \geq d(x', x^*).$$

Property (iii) is referred to as the *triangle inequality*. If only (ii) and (iii) were in force together with a weaker version of property (i), namely,

$$\text{(iv) } x' = x'' \qquad \text{implies} \qquad d(x', x'') = 0,$$

then d would be called a *pseudo-metric*. The question arises as to whether any of the transposed measures

$$I - m^j(x', x''), \tag{13}$$

for $j = 1, ..., 5$, have any metric characteristics.[13] To begin with, it is obvious that property (ii) holds in all cases. Furthermore, it is equally obvious that, in general, $x' = x''$ implies

$$I - m^j(x', x'') = 0,$$

but not conversely, for every j. Hence, as a rule, the transposed measures of (13) can, at most, be pseudo-metrics. But $I - m^1$, $I - m^2$ and $I - m^3$ do not satisfy the triangle inequality. Focusing on $I - m^1$, for example, suppose that x' and x'' share equivalence classes under all I orderings, that x'' and x^* also share equivalence classes under all orderings, but that x' and x^* have no common equivalence classes under any ordering. Then the left-hand side of the triangle inequality analogous to (iii) would vanish while the right-hand side would be I. As the proposition below shows, such examples cannot arise with $I - m^4$ and $I - m^5$.

[13] That (13) is an appropriate formulation of the measures of closeness for answering this query can be seen by replacing m^d and D in (11) with, respectively, m^j and I, and then solving (11) for d.

Theorem 4.[14] The measures $I - m^4$ and $I - m^5$ are both pseudo-metrics on $X \times X$.

Proof:

Since all other pseudo-metric properties hold for both $I - m^4$ and $I - m^5$, it is only necessary to consider the triangle inequality. In the case of $I - m^4$ this inequality is

$$[I - m^4(x', x'')] + [I - m^4(x'', x^*)] \geq I - m^4(x', x^*), \tag{14}$$

for all x', x'', and x^* in X. To establish (14) it is sufficient to show that for every i, the inequality obtained from (14) by setting $I = 1$ and replacing each function value m^4 by the ith term in the sum defining that function value in the definition of m^4 (i.e., equation (4)), is sustained. For a given specification of x', x'', x^* and i, this latter inequality reduces to

$$\frac{1}{b_i - 1} g(x', x'', i) + \frac{1}{b_i - 1} g(x'', x^*, i) - \frac{1}{b_i - 1} g(x', x^*, i) \leq 1. \tag{15}$$

There are 7 cases to consider. First, if x', x'', and x^* are all in the same equivalence class under ordering β_i, then the expression to the left of the inequality sign in (15) is 1. Second, if only x' and x'' share an equivalence class under β_i, then the second and third terms in the expression to the left of the inequality sign in (15) are equal, and that expression again reduces to unity. A similar argument applies to the third case in which x'' and x^* are the only pair out of x', x'', and x^* to be in the same equivalence class under β_i. Fourth, if only x' and x^* share an equivalence class under ordering β_i, then the first two terms in the expression to the left of the inequality sign in (15) are equal, and that expression now becomes

$$\frac{2}{b_i - 1} g(x', x'', i) - 1 \leq 1.$$

The last three cases are concerned with situations in which x', x'', and x^* all lie in distinct equivalence classes under ordering β_i. Case 5 arises when the equivalence class containing x'' lies between those containing x' and x^*. Here

$$g(x', x'', i) + g(x'', x^*, i) = g(x', x^*, i) + 1,$$

[14] Applied to the special case of the Kemeny-Snell measure, Theorem 4 says that $I - \bar{m}^4$ is a pseudo-metric. But the definition of $\bar{m}^4$ clearly implies that $I - \bar{m}^4$ is also a metric. This last result, with $I - \bar{m}^4$ replaced by $2(I - \bar{m}^4)$, is due to Kemeny and Snell [9, p. 16].

so that the expression to the left of the inequality in (15) condenses to

$$\frac{1}{b_i - 1} \leq 1.$$

In Case 6, the equivalence class containing x' falls between the equivalence classes containing x'' and $x*$. When this happens,

$$g(x', x'', i) + g(x', x*, i) = g(x'', x*, i) + 1.$$

Now the expression to the left of the inequality in (15) is

$$\frac{2}{b_i - 1} g(x', x'', i) - 1 \leq 1.$$

Case 7, where the equivalence class containing $x*$ is between those containing x' and x'', is handled analogously.[15]

All possibilities having been covered, it follows that $I - m^4$ is a pseudometric. A similar argument applies to $I - m^5$.

Q.E.D.

The second main issue to be explored in this section has to do with the role that orderings and the equivalence classes they generate play in the assignment of meaning to the idea of closeness. Recall that all of the notions (measures) of closeness introduced in Section I are based on the existence of I orderings, $\beta_1, \ldots, \beta_I$, where β_i is reflexive and transitive for $i = 1, \ldots, I$. As described earlier, each β_i determines a collection of mutually exclusive and exhaustive equivalence classes that partitions X, along with another relation that at least partially orders the equivalence classes defined by β_i. Measures m^4 and m^5 require, in addition, that the latter ordering of equivalence classes be linear. Rather than beginning with the orderings β_i and deriving the ordered collections of sets partitioning X from them, the argument just as easily could have been started by assuming the existence of partitions whose sets are partially (and, where appropriate, linearly) ordered. It then would have been possible to derive suitable reflexive and transitive orderings β_i from them. (Indeed, this was the approach used to obtain $\bar{m}^1$ and the Kemeny-Snell measure $\bar{m}^4$ at the end of Section I.) In other words, assuming the existence of the β_i is equivalent to assuming the existence of the requisite partitions.

The significance of these orderings and partitions in giving meaning to the idea of closeness can best be understood by examining the kinds of things that

[15] Removing the requirement of Cases 6 and 7 that all equivalence classes under ordering β_i are distinct, Cases 2 and 4 could be regarded as special situations of Case 6, and Cases 3 and 4 could be viewed as special circumstances of Case 7.

can occur in their absence. One way of doing this is to suppose that the β_i exist and are reflexive but not transitive. Alternatively, the partitions of X may be replaced by collections of sets such that in each collection there are at least two overlapping sets, and the union of all sets in every collection is still X. Although the former modification in the assumption about the orderings is implied by the latter modification in the assumption about the partitions of X, the two are not equivalent. In any case, it is not hard to provide an example that satisfies both modified assumptions simultaneously. The following is such an illustration for the circumstance in which there is only one ordering ($I = 1$).

Let X consist of all countries of the world and let μ be the "borders on" relation defined by, $x' \mu x''$ if and only if country x' borders on (i.e., shares a land boundary with) country x'', for all x' and x'' in X. Thus with x' representing the U.S., say, and x'' indicating Canada, the pair (x', x'') would be in μ since the U.S. and Canada share a common border. Of course, an island country such as Japan does not border on any other country. Taking each country to border on itself, μ is reflexive (and symmetric). But it is not transitive. The relation μ may also be used as the basis for constructing an appropriate collection of sets. Thus, for each country, consider the set of all countries, including itself, on which that country borders. Denote the collection of all of these sets, one set for each country, by C. Many of the sets in C overlap and the union of all of them is X. Therefore μ and C violate, respectively, the original properties of orderings and partitions as described above.

In spite of the violations, one might still want to use such a framework as a basis for defining closeness among countries. However, because the sets of C overlap and hence do not constitute a partition of X, there are serious difficulties with this approach. To see why, focus for a moment on the measure m^1. In the present context, m^1 would be defined as before except now with respect to the overlapping sets of C rather than with respect to a partition of X. And, since there is only one ordering, the value of m^1 for each pair of countries is the number of sets of C that contain both members of the pair. Under the previous arrangement, then, the U.S. appears in three sets of C ((i) the U.S. borders on itself, Canada, and Mexico, (ii) Canada borders on itself and the U.S., and (iii) Mexico borders on itself, the U.S., Belize and Guatemala); Japan, being an island, appears in one set of C (namely, that set containing the single element "Japan"); and the pair consisting of the U.S. and Canada appears in two sets of C. Therefore,

$$m^1(U.S., U.S.) = 3,$$

$$m^1(Japan, Japan) = 1,$$

and

$$m^1(U.S., Canada) = 2.$$

This means that the U.S. is closer to itself than Japan is to itself and, perhaps still more worrisome, that the U.S. and Canada are closer together than Japan is to itself. These statements contradict our intuition about the meaning of closeness in a most fundamental way. Such a conceptualization of m^1, therefore, is not very satisfying.

Similar problems arise with analogous reformulations of m^2 and m^3. Measures m^4 and m^5 cannot be defined in this context without introducing a linear ordering of the sets in C, and even if one were found, the definition of these measures would have to be amended to allow for the same pair of countries appearing in more than one class of C. In any event, counter-intuitive peculiarities like those described above are unlikely to go away.

Thus, regardless of whether transposed measures of closeness are pseudometrics, reflexive and transitive orderings and the partially or linearly ordered equivalence classes that they generate are essential if the abstract definition of the notion of closeness is to be consistent with what intuition says the idea of closeness of objects should mean. Attention now turns to an example of the calculation of m^1 through m^5 (as originally characterized in Section I) in terms of actual data.

IV

In order to investigate the relationship between various economic, political, and social factors (mostly not cardinally quantified) on one hand, and economic development on the other, Adelman and Morris [1] ordered 74 less developed countries according to 41 criteria such as the "degree of social tension," the "extent of political stability" and the "level of modernization of industry" for the years 1950-1964. Although Adelman and Morris had other calculations in mind,[16] their data are ideally suited for use in computing closeness among countries in conformity with the measures defined in Section I. In applying these measures to the Adelman-Morris data, the objects of the set X are the 74 countries as listed in Table 1. Only 40 of the original 41 orderings

[16] Adelman and Morris assigned numbers to their rankings and then employed them in a factor analysis to determine "systematic underlying associations" [1, p. 4]. In spite of the fact that this procedure has been criticized on the grounds that the results of factor analyses with ordinal data depend on the scales on which the ordinal data are measured (e.g., Katzner [8, pp. 44-47]), there is clearly no such problem in using the data as long as its ordinality is respected.

Table 1. Countries

Afghanistan	Ethiopia	Liberia	South Africa
Algeria	Gabon	Libya	South Korea
Argentina	Ghana	Malagasy	South Vietnam
Bolivia	Greece	Malawi	Sudan
Brazil	Guatemala	Mexico	Surinam
Burma	Guinea	Morocco	Syria
Cambodia	Honduras	Nepal	Taiwan
Cameroun	India	Nicaragua	Tanganyika
Ceylon	Indonesia	Niger	Thailand
Chad	Iran	Nigeria	Trinidad
Chile	Iraq	Pakistan	Tunisia
Columbia	Israel	Panama	Turkey
Costa Rica	Ivory Coast	Paraguay	Uganda
Cyprus	Jamaica	Peru	United Arab Republic
Dahomey	Japan	Philippines	Uruguay
Dominican Republic	Jordan	Rhodesia	Venezuela
Ecuador	Kenya	Senegal	Yemen
El Salvador	Laos	Sierra Leone	Zambia
	Lebanon	Somali Republic	

Source: Adelman and Morris [1, pp. 10,11]

are included ("per capita GNP in 1961" is dropped) and these appear in Table 2. For present purposes the relative importance of these orderings (i.e., the importance ranking) is taken, arbitrarily, to be descending as one reads down the table (left-hand column first). Thus 40, the most important ordering, is the "size of the traditional agricultural sector" and 1, the least important ordering, is the "structure of foreign trade."

It should be pointed out that Adelman and Morris present each ordering by grading every country in Table 1 according to the concept that characterizes that ordering. The grades run in sequence, A^+,A,A^-,B^+,B,B^-,...,E^+,E,E^-,F^+, F,F^-, where A^+ is the highest grade possible. No ordering, however, has a country assigned to every grade. Thus, for example, the ordering "size of the traditional agricultural sector" has no country with the grade D^+, and no country with a grade below D^-. To be consistent with the constructions of Section I, for any ordering, a grade without a country can not define an equivalence class under that ordering. Alternatively put, equivalence classes arise only in

Table 2. Orderings

Size of the traditional agricultural sector	Extent of leadership commitment to economic development
Extent of dualism	Extent of political stability
Extent of Urbanization	Rate of growth of real per capita GNP: 1950/51-1963/64
Character of basic social organization	Abundance of natural resources
Importance of the indigenous middle class	Gross investment rate
Extent of social mobility	Level of modernization of industry
Extent of literacy	Change of degree of industrialization since 1950
Extent of mass communication	Character of agricultural organization
Degree of cultural and ethnic homogeneity	Level of modernization of techniques in agriculture
Degree of social tension	Degree of improvement in agricultural productivity since 1950
Crude fertility rate	Level of adequacy of physical overhead capital
Degree of modernization of outlook	Degree of improvement in physical overhead capital since 1950
Degree of national integration and sense of national unity	Level of effectiveness of the tax system
Extent of centralization of political power	Degree of improvement in the tax system since 1950
Strength of democratic institutions	Level of effectiveness of financial institutions
Degree of freedom of political opposition and press	Degree of improvement in financial institutions since 1950
Degree of competitiveness of political parties	Rate of improvement in human resources
Predominant basis of the political party system	Structure of foreign trade
Strength of the labor movement	
Political strength of the traditional elite	
Political strength of the military	
Degree of administration efficiency	

Source: Adelman and Morris [1, pp. 16,17]

correspondence to grades that are assigned to at least one country. In the case of "size of the traditional agricultural sector," then, there are 11 equivalence classes. Moreover, in this case the equivalence classes associated with C^- and D are adjacent and, say, the equivalence class identified with C^- is the only one between those corresponding to C and D.

Each measure of closeness, m^1 through m^5, provides ordinal numbers that

Table 3. Measured closeness of selected pairs of countries

	m^1	m^2	m^3	m^4	m^5
Score	30	29.805	6	38.477	38.381
Pair	Chad, Niger	Chad, Niger	Greece, Uruguay	Chad, Niger	Chad, Niger
Score	26	24.415	6	36.452	36.716
Pair	Nepal, Yemen	Nepal, Yemen	Iran, Iraq	Israel, Japan	Greece, Japan
Score	22	24.146	5	36.038	36.306
Pair	Israel, Japan	Greece, Uruguay	Philippines, U.A.R.	Ethiopia, Nepal	Israel, Japan
Score	22	22.049	4[a]	36.035	35.789
Pair	Guinea, Niger	Guinea, Niger	Ivory Coast, Kenya	Greece, Japan	Jamaica, Trinidad
Score	22	21.366	4[a]	35.899	35.722
Pair	Ethiopia, Yemem	Israel, Japan	Cameroun, Tangan.	Nepal, Yemen	Afghan., Ethiopia
Score	0	0	0	8.314	8.409
Pair	Chile, Nepal	Turkey, S. Viet.	Afghan., Burma	Ethiopia, Japan	Ethiopia, Japan

Score	0	0	0	8.306	7.815
Pair	Chile, Iran	Guinea, Venezu.	Afghanistan, Brazil	Israel, Nepal	Israel, Yemen
Score	0	0	0	7.663	7.662
Pair	Lebanon, Thai.	Dahomey, Turk.	Afghan., Bolivia	Japan, Nepal	Israel, Nepal
Score	0	0	0	7.603	7.594
Pair	Cambodia, Japan	Jamaica, Laos	Afghan., Argentina	Israel, Yemen	Japan, Yemen
Score	0	0	0	7.137	7.135
Pair	Mexico, Nepal	Brazil, Chad	Afghan., Algeria	Japan, Yemen	Japan, Nepal
Pairs with					
zero scores	56	56	2261	0	0
same scores	2698	2644	2700	0	0
Number of					
distinct scores	25	365	7	2701	2701
one-pair scores	3	57	1	2701	2701

[a] The score of the pair "Niger, Yemen" is also 4

rank each pair of the 74 countries according to their closeness. Since there are 2,701 pairs in all, it is not practical to list the measured closeness of every pair under every measure. Instead, Table 3 indicates the five (or, in one case, six) pairs scoring the highest measured closeness under each measure, five of the many pairs with the lowest score under m^1 through m^3, and the five pairs with the lowest scores under m^4 and m^5. The table also specifies the measured closeness scores of all of the pairs it contains and, for each measure, gives the total number of pairs having a zero score, the total number of pairs having the same score as at least one other pair, the number of distinct scores, and the number of distinct scores that are associated with exactly one pair.

There are several things that ought to be noted in Table 3. First, many pairs score zero measured closeness under m^1, m^2, and m^3. The 15 such pairs appearing in the table were selected arbitrarily as a result of the algorithm used for computation of the scores. According to Section I, any pair scoring zero under m^1 also scores zero under m^2, and conversely. Furthermore, any pair scoring zero under m^1 (or m^2) necessarily scores zero under m^3. The converse of this second proposition however, is not true. Taken together, these assertions imply that any pair with a zero score in columns m^1 or m^2 in Table 3 could also be listed with the zero scorers in the remaining two columns among m^1, m^2, and m^3.

Second, the number of pairs having the same score as at least one other pair under each measure in Table 3 includes the number of pairs with zero scores under that measure. Again, pairs having the same score are listed arbitrarily so that the order of the two pairs scoring 6 under m^3 could be reversed, and the three pairs scoring 4 could be presented in any one of six ways.

Third, the large number of pairs with shared scores observed for m^1 and m^3 is to be expected. In the case of m^1, for example, because there are exactly 40 orderings, there can be only 41 integer values that are assigned to 2,701 pairs. Table 3 indicates that above score 22, sixteen of these are not used. Clearly, then, the only way to allocate the remaining 25 integers (and according to the table, all of these are used) among so many pairs is to have a large number of common scores. Note that m^3 uses only seven integers.

Fourth, the number of distinct scores minus the number of scores associated with exactly one pair gives the number of scores that are identified with more than one pair. And the number of pairs having the same score as at least one other pair plus the number of scores associated with exactly one score equals the total number of pairs, or 2,701.

Fifth, it is important to emphasize that both the absolute size of and the differences between scores is irrelevant. All that matters is the ordering among pairs that these measures define. It is interesting to observe, moreover, that restricting attention to m^1, m^2, m^4, and m^5, the pair Chad-Niger has the highest score under all four measures, the pair Israel-Japan appears among the top five scorers under each of them, and the pair Nepal-Yemen scores in the top five under all but one. In addition, the pairs Ethiopia-Japan, Japan-Nepal, Japan-Yemen, Israel-Nepal, and Israel-Yemen constitute the bottom five scorers under both m^4 and m^5. Of course, not much can be made of these results. A judicious rearrangement of the importance ranking of the original 40 orderings is capable of knocking any of the five highest scoring pairs under m^2 or m^5 out of the top five, or raising any of the five lowest scoring pairs under m^5 from the bottom five.

Another way to contrast any two measures is to analyze their closeness by employing the number-of-identically-ordered-pairs[17] measure $\bar{m}^1$ or the Kemeny-Snell measure $\bar{m}^4$ described in Section I. For each coupling of measures, this calculation requires 3,646,350 comparisons of ordered pairs. The number of identically ordered pairs for all two-measure combinations[18] appears in Table 4. Since these numbers are very large, reaching to a maximum of 3,646,350, they are also expressed in the table as percentages of the total number of comparisons. The corresponding Kemeny-Snell scores[19] are given in Table 5. (The percentages in Table 5 are also percentages of the total number of comparisons.) Although certainly not independent of the importance ranking of the original orderings, the combinations of m^1 and m^2, and of m^4 and m^5, have the highest scores in both tables. Not surprisingly, the combinations involving m^3 have the lowest. As required by the analysis of Sections I and II, the scores in Table 5 are at least as large, respectively, as those in Table 4, and the pair (m^4, m^5) has the same score in both tables. Additional ways

[17] Recall that the pairs (country Q, country R) and (country U, country V) are ranked in the same pairwise order under, for example, m^1 and m^2, provided that if countries Q and R are said to be closer than countries U and V with m^1, say, then countries Q and R are also said to be closer than countries U and V with m^2.

[18] These numbers were obtained by using the Kendall τ option of the non-par corr subprogram of SPSS, which allows for the presence of ties generated by equal scores of measured closeness. The resulting τ coefficients were then converted to numbers of non-tied, identically ordered pairs using a standard transformation. Total numbers of identically ordered pairs were then found by adding in the number of pairs that were simultaneously tied under the two measures compared in each case.

[19] It is not hard to show that these scores may be calculated by adding half of the total number of ties occurring in each of the two measures compared in each case to the numbers of non-tied, identically ordered pairs obtained as described in n.18 immediately above. This was the method employed in Table 5.

Table 4. $\bar{m}^1$— numbers of identically ordered pairs*

	m^1	m^2	m^3	m^4	m^5
m^1		3,146,360 (86.3)	1,025,938 (28.1)	2,863,047 (78.5)	2,815,816 (77.2)
m^2			875,179 (24.0)	2,937,645 (80.6)	2,974,770 (81.6)
m^3				809,290 (22.2)	832,067 (22.8)
m^4					3,391,288 (93.0)
m^5					

* Percentages in parentheses

of investigating the closeness of pairs of these measures are possible but not pursued here.

The preceding discussion has defined and examined different ways of measuring closeness of not-necessarily-quantifiable elements of a given set. In the course of doing this, it has been noted that other, more mathematically complex measures could also be devised. All such measures of closeness are potentially useful to social scientists in a number of ways. First, they enlarge the descriptive power of social science by providing a technique that enables more complete descriptions of economic and social reality. It is clear from the above that adopting any of the measures m^1 through m^5 permits descriptive statements about less developed countries during the 1950s and early 1960s that would not otherwise be possible. Second, the availability of measures of closeness expands the capacity of social scientists to include non-quantifiable variables in their models and theories. Decision criteria for locating a plant, say, could perhaps allow for things like the nature and quality of transportation facilities and the skills and quality of the labor force. And, in general, were the descriptive and analytical force of social science to be so enhanced, broader policy recommendations could not be far behind.

Table 5. $\tilde{m}^4$— Kemeny-Snell measures*

	m^1	m^2	m^3	m^4	m^5
m^1		3,292,932 (90.3)	2,242,965 (61.5)	3,007,802 (82.5)	2,960,571 (81.2)
m^2			2,173,429 (59.6)	2,945,198 (80.8)	2,982,314 (81.8)
m^3				2,112,762 (57.9)	2,135,539 (58.6)
m^4					3,391,288 (93.0)
m^5					

* Percentages in parentheses

References

1. Adelman, I., and C. T. Morris, *Society, Politics and Economic Development* (Baltimore: Johns Hopkins Press, 1967).
2. Birnberg, T. B., and S. A. Resnick, *Colonial Development: An Econometric Study* (New Haven: Yale University Press, 1975).
3. Brzezinski, Z., and S. P. Huntington, *Political Power: USA/USSR* (New York: Viking, 1964).
4. Ellman, M., *Collectivisation, Convergence and Capitalism: Political Economy in a Divided World* (London: Academic Press, 1984), Ch. 18.
5. Feinstein, I. K., and K. H. Murphy, *College Algebra* (Ames: Littlefield-Adams, 1957).
6. Gregson, R. A. M., *Psychometrics of Similarity* (New York: Academic Press, 1975).
7. Hoover, E. M., *An Introduction to Regional Economics*, 2nd ed. (New York: Knopf, 1975).
8. Katzner, D. W., *Analysis without Measurement* (Cambridge: Cambridge University Press, 1983).

9. Kemeny, J. G., and J. L. Snell, *Mathematical Models in the Social Sciences* (New York: Blaisdell, 1962).
10. Kerr, C., *The Future of Industrial Societies: Convergence or Continuing Divergence* (Cambridge: Harvard University Press, 1983).
11. Kruskal, J. B., and M. Wish, *Multidimensional Scaling* (Beverly Hills: SAGE, 1978).
12. Kuznets, S., *Population, Capital and Growth* (New York: Norton, 1973).
13. Lauterbach, A., "The 'Convergence' Controversy Revisited," *Kyklos* 29 (1976), pp. 733-754.
14. Meyer, A. G., "Theories of Convergence," in *Change in Communist Systems*, C. Johnson, ed. (Stanford: Stanford University Press, 1970), pp. 313-341.
15. Pfanzagl, J., *Theory of Measurement*, 2nd ed. (Würtzburg-Vienna: Physica-Verlag, 1971).
16. Sneath, P. H. A., and R. R. Sokal, *Numerical Taxonomy: The Principles and Practice of Numerical Classification* (San Francisco: W. H. Freeman, 1973).
17. Spector, B. I., "A Social-Psychological Model of Position Modification: Aswan," in *50% Solution*, I. W. Zartman, ed. (Garden City: Anchor/Doubleday, 1976), pp. 343-371.
18. Spulber, N., and I. Horowitz, *Quantitative Economic Policy and Planning* (New York: Norton, 1976).
19. Tinbergen, J., "Do Communist and Free Economies Show a Converging Pattern?" *Soviet Studies* 12 (1961), pp. 333-341.
20. Zartman, I. W., *50% Solution* (Garden City: Anchor/Doubleday, 1976).

6
The Role of Formalism in Economic Thought, with Illustration Drawn from the Analysis of Social Interaction in the Firm[1]

Economists tend to use the word "analysis" rather glibly to describe the things that they do. The list of these things is long, including verbal description, numerical manipulation, model building in its many forms, and so on. In all usages, however, the underlying goal of analysis is the same: to make sense out of or to understand worldly phenomena. And in all cases, analysis proceeds by organizing and explaining the thoughts one has about the phenomena in question.

The most widespread approach to analysis in economics is called *formalism*. To economists, a formalist analysis consists of identifying (usually quantifiable) variables, assuming the existence of relations among them, assuming

[1] The Reconstruction of Economic Theory, P. Mirowski, ed. (Boston: Kluwer-Nijhoff, 1986), pp. 137-177.

The author would like to thank Robert W. Drago, Philip Mirowski, and Douglas Vickers for their help.

that the relations exhibit certain properties or characteristics, and working out at length the implications of all of these assumptions. Such analyses may also concern themselves with maximization, and with solutions and proofs of existence of solutions for some system of (simultaneous) relations.

This essay explores the role of formalism in economic thought: where it came from, what it does, and what are its prerequisites and limitations, its power and potential. The argument of the essay is illustrated with an analysis of the social interactions among employees in the economic firm.

It should be made clear at the outset that what follows is neither an essay on methodology nor on epistemology. Most methodologies and epistemologies appearing in economics today make room for formalist constructions in analysis, although they use and interpret such structures in a variety of different ways (Katzner [15]). And in all cases, whatever the methodological and epistemological foundation of an investigation, if formalism is to be employed, certain issues have to be faced. These latter issues are the focus of attention here.

History

A quick glance at the current issue of almost any modern economics journal reveals the pervasiveness of formalism in economic analysis. But the appearance of formalism in economics is only a late development in the long evolution of formalism as a mathematical school of thought. The emergence of formalism in the history of mathematics has been chronicled recently by Kline [17]. His story follows:

All ancient civilizations sought truths: truths about the properties of the physical world, truths about the nature of man and his behavior, etc. Most obtained these truths from theology. The Greeks, however, thought that the mind of man, aided by observation, is also capable of discovering truths. Moreover, since (the Greeks believed) the universe is designed according to mathematical principles, and since the relationships among numbers underlie and unify nature, truths may be learned through the application of mathematics. This reasoning was based on three precepts: First, mathematics is concerned with abstractions, and one abstract concept would encompass the essential features of every physical occurrence of that concept. Second, all discussion would begin with axioms or self-evident truths that no one could doubt. And third, each conclusion was to be derived deductively from the axioms. In their search for the mathematical laws governing the universe, the Greeks created, among other things, Euclidean geometry.

From the ancient Greeks up to the beginning of the nineteenth century A. D., Western thinkers (with a few exceptions) thought that all known truths about our physical world were described by Euclidean geometry. Furthermore, any unknown truths about physical reality were merely parts of Euclidean geometry that had not yet been detected. All of this was shattered in the nineteenth century with the discovery that non-Euclidean geometries could also be used to accurately represent the properties of physical actuality. Hence Euclidean geometry is not necessarily the true description of real physical space. Although the Greek program of employing mathematics to reveal truths about the world had been extraordinarily useful, it did not reveal truths in the sense originally intended. Axioms could no longer be regarded as unquestionable self-evident truths. They may be suggested by experience but they, along with the conclusions to which they deductively lead, still have only limited applicability.

About the same time that mathematicians began to understand that the mere usage of mathematics did not necessarily yield truths, they also realized that their discipline had evolved over the years in a sloppy haphazard fashion, leaving many poorly understood concepts and numerous logical errors. Consequently, the second half of the nineteenth century witnessed their attempt to correct these deficiencies by axiomatizing their arguments. Such efforts led to the recognition of at least three noteworthy principles: First, all deductive systems necessarily contain undefined terms. Second, every set of axioms should be shown to be consistent, that is, not permit the derivation of contradictory propositions from it. Finally, each individual axiom in any set of axioms should be independent of (not derivable from) the remaining axioms in that set.

By 1900 mathematicians believed that they had completed the reconstruction of their arguments in axiomatic terms. But almost immediately contradictions were uncovered in their new mathematics. In response to this state of affairs four schools of thought arose, each claiming to provide a contradiction-free approach to the nature of mathematics. According to the logistic school, all mathematics was secured from logic. Since the laws of logic constituted a body of consistent truths, so did mathematics. The set-theoretic school claimed that all mathematics was derived from a consistent theory of sets. The latter could be obtained by restricting the type of sets that were admitted for discussion. The intuitionist school asserted that mathematics was independent of the real world. Mathematical thinking consisted of mental construction of its own universe based on fundamental mathematical intuition. Intuition, not logic, also determined the soundness of argument. One did not deduce from axioms. Rather, to do valid mathematics was to construct entities in a finite number of steps. Defining sets by describing the characteristics of their elements and using non-constructive proofs of the existence of things were not legitimate. Consistency was furnished by correct thought as judged by intuition.

The last of the schools of thought was the formalist school. Contrary to all of the other approaches, mathematics to the formalist was a collection of formal systems, each with its own concepts, axioms, and theorems. All axioms (both logical and mathematical) were expressed as formulas or collections of mathematical symbols. All deductions were manipulations of formulas according to the specified logical axioms. And every formal system had to be shown to be consistent within itself.

Each of these four schools vigorously attacked the others. Because interest here centers on formalism, it is worth noting at this juncture two criticisms leveled against the formalist school. On one hand, their mathematics was labeled as abstract and having little meaning in actuality. Infinite sets, for example, were a part of the mathematics of the formalist school, and were (and are) totally foreign to human experience. On the other hand, the consistency of a formal system did not guarantee the existence in the real world of things (such as equilibrium price vectors) proved by formalists to exist in non-constructive existence theorems. Discussion will return to these points later on.

All of the four schools made claims of consistency. The intuitionists based consistency on intuition. The remaining three groups either asserted that their axioms led to consistency or believed that their axioms were sufficient to establish it, although they had no proof. But in 1931, Gödel showed that the consistency of any mathematical system sufficiently wide so as to include the arithmetic of whole numbers can never be established. He also demonstrated that in such a system there always is at least one proposition which, together with its negation, cannot be proved. Thus for the logicists, set-theorists, and formalists, who relied on axiomatic foundations, no system of axioms permitted proof of all theorems that fell within its structure. Moreover, there was no guarantee that contradictions could not arise in any of their systems. The principle that all systems should be consistent was impossible to enforce.

Gödel's results (combined with others that emerged at roughly the same time on the unprovability of specific propositions) fragmented mathematicians into an even greater number of competing factions. Many of these, including the formalist school, persist to this day.

The introduction of formalism in economics is relatively new. To be sure, functions have been maximized and systems of simultaneous equations have been solved as far back as Cournot [5]. And many later nineteenth century economists such as Jevons [13], Pareto [24], and Walras [32] subsequently applied mathematics to the study of economic phenomena. But all of this occurred before the emergence of the formalist school in the early years of the twentieth century. It is only very recently that the formalist approach, whereby axioms are explicitly postulated and their implications derived, appeared as a method of analysis in economics. The culmination of the transference of formalism from mathematics to economics appeared in 1959 in Debreu's *Theory of Value* which is still regarded by many as the apotheosis of the axiomatic method in economics. Debreu may also have been the first economist to expressly acknowledge and sanction formalism. In the Preface to the *Theory of Value* he wrote:

> The theory of value is treated here with the standards of rigor of the contemporary formalist school of mathematics .... Allegiance to rigor dictates the axiomatic form of the analysis where the theory, in the strict sense, is logically entirely disconnected from its interpretations. (Debreu [6, p. viii].)

Another aspect of the appearance of formalism in economics is the focus by economists almost exclusively on quantifiable aspects of the thing under investigation. Now quantification is neither a necessary nor a sufficient condition for formalism. Indeed, it is possible to do a formalist analysis without any sort of quantification at all (see Katzner [14] and Essay 4 in this volume). But by the time that Cournot started what eventually became a movement toward formalism, virtually all economists employing mathematics in their trade had accepted the equivalent of Lord Kelvin's dictum:

> ... when you can measure what you are speaking about and express it in numbers, you know something about it; but when you cannot measure it, when you cannot express it in numbers, your knowledge is of a meager and unsatisfactory kind: it may be the beginning of knowledge, but you have scarcely, in your thoughts, advanced to the stage of *science*, whatever the matter may be. (Thomson [31, pp. 80,81].)

Thus the introduction of mathematics and later of formalism in economics seems to have gone hand in hand with quantification.

The Prerequisites of Formalism

As described above, formalist analysis usually begins with the specification of variables and relations among them. But before even arriving at this starting gate, considerable abstraction and discipline of thought are required just to be able to accomplish the necessary specifications. The statement, "Let there be J variables and I relations among them," can and should be justified. And so discussion now focuses on what has to be done to set the stage for a formalist analysis. In anticipation of subsequent argument, a certain kind of intellectual tension is worthy of mention at the beginning.

Meyerson [21, Chs. 1,2] has argued that when thinking about the world in terms of discrete objects and discrete laws (relations among objects), both the objects and the laws are not changed by displacing them in space. Nor are these laws modified by the passage of time, that is, they persist unaltered through time.[2] Furthermore, to be able to understand the assertion, "An event happening to object *A* causes or determines another event happening to object *B*," it must also be supposed that *A* and *B* persist without transformation over time as well. But the nature of our world is such that changes in *A* and *B* are perceived as time moves on. These perceptions, then, can only reflect "apparent transformation" which, at a deeper level, does not actually occur. Hence there is always a tension that can never be completely overcome between what an analyst thinks and what he sees.

Similarly with change itself. To think about change in such a context requires that evolving reality be reduced to discrete laws that govern its metamorphosis. These laws are set against fixed objects and environments that are inviolate through time and which, on account of their constancy, permit change to be detected by comparison and contrast. This kind of change is called displacement or motion. But as before, apparent change is still perceived in the "fixed" objects and environments, and the tension between what one thinks and sees remains.

The Dialectical Nature of Thought

This tension (and others) reflects, in part, the dialectical characteristics embedded in the processes of thought. To see what is involved, notice first that in certain cases, the human mind is perfectly capable of sharply delineating the boundaries of an idea. The result is what Georgescu-Roegen [10, pp. 43-45] has called an arithmomorphic concept. Such concepts have the property that they can be clearly distinguished and separated from all others. They are distinctly discrete and there is no overlap between them and their opposites. The

[2] This essay, like others in the present volume, is focused in the context of logical time described in the introductory essay above. But, as indicated there, its argument (as with those of the other essays reprinted here) is largely independent of that context, and only very minor and mostly obvious modifications are required to reset it for an environment of historical time.

velocity of a moving object is an arithmomorphic concept as is the weight of a pot of water and the length of a train. It should also be understood that non-quantifiable ideas, such as the notion of a human being or a country, also have expressions in arithmomorphic form.

On the other hand, there are concepts whose boundaries human powers seem unable to clearly and precisely define. Exact characterizations are either arbitrary in that they do not conform to standard notions or are extraordinarily difficult to employ. Where, for example, does one quality of experience leave off and another begin? Democracy and non-democracy are two different ideas, each with a variety of shades of meaning and, what is more important, with certain shades of democracy overlapping certain shades of non-democracy. Concepts such as these may be referred to as dialectical (Georgescu-Roegen [10, pp. 45-47]). Dialectical notions are distinct, though not, as their arithmomorphic counterparts, discretely so. Each is surrounded by its own penumbra of meanings. Any dialectical concept is distinguishable from all others (including its opposite), since no two penumbras can be identical. But, although impossible with arithmomorphic concepts, a country can be both a democracy and a non-democracy at the same time.

Now formalism, as it appears in economics, is clearly based on arithmomorphic concepts. But with dialectical contexts, since a thing can be both A and not A at the same time, the formalist rules for constructions and deductions do not apply. In particular, deductive logic can not be employed because it requires the discrete distinction of the objects on which it operates. One may still, however, make assumptions and reason with dialectical ideas, as the following passage due to Russell shows:

> Not only are we aware of particular yellows, but if we have seen a sufficient number of yellows and have sufficient intelligence, we are aware of the universal *yellow*; this universal is the subject in such judgements as "yellow differs from blue" or "yellow resembles blue less than green does." And the universal yellow is the predicate in such judgements as "this is yellow" .... (Russell [27, p. 212].)

Dialectical reasoning can be checked in at least two ways (Georgescu-Roegen [10, p. 337]). The first is by use of the ancient Socratic method: systematic questioning of all aspects of argument. The second is by working through arithmomorphic similes. Dialectical reasoning can often be likened to various arithmomorphic arguments, although none of these test arguments is ever capable of replacing the original in its entirety. Error uncovered by either the Socratic method or the employment of deductive logic in an arithmomorphic simile clearly casts doubt on the original dialectical reasoning. But even though it provides a certain comfort and satisfaction, a lack of detection of error does not imply correctness.

Most important concepts in economics are really dialectical in character. In actuality, for example, there is generally no such thing as the single, unique price of a good.[3] Rather, any commodity usually has an entire penumbra of prices at which it is sold. Moreover, because of the great variety of forms in which commodities normally can be produced, the line marking the "end" of one commodity and the "start" of another is often difficult to determine. Thus in saying that certain goods are sold in certain markets at certain prices, the underlying conceptual referents of "goods," "markets," and "prices" are purely dialectical. Other examples of dialectical concepts are the preferences of an individual, the technology of production, and the various forms of competition that may appear in markets, etc.

Formalist analysis in economics abstracts from such concepts to secure discretely distinct (arithmomorphic) notions which are then converted into variables. It is among these kinds of variables that formalist relations are defined and manipulated. As will be seen below, the relations themselves may be viewed as abstractions from underlying dialectical processes. In this sense, formalisms in economics may be described as arithmomorphic similes extracted from a dialectical base.

Arithmomorphic Abstraction

Consider a dialectical idea such as the price of good x, and suppose the arithmomorphic notion of the price of x is drawn from it. Suppose further that the arithmomorphic price of x is permitted to range over all non-negative real numbers. Thus the arithmomorphic variable called "price of x" is obtained. An arithmomorphic variable, then, is defined by extracting an arithmomorphic concept from a dialectical one and specifying the collection of discretely distinct realizations or values that the concept may possess.

Although the variable "price of x" is quantitative, there is nothing in the construction of an arithmomorphic variable requiring that measurement be possible. To illustrate, from the dialectical notion of the form of competition in the market for x, extract an arithmomorphic counterpart. On 3-by-5 cards, say, write down descriptions of each of the various forms of competition that may appear in the market for x — one description on each card. Take these descriptions to be discretely distinct even though the prose on each card may

3 See Bausor [1] and Mirowski [22].

appear to be imprecise and fuzzy. Assume that the relevant group of investigators agrees that this collection of descriptions is appropriate for the purpose at hand. Then the variable "form of competition in the market for x" may be defined as that which takes on as values the description on any 3-by-5 card in the collection. Another example of such a variable (and one employed in the sections on the firm below) is the (set of) activities in which an employee engages while at work. Each of its variable values, too, may be thought of as a description on a 3-by-5 card.

The question of whether the 3-by-5 cards in a given collection of variable values can be supplanted by numbers that meaningfully measure the descriptions on them in some way is a separate matter. To answer it requires formalisms that are entirely different from those employed in the analysis of the particular economic phenomena under scrutiny. Measuring the descriptions on the 3-by-5 cards implies that all of the important information on the cards is encapsulated in certain abstract properties, and that the specific form in which these properties arise in the description on any one card permits that card to be replaced by a single number conveying the same information as on the card.[4] For example, if each card described a person of a certain "oldness," and if oldness were all that mattered, then a number representing the age of the person described could possibly be substituted for the description on the card. The formal conditions under which such replacement is valid in general are complex. To be able to measure ordinally, say, requires the presence of a reflexive, transitive, and total ordering relation defined among the 3-by-5 cards such that the interval topology, based on the equivalence classes generated by this ordering, has a countable base. The details and the requisites for other forms of measurement are not considered here.[5] Suffice it to say that the more (relevant) information on the card that is not reflected by the number assigned to the card, and the more extraneous information entrapped by the number itself, the less meaningful the measure. Thus the price of x is not a good measure of the quality of the commodity x since the price of x contains information having nothing to do with the quality of x, and there are many aspects of the quality of x that need not be mirrored in its price. In any case, it has already been noted that measurement is not a prerequisite of formalism, and none is assumed in present discussion. Arithmomorphic variable values then, are generally viewed as descriptions on 3-by-5 cards that are discrete and unchanging over time.

Suppose now that the variables and relations for a formalist analysis have

4 An expanded discussion may be found in Katzner [14, Sec. 2.2].

5 See, for example, Pfanzagl [25].

been distilled from their dialectical foundations. (The extraction of arithmomorphic relations from dialectical processes is the topic of the subsection "From Processes to Functions" below.) Several issues concerning the properties of the spaces of variable values, the meaning of the relations defined on them, and the apparatus for the manipulation of these relations still have to be discussed. In the next few paragraphs each is considered in turn.

Specification of spaces of variable values (the sets over which the variables range) and the properties these spaces are to possess is one of the important elements in proceeding to the start of any formal analysis. Indeed, Hofstadter [12, pp. 611-613] has suggested that the proper choices in this regard may be crucial to the solution of many real problems. Economists, however, have tended to ignore the issue. When variables are quantifiable, the relevant spaces are almost always taken to be Euclidean. Other possibilities are seldom considered, in spite of the proven usefulness of non-Euclidean spaces for analyzing the physical world. As of now, non-quantifiable spaces have hardly been employed in formal analysis in economics, and there is still much to learn about them. One specification of such a space has been given by Katzner [14, Sects. 3.2,3.3]. In any case, the specification of the space over which a variable ranges contains implicit theoretical statements about the variable itself.

Also implicit in the specification of spaces and their properties are rules for manipulation of the variable values. The weakest rule that one can give is a scheme for classification. Somewhat stronger is the designation of order, that is, the imposition of an ordering relation among the elements of the space.[6] Thus in the section on social interaction below, values of the variable "activities in which a worker engages while on the job" are classified by certain "rule sets" and ordered according to their impact on output. With enough quantification present, the arithmetic operations of addition, subtraction, multiplication, and division provide still further manipulative tools.

It should also be noted that although an infinite number of descriptions on 3-by-5 cards can never be written down, infinite collections (both countable and uncountable) of such cards can certainly be imagined. Economists and other social scientists do so all the time (Katzner [14, Sec. 7.2]). Infinite sets of non-quantifiable elements may be accepted in the same sense that infinite sets of numbers are employed in quantitative contexts: Such sets exist only in the minds of investigators and have no basis in reality. In this way, the set of all values of the variable "activities in which a worker engages while on the job" is thought of as a possibly uncountable set in the section on social

[6] Specification of order alone does not, in general, imply (ordinal) measurement as the term is commonly used (Pfanzagl [25, pp. 75,79]).

interaction. Recall that such conceptualizations are the source of one of the criticisms aimed at the formalist school many years ago.

Arithmomorphic relations among arithmomorphic variables are frequently expressed as mathematical functions. And, of course, the definition of function does not rely on measurement: Let y and x be two variables defined over sets called, respectively, the domain and range. (These may actually be vectors of variables such as $y = (y_1, ..., y_J)$ and $x = (x_1, ..., x_I)$.) Then the function f, often written as

$$x = f(y),$$

is a rule which assigns to each element of the domain a unique element in the range. When y and x are not quantifiable, f is defined by indicating which value of x is associated to each value of y. This is the meaning of the functions involving non-quantified variables used to analyze social interaction in the firm subsequently in the section on such social interaction below. In the numerical case, f may be characterized either by listing the associations between x and y or by summarizing them in a formula such as

$$x = f(y) = y + 2.$$

Consider, for a moment, the latter. The formula $x = y + 2$ is generally taken to be a rule which indicates that values of x are obtained from values of y by adding the number 2. But according to Wittgenstein (see Wright [35, pp. 21-38]), it can not be said that every time one sees $x = y+2$, one is committed to interpret its meaning in this way. Individuals are always free to choose their interpretation at each encounter. There is no reason why a person could not invoke the above interpretation of $x = y + 2$ today and employ an entirely different one tomorrow.

Naturally, individuals can be trained to understand $x = y + 2$ in a certain way. Or they can negotiate over its meaning and possibly agree on an interpretation. But someone else with another kind of training or not a party to the negotiated agreement may well come along and comprehend the meaning of $x = y + 2$ differently. This is because each individual learns meanings by making inductive inferences from past experience. These understandings are one's own and can never be conveyed to another. For two persons to arrive at the same meaning, then, they must have the same experiences and must make the same, inferences from them — an unlikely occurrence in the absence of negotiation or similar training.

The upshot is that the relations of any formalist analysis are always subject to new interpretations and changed meanings, and such is the case even if the dialectical foundation from which it springs were to remain constant. Thus the same formalist analysis of a given phenomenon at two separate times can not guarantee the same conclusions in advance. Formalism, then, can not be said to provide an absolute standard against which the conclusions of other types of analyses can be compared.

It remains, in this subsection, to consider the rules for manipulating the relations of a formalist analysis. As with the formalist school, these rules turn on the principles of deductive logic. Although deductive logic has no relevance in the underlying dialectical base of the analysis, its force upon application in arithmomorphic abstractions is well known.

The most fundamental operation that can be performed on functions is composition or elimination of variables by substitution. Thus, two functions f and g, say

$$x = f(y) \qquad \text{and} \qquad y = g(z),$$

may be combined into h by eliminating y:

$$x = h(z),$$

where

$$h(z) = f(g(z))$$

and h is referred to as the *composition* of f and g. To be useful, function composition must exhibit two characteristics: It must be closed, that is, the composites it produces must always be functions, and it must be associative.[7] The simplest algebraic structure conforming to these properties is called a *semigroup*.[8] Hence the least that can be postulated about the functions of a formalist analysis is that they are elements of a semigroup under function composition.[9]

Additional techniques for manipulating functions may also be introduced. Inverting functions to obtain inverses and partial inverses is a possibility (Katzner [14, Ch.4] and Essay 4 in this volume). In the quantifiable, case functions may also be added, subtracted, multiplied, divided, differentiated, integrated, and so on. Clearly, each insertion of a new manipulative rule complicates the algebraic structure required to support formalist analysis.

It should be emphasized that the postulation of a semigroup structure does not imply the presence of ordinal, cardinal, or ratio measures. First of all,

---

7 For example, if $w = e(x)$, $x = f(y)$, and $y = g(z)$ are three functions, then associativity of function composition means that eliminating first x and then y gives the same result as eliminating y first and then x.

8 A semigroup is a nonempty set on which a closed and associative operation has been defined.

9 See Mirowski [22].

the conditions for the existence of such measures are not all met by semigroup structures. And second, the functions of the semigroup may express the substantive relations of the analysis rather than the relations required for the construction of numerical scales. Thus the convenience of numerical representations, with their attendant arithmetic tools of manipulation, is not necessarily available. What is at hand are the discrete variable values and the functions or laws relating them, both of which persist as constants through time, the operation of composition for manipulating functions which is closed and associative, plus any other elements such as inverses that may be introduced for analytical purposes. All dialectical facets of thought have been exorcised.

Time and Change

As far as human capacity to sense nature is concerned, there is no such thing as an "instant of time." Rather, time is perceived as a series of imprecise and overlapping durations in which the future becomes the inexactly felt present and then slips into the past. It is a dialectical concept (Georgescu-Roegen [10, pp. 69-72]). The idea of instants of time (or discretely distinct time periods) all lined up one after the other is an arithmomorphic abstraction. It permits identification of the linear continuum as the standard reference for keeping track of the movement of time. The use of dynamic equations (differential or otherwise) in formalist analysis depends on it.

Time and change are tightly interwoven; one can hardly be discerned without the other. Change, unobservable at an instant of time, is capable of detection only over durations. Although the distinction between sameness and change rests ultimately in the beholder, judgments as to whether a change has actually occurred turn on the relation of the thing in question to its "other." Change can only appear in contrast to the environment in which it is set. And because there are no clear-cut boundaries delineating where it begins and ends, change, like time, is dialectical in character (Georgescu-Roegen [10, pp. 63,69]).

One way of describing change is with the notion of process (Georgescu-Roegen [10, pp. 213-215]). A process involves something happening, certain events or changes taking place over time. Each process is defined by the happenings that make it up. All remaining events constitute the process' environment. The process itself can only be understood in terms of the relationship between these two collections of occurrences which dialectically overlap each other.

To extract an arithmomorphic analytical representation of a given process, that is, to reduce change to motion or displacement as described earlier, an

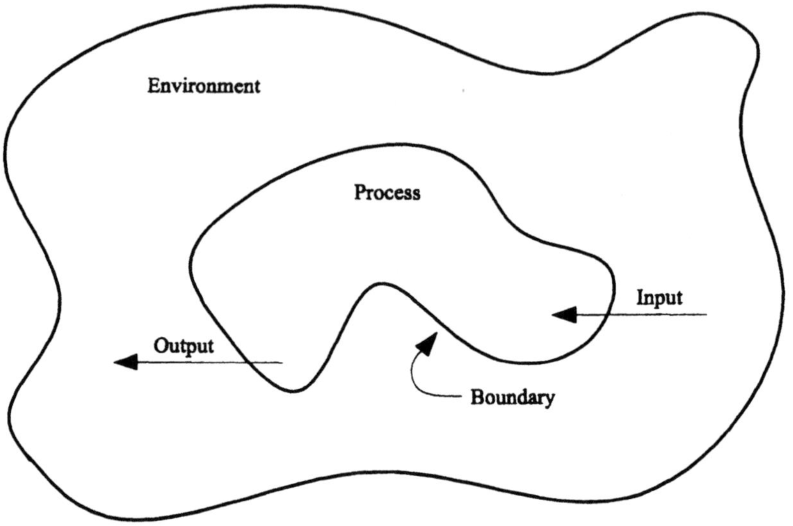

Figure 1

arithmomorphic boundary partitioning reality is drawn between the process and its environment. (Figure 1 provides a schematic illustration.) Included in this boundary is a specification of the finite (arithmomorphic) period of time over which the process is considered. Neither occurrences entirely within the process nor entirely within its environment can be seen. Only arithmomorphic objects crossing the boundary that remain unchanged over time are capable of observation. (Recall that any change actually perceived in these arithmomorphic objects is regarded as merely apparent change having no significance.) Thus the analytical representation of the process consists of the record of boundary crossings over the interval of time in question. Elements crossing from the environment to the process are called *inputs*; those passing from the process to the environment are *outputs*. (In Figure 1, only one input arrow and one output arrow are drawn. These are intended to represent schematically all inputs into and outputs from the process.)

Observe that in taking the analytical representation of a process to be an arithmomorphic boundary, all intentions of analyzing what goes on within the process must be given up. Of course, it is always possible to peer "inside" the process by drawing a second arithmomorphic boundary and dividing the original process into two subprocesses, so that the output of one subprocess pro-

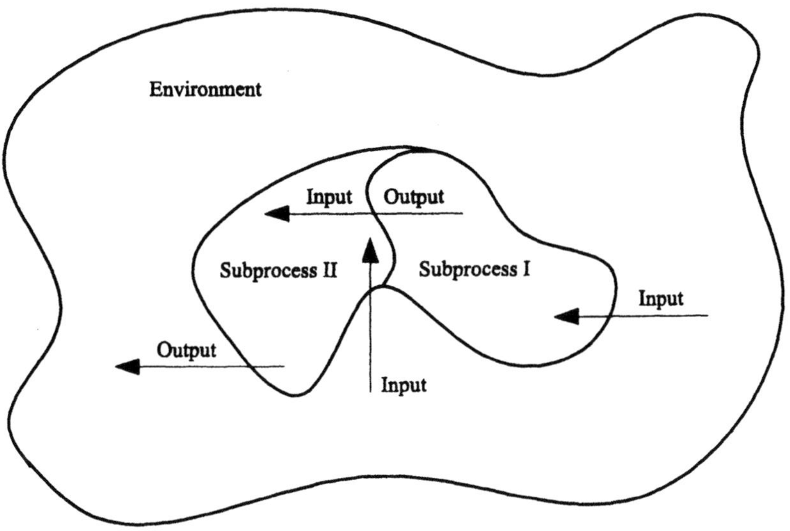

Figure 2

vides part or all of the input for the other (Figure 2). But the two subprocesses are themselves independent processes, and the events occurring within each remain hidden from view. Note also that since a process is considered to have only a finite duration, whatever transpired before and whatever might happen after the relevant time period is ignored.

From Processes to Functions

Just as the variables of formalist analysis may be seen as emerging from dialectical concepts, so may the functions of formalist analysis be thought of as extractions from dialectical processes. Although the reduction of dialectical processes to arithmomorphic analytical representations of them has been described in the previous subsection, additional steps are needed to convert the latter into functions. These steps are now considered with special reference to the case of neoclassical production for illustrative purposes. The production function appearing in the following section as equation (2) is of the same sort as that derived here.

Let an analytical representation of a dialectical process be given and suppose the interval of duration is $\{t : 0 \leq t \leq t^0\}$, where t is a real (arithmomorphic) variable representing time. (It is convenient, henceforth, to use the term "process" synonymously with its analytical representation.) Thus the process (that is, its analytical representation) starts at $t = 0$ and ends at $t = t^0$. The first step is to thin all boundary crossings to not-necessarily-quantifiable arithmomorphic entities. If there are J distinct arithmomorphic input-boundary-crossing variables indexed by $j = 1, ..., J$, and if $y_j(t)$ denotes the value of input variable j at time t (that is, an input boundary crossing at t), then the vector of input boundary crossings at t is $y(t) = [y_1(t), ..., y_J(t)]$, and the collection of all input boundary crossings for the duration of the process is

$$Y = \{y(t) : 0 \leq t \leq t^0\}.$$

Similarly, with $x_i(t)$ representing the value of output variable i at time t, where $i = 1, ..., I$, and with $x(t) = [x_1(t), ..., x_I(t)]$ the complete set of output boundary crossings for the process appears as

$$X = \{x(t) : 0 \leq t \leq t^0\}.$$

The pair (Y, X) is one (arithmomorphic) description of the process.

The representation of a process as the culmination of all input and output boundary crossings encompasses several special instances which are worthy of brief mention (see Georgescu-Roegen [10, pp. 215-217]). To begin with, some inputs might enter the process and, like catalysts in a chemical reaction, subsequently exit without noticeable change. This can be captured by the statement that

$$x_i(t + k) = y_j(t),$$

for appropriate i and j, and some positive real number k. In another instance, some entering inputs could be completely "used up" by the process and never exit as outputs, while certain exiting outputs produced by the process may have no counterpart as entering inputs. Lastly, inputs might be modified or only partially used up by the process, and hence exit in a somewhat different form from that in which they entered. Here the entering inputs may be regarded as different variables from the exiting outputs. These special cases find illustration in the production process of growing corn, in which land is often described as an input that is unchanged by the process; rain an input that is completely used up; ears of corn an output that does not appear as an input; and an entering spade that exits with increased wear, an input that is modified by the process.

It is also possible in a production process to divide inputs into two categories: those that are flows per unit of time (such as seed and fertilizer in the corn example) and those that are "agents" that use or act on the flows (like labor and spades). But such a distinction is not worth pursuing in the present discussion (Georgescu-Roegen [10, pp. 219-234]).

Of course, a process need not always be depicted by the same pair (Y, X), although only one pair can be observed for every process. Conceptually, for any given process, different input values of the same variables at the same times — that is, different sequences of input boundary crossings — would generally give rise to different sequences of output boundary crossings or output variable values. Let $\mathcal{Y}$ be the set of all conceivable sequences, Y, of input variable values, and $\mathcal{X}$ be the collection of all possible sequences, X, of output variable values. Then the complete arithmomorphic analytical representation of the process is the set of ordered pairs $f(Y, X)$, where X is in $\mathcal{X}$, Y is in $\mathcal{Y}$, and the ordered pair (Y, X) is in $f(Y, X)$ provided that X is the output sequence when Y is the input sequence. (To speak about neoclassical production, one would have to add a condition of efficiency or maximization in the specification of f.) If correspondences such as f are to be the functions employed in a formalist analysis, then the distillation from the original dialectical process stops here.

Otherwise, the next step in reducing a process to a function is to focus attention on one of the output variables and ignore all others. Dropping the subscript on x, let $x(t)$ now represent the value of the selected output variable at time t. Keep $y(t)$ as before. Assuming that the ordered pairs in $f(Y, X)$ associate exactly one X in $\mathcal{X}$ to each input sequence Y in $\mathcal{Y}$, the relation f becomes a function and may be written as

$$X = f(Y).$$

However, f is not a function in the usual sense. To see why, observe that Y and X actually describe, respectively, a vector of functions of t and a (scalar) function of t. These functions are frequently denoted by the previously introduced symbols $y(t)$ and $x(t)$. Thus f is really a functional, mapping functions y into a single function x, or

$$x = f(y),$$

where the functional argument t, though present, has been excluded to simplify notation (Georgescu-Roegen [10, p. 236]).

Occasionally, functionals are taken as the functions in a formalist analysis by economists. More often, however, ordinary functions are employed. The final step in securing such functions is to make assumptions about the nature of the $y(t)$ and $x(t)$. Indeed, appropriate specification of $\mathcal{Y}$ and $\mathcal{X}$ is capable of turning f into either a static or dynamic function. If, for example, one were to suppose that

$$y(t) = y(t') \qquad \text{and} \qquad x(t) = x(t'),$$

for all t and t', and for all $y(t)$ in $\mathcal{Y}$ and $x(t)$ in $\mathcal{X}$, then all functions $y(t)$ and $x(t)$ are constant functions, and the functional f becomes an ordinary function of (not-necessarily-quantifiable) arithmomorphic variables that are independent of time. This may also be written as

$$x = f(y),$$

where y and x are now interpreted as ordinary time-independent vector and scalar variables.

It is clear, then, that the arithmomorphic functions employed by economists in formalist analyses may be viewed as extractions from dynamic, dialectical processes. Following the above path in the case of neoclassical production, the initial process is diluted to a static, technical structure that merely indicates possible (efficient) ways to combine inputs into outputs. Naturally, the deletion of time precludes serious discussion of change.

Social Interaction in the Economic Firm: An Example of Formalism

The next task is to provide an example of a formalist analysis. This will not only illustrate what formalism can do, but will also serve as the basis for subsequent discussion of its power and limitations. To fully display the depth of formalist argument, it is necessary that the example be both detailed and complete. Furthermore, to be able to distinguish the power of formalism as distinct from that of quantification (remember that arithmomorphic extraction does not imply measurement), the example focuses almost exclusively on non-quantifiable entities. In presenting the example, the preceding section's derivations of concepts, variables, and functions from their corresponding dialectical thought-forms are not repeated for each concept, variable, and function employed. Rather, all such derivations are taken as having already been accomplished, and discussion begins with these concepts, variables, and functions in their arithmomorphic state ready for use.

The model in the example set out below provides the foundation for the argument of Essay 11 and is revisited, in part, therein. A streamlined and modified version also appears in Essay 10.

The Problem

The idea of *production function* is one of the cornerstones on which the neo-classical theory of the perfectly competitive firm rests. Given technology, a production function describes the maximum output obtainable from every possible combination of inputs. In one common version, the theory postulates certain non-negativity, smoothness, increasingness, and convexity traits of technology which are represented as properties of the production function. It then supposes that the firm, being faced with "fixed" market prices, bases input and output decisions on profit maximization. Thus the firm's input demand and output supply are derived as functions of input and output prices. The characteristics of these latter functions, i.e., the so-called comparative-statics propositions, are deduced from the initial restrictions placed on the production function.

As pointed out earlier, this theory has no choice but to treat the production process as a "black box." And the theory clearly draws the boundary of the process in such a way that inputs go in, output comes out, and no questions are asked in between. But unfortunately, it is equally clear that, in addition to inputs and technology, production also depends on the specific people involved in the production process and on what they do and do not do while employed. Individuals, after all, are hired to perform particular tasks within the limits of certain rules. A salesman has to decide how to approach and deal with prospective buyers; a carpenter may have to choose the order in which wood is cut and nailed together. Hence with the same technology and numerical input quantities, output can vary significantly according to whether the rules are reasonable, the extent to which the relevant individuals are willing to follow them, and the extent to which they foster cooperation within the firm. Cases in which output has lagged at certain times due to non-technological "internal" problems even in the most well-supplied and technologically "advanced" firms are observed often.[10] At the opposite extreme, productivity has been known to soar during periods in which other social arrangements obtained.[11] These issues can only be considered by drawing the boundary of the production process somewhat differently.

The formalist analysis presented here attempts to begin such a program

[10] One of the more notorious examples centers around the famous strike at General Motors' Lordstown plant. At the time, this plant was supposed to be the technological showcase for the American automobile industry. But in 1972 things went awry. (See Rothschild [26, Ch. 4] and O'Toole [23, pp. 89-93]).

[11] The Eagle Project at the Data General Corporation would appear to illustrate the point. (See Kidder [16]).

by developing an economic model of the "perfectly competitive" firm which attempts to account for a small part of the social interaction naturally occurring among employees. Non-labor inputs are treated in the traditional fashion. But rule structures, influence, cooperation of workers, and incentive schemes are introduced[12] and the potential for still further generalization is suggested. Both individuals and the firm itself are taken to be maximizers. Input demand and output supply functions are derived and their (comparative statics) properties relating to modifications in workers skills and preferences are studied. The meaning and importance of Pareto optimality (efficiency) within production also is considered. The argument follows in the tradition of Coase [4], Dunlop [8], Leibenstein [18], and Simon [29], formalizing and pursuing many of their ideas. It draws heavily on Gintis and Katzner [11].

The Firm

Let there be K workers in the firm and index them by k, where $k = 0, ..., K$. Designate the director by $k = 0$. Assume lines of authority are pyramidal (with the director at the top) so that every worker $k \neq 0$ has exactly one supervisor. All workers except those at the bottom end of a line of authority have at least one subordinate. Any worker who supervises k, or the supervisor of k, or the supervisor of the supervisor of k, etc., is said to be *above* k in authority. Of course, the director is above all $k \neq 0$, and k is *below* all those above him. The *co-workers* of k are those workers who have the same supervisor as k. The set of all workers can be partitioned into non-overlapping and exhaustive subsets, each of which is a class of all mutual co-workers. Suppose there are J such classes enumerated by $j = 1, ..., J$.

As an illustration, consider the pyramid drawn in Figure 3. There are 19 workers, each denoted by a dot and assigned a number. The dot associated with 0 represents the director. Lines indicate the flow of authority from the director on down. Thus worker 3 supervises 7 and 8 and, in turn, is supervised by the director. Persons 5, 1, and 0 are all above worker 11, while 17, 18, and 19 are below him. There are 9 co-worker classes: $\{1, 2, 3\}$, $\{4, 5\}$, $\{6\}$, $\{7, 8\}$, $\{9, 10\}$, $\{11\}$, $\{12, 13, 14, 15\}$, $\{16\}$, and $\{17, 18, 19\}$. Observe that worker 5 is neither above nor below persons 2, 6, and 10. Nor is he a co-worker of these individuals.

Each worker k supplies labor time e_k to the firm. All units of labor time coming from the same person are homogeneous and can not exceed some maximum. During time supplied, the employee performs activities or acts a_k which

[12] The role of individual personality traits, though potentially significant (Filer, [9]), is ignored.

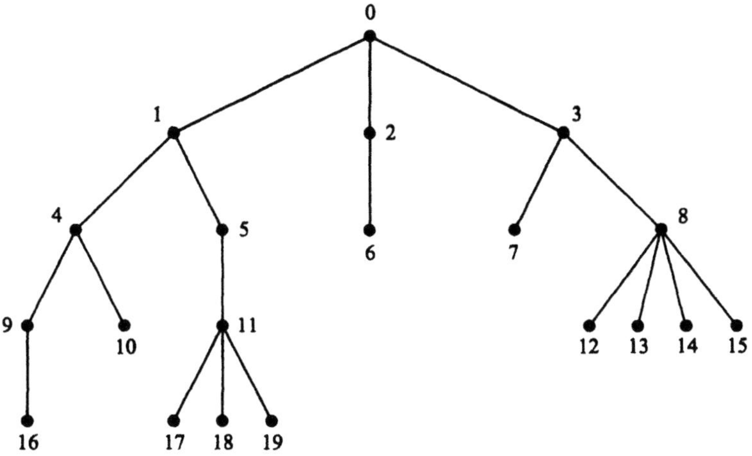

Figure 3

fall within the terms of the work contract.[13] These activities involve social interactions among employees and are limited by the technological imperatives of production. It is not necessary that the a_k be quantifiable: As described earlier; the only restriction is that each "value" of a_k be capable of distinct, discrete verbal description. The collection of values over which a_k may range is called k's *activity* set and is denoted by A_k. Write $a = (a_1, ..., a_K)$ and $A = A_1 \times \cdots \times A_K$. In addition to activities, each worker also provides rules that constrain the activities of all workers below him. The furnishing of rules may be thought of as an "administrative" activity separate from all other activities and singled out for special attention. Recalling the example of Figure 3, worker 5 say, receives rules from 1 and 0, and issues rules for 11, 17, 18, and 19. Such rules are defined by the subsets of the activity sets they determine. Rules may be so restrictive as to dictate exactly what must be done (i.e., select a single element from the relevant activity set) or they may allow for considerable flexibility and choice. Moreover, the nature of the rules so promulgated may be legally limited.[14]

It is worth remembering at this point how far these notions of activities and rules really are from their underlying dialectical counterparts. All of the

[13] A similar variable is introduced and described by Whyte [33, p. 192].

[14] It is interesting that at least one observer has identified rule changes dictated from above as one of the chief causes of the 1972 Lordstown plant strike (O'Toole [23, p. 91]). See n. 10 on p. 131.

subtle variations in activities in which one activity overlaps another have disappeared in the discretization of the values that the variable "activity" may take on. Either a worker does a particular job or he does not — there is no in-between. The designation of rules as a subset of these activity variable values, then, imposes greater rigidity and less flexibility in communication among persons than one would, as a practical matter, expect. That is, the nuances of the rules themselves, as well as those of the way in which they are transmitted, are necessarily lost in the formalization of this kind of human interaction.

Consider the rules received by person k from above. If k is above $k' \neq 0$, let $R_{kk'}$ vary over possible rules prescribed by k for k'. Then $R_{kk'} \subseteq A_{k'}$. The collection of rules imposed on k' by all persons above him (including the director) is

$$\rho_{k'} = \bigcap_{k} R_{kk'}, \tag{1}$$

where the intersection is taken over all k above k'. Note $\rho_{k'} \subseteq A_{k'}$. It is not necessary that the sets $R_{kk'}$ be nested, that is, become smaller, as k moves from 0 to k' — although in practice, actual rule sets may wind up having this property. If, for example, the director wants to have certain things done in certain ways, then he promulgates rules for all workers ensuring that his wishes are met. Rules issued by persons between the director and k' may permit more freedom than the directors rules. But k' is constrained by the director's more restrictive rules anyway and can not take advantage of larger rule sets even if issued by intermediate persons above him. Of course, for a sequence of rules imposed on k' to be viable (consistent), $\rho_{k'}$ cannot be empty. Assume that workers obey all rules handed down from above and that there are no monetary costs associated with the implementation of any rule.

Persons not at the bottom of the pyramid of authority post rules for all individuals below them. Let r_k be the vector of rules issued by worker k. The components of r_k are the $R_{kk'}$ for appropriate k'. Take r_k to vary over some admissible set, $\mathcal{R}_k$, of vectors of rules. For notational simplicity write $r = (r_1, ..., r_K)$ and $\mathcal{R} = (\mathcal{R}_1, ..., \mathcal{R}_K)$, where it is understood that if, say, k' has no workers below him then $\mathcal{R}_{k'}$ is empty and $r_{k'}$ has no meaning. Both $\mathcal{R}$ and the director's rule vector, r_0, are presumed given.

Output, in the present context, depends on quantities of labor time and non-labor inputs employed by the firm as well as on activities (consistent with rules received from above) and rules for subordinates chosen by workers. Suppose, insofar as their contribution to output is concerned, the firm regards all individuals from the same co-worker class as more-or-less identical. The labor hours contributed by co-worker class j may be viewed as homogeneous and combined in

$$z_j = \sum_k e_k,$$

where the sum is taken over all persons in class j. Let y_i represent quantities of non-labor input i, where $i = 1, ..., I$, and let x denote output. Write $y = (y_1, ..., y_I)$ and $z = (z_1, ..., z_J)$. Then the firm's production function is given by

$$x = f(y, z, a, r), \tag{2}$$

defined for all $y > 0$, $z > 0$, a in A and r in $\mathcal{R}$. Actually since it only serves to limit the values that a can take on and does not affect output directly, r need not be listed as an argument of f. But retaining r in the production function introduces no difficulties and at the same time provides convenience and suggestiveness that is useful below. In the currently fashionable theory of the firm, y and z are picked by the firm and the presence of a and r are ignored. The following retains selection of y and z within the province of the firm but views the choice of a and r (except r_0) as coming from workers, where not all workers have the same power of choice over both rules and activities.[15] Determination of y and z are considered first for fixed (but not-necessarily-quantifiable) values of a and r.

Let the firm pay each employee k a wage w_k per unit of time according to the incentive function W_k where

$$w_k = W^k(a_k, r_k), \qquad k = 1, ..., K, \tag{3}$$

and W^k is defined on $A_k \times \mathcal{R}_k$. Non-monetary incentives such as the possibility of promotion and guaranteed long-term employment are not considered. Because rules dictated from above restrict person k to a subset ρ_k of A_k (recall equation (1)), some wages w_k might not actually be available to him. Moreover, since the firm makes no distinctions between co-workers, it is reasonable to require that for any pair of workers k' and k'' in the same co-worker class, incentive functions reward equal work with equal pay. Let "equal work" be defined for k' and k'' in terms of some equivalence relation $\ominus_{k'k''}$ on $(A_{k'} \times \mathcal{R}_{k'}) \times (A_{k''} \times \mathcal{R}_{k''})$. Then the firm provides equal pay for equal

[15] Since the presence of real capital assets among the components of y could be taken to mean that, in selecting y, the firm is choosing its long-run optimum structure, the question arises of whether workers' choices of a_k and r_k can be expected to remain constant throughout the lives of the assets. This issue, however, is ignored in subsequent discussion.

work when for all $(a_{k'}, r_{k'})$ in $(A_{k'} \times \mathcal{R}_{k'})$ and all $(a_{k''}, r_{k''})$ in $(A_{k''} \times \mathcal{R}_{k''})$,

$$(a_{k'}, r_{k'}) \textcircled{=}_{k'k''} (a_{k''}, r_{k''})$$

if and only if

$$w_{k'} = w_{k''}.$$

Supposing, moreover, that all workers in each co-worker class execute equal work, there are only J distinct wage rates paid by the firm namely, $w_1, ..., w_J$. Note the aforementioned fixity of (a, r) in the production function (2) now implies that the w_j play the role of given parameters. Under these conditions the profit, π, of the firm is expressed as

$$\pi = qf(y, z, a, r) - p \cdot y - w \cdot z,$$

where p is an I-vector of non-labor input prices, $w = (w_1, ..., w_J)$, q denotes the price of the output, and the dot indicates "inner product." To keep matters simple, the director is paid out of profits rather than provided a wage.

The selection of incentive functions W^k by the firm (or its director) deserves comment. On one hand, the W^k may be constant functions assigning the same wage to every (a_k, r_k). Alternatively, those values of $(a, r) = (a_1, ..., a_K, r_1, ..., r_K)$ which enhance the productivity or profitability of the firm may be rewarded with a higher wage by the W^k. In the latter case, however, suppose that for fixed values of q, $p_1, ..., p_I$, y, and z, output is higher at (a', r') than at (a'', r''). If profit is also to be larger at (a', r'), then it is necessary for the firm to set the W^k so that the additional wages paid employees at (a', r') over those paid at (a'', r'') are less than the additional revenue received at (a', r'). Were this not always the case, then the most productive (a, r) need not be the most profitable, and hence moving to increase productivity might reduce profitability. Formally, the collection of incentive functions $\{W^k\}$, one for each employee $k = 1, ..., K$, is said to be *profit-efficient*[16] whenever

$$f(y, z, a', r') \geq f(y, z, a'', r'')$$

implies

$$qf(y, z, a', r') - p \cdot y - \sum_{j=1}^{J} z_j W^j(a', r') \geq$$

[16] This definition of profit efficiency is slightly different from that given by Gintis and Katzner [11] in that here the weak instead of the strong inequality is employed.

$$qf(y,z,a'',r'') - p \cdot y - \sum_{j=1}^{J} z_j W^j(a'',r''),$$

for all (a',r') and (a'',r'') in $A \times \mathcal{R}$, and all $y > 0$ and $z > 0$, where W^j is a representative incentive function for co-worker class j. Profit-efficient incentives, then, have the property that productivity increases due to changes in (a,r) always are translated into greater profit. Note that in addition to incentives which provide wage raises that are smaller then resulting revenue increases, all collections of constant incentive functions are also profit efficient.

As usual, p and q are determined in perfectly competitive input and output markets. Continuing with the restriction that a, r, and hence w are fixed, assume further that f, as a function of y and z, has sufficient non-negativity, smoothness, increasingness, and convexity properties to validate the propositions stated below. Now let x, y, and z be chosen so as to maximize π. Then in the traditional way, values of marginal products at the maximum are equated to input prices:

$$qf_i(y,z,a,r) = p_i, \qquad i = 1,...,I,$$

$$qf_{I+j}(y,z,a,r) = w_j, \qquad j = 1,...,J,$$

where p_i, is the price of input i and f_i (or f_{I+j}) is the partial derivative of f with respect to its ith (or $I + j^{\text{th}}$) argument. Solving and substituting the solution into (2) yields the ordinary input demand and output supply functions,

$$y_i = h^i(q,p,a,r), \qquad i = 1,...,I,$$

$$z_j = h^{I+j}(q,p,a,r), \qquad j = 1,...,J, \tag{4}$$

$$x = h^{I+J+1}(q,p,a,r),$$

except that here x, y, and z also depend on a and r. As long as the latter remain fixed, the well-known comparative statics properties of such functions apply. To the extent that the given vector (a,r) does not reflect equal work by all pairs of workers in the same co-worker class, these results must be modified accordingly.

Thus even in this more general setting, the time-honored theory of the economic firm remains essentially intact. But it now is embedded in a world which recognizes that individuals are responsible for carrying out the activities of production, and that the way these responsibilities are met is a significant element in determining the firm's output and profitability. The coordination and accomplishment of the activities of production alone, without direct reliance on a price mechanism for guidance is, according to Coase [4, pp. 388,389], the distinguishing feature in the economists notion of a firm. The next section looks at the individuals decision making and at some of the coordinating instruments that bring the activities of production to fruition.

Workers

Two coordinating instruments, of course, have already been built into the model. First, rules are issued from the director down through the pyramid of authority and these serve to define the activity limits within which each worker may operate. Second, an incentive function (equation (3)) is furnished for each worker in an attempt to induce him to choose, within boundaries set by the rules imposed upon him, those activities and rules for others that are best from the point of view of the firm. A third coordinating instrument, introduced here, is the leadership and influence exercised by supervisors in their provision of information, training, encouragement, and advice to subordinates. Such leadership is needed to support supervisors' authority since the latter often is insufficient to guarantee "correct" choices of activities and rules by subordinates (see Simon [28, pp. 14,15]). This last coordinating instrument is accounted for by supposing that each worker $k \neq 0$ perceives a goals and premises (g-p) function

$$g_k = G^k(a_k, r_k) \tag{5}$$

on $A_k \times \mathcal{R}_k$, in which g_k varies over ordinal numbers expressing what he thinks to be the preferences of his supervisor for points in $A_k \times \mathcal{R}_k$. The G^k are taken to be given and the characteristics they might be expected to possess are not discussed. G-p functions are independent of incentive functions. They rely on social rather than economic pressures for their effect.

It should be noted in passing that, among other things, workers may also be influenced by the values of their co-workers, and by the information (relevant for their job or otherwise, true or false) circulating around the firm. These kinds of social interactions are not difficult to include; but since, in light of present purposes, there is little to be gained by doing so, the necessary effort is not worth expending.[17] Instead, attention now focuses briefly on workers' decisions.

To complete the above description of the economic firm, workers are required to choose the activities they perform and the rules they issue. Generally

[17] The interested reader is referred to Gintis and Katzner [11].

these are picked simultaneously along with labor time supplied and consumption. It will simplify matters considerably, however, if decisions regarding activities and rules are kept both separate from and prior to those concerning labor supply and consumption. In each case the worker is assumed to be a constrained utility maximizer. Observe that once activities and rules are obtained (as described below) the worker can treat his wage per unit of time as a fixed parameter according to equation (3). Hence the calculation of labor time e_k, for every worker $k \neq 0$, proceeds in the usual manner by maximizing a utility function over consumption-leisure space subject to an appropriate budget constraint.

Turning to the selection of activities and rules, worker k's ($k \neq 0$) utility function is written to make the role of incentives and influences explicit: Let

$$\mu_k = u^k(a_k, r_k, w_k, g_k) \tag{6}$$

be defined for all appropriate values of (a_k, r_k, w_k, g_k). Substitution of (3) and (5) into (6) yields

$$\mu_k = U^k(a_k, r_k), \tag{7}$$

where

$$U^k(a_k, r_k) = u_k(a_k, r_k, W^k(a_k, r_k), G^k(a_k, r_k))$$

and $k = 1, ..., K$. Suppose (a, r) emerges uniquely from the simultaneous maximization[18] of $U^k(a_k, r_k)$ for all $k \neq 0$, subject to the constraints that a_k is consistent with all rules imposed from above, i.e., a_k is in ρ_k, for $k = 1, ..., K$. Recall that the ρ_k consist of intersections (equation (1)) of certain components of r. Obviously, the latter constraints ensure that every ρ_k coming out of these K maximizations is non-empty. Thus workers choose internally consistent values for (a, r), the firm hires a vector (y, z) as indicated at the end of the last subsection, and the firm's output and profit are determined.

The assumption of prior determination of (a, r) also permits a simple explanation of the functioning of labor markets. In labor market j (there is one for each wage) the supply of labor is generated by aggregating over workers participating in that market. The behavior of each is based on a utility-maximizing, consumption-leisure choice as indicated above. Labor demand is secured as the sum across firms of the relevant functions derived from profit maximization, as in (4). (It is necessary to suppose here, as it is within the single firm, that all workers in the market, regardless of where they work, do "similar" jobs

---

[18] Conditions that ensure that functions of non-quantifiable variables can be maximized uniquely are discussed in Katzner [14, Sec. 5.4].

and are rewarded with the same pay.) The market wage w_j is obtained from appropriate components of the predetermined vectors (a, r) for all participating firms in conjunction with incentive functions like (3). If this wage is too low so that demand is greater than supply, then firms adjust incentive functions so that the same work receives a higher wage. If the market wage is too high, competition among workers alters incentive functions obversely. Thus, although relative incentive scales are maintained to encourage the worker to behave (while on the job) in the interest of the firm, their absolute levels are varied to equilibrate demand and supply.

At this point, three implicit assumptions ought to be brought out into the open. First, only social interaction among workers connected along lines of authority is considered here. Such interaction appears in the issuance and acceptance of rules and incentives, in the attempt by supervisors to influence subordinates through goals and premise functions, and in the response of workers to these elements as reflected by their choices of activities and rules for others. Social interaction among co-workers, such as the interplay of personal values and the sharing of information mentioned earlier, has been ruled out. Were this not done, individual utility maximization could be more complex since decisions made by one person might then depend on those made by others. Second, upon selection of activities from utility maximization, each worker k is presumed to carry out his chosen activity a_k according to expected standards. In other words, performance is not determined separately after the selection of all (a_k, r_k). If performance were permitted to vary, then output could not yet be found from the production function (2) as described above since the vector (a, r) actually performed would still not be known. Third, it is supposed that each subordinate and his supervisor has identical perceptions of the formers activity set, of the rules prescribed by the latter for the former, and of the preferences of the supervisor for points in the subordinate's set $A_k \times \mathcal{R}_k$ (as appearing in the g-p function facing the subordinate). Thus confusion resulting from differing perceptions is precluded. The Wittgensteinian possibility that a subordinate conceives of his job in different qualitative terms from his supervisor (e.g., applies paint to a wall less thickly than the supervisor expected), and hence induces an unexpected quality to the firm's output, does not arise.

Skill and Preference Modification

It is now time to examine some of the comparative statics properties of input demand and output supply functions (equations (4)) with respect to (a, r) and the functions W^k, G^k, and U^k lying implicitly in the background. To do so, however, first requires the development of analytical structure. In the traditional theory of the firm, such structure — upon which derivations of comparative-statics propositions with respect to q and p rest — is found in conventional economic concepts like "isoquant," in the non-negativity, smoothness, increasingness, and convexity characteristics of production as a function of input magnitudes, and also in the commonly used traits of quantitative spaces and functions that permit such things as differentiation and the definition of numerical order. Clearly none of this is available here and it is therefore necessary to start from scratch.

Discussion begins with three notions of order. Fix $k \neq 0$. For any a'_k and a''_k in A_k, write $a'_k \geq a''_k$ whenever replacement of a''_k by a'_k in the firm's production function does not lower output no matter what the values of the remaining components a_{k^0} in (a, r), where $k^0 \neq k$. Next, for any pair of non-empty, admissible rules R'_{kk^0} and R''_{kk^0} imposed by k on k^0, define $R'_{kk^0} \geq R''_{kk^0}$ provided that $R'_{kk^0} \subseteq R''_{kk^0}$ and if a'_{k^0} is in R'_{kk^0} and a''_{k^0} is in $R''_{kk^0} - R'_{kk^0}$, then $a'_{k^0} \geq a''_{k^0}$. In other words, R'_{kk^0} restricts k^0 to a subset of R''_{kk^0} on which output is at least as high as that at any point of $R''_{kk^0} - R'_{kk^0}$. Take $r'_k \geq r''_k$ to mean $R'_{kk^0} \geq R''_{kk^0}$ for all k^0 below k. Finally, for all (a'_k, r'_k) and (a''_k, r''_k), put $(a'_k, r'_k) \geq (a''_k, r''_k)$ if and only if both $a'_k \geq a''_k$ and $r'_k \geq r''_k$. All three relations are reflexive, transitive, and antisymmetric; and all generate the usual derivative relations $>$ and $=$ appropriately defined (see Gintis and Katzner [11, pp. 283,284]). Confusion will not arise by employing the same symbol of order, namely $\geq$, for all three meanings. (Note that $\geq$ also refers to "greater than or equal to" when numbers are involved.) Context determines the appropriate interpretation.

The following concepts provide a vocabulary in terms of which subsequent comparative statics propositions emerge. The incentive function W^k is called *non-decreasing on* A_k whenever $a'_k \geq a''_k$ ensures the numerical inequality $W^k(a'_k, r_k) \geq W^k(a''_k, r_k)$, for any a'_k, a''_k, and r_k. It is said to be *non-decreasing on* $A_k \times \mathcal{R}_k$ as long as $W^k(a'_k, r'_k) \geq W^k(a''_k, r''_k)$ arises from $(a'_k, r'_k) \geq (a''_k, r''_k)$, for every a'_k, a''_k, r'_k and r''_k. Similarly, G^k can be non-decreasing on A_k or $A_k \times \mathcal{R}_k$. Now worker $k \neq 0$ is *incentive motivated* if for all a'_k, a''_k, r'_k and r''_k, the numerical inequality

$$W^k(a'_k, r'_k) \geq W^k(a''_k, r''_k)$$

implies (recall equation (7))

$$U^k(a'_k, r'_k) \geq U^k(a''_k, r''_k).$$

He is *vertically influenced* when

$$G^k(a'_k, r'_k) \geq G^k(a''_k, r''_k)$$

(also a numerical relation) forces

$$U^k(a'_k, r'_k) \geq U^k(a''_k, r''_k),$$

again for all a'_k, a''_k, r'_k and r''_k. And he *internalizes the values of the firm* provided that for all a'_k, a''_k, r'_k and r''_k, if $(a'_k, r'_k) \geq (a''_k, r''_k)$, then

$$U^k(a'_k, r'_k) \geq U^k(a''_k, r''_k).$$

The last three definitions respectively depict worker k's preferences as receptive to incentives, influence, and the expansion of output. With W^k and G^k non-decreasing on $A_k \times \mathcal{R}_k$ any person k exhibiting one or more of these characteristics cooperates naturally in the carrying out of production within the firm.

Suppose that the preferences of worker k are permitted to vary. Let $\mathcal{U}^k$ be a class of utility functions each of which represents a unique preference-order possibility for k. Thus $\mathcal{U}^k$ contains no increasing transformations of any of its elements. Likewise, take $\mathcal{W}$ to be a collection of admissible incentive functions. Consider any $\bar{U}^k$ and $\hat{U}^k$ in $\mathcal{U}^k$ and use the symbolism $(\bar{a}_k, \bar{r}_k)$ and $(\hat{a}_k, \hat{r}_k)$ to denote the (unique) vectors chosen by constrained utility maximization from, respectively, $\bar{U}^k$ and $\hat{U}^k$. If

$$(\bar{a}_k, \bar{r}_k) \geq (\hat{a}_k, \hat{r}_k),$$

then $\bar{U}^k$ is said to *dominate* $\hat{U}^k$. Alternatively, k is referred to as being *more highly motivated by incentives* under $\bar{U}^k$ than under $\hat{U}^k$ provided

$$W^k(\bar{a}_k, \bar{r}_k) \geq W^k(\hat{a}_k, \hat{r}_k),$$

for all W^k in $\mathcal{W}$. In the former instance, preferences dominate when they generate more productive choices; in the latter, k is more highly motivated by incentives under certain preferences if choices based on these preferences lead to larger wages regardless of the incentive function. The idea that k can be *more highly motivated by influence* under $\bar{U}^k$ than under $\hat{U}^k$ is described analogously.

The last definitions introduced here have to do with the skills of the worker. Let $A_k \subset \tilde{A}_k$, where $A_k \neq \tilde{A}_k$, for some k. Person k is said to have become *more skilled* if the following two conditions are met: (i) $\tilde{A}_k$ is substituted for A_k in making his decisions, and (ii) for all $(\tilde{a}_k, \tilde{r}_k)$ and (a_k, r_k) such that

$\tilde{r}_k \geq r_k$, if a_k is in A_k and $\tilde{a}_k$ is in $\tilde{A}_k - A_k$, then $(\tilde{a}_k, \tilde{r}_k) \geq (a_k, r_k)$. Skills are thus improved when act sets expand to include activities leading to increased output. But this definition by itself guarantees neither that k will use his new skills (i.e., actually choose an act from $\tilde{A}_k - A_k$) nor that co-workers will not attempt to subvert them. As will be seen momentarily, the first possibility can be prevented by invoking one of the notions of cooperation discussed above. To handle the second requires a final concept: The firm is *receptive to new skills* of k whenever, upon substitution of $\tilde{A}_k$ for A_k in the simultaneous constrained maximization of all U^k, the ρ_k (defined in equation (1)) generated by that maximization contain at least one element of $\tilde{A}_k - A_k$.

Several properties of the firm's output supply function h^{I+J+1} (from (4)) with respect to a, r, W^k, G^k, and U^k can now be described. Each assumes that workers are in a utility-maximizing stance and asks what happens to output when certain things change and appropriate maximizations are repeated. Labor time and non-labor inputs, that is (y, z), are assumed fixed. The properties are listed below in a series of six propositions. Proofs are available elsewhere.[19]

Theorem 1. Let the firm be receptive to new skills of k and suppose k internalizes the values of the firm. If k becomes more skilled and no other worker alters his chosen acts and rules, then output either rises or remains unchanged.

Theorem 2. Let the firm be receptive to new skills of k and let W^k be non-decreasing on A_k. Suppose k is incentive motivated. If k becomes more skilled and no other worker alters his chosen acts and rules, then output either rises or remains unchanged.

Theorem 3. Let the firm be receptive to new skills of k and let G^k be non-decreasing on A^k. Suppose k is vertically influenced. If k becomes more skilled and no other worker alters his chosen acts and rules, then output either rises or remains unchanged.

Theorem 4. Let k change preferences. If the new utility function dominates the old and if no other worker alters his chosen acts and rules, then output either rises or remains unchanged.

Theorem 5. Let k change preferences and W^k be non-decreasing on A_k.

[19] Except for the last, these propositions roughly correspond to Theorems 7-11 (or, in the reprinted version, 11.3-1 to 11.3-5), respectively, in Gintis and Katzner [11]. Because they are concerned with profit instead of output, in each case Gintis and Katzner require the extra hypothesis of profit efficiency. The proofs of Theorems 1-5 here essentially carry over from those in Gintis and Katzner, with the last step involving profit efficiency omitted. The proof of Theorem 6 is analogous to that of Theorem 5.

If k is more highly motivated by incentives under the new utility function and if no other worker alters his chosen acts and rules, then output either rises or remains unchanged.

Theorem 6. Let k change preferences and G^k be non-decreasing on A_k. If k is more highly motivated by influence under the new utility function and if no other worker alters his chosen acts and rules, then output either rises or remains unchanged.

To the extent that the weak inequalities ($\geq$) in the previous list of definitions are replaced, in Theorems 1-6, by their associated strong inequalities ($>$), the conclusions of these theorems can be strengthened to assert that output must rise. If, in addition, incentives are profit-efficient, then profit must increase or remain constant with output.

Thus, in the narrow context of this arithmomorphic model and with the deletion of all dialectical possibilities, new skills and new preferences will, under certain conditions, increase output and profit. Alternatively put, in choosing among individuals to fill its positions, the firm should be interested not only in skills but in other attributes, like incentive motivation, as well. Further comparative statics questions — such as (i) if output is fixed and labor time and non-labor inputs vary, what is the impact of alterations in skills and preferences? and (ii) in what ways are Theorems 1-6 and the answer to (i) affected by permitting x, y, and z to all change simultaneously? — require still additional structure and are not pursued here. The problem of how to select the incentive functions W^k so as to maximize profit given individual utility functions also is ignored. Instead, attention now turns to the issue of efficiency within the firm.

Internal Pareto Optimality

It is well known that under certain conditions in a perfectly competitive economy, equilibrium is Pareto optimal. Thus, with initial endowments given, with consumers buying output quantities and supplying factor quantities so as to maximize utility subject to their budget constraints, with firms selling output quantities and buying input quantities so as to maximize profit, and with supply equal to demand in all markets, quantities of outputs and inputs can not be redistributed among consumers and firms without lowering some output or making at least one person worse off. This proposition is fundamental to the Walrasian vision of microeconomic reality. Its significance lies in the efficiency property it imparts to equilibrium distributions of inputs, outputs, and consumption. For to say such a distribution is Pareto optimal means that the utility (or output) level of any one consumer (or, respectively, firm) achieved in the distribution is the largest possible given the remaining allocations of the distribution. In other words, perfect competition "wastes" nothing at equilibrium. Thus, as suggested by Smith [30, p. 423], the "invisible hand," which coordinates market behavior based on maximization, leads individuals to an end which they do not intend and which benefits society.

Previous discussion has attempted to analyze more completely the production process within the perfectly competitive firm by drawing its arithmomorphic boundary so as to more fully describe how production takes place. A model accounting for part of the social interaction of employees in their jobs has been proposed. Each worker picks rules for those beneath him and likewise is constrained in the selection of this own activities by rules imposed from above. In making these choices workers also are subjected to various influences and incentives. As indicated, everything takes place in the context of rationality and perfect competition. And so, with individuals still making decisions on the basis of maximization, the traditional question once again arises concerning the end toward which workers and the firm are lead by the nonmarket invisible hands that, under varying circumstances, coordinate behavior internally within the firm: Is it wasteful or efficient?[20]

The first thing to notice is that efficiency in the economy is entirely independent of efficiency within the firm. Pareto optimality may arise in the distribution of consumption, output, and input quantities with considerable waste in production itself. Obversely, decisions concerning activities and rules could result in efficient production even when the optimality of economy-wide equilibrium fails — perhaps due to the presence of monopoly or other market imperfections. (Previous argument may be modified in the traditional manner to accommodate whatever form of imperfect competition one might wish to impose on the firm.) In what follows, then, interest centers on efficiency in production only. As before, the vector (y, z) is taken to be fixed. Notation is simplified by abbreviating the production function (equation (2)) to

$$x = f(a, r).$$

The same analytical structure introduced to develop the comparative statics of input demand and output supply functions (see the previous subsection) is employed.

Let *g-p* (goals and premise) functions G^k and incentive functions W^k be given for every $k \neq 0$. Write $a^0 = (a_1^0, ..., a_K^0)$ and $r^0 = (r_1^0, ..., r_K^0)$. A

[20] Leibenstein [18, p. 95] has coined the term X-inefficiency to refer to whatever wastefulness might be present.

vector (a^0, r^0) in $A \times \mathcal{R}$ is called *internally Pareto optimal in production*, or just *Pareto optimal*, provided that there is no other (a, r) in $A \times \mathcal{R}$ such that

$$U^k(a_k, r_k) \geq U^k(a_k^0, r_k^0)$$

for all $k = 1, ..., K$,

$$U^k(a_k, r_k) > U^k(a_k^0, r_k^0)$$

for at least one $k = 1, ..., K$, and

$$f(a, r) \geq f(a^0, r^0),$$

where all inequalities refer to numerical relations. Thus at a Pareto optimum, no reorganization of production in terms of activities and rules can make one worker better off, and no other worker worse off, without lowering output. Note that the director is not included in this concept of Pareto optimality.

On the basis of notions of incentive motivation, internalization of the values of the firm, and vertical influence defined earlier, different sets of conditions sufficient for Pareto optimality obtain. These are stated as three propositions. The parallel between them and Theorems 1-3 above is worth noting. Once again, proofs are ignored.[21] It is convenient to prescribe one assumption beforehand, namely, that both the $\geq$ on A_k and the $\geq$ on $\mathcal{R}_k$ be total for every $k \neq 0$. (Note this implies that $\geq$ is total on $A_k \times \mathcal{R}_k$, for all $k = 1, ..., K$.) In consequence, the characterizing implication in each of the definitions of non-decreasingness of W^k and G^k on $A_k \times \mathcal{R}_k$, incentive motivation, internalization of the values of the firm, and vertical influence points in both directions. Thus, for example, W^k is now non-decreasing on $A_k \times \mathcal{R}_k$ whenever

$$(a'_k, r'_k) \geq (a''_k, r''_k)$$

if and only if

$$W^k(a'_k, r'_k) \geq W^k(a''_k, r''_k),$$

[21] Theorems 7 and 8 are more or less identical to, respectively, Theorems 5 and 6 (or, 11.2-5 and 11.2-6 in the reprinted version) in Gintis and Katzner [11]. As previously indicated in n. 19 on p. 143, proofs of the former are essentially the same as those of the latter. The proof of Theorem 9 is similar to that of Theorem 8.

The deduction that $d'_w \textcircled{\geq} d^0_w$ in the proof of Theorem 5 given by Gintis and Katzner requires $\textcircled{\geq}$ to be total on D_w (their notation). Totality of $\textcircled{\geq}$, however, follows from totality of $\geq$ on A_k and of $\geq$ on $\mathcal{R}_w$ — assumptions that were left out of the original. This omission is remedied here in the remainder of the present paragraph. It also has been corrected in the reprinted version of the paper.

for all a'_k, a''_k, r'_k, and r''_k. With the totality of $\geq$ on the A_k and $\mathcal{R}_k$ in force, the propositions are as follows:

Theorem 7. Let incentives be profit-efficient and suppose all workers internalize the values of the firm. If (a^0, r^0) maximizes profit over $A \times \mathcal{R}$, then (a^0, r^0) is Pareto optimal.

Theorem 8. Let incentives be profit-efficient, let all workers be vertically influenced, and suppose G^k is non-decreasing on $A_k \times \mathcal{R}_k$ for each $k = 1, ..., K$. If (a^0, r^0) maximizes profit over $A \times \mathcal{R}$, then (a^0, r^0) is Pareto optimal.

Theorem 9. Let incentives be profit-efficient, let all workers be incentive motivated, and suppose W^k is non-decreasing on $A_k \times \mathcal{R}_k$ for each $k = 1, ..., K$. If (a^0, r^0) maximizes profit over $A \times \mathcal{R}$, then (a^0, r^0) is Pareto optimal.

Each of the above theorems assumes as one of its hypotheses that (a^0, r^0) maximizes profit over $A \times \mathcal{R}$. This supposition by itself is not enough to guarantee Pareto optimality. Although it implies that $(a_k^0, r_k^0) \geq (a_k, r_k)$ for every (a_k, r_k) in $A_k \times \mathcal{R}_k$ and all $k \neq 0$, to establish the propositions still requires that (a_k^0, r_k^0) also maximize each workers utility. This is ensured by the remaining assumptions.

An answer to the big question, namely, "Under what conditions does internal equilibrium within the firm result in Pareto optimality?" is now within easy reach. Recall *g-p* functions, incentive functions, and production functions are given along with the pyramid of authority, the directors rules, and individual activity and admissible rule sets. Workers alone choose their acts and the rules they issue. In conformity with earlier argument, then, *internal equilibrium* is defined as a vector $(\bar{a}, \bar{r})$ such that $(\bar{a}_k, \bar{r}_k)$ maximizes the utility of worker k subject to (a_k, r_k) being within the collection of all rules, ρ_k, imposed upon him from above, where $k = 1, ..., K$. According to earlier assumptions alluded to but not spelled out, such an equilibrium always exists. Let $\bar{\rho}_k$ be the constraint set determined by $(\bar{a}, \bar{r})$ for $k \neq 0$. Now if, in addition to the hypotheses of Theorems 7, 8, or 9, the profit-maximizing vector (a_k^0, r_k^0) also lies in $\bar{\rho}_k$ for all $k \neq 0$, then in every case, $(a_k^0, r_k^0) = (\bar{a}_k, \bar{r}_k)$. Hence internal equilibrium is Pareto optimal. Evidently, internalization of the values of the firm, vertical influence, and incentive motivation, each in its own way, makes some contribution towards preventing wastefulness in the carrying out of production.

The Limits of Formalism

The study of social interaction in the economic firm just considered displays all of the characteristics of a formalist analysis. It has concepts such as profit efficiency and incentive motivation, and variables like firm profit and workers' activities. Its axioms include assertions about the existence of production and utility functions, each having enough properties to permit appropriate maximization, along with statements about certain ordering relations among activities and rules, also with specific properties. Functions are manipulated by composition or substitution of variables (for example, in passage from equation (6) to equation (7)), addition, and multiplication (recall the definition of profit efficiency). Variable and function values[22] are manipulated by classifications (the designation of rule sets), by the aforementioned ordering relations (as in the definition of non-decreasing incentives), and by ordinary arithmetic operations (see the definition of firm profit). And deductive reasoning is employed throughout.

The main implications obtained by applying manipulative procedures and deductive reasoning to the concepts, variables, and axioms, are the assertions about the impact on output (and profit) of skill and preference modification among employees, and about the relationship between profit and utility maximization and internal equilibrium on one hand, and internal Pareto optimality on the other. The first group of implications are summarized in Theorems 1-6; the second in Theorems 7-9 and the subsequent conclusion linking internal equilibrium within the firm to internal Pareto optimality. Still further implications also could have been explored. For example, a version of the proposition that becoming more skilled increases a workers wage could be established (Becker [2]), and by lifting the previously imposed requirement that rules are costless to implement, the optimum firm size could be calculated (Calvo and Wellisz [3], Williamson [34]).

As argued in the section on prerequisites, all of the concepts, variables, and functions employed in this analysis are distinctly discrete arithmomorphic extractions from non-discrete dialectical entities. (Similarly, the notion of country employed in Essay 5 is an arithmomorphic extraction from the dialectical reality that encompasses all of the properties from which it is constituted.) In addition, none of the manipulative rules of classification, order, composition, arithmetic operations, and even deductive reasoning has any basis at all in the underlying dialectical scheme. Each is an abstract notion introduced solely for the purpose of generating implications. Different arithmomorphic extrac-

22 Actually, function values are special instances of variable values.

tions, different manipulative rules, and hence different implications can not be ruled out. There can be little doubt, then, that the old criticism of the formalist school, which arises because of the abstractness of the formalist approach and which, as a consequence, questions its relevance in studying reality, has not been escaped in the application of formalism in economics. The results that one obtains by using formalism in economics are necessarily somewhat removed from ordinary life.

The complaint that formalism is too abstract clearly derives from the loss of dialectical content required for the construction of formalist models. A small portion of this loss has been described specifically for the model concerned with social interaction as the loss resulting from the fact that only certain very special kinds of activities and rules are permitted. All other variables in the model involve similar losses. Moreover, additional losses of dialectical content emerge from the functions employed. Still further losses come from the abstraction that maximization is the driving force behind firm and worker behavior. Since every one of these abstractions is arbitrary, and since none of them can be justified as the "correct" representation of reality, the criticism that the model is some distance away from describing the actual social interactions in the economic firm can not be dismissed out of hand. It is not that the specific assumptions of some formalist models are better than others. Rather, it is that all such sets of assumptions (each of which serves as the basis for a separate formalist model) are constrained by the arbitrary limits imposed so as to be able to use formalism in the first place.

Note that measurement is not at issue here. The same problem of the relationship of the real world to the constructs, axioms, and implications of formalist analysis turns up regardless of whether the variables employed may legitimately be represented by numbers. Attacking the meaningfulness and appropriateness of certain numerical quantifications is certainly not the same thing as an assault on the use of formalism. But since, as has already been pointed out, measurement requires its own (independent) formalisms, any difficulties relating to formalism in general necessarily pertain to the use of formalism to derive measures in particular. Thus, as is the case with all formalist argument, one may also ask about the real-world relevance of introducing abstract measures into the investigation of actuality.

The second criticism of formalism invoked by the opponents of the formalist school, namely that non-constructive proofs of existence may establish the abstract existence of entities in models but can never establish the existence of such entities in reality, is also germane to the application of formalism in economics. Hence, to show — the proof is non-constructive — that internal equilibrium always exists as the outcome of utility maximization on the part of each worker (a proposition asserted but not proved in an earlier section) is not to demonstrate the existence of internal equilibrium in a real firm. Economists often fill such a gap between what is shown to exist in a model and what is seen to exist in reality by interpreting the latter as the former. In other words, what one would observe by looking at an actual firm at any moment would be identified as an internal equilibrium. This, then, permits the assertion that the model explains what is seen. As a further illustration, observations of price and quantity sold in a particular market during a period of time are frequently understood as equilibria in a model of the market containing demand and supply functions.[23] That is, the observations are explained as the outcome of the interaction of demand and supply.

Thus, to the extent that formalist analysis in economics employs non-constructive entities, interpretation of these entities is essential if the links between the analysis and actuality are to be comprehended. The formalist approach itself gives no clues or standards for determining what these interpretations should be. And of course, different interpretations yield different explanations of the same thing.

In addition to the above limitations, formalism also faces the Wittgenstein problem that the meanings of the relations of a formalist analysis are not absolute and unchanging over time: One is not committed to the same understandings of them each moment they come up.

It should be emphasized that all of these limitations emerge solely from the particular discipline that formalism imposes on our mental forms. Thus the issue of relevance of formalist analysis in understanding reality derives from the things that have to be thrown out, the concessions that have to be made, in order to proceed from dialectical foundations and arrive at the abstract starting gate where formalist analysis can begin. The reason for caution over the meaning of formalist relations may be attributed to the abstraction procedure, which results in functions that are deceptively well defined. Lastly, the necessity for interpretation of non-constructive entities emerges from the abstract manipulative rules that are employed in leaving the starting gate and developing formalist analyses.

---

[23] In this case, there are other well-known interpretations. For example, the observations may be thought of as lying on a "dynamic" time path which is converging to equilibrium. See Sect. I of Essay 3 in this volume.

The Power of Formalism

And what, then, can be said for the use of formalism in economics? To be sure, formalist analysis may always be employed in arithmomorphic similes to look for error in dialectical reasoning. But it also has a broader application in the building of arithmomorphic metaphors of dialectical experience. Metaphors in economics serve as both an instrument of thought and as a device for communicating meaning (McCloskey [20]). Their force lies in that they transfer the sense of one persons vision to another. They are figures of communication in which one thing, say thing *A*, is likened to a different thing, call it thing *B*, by speaking of *A* "as if" it were *B*. A market operates as if to equate demand and supply. Economic analysis is heavily metaphorical and formalism provides one way of developing metaphors.

And these metaphors are powerful! They permit an analyst to focus his or her thoughts in a concrete and precise fashion on variables and relations that seem important by current professional standards.[24] In the example of formalism given earlier, the production function incorporates the idea that inputs are related to output. But production is more than just a technological process: Social interactions among employees are entangled in its structure and influence both output and firm profit. Confining attention in this manner permits the drawing of specific conclusions about the effects of improved worker skills on the output and profit of the firm, and about the efficiency of the production process itself. The model and these conclusions constitute an "ideal type" or mental construction which isolates what are thought to be "fundamental" forces of reality for study by themselves in the absence of the "secondary" and still less important forces also thought to be present. Hence the investigator can gain an understanding of the ideal system functioning alone as a "first step" in his exploration of reality. At a later stage (and this is rarely attempted by those employing formalism) dialectical reality may be introduced and the initial formalism abandoned.

These metaphors also provide standards for judging real-world behaviors; that is, in our earlier example, standards for deciding whether actual firm and worker behavior is, in fact, maximizing. Lastly, the metaphors are relatively easy for those who wish to pursue similar analyses within the formalist framework to modify and extend as new techniques, new concepts, and new assumptions are introduced. Again referring to the earlier example, novelty appears in the use of non-quantifiable variables and in the formalization of the idea that

[24] Current professional standards are determined by a complex social and historical interaction among present and the work of past economists involving, in part, the techniques of analysis themselves.

social interaction among employees is, in certain specific ways, significant in production.

But formalist metaphors are still extractions from dialectical perceptions of reality. They are abstract. They often contain non-constructive entities requiring interpretation. And so on. Hence such metaphors can only be regarded as very crude "approximations" of the real world. With this in mind, an epilogue to our discussion of the optimality of internal equilibrium might run as follows:

According to Theorems 7-9, internalization of the values of the firm, vertical influence, and incentive motivation each helps to prevent wastefulness in production. But none, by itself, is enough. And the very real possibility exists that actual economic behavior may not reasonably fit any of them. Moreover, the assumptions of totality of $\geq$ on each A_k, and on each $\mathcal{R}_k$ and of output-maximizing (a_k^0, r_k^0) lying in $\bar{\rho}_k$, are equally tenuous. The first insists on a kind of independence among the activities of workers. The second throws out all rule sets from each $\mathcal{R}_k$ except those that form a certain kind of nested sequence under set inclusion. And the third requires that rules issued by different persons also line up in a very special way. The Lordstown case[25] is an example in which the hypotheses of these theorems generally do not seem to apply. In reality, the forces allocating activities and rules within actual firms may be insufficient to secure the non-wastefulness of internal equilibrium.

Marshall was similarly circumspect in his view of the demand-supply analysis of an isolated market:

> The theory of ... equilibrium ... of demand and supply helps indeed to give definiteness to our ideas; and in its elementary stages it does not diverge from the actual facts of life, so far as to prevent its giving a fairly trustworthy picture of the chief methods of action of the strongest and most persistent group of economic forces. But when pushed to its more remote and intricate logical consequences, it slips away from the conditions of real life. (Marshall [19, p. 461])

Why is formalism as a general approach so compelling and appealing to economists? One reason is the power (described above) of the metaphors it is able to produce. Moreover, in the arithmomorphic contexts in which it is set, formalism has rendered errors in deductive reasoning easier to detect; it has deepened understanding; and it has increased the simplicity, elegance, and generality of argument. It has provided a clear and precise way of organizing thoughts and it has made available the efficient language of mathematics

[25] See nn. 10 and 14 on, respectively, pp. 131 and 133.

for use in developing and reporting research (Debreu [6, p. viii], [7, p. 275]). And, most important, it has led to what are considered to be significant arithmomorphic results.

Citing the fact that the subject does not have a unique, rigorous, logical structure, Kline characterizes mathematics as "... a series of great intuitions carefully sifted, refined, and organized by the logic men are willing and able to apply at any time" (Kline [17, p. 312]). These intuitions have had an enormous impact on economics, largely entering our discipline through formalist analyses. Even though mathematics may be inconsistent, even though the correct foundation for it may never be determined, and even though it is incomplete, mathematics has still been effective in various fields — and no one knows why (Kline [17, p. 7]). Mathematics, after all, has been instrumental in sending man to the moon. In the guise of formalism, it has been employed throughout economics. Also as formalism, it appears in the study of social interaction in the firm. Perhaps the most important accomplishment of mathematical formalism in economics is the demonstration of the possibility of coherence in a world of individuals motivated solely by their own self-interest. While not as spectacular as placing a man on the moon, this may still be regarded as progress.

References

1. Bausor, R., "Time and Equilibrium," in *The Reconstruction of Economic Theory*, P. Mirowski, ed. (Boston: Kluwer-Nijhoff, 1986), pp. 93-135.
2. Becker, G. S., *Human Capital* (New York: National Bureau of Economic Research, 1975).
3. Calvo, G. A., and S. Wellisz, "Supervision, Loss of Control, and the Optimum Size of the Firm," *Journal of Political Economy* 86 (1978), pp. 943-952.
4. Coase, R. H., "The Nature of the Firm," *Economica* n.s. 4 (1937), pp. 386-405.
5. Cournot, A., *Researches into the Mathematical Principles of the Theory of Wealth*, N. T. Bacon, trans. (New York: Kelley, 1960).
6. Debreu, G., *Theory of Value* (New York: Wiley, 1959).
7. ________, "Economic Theory in the Mathematical Mode," *American Economic Review* 74 (1984), pp. 267-278.
8. Dunlop, J. T., *Industrial Relations Systems* (New York: Holt, 1958), Ch. 1.

9. Filer, R. K., "The Influence of Affective Human Capital on the Wage Equation," in *Research in Labor Economics*, v. 4., R. G. Ehrenberg, ed. (Greenwich: JAI Press, (1981), pp. 367-416.
10. Georgescu-Roegen, N., *The Entropy Law and the Economic Process* (Cambridge: Harvard University Press, 1971).
11. Gintis, H., and D. W. Katzner, "Profits, Optimality and the Social Division of Labor in the Firm," in *Sociological Economics*, L. Lévy-Garboua, ed. (London: SAGE, 1979), pp. 269-297. Reprinted as Ch. 11 in D. W. Katzner, *Analysis without Measurement* (Cambridge: Cambridge University Press, 1983).
12. Hofstadter, D. R., *Gödel, Escher, Bach: An Eternal Golden Braid* (New York: Basic Books, 1979).
13. Jevons, W. S., *The Theory of Political Economy*, 5th ed. (New York: Kelley, 1965).
14. Katzner, D. W., *Analysis without Measurement* (Cambridge: Cambridge University Press, 1983).
15. ________, "Alternatives to Equilibrium Analysis," *Eastern Economic Journal* 11 (1985), pp. 404-421.
16. Kidder, T., *The Soul of a New Machine* (Boston: Little Brown, 1981).
17. Kline, M., *Mathematics: The Loss of Certainty* (New York: Oxford University Press, 1980).
18. Leibenstein, H., *Beyond Economic Man* (Cambridge: Harvard University Press, 1976).
19. Marshall, A., *Principles of Economics*, 8th ed. (New York: Macmillan, 1948).
20. McCloskey, D. N., "The Rhetoric of Economics," *Journal of Economic Literature* 21 (1983), pp. 481-517.
21. Meyerson, E., *Identity and Reality*, K. Loewenberg, trans. (New York: Dover, 1962).
22. Mirowski, P., "Mathematical Formalism and Economic Explanation," in *The Reconstruction of Economic Theory*, P. Mirowski, ed. (Boston: Kluwer-Nijhoff, 1986), pp. 179-240.
23. O'Toole, J., *Work, Learning and the American Future* (San Francisco: Jossey-Bass, 1977).
24. Pareto, V., *Manuel d'economie politique*, A. Bonnet, Fr. trans. (Geneva: Droz, 1966).
25. Pfanzagl, J., *Theory of Measurement*, 2nd ed. (Würzburg-Vienna: Physica-Verlag 1971).

26. Rothschild, E., *Paradise Lost: The Decline of the Auto-Industrial Age* (New York: Random House, 1973).
27. Russell, B., "Knowledge by Acquaintance and Knowledge by Description," in *Mysticism and Logic and Other Essays* (London: Allen & Unwin, 1959), pp. 209-232.
28. Simon, H. A., *Administrative Behavior*, 2nd ed. (New York: Macmillan, 1957).
29. Simon, H. A., *Models of Man* (New York: Wiley, 1957).
30. Smith, A., *An Inquiry into the Nature and Causes of the Wealth of Nations* (New York: Random House, 1937).
31. Thomson, Sir W. (Baron Kelvin), "Electrical Units of Measurement," lecture delivered on May 3, 1883. In *Popular Lectures and Addresses*, v. 1 (London: Macmillan, 1891), pp. 80-143.
32. Walras, L., *Elements of Pure Economics*, W. Jaffé, trans. (Homewood: Irwin, 1954).
33. Whyte, W. F., *Money and Motivation* (New York: Harper & Row,1955).
34. Williamson, O. E., "Hierarchical Control and Optimum Firm Size," *Journal of Political Economy* 75 (1967), pp. 123-138.
35. Wright, C., *Wittgenstein on the Foundations of Mathematics* (Cambridge: Harvard University Press, 1980).

7

Institutionally Determined Parameters in Economic Equations[1]

The idea that economic events are shaped by economic, political, social, and other institutions is rather old. In modern times, one of its more common appearances is in statements of the form, "Parameters δ, ρ, and λ in the equations under consideration are institutionally determined." Thus, for example, the speed of adjustment in market stability analyses is said to emerge from the particular market institutions present in the economy and, in macroeconomic studies, the rate of change in the money supply is alleged to depend on the institutional arrangements between central banks and commercial banks. But in practice, the way in which the relevant institutions actually produce these parameters is usually not considered. Most often the assertion that a parameter is institutionally determined seems to be a short way of saying that the parameter, although capable of change by human action as opposed to nature, is exogenous to the system under consideration. In this manner the parameter can be disposed of without having to deal explicitly with it. Thus, in such situations, authors are content merely with the vague assertion that institutional

[1] *Économie Appliquée* 43 (1990), pp. 35-52. Reprinted with permission of the publisher: Institut de Sciences Mathématiques et Economiques Appliquées, Paris.

The author would like to thank Samuel Bowles, Michael Krüger and Douglas Vickers for helpful comments and suggestions.

changes cause shifts in parameter values and to leave matters at that.[2] The precise modifications that occur and the exact manner in which these modifications influence the numerical sizes of the parameters is left up in the air. The purpose of the present paper is to explore what it might mean to say that a parameter in an equation is institutionally determined.

Of course, not all parameters in all equations need be viewed as institutionally determined. For example, the parameters in a firm's production function are usually described as the product of technology or nature; in deriving market demand functions, the number of individuals in the market is often taken to be an exogenously given fact; the initial conditions in differential or difference equations are sometimes assumed to be set historically; and so on. Thus, in addition to being institutionally determined, parameters can also be thought of as the result of, among other things, technology, nature, history, or exogenous fact. Only those that are institutionally determined are of interest here.

All institutionally determined parameters appear as numbers in numerical economic equations. Some of these parameters, such as, perhaps, the rate of change in the money supply, emerge already in usable numerical form from the flux of institutional interaction. Sometimes, too, the institutional interaction itself is numerically describable. More commonly, however, institutional interaction seems to be non-quantifiable and to produce qualitative results that then have to be transformed into numbers. The present approach is to focus on the qualitative, more general, situation and to think of the quantified instances as arising as special cases. For each institutionally determined parameter (or collection of parameters), a model has to be built to explain from where it comes and a method of translating the outcomes of that model into single real numbers for use as parameter values in an equation has to be given. The translating of outcomes into numbers, it turns out, may not be possible to accomplish except in an *ad hoc* or arbitrary manner. Moreover, the model itself may have its own underlying parametric structure that relocates the explanation of the original parameter on a different level. In this latter case, the phrase "institutionally determined parameter" can have meaning only if the underlying parameters are not themselves institutionally determined.

This paper, then, attempts to show what has to be done so that institutions can be analyzed and explicitly included as part of the formal structures relating to parameters in models of economic activity. It does so by providing a simple example in which an institutional substructure directly determines the numerical value of a parameter in an equation describing a specific economic

[2] For example, Gordon, Weisskopf, and Bowles [5, p. 153] state without explanation that "The expected profit rate depends on the effectiveness of those institutions which make up a given SSA [social structure of accumulation]. The level and pattern of investment depends upon the SSA and the expected profit rate."

phenomenon. The example itself, in so far as the institutional interaction it depicts is concerned, is abstract in character. Moreover, only a rather modest and incomplete particularization of the interaction is cited from another context in the economics literature. This is because the purpose of constructing the example is not so much to furnish a detailed analysis of a concrete situation as it is to clarify the logical steps that are required, and the difficulties that are encountered, in giving meaning to the assertion that a parameter in an equation is institutionally determined.

I

The example to be considered consists of an equation describing the so-called business or trade cycle. Although there are a number of different kinds of business cycles that might be analyzed and various ways to approach them,[3] the perspective taken here is to follow Hansen [7, Ch. 2] in thinking of a relatively short-term cycle superimposed on a longer-term one. The combined cycle is described in terms of a sequence of solutions of differential equations, each involving the same single variable, real national income. The short-term cycle is the result of economic forces working themselves out as they interact over time against the fixed institutional constraints that appear as parameters in the differential equations. The long-term cycle is generated by independent institutional transformations that result in parameter shifts.

Such a view of the business cycle is similar to that of Gordon, Weisskopf, and Bowles [5]. In their analysis the reproductive and non-reproductive, that is, short-term, cycles generate upturns and downturns endogenously through their own internal dynamics. The upturns and downturns of the long-term cycle, however, are accompanied by institutional variations that affect the profitability of firms and the process of capital accumulation. The set of institutions involved are referred to as the social structure of accumulation. They create the environment in which profitability is estimated and decisions to invest are made. Thus long-term expansions are founded on the ability of the social structure of accumulation to sustain sufficient profitability and accumulation, while long-term declines are caused by the substantial erosion of this same ability. The trough of the long-term cycle lasts until the social structure of accumulation is able, once again, to call forth enough accumulation and growth. A parallel statement explains the length of long-term cycle's peak.

One way to obtain a concrete, short-term cycle is with the mathematical

3 See, for example, van Duijn [4].

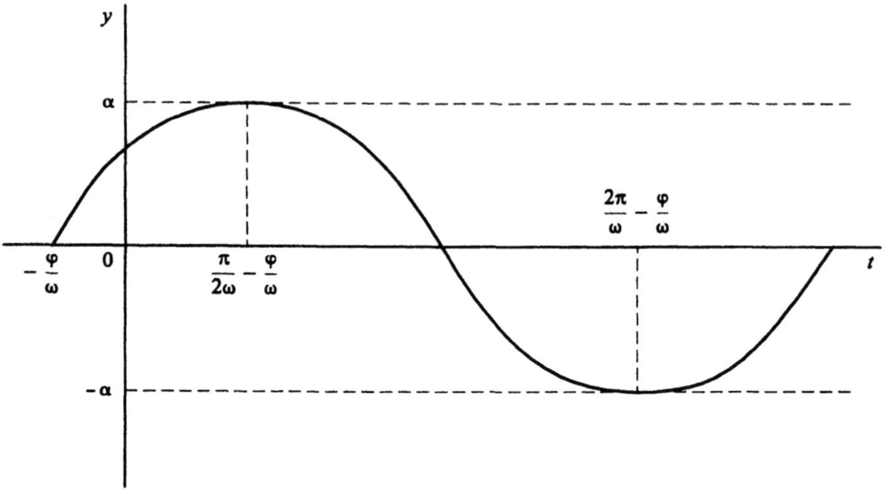

Figure 1. Short-term cycle ($\theta = 0$)

equation

$$y = \alpha e^{\theta t} \sin(\omega t + \varphi), \tag{1}$$

where y represents real national income, $t \geq 0$ is time, α, θ, ω, and φ are parameters, and e is the base of natural logarithms. Assume that $\alpha \neq 0$ and $\omega \neq 0$. The graph of (1) is a sine curve over time whose period is $2\pi/\omega$, whose amplitude at its first peak is

$$\alpha e^{(\theta/\omega)[(\pi/2)-\varphi]},$$

and whose phase is $-\varphi/\omega$. If $\theta = 0$, then the amplitude is the same constant α at all peaks and troughs. Thus each of the parameters α, θ, ω, and φ play a specific role in characterizing the nature of the cycle defined by (1): α is the amplitude when $\theta = 0$, θ is the factor that determines the damping or expansion of the amplitude as t increases with $\theta \neq 0$, ω sets the period, and φ fixes the phase once the period is given. An illustration in which $\theta = 0$ appears in Figure 1. Generally, in subsequent discussion, the values of α, θ, ω, and φ (along with the trend parameters introduced below) are viewed as determined independently of each other by institutional interaction.

A simple way of superimposing this short-term cycle onto a long-term cycle is to add a linear trend to (1) as follows:

$$y = \alpha e^{\theta t} \sin(\omega t + \varphi) + bt + c, \tag{2}$$

where b and c are also parameters. Then when $b > 0$, the trend of the short-term cycle is upward as it oscillates about a line of positive slope. Similarly, a negative b means that the short-term cycle has a downward trend. When $b = 0$, the trend is neither upward nor downward. A long-term cycle is formed by varying the parameters b and c in such a fashion that a cyclical pattern of trends emerges.

To see what is involved in a simple case, suppose that α, θ, ω, and φ remain fixed over time while b and c vary only at the points of some sequence $\{t^n\}$, where $t^0 = 0$ and $t^n > t^{n-1}$, for $n = 1, 2, \ldots$. For the moment, the selection of the time-points to be included in $\{t^n\}$ should be viewed as arbitrary. Discussion will return to this issue later on. Denote the values of b and c on the interval $t^{n-1} \leq t < t^n$ by, respectively, b^{n-1} and c^{n-1}. Each pair (b^{n-1}, c^{n-1}) defines a linear trend-line, $y = b^{n-1}t + c^{n-1}$, over $t^{n-1} \leq t < t^n$, where b^{n-1} is the slope of the trend-line and c^{n-1} is its vertical intercept if extended to $t = 0$. A combined trend-line over the two consecutive intervals, $t^{n-1} \leq t < t^{n+1}$, can be defined only if the trend-lines over $t^{n-1} \leq t < t^n$ and $t^n \leq t < t^{n+1}$ meet at $t = t^n$. To ensure such an intersection for every n, assume that for all $n > 1$,

$$c^n = (b^{n-1} - b^n)t^n + c^{n-1}. \tag{3}$$

Then the trend line on the interval $t^{n-1} \leq t < t^n$ is, as indicated above,

$$y = b^{n-1}t + c^{n-1},$$

and, from (3), that on $t^n \leq t < t^{n+1}$ is

$$y = b^n t + (b^{n-1} - b^n)t^n + c^{n-1}.$$

Since the y-values of these expressions are the same at $t = t^n$, the two trend lines must come together there. Note also that specification of c^0 and b^n for all $n \geq 0$ is enough to determine all remaining c^n (where $n \geq 1$) according to (3). Under the above assumptions, then, the collection of trend lines obtained as n increases form a continuous, piece-wise linear curve. When the latter curve assumes an appropriate cyclical shape, this defines the long-term cycle that is taken to underlie equation (2). An illustration may be found in Figure 2.

Of course, on the interval $t^{n-1} \leq t < t^n$, (2) becomes

$$y = \alpha e^{\theta t} \sin(\omega t + \varphi) + b^{n-1}t + c^{n-1},$$

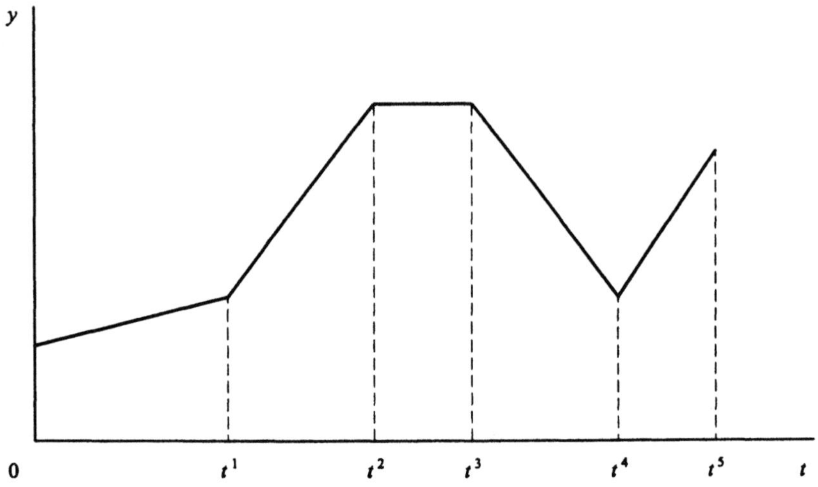

Figure 2. Long-term cycle

while on $t^n \leq t < t^{n+1}$ it is

$$y = \alpha e^{\theta t} \sin(\omega t + \varphi) + b^n t + (b^{n-1} - b^n)t^n + c^{n-1}.$$

Again, the y-values in both of these expressions are identical when $t = t^n$. Therefore, in spite of the shifts in the parameters b^n and c^n over time, the curve secured by superimposing the short-term cycle on the long-term cycle is continuous. It is also differentiable except, generally, at the points of $\{t^n\}$. A picture illustrating the combined cycle when $\theta = 0$ is given in Figure 3. The combined cycle, then, is characterized by the collection of equations

$$y = \alpha e^{\theta t} \sin(\omega t + \varphi) + b^n t + c^n, \tag{4}$$

each defined on the interval $t^n \leq t < t^{n+1}$, for $n = 0, 1, 2, ...$ Parameters are allowed to take on only those values that ensure $y \geq 0$ for all t.

Now equation (4) may be perceived as reflecting both "economic" and "non-economic" forces. One approach to conceptualizing this idea is to observe that for each n, (4) is a solution of the differential equation

$$\frac{d^2y}{dt^2} - 2\theta\frac{dy}{dt} + (\omega^2 + \theta^2)y = (\omega^2 + \theta^2)(b^n t + c^n) - 2\theta b^n, \tag{5}$$

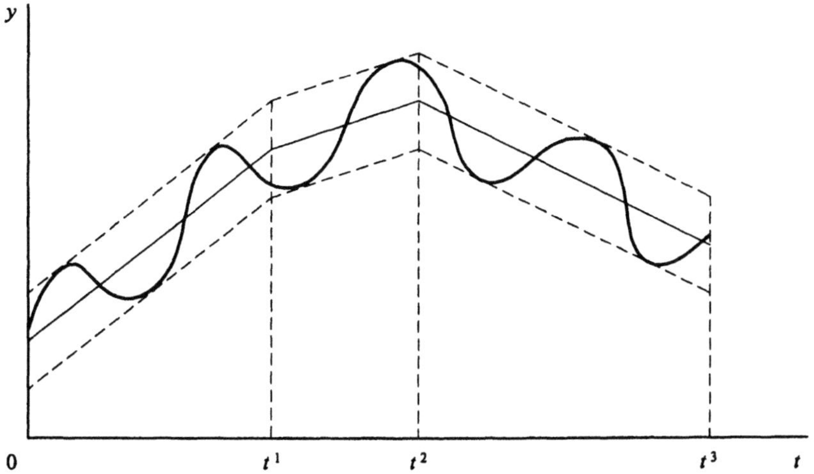

Figure 3. Combined cycle ($\theta = 0$)

on the interval $t^n \leq t < t^{n+1}$. The homogeneous version of (5), viz.,

$$\frac{d^2y}{dt^2} - 2\theta\frac{dy}{dt} + (\omega^2 + \theta^2)y = 0, \tag{6}$$

may be thought of as generated by economic forces alone in the absence of independent outside pressures. That is, equation (6), which describes the motion of real national income over time, is derived as the resolution of a system of equations that models the relevant economic forces at work. Thus, in this interpretation, θ and ω are purely economic parameters emerging from purely economic institutions. Independent, non-economic institutional constraints, in part represented by b and c, are introduced as interacting with θ and ω in the term $(\omega^2+\theta^2)(b^n t+c^n)-2\theta b^n$ on the right-hand side of (5). Although the precise nature of their determination is not considered here, assume that the values of α and φ are also independently and institutionally set. Then the parameters of equation (4) can be separated into two distinct groups: those identified with institutions that are classified as economic, and those that are secured through other kinds of institutions. Note that (5) modifies over time while (6) does not and that, unlike the other parameters, specific values of α and φ have no impact on either (5) or (6). Thus, in the present case, the period of the short-term cycle and its amplitude-damping (or expansion) factor are determined by economic institutions; and the amplitude when $\theta = 0$, the phase (given ω), and the trend (i.e., the long-term cycle) depend on non-economic institutions.

Of course the example described here is highly specialized. Not only are the forms of the equations rather simplistic but so is the separation of the economic institutions determining θ and ω from the non-economic institutions that fix α, φ, and the b^n and c^n. Moreover, the requirement that α, θ, ω, and φ remain constant over time is rather restrictive. Nevertheless, the stage is now set for an analysis of how a parameter can be said to be institutionally determined. Although subsequent discussion centers only on the setting of the values of the b^n, as pointed out earlier, if the value of c^0 is taken as given (it may be viewed as, say, fixed by history), then specification of the values of all of the b^n determines, from (3), the values of the c^n for every $n \geq 1$. The fact that b^n has been classified above as a non-economic parameter is of no consequence. An argument similar to that which follows could be made for any parameter, economic or non-economic.

II

There are many ways to characterize the notion of institution. For example, Brown and Selznick [2, p. 27] take an institution to be an organization that has a special purpose, serves public rather than private interests, and conducts its activities in an accepted, orderly, and enduring way. Davis and North [3, p. 7] describe an (economic) institution as "... an arrangement between economic units that govern[s] the ways in which these units can cooperate and/or compete," and Boland [1, p. 51] defines the concept as any constraint on individual behavior that is established as a result of the collective action of many individuals. A fourth alternative is given by Schotter [9, p. 11]: An institution is "... a regularity in social behavior that is agreed to by all members of society, specifies behavior in specific recurrent situations, and is either self-policed or policed by some external authority." Thus firms, markets, government agencies (or government itself), churches, and clubs are all institutions. As they stand, however, these approaches are too vague and general to be of use in explaining how institutions interacting with each other determine something as concrete as specific parameter values. Hence the notion of institution employed here is necessarily an extract from one of these (or another) general conceptualizations that is more precise and restrictive.[4] In particular, it abstracts from reality

[4] For purposes of analysis, Schotter, too, introduces a more exact and confining notion, namely

in such a way as to focus attention on the relations that might exist among the elements that make up the institution. Expressed in formal language, the idea is as follows: An institution is an abstract functional relation among variables appropriate to the underlying general conceptualization of institution that has been chosen.[5]

Relations of this sort, however, are not easy to describe because, as indicated at the outset, the variables involved are taken to be not quantifiable.[6] (How, for example, is the institution of private property to be represented numerically?) Instead of numbers, non-quantifiable variable values take the form of discretely distinct verbal descriptions (in the private property case they appear, perhaps, as descriptions of legal codes, descriptions of attitudes, etc.). Furthermore, to the extent that a non-quantifiable institutional relation is concretely specified, such a specification can indicate only a few of the points or vectors of variable values (each vector consists of one verbal description for each variable) that lie in it. The mechanics of dealing with the non-quantifiable have been discussed elsewhere.[7] A partial illustration is presented later on.

Formally, then, an institutional relation, that is, an *institution*, is an ordinary mathematical function defined on a suitable, non-quantifiable domain. Assume there are J such relations that go into the fixing of the institutionally determined parameter b of equation (2). (This, remember, is the only parameter of (2) to be considered here.) Denote the jth function or institution by F^j and suppose it involves I variables and its own vector of parameters p as follows:

$$z_j = F^j(z_1, ..., z_{j-1}, z_{j+1}, ..., z_I, p). \tag{7}$$

As will be seen momentarily, p plays an important role in the subsequent explanation of b. Assume without loss of generality that the remaining functions are made up of the same variables and parameters so that the set of institutions determining b is constituted by (7) with $j = 1, ..., J$. Now under certain conditions,[8] which include the requirement that $I = J$, the simultaneous interaction of the institutional relations of (7) determines the vector $z = (z_1, ..., z_I)$ as a function of the parameters p:

$$z = G(p). \tag{8}$$

---

the equilibrium convention or pattern of behavior in play that players develop upon repeated plays of a certain kind of game [9, pp. 58,59].

[5] This definition may be employed regardless of whether one approaches the notion of institution from the perspective of methodological individualism or not.

[6] Recall that quantifiable situations are regarded as special cases.

[7] See Katzner [8] and Essay 4 in this volume.

[8] Katzner [8, Sect. 5.1].

In other words, simultaneous institutional activity given p, fixes a unique value for z. The next step is to consider the problem of mapping z into b.

Before doing so, however, note that to actually come up with the J relations of (7) and (or) (8) requires that agreement be reached on a number of difficult issues. These include the following: (i) What are the relevant variables and parameters to use in describing the institutions whose interaction is eventually to explain b? (ii) What values do each of these variables and parameters take on? And (iii), how, for each institution j, are the variable values assumed by z_j related to those of the remaining z_i and those of p or, in other words, how is each of the functions F^j defined? Under the assumption of solvability, the last question can be simplified so that its focus is only on the specification of G. Although the working out of generally agreed-upon answers to these questions will not be easy, it should be pointed out that similar issues arise and are resolved, at least implicitly, when all variables and parameters are quantified. If this is not obvious in any particular quantitative study, it is only because the agreed-to answers have already been worked out by others in the (perhaps distant) past and, in that form, have implicitly been accepted for the study at hand.

Returning to the problem of relating b to z, and hence to p, observe that, although a general function could be constructed, the only values of b that are of interest in the present case are the b^n from (4), for $n = 0, 1, 2, ...$ Let values of p be observed only at the time points of $\{t^n\}$. Denote the values of p at each t^n by p^n. Then G, through (8), defines a corresponding sequence of values of the vector z, namely $\{z^n\}$. Of course the institutions themselves, that is, the number J and the functions $F^1, ..., F^J$, and hence G, along with the number and type of variables, $z_1, ..., z_I$, could also undergo transformation through time. But to keep matters simple, these kinds of alterations are ignored.

Suppose next, that in relation to what is thought to be happening over time with respect to the combination of economic forces and institutions under investigation (that is, in the present case, the macroeconomy), some subsequence of points of $\{z^n\}$ can be classified as a sequence containing only "break points" and "balance points." A point z^n, where $n > 0$, is a *break* point (or, for short, just *break*) if $z^n \neq z^{n-1}$ and z^n is also associated with a "radically opposite" economic environment from z^{n-1} according to mutually agreeable criteria. Each break reflects a fundamental change in the outcome of institutional interaction from that which precedes it. Alternatively, z^n, for $n \geq 0$, is a *balance* point (or *balance*) if it corresponds to regular and repeating patterns (as defined, again, by mutually agreeable criteria) in the economic environment over the period $t^n \leq t < t^{n+1}$. Thus breaks are identified with deep reversals in economic direction, while balances indicate pauses in the core of evolutionary change. (For convenience, the "direction" of a balance may be taken to be the same as that of the first non-balance that precedes it when, of course, the latter exists.) Such breaks and balances might also be observable in the associated underlying subsequence of $\{p^n\}$ that produced them through (8).

Let a real-valued function, M, be constructed on the elements of $\{z^n\}$ such that for all $n \geq 0$,

i. z^n is a balance point if and only if $M(z^n) = 0$.

ii. If z^n is a break point, then $M(z^n)$ and $M(z^{n-k-1})$ are of opposite sign, where k is the number of balance points immediately preceding z^n.

iii. If $z^{n'}$ and $z^{n''}$, where $n' < n''$, are neither break nor balance points, and if no z^n, for $n' < n < n''$, is a break point, then $M(z^{n'})$ and $M(z^{n''})$ have the same sign.

Define b^n in equation (4) by setting

$$b^n = M(z^n), \tag{9}$$

for all $n \geq 0$. (With c^0 given, the definition of c^n remains as in (3).) Thus, if there is a break at t^n, and if the b^n just before the break are non-negative with at least one of them positive, then at the break (for example, t^3 in Figure 2 or t^2 in Figure 3) the b^n become negative. Likewise, if the b^n are non-positive with at least one of them negative beforehand, then afterwards they are positive (t^4 in Figure 2). Hence the peaks and troughs of the long-term cycle described in Section I are associated with and only with breaks. At balances (for example, t^2 in Figure 2) the economy is merely resting for a while before following an upward or downward trend.

Implicitly, the b^n have been assumed to possess sufficient properties so as to permit the mathematical manipulation required for them to appear as parameters in (4). In particular, the b^n as numbers have the potential to be ordered according to their size and to be combined by addition. Under certain conditions, then, M might be thought of as a function that "measures" the outcome of institutional interaction on a cardinal scale. This would necessitate the specification of an ordering and an operation of "combination," each with certain traits, among the values that z^n may assume such that, on the cardinal scale, the ordering would be reflected in the ordering of real numbers and the combination operation would manifest itself as addition.[9] But clearly, the meanings of these underlying constructs are likely to be quite difficult to penetrate.

In any case, by postulating the existence of suitable functions F^j, where $j = 1, ..., J$, and M, the parameters b^n that characterize the long-term cycle in (4) are determined through (9) by the interaction of institutions (7) as p modulates. If one could specify the F^j and M having the requisite properties, and the appropriate values of p in advance, then it would be possible to predict the long-term cycle. In order to do so, however, it would be necessary (i) to select an appropriate sequence of moments $\{t^n\}$, (ii) to develop and justify a particularization of (7) for each j (or, alternatively, of (8)), and (iii) to furnish a concrete way of mapping solution values z^n into numbers b^n that provides a sequence of breaks and balances. The second is, probably, the easiest of the three, considering that there have been attempts, as illustrated below, to study the nature of institutions and their interactions. But at present, there is not much known concerning how to accomplish the first and the third, i.e., how to construct a reasonable $\{t^n\}$ and M *a priori*. Given the current state of knowledge, any such specification of $\{t^n\}$ and M is likely to have a ring of arbitrariness about it — and this is true regardless of whether the z^n are quantifiable or non-quantifiable. The difficulty may be that sufficient information for a proper determination of $\{t^n\}$ and M is not obtainable. If so, then the only practical way of linking parameter values b^n with institutional-solution values z^n would be on an *ad hoc* basis. That is, the relevant values of b^n would be found by fitting equation (4) to existing data. This would also, of course, pick out an appropriate, finite, starting subsequence for the sequence $\{t^n\}$. At the same time the values of z^n would be secured from a particularization of (7), for each j, or (8). Then M would be defined by associating b^n with z^n for all n, and the presence of breaks and balances would be revealed in the picture of the long-term cycle that emerges.

The particularizing of (7) or (8) finds partial illustration in the Gordon-Weisskopf-Bowles [6] discussion of the social structure of accumulation in the U.S. economy between, approximately, 1945 and 1980. Although neither the institutional relations of equation (7) nor their resolution into (8) are described, Gordon, Weisskopf and Bowles nevertheless identify four variables that could serve as the arguments of the F^j, and loosely trace out the resolved solution values (i.e., the z^n) that they observe for the period. The four variables are as follows: (i) the particularities of the informal arrangement, called the "capital-labor accord," between capital and labor that defines, in very general terms, management's control over labor and the rewards that labor receives in ex-

[9] See, for example, Katzner [8, Sect. 2.2].

change; (ii) the characteristics of American influence in the world economy; (iii) the nature of the compromise, referred to as the "capital-citizen accord," which specifies the extent to which capital can be held socially accountable to society at large; and (iv) the qualities of competition among capitalists.

Without attempting to determine breaks and balances, Gordon, Weisskopf and Bowles argue that the outcome of the institutional interaction summarized in (8) up to the mid 1960s produced a capital-labor accord that assured labor submission and cooperation (including rising productivity) in exchange for rising real wages, improved working conditions, and greater job security. It also led to dominance of the U.S. in the world economy, a relatively *laissez-faire* attitude on the part of society toward business activity, and moderation of competition among capitalists. The particular values of z^n so obtained resulted in considerable accumulation and growth, or in other words, to associated values of b^n that were positive and relatively large. After the mid 1960s, the emerging values of z^n did not support accumulation and growth as well and the corresponding values of b^n began to decline.

III

The last step in imputing meaning to the idea that the parameters b^n of (4) are institutionally determined is to recognize explicitly the internal dynamic that, until now, has been implicit as it works itself out among the values of the vector of parameters p. Let this be represented in the form

$$p^{n+1} = H(p^n, \mu), \tag{10}$$

where μ is an independent parameter (or vector of parameters) of H, $n = 0, 1, 2, \ldots$, and H is a periodic functional relation that defines the movement of p over the time points of the sequence $\{t^n\}$. (The presence of μ in (10) is significant and will be discussed below.) It is H that determines $\{p^n\}$ upon specification of an initial value p^0. Then, through the institutional interaction that defines (8), the sequence $\{p^n\}$ is mapped into $\{z^n\}$. And finally, $\{z^n\}$ is converted into numbers $\{b^n\}$ according to (9). It follows that the long-term cycle is ultimately generated by the dynamic of (10).

Observe that by restricting (8) to the points associated with the sequence $\{t^n\}$ and combining it with (9), the b^n can be related directly to the p^n:

$$b^n = R(p^n),$$

where for all p^n,

$$R(p^n) = M(G(p^n)).$$

Moreover, if R has an inverse (denote it by R^{-1}), then the dynamic of (10) can be expressed in terms of the b^n:

$$b^{n+1} = S(b^n, \mu), \tag{11}$$

where

$$S(b^n, \mu) = R(H(R^{-1}(b^n), \mu)),$$

for all $n \geq 0$. In a similar way, this dynamic can also be articulated with respect to the z^n.

From the present perspective, it is clear that the question of the existence of long-term cycles depends, at least in theory, on the properties of H. If, to illustrate, (10) had a *stationary* path for some μ, i.e., a point $\bar{p}$ such that

$$\bar{p} = H(\bar{p}, \mu),$$

and if $\{p^n\}$ converged[10] to $\bar{p}$, then eventually all long-term cycles (if there were any) would have to disappear. The sequence $\{p^n\}$ is called *cyclic* (not to be confused with the term "cycle" as used previously) if there exists an integer $k > 0$ such that

$$p^n = p^{n+k},$$

for all $n \geq 0$. If $\{p^n\}$ is cyclic, then it contains a finite number of distinct terms. (On the other hand, if $\{p^n\}$ contains a finite number of distinct terms, then $\{p^n\}$ is cyclic only when it does not converge to a stationary path.) Generally, knowing only that $\{p^n\}$ is cyclic is not enough to guarantee that a long-term cycle exists. To have a long-term cycle requires, in addition, that at least one term different from p^0 be a break. Otherwise the b^n could merely repeat the same positive numbers, say, over and over again.

In a sense, however, the reduction of the dynamic behavior of b^n to the level of the behavior of p^n as described here does not help as much as one would like. For the purpose of the analysis is to explain the pattern of values assumed by the institutionally determined parameter b^n in (4). Clearly that explanation,

---

[10] It is possible to give rigorous meaning to the notion of convergence, even in the absence of measurement. See Katzner [8, Sect. 3.2] and Essay 4 in this volume.

as summarized in (11), can be substituted into (4) to give

$$y = \alpha e^{\theta t}\sin(\omega t + \varphi) + S(b^{n-1}, \mu)t + c^n, \tag{12}$$

where, as previously indicated, c^n could be expressed in terms of the b^{n-k} (for $0 \leq k \leq n$) and c^0. But now (12) has a new parameter in place of b^n, namely μ, that may be institutionally determined and, if so, still requires explanation. Of course, if μ is fixed by technology, nature, history, or exogenous fact, then there is no problem. Otherwise, although one may be able to learn something about the determination of the b^n through the specification of a model of the sort described here, the explanation of the pattern of values assumed by the b^n is not completely satisfying because it merely substitutes one institutionally determined parameter for another.

There are at least two possible ways out. On the one hand, if it seems reasonable, the parameter μ could be dropped from the conceptualization of H in (10) so that the description of the underlying dynamic is all-encompassing and does not rely on an unexplained, institutionally determined parameter.[11] On the other, it might be appropriate to reformulate the approach itself so as to determine y and b simultaneously. This would require something like the following: Revert to the full, continuous-time version of the national income equation in (2). Replace the argument p of the F^j in (7) with y, thereby transforming (8) into

$$z = G(y). \tag{13}$$

Redefine M in (9) to include all values of z (not only those values z^n that are associated with time periods $n = 0, 1, 2, ...$) in its domain and write

$$b = M(z). \tag{14}$$

Next combine (2), (13), and (14) to obtain

$$y = \alpha e^{\theta t}\sin(\omega t + \varphi) + M(G(y))t + c. \tag{15}$$

Then solve (15) to express y as a function of t and the remaining parameters, and observe that the solution still produces fluctuations in y and that the parameter b does not appear in it. However, this elimination of the institutionally determined parameter b occurs precisely because b is no longer a parameter. Its value still depends, in part, on the institutional interaction defined by (13),

[11] In the special case in which all variables are quantifiable, so that (10) would take the form of a difference equation, elimination of μ would mean that any numbers, i.e., parameters, appearing as coefficients or powers in (10) could not be thought of as institutionally determined. Of course, coefficients and powers are not present in non-quantitiable specifications of (10).

but that value is now determined endogenously with the value of y at each t. Hence it is not an "institutionally determined *parameter*" any more.[12] In other words, under these conditions the phrase "institutionally determined parameter" itself has no meaning because any imputation of meaning requires that either the parameter is "explained" in terms of an infinite regress, which is no explanation at all, or the parameter has to be simultaneously determined along with the endogenous variables of the model and this, in turn, destroys its status as an institutionally determined parameter.

Thus the assertion that the parameter b^n is institutionally determined not only rests on the construction of a model of institutional interaction, and on a method of associating the resolutions of the modeled institutional interactions with single real numbers, but it also implies the existence of an underlying dynamic process that generates the long-term cycle in (4). The latter process has its own properties and, if it depends on its own parameter values, then these parameter values cannot themselves be institutionally determined. Clearly the complexity of this explanation of b^n increases as the remaining institutionally determined parameters α, θ, ω, φ and c^0 in (4) are brought into the picture and permitted to be simultaneously and interdependently set along with b^n. In general, an underlying structure will be present in any analysis of the institutional determination of parameters in economic equations, and different investigations will encounter different underlying structures. Whether or not an actual examination of the underlying structure is worth while in any particular investigation turns on the purposes of that investigation and on the results that might be obtained from such an examination. But regardless of the situation, the effort to link a specific numerical parameter in an economic equation to concrete institutional interactions is not a simple task.

References

1. Boland, L. A., *The Foundations of Economic Method* (London: Allen & Unwin, 1982).
2. Brown, L. and P. Selznick, *Sociology*, 2nd ed. (Evanston: Row Peterson, 1958).
3. Davis, L. E. and D. C. North, *Institutional Change and American Economic Growth* (London: Cambridge University Press, 1971).

[12] Note that, in this example, the simultaneous determination of y and b blurs the distinction between the long run and the short run since the trend b is now set at each instant t and is not necessarily constant over intervals of time.

4. v. Duijn, J. J., *The Long Wave in Economic Life* (London: Allen & Unwin,1983).
5. Gordon, D. M., T. E. Weisskopf, and S. Bowles, "Long Swings and the Nonreproductive Cycle," *American Economic Review* 73, no.2 (May, 1983), pp. 152-157.
6. ________, "Power, Accumulation, and Crisis: The Rise and Demise of the Postwar Social Structure of Accumulation," in *The Imperiled Economy*, Book I, *Macroeconomics from a Left Perspective*, R. Cherry, *et al*, eds. (New York: Union for Radical Political Economics, 1987), pp. 43-57.
7. Hansen, A. H., *Business Cycles and National Income*, expanded ed. (New York: Norton, 1964).
8. Katzner, D. W., *Analysis without Measurement* (Cambridge: Cambridge University Press, 1983).
9. Schotter, A., *The Economic Theory of Social Institutions* (Cambridge: Cambridge University Press, 1981).

8
The Misuse of Measurement in Economics[1]

Some years ago, Friedrich Hayek [11] complained about the tendency he observed in economics to disregard as unimportant and irrelevant that which, at the time of inquiry, did not appear to be amenable to measurement. Economists seemed to believe that, in confluence with Kelvin 's famous but dubious dictum,[2] the only way to live up to the scientific requirements of economic analysis was to work with numerical measures even when knowing they only captured a small portion, if that, of the important facets of the issue at hand. By this standard, wrote Hayek [11, p. 3], "... there ... may well exist better 'scientific' evidence for a false theory, which will be accepted because it is more 'scientific,' than for a valid explanation, which is rejected because there is no[t] sufficient quantitative evidence for it." He then went on to say [11, p.

---

1 *Metroeconomica* 49 (1998), pp. 1-22.

Thanks are due to Samuel Bowles, Herbert Gintis, Douglas Vickers, and Cleve Willis for their useful and insightful comments.

2 "... when you can measure what you are speaking about and express it in numbers you know something about it; but when you cannot measure it, when you cannot express it in numbers, your knowledge is of a meagre and unsatisfactory kind: it may be the beginning of knowledge, but you have scarcely in your thoughts, advanced to the stage of *science*, whatever the matter may be (Kelvin [21, p. 80]). Doubts raised about the dictum have been described in Katzner [17, p. 25, n. 7 (this volume, Essay 2, p. 29, n. 7)]. Elsewhere in this volume and in [15], Katzner shows that it is possible to be "scientific" even when numerical measures are not available.

5], "I prefer true but imperfect knowledge ... to a pretence of exact knowledge that is likely to be false. The credit which the apparent conformity with recognized scientific standards can gain for seemingly simple but false theories may ... have grave consequences."

Since Hayek's warning, however, matters in economics have only moved in a direction in which he probably would not have approved. For in addition to the general omission of important elements because numerical measures of them are not known, it has now become commonplace in certain areas to introduce what many would regard as the non-quantifiable and partially quantifiable (e.g., ordinally measured) by treating them as if they were fully quantifiable (i.e., at least cardinally measured).[3] Thus, for example, Boulding [7, p. 32] includes variables representing "virtues," "vices," and "goodness" in a fully-quantified mathematical equation, Azzi and Ehrenberg [3, p. 33] do something similar with the "expected value of afterlife consumption," and so does Akerlof with the "quality" of an automobile [1, p. 490] and a persons "reputation" [2, p. 754]. Becker and Lewis [5] maximize a utility function (subject to constraint) with respect to fully-quantified "child quality" and other variables. In addition, all of the literature on efficiency wages (and related issues) and some of that pertaining to the principal-agent problem employs fully-quantified mathematical models in which the questionably quantifiable variable "effort" plays a major role.[4] Another aspect of what might be called this misuse of measurement in economics is the appearance of fully-quantified proxy variables[5] in place of and as "approximations" of the variables for which no measures (ordinal, cardinal, or ratio) or only "fractional" or "incomplete" measures are available. Kalt and Zupan's [13, p. 287] substitution of a particular rating scale (based on voting) for a senator's "ideology," Fair's [10, pp. 52-58] replacement of an individual's wage by his or her occupation and education, Barro's [4, p. 432] use of the number of revolutions and coups, and the number of political assassinations, as indicators of a country's political stability, and Helliwell and Putnam's [12, p. 297] "measures" of social capital illustrate the phenomenon. In practically all such cases the authors make no attempt to justify the measurement they employ.

The purpose of this paper is to examine some of the implications of these

[3] That is, non-quantified or ordinally quantified variables appear perhaps along with cardinally or ratio quantified variables in the same analysis. No distinction between or discussion about the nature of the quantification of the variables is given, and standard mathematical techniques usually reserved for at least cardinally quantified variables are applied everywhere. For present purposes, the absence of any discussion of measurement is taken to imply that in those analyses all variables are treated as if they were fully quantified.

[4] See, for example, Currie and Steedman [8].

[5] For a definition of the term "proxy variable," see n. 12 of Essay 1 on p. 10.

measurement practices. In particular, it explores the kinds of things that can go wrong when variables that are only ordinally measured are treated as if they were cardinally quantified. In this vein, it has already been shown elsewhere that the application of increasing transformations to ordinal data (which, of course, has no impact on the information content of that data) can reverse the signs of estimated coefficients in regression analysis, and can change the number of variation-explaining factors that emerge from factor analysis (Katzner [15, pp. 44-48]). A question has also been raised about the sense of empirically measuring things like the quality of life without having any prior notion of what that concept might mean (Katzner [14, pp. 21-29]). The present argument, however, is more concerned with theoretical than with empirical matters. After a brief introduction to four basic types of measurement, it concentrates on the difficulties associated with using ordinal variables as cardinal variables in models that really require all variables to be at least cardinally quantified. Specifically, the determination of dependent variable values in functional equations, the derivatives of functions reflecting both slope and curvature, and certain maximization problems are examined. Efficiency wage models are given especially close scrutiny. The use of proxy variables is then taken up, and the paper closes with a general comment about an alternative to the procedure of treating non-quantified and partially quantified variables as if they were fully quantified. The principal conclusion is that in many cases, if not in most, the use of both ordinally calibrated variables as if they were fully quantified and proxy variables in economic analysis results in constructions that are without meaning, significance, and explanatory power. Treating ordinal variables as cardinal or ratio variables and ignoring the limitations of proxies can mislead an investigator into thinking that an analysis has shed light on the real world. Economists, then, have to be very careful when introducing ordinal variables and proxies into their models.

At the outset, it should be noted that subsequent discussion takes the main purpose of economic analysis to be explanation. From a theoretical vantage point, that purpose is achieved by the construction of models to explain behavior that, at least in principle, is capable of observation. Explanation can be general without linking specific observations to a particular realization of the model through the detailing of functional forms and parameter values. In this case, observations are merely interpreted as being explained by some realization without indicating which one. Explanation becomes concrete when a particular realization is specifically identified, perhaps through estimation, with a particular set of observations. Prediction is viewed as a by-product of concrete explanation which may or may not be pursued in any given analysis.

Prediction by itself is insufficient for explanation because it cannot rule out the possibility of spurious coincidence of observations and predictors. In any case, the issue of using an ordinal variable as if it were fully quantified for prediction purposes only is also taken up at the end of the paper.

I

All economic objects have properties. Measurement is the assignment of numbers to the realizations of those properties.[6] Thus, for example, the property of "heaviness" is measured as weight in, say, pounds or kilograms. There are four basic kinds of measurement: nominal, ordinal, cardinal or interval, and ratio. Nominal measurement only identifies categories (such as, in the previous example, heavy and light) in which objects have been placed according to the property. Ordinal measurement not only reflects the categories of nominal measures but also the ordering of the objects by the property. (Hence object A is heavier than object B if and only if A has more weight than B.) Cardinal measurement is ordinal measurement which also permits the numbers identified with combined objects to be obtained as the sum of the separate numbers assigned to each. (Thus the heaviness of A and B combined is measured as the sum of the weights of A and B separately.) And finally ratio measurement encompasses all of the elements of cardinal measurement and, in addition, permits assertions such as the heaviness of A as measured by its weight is three times that of B. The main difference between cardinal and ratio measurement is that in the latter case, the position of the zero never changes regardless of whether, in the above example, the measurement is in pounds, ounces, or kilograms. This is not true with cardinal measures of, say, temperature where 0° in Centigrade is 32° Fahrenheit, and 0° in Fahrenheit is about $-18°$ Centigrade.[7]

The numbers of nominal, ordinal, cardinal, and ratio measures are all drawn from scales. These scales reflect the properties described above.[8] Thus it is well-known that nominal scales are completely arbitrary. The only requirement is that a different number be assigned to each category. Ordinal scales

[6] For a more detailed discussion, see Katzner [15, Sect. 2.2].

[7] Temperature measures satisfy a more general version of the cardinality property than that described above for weight: Consider two objects A and B each having a different manifestation of the property "hotness." Let A and B be combined by transfering energy from the warmer object to the cooler one until they both have the same hotness. Then the hotness of A and B combined is measured as the *weighted* sum of the temperatures of A and B separately. For the special case in which both objects have the same "specific heat," the weight assigned to each is its mass divided by the total mass of A and B taken together.

[8] Katzner [15, Sect. 2.2].

(e.g., ordinal utility scales) are unique up to increasing, continuous transformations. Using the square or logarithm of the numbers, μ, on an ordinal scale (provided all scale values are positive) is equivalent to, and conveys the same information as, the original numbers. Such transformations, referred to below as *permissible* or *admissible* transformations, may be written as $T(\mu)$ and, assuming they exist, the first-order derivatives $T(\mu) > 0$ everywhere except, possibly, at "isolated" points where they may vanish. Cardinal scales (e.g., the Centigrade and Fahrenheit scales) are unique only up to increasing, linear transformations like $T(\mu) = \alpha\mu + \beta$ (where $\alpha > 0$), and ratio scales (e.g., pound and inch scales) are unique up to increasing, linear transformations for which $\beta = 0$. In these latter cases, the admissible transformations of scale are the $T(\mu) = \alpha\mu + \beta$ and $T(\mu) = \alpha\mu$, respectively.[9]

To examine what can happen when a variable legitimately measured only on an ordinal scale is regarded as a variable measured on a cardinal or ratio scale, focus attention on the variable "effort." Assume, for the sake of argument, that effort can be understood as a unidimensional concept permitting scalar rather than vector representation, and suppose that effort can legitimately be measured on an ordinal scale.[10] For effort to be cardinally measured it would be necessary to describe how the combination of two manifestations of effort calibrated on the same effort scale could be combined so that the combined manifestations could be gauged as the sum of the measures of each separately. This is accomplished for physical properties such as longness by marking off the lengths of two objects separately on a ruler, then placing them end-to-end and marking off their combined lengths as the sum of the two individual lengths. But in the case of effort, since there are no generally accepted yardsticks (like rulers, balances, or columns of mercury) with respect to which an analogous combination operation can be performed, at present it is hard to see how effort could be measured cardinally. It is not good enough to proceed on the basis of a belief that effort is cardinally calibrated and that eventually a cardinal scale for it will be found. For until such a scale becomes available (if, indeed, one ever does), there is no way to be sure that analyses that rest on that belief have anything to do with the real world. Moreover, if it were permissible under these conditions to assume that effort were a cardinally quantified vari-

[9] Mathematicians often describe $T(\mu) = a\mu + \beta$ as an affine transformation. When doing so, the word "linear" would be applied only for the case in which $\beta = 0$.

[10] The first of these assumptions is questionable; the second, at least in so far as the presence of ordinality is concerned, potentially so. Currie and Steedman [8, p. 136] cast doubt on the former. To justify the latter, it would be necessary to verify that the sufficient conditions guaranteeing the existence of ordinal scales are in force. See Katzner [15, p. 40]. In any case, there is little harm in making such assumptions for present purposes.

able, then any variable, no matter how farfetched, for which cardinal measures are not yet known, such as, for example, love, fear, self esteem, etc., could be treated as if it were cardinally appraised. And the gains from such practices are likely to be regarded as suspect. Thus, it would seem, those who would analytically employ effort as a cardinal variable would need to demonstrate how an appropriate cardinal scale can be constructed.[11] Regardless, effort is taken as only an ordinal variable here in order to illustrate the difficulties that can arise when an ordinally calibrated variable is treated as if it were cardinally gauged. Denote the ordinal effort variable by the symbol e and assume that e can range over all non-negative real numbers.

Consider an equation, e.g., a production function, of the form

$$x = f(e), \tag{1}$$

where x is a scalar variable quantified on a ratio scale and f is a real-valued function. Of course, the value of x depends on the value of e which reflects the effort that the number e represents. But the value of e depends on the scale on which effort is measured, and hence so does x. Applying a permissible transformation to that scale, that is, substituting $T(e)$, where $T'(e) > 0$ everywhere, in place of e in (1), gives

$$x = F(e) = f(T(e)). \tag{2}$$

Equation (1) may be viewed as a special case of (2) in which T is the identity transformation. Were effort measured on a cardinal scale (in which case, recall, $T(e) = \alpha e + \beta$, where $\alpha > 0$), then a value for x given e could be found relative to the units in which effort is calibrated and the position of the zero on the effort scale. But effort is measured only ordinally and, for that reason,

---

11 An individual's output per hour, for example, might be thought of as a "measure" of his effort per hour. But since output (which is appraised on a ratio scale) depends, in addition to effort, on many things like the capacity of the individual, job conditions, the technology available, etc., it is usually not possible to determine, in a theoretically meaningful way, what portion of output represents effort alone. Alternatively, effort per hour might be "measured" by the number of minutes per hour actually spent working divided by 60 (this is similar to Weisskopf, Bowles, and Gordon [22, p. 393]), or the sums of times (e.g., minutes) actually required to do specific tasks relative to standard, predetermined times (Bennett and Smith-Gravine [6] and Schor [18, pp. 4-7]). The latter, too, are ratio measures like weight and length. But as with output per hour, it may be argued that they do not mirror exactly what is meant when speaking of effort. And were any to be employed as a proxy for effort, their use would be subject to the difficulties described in Section III below. For these reasons, and also because none of the three has yet gained general acceptance as a measure of effort, they may be regarded as inadmissible as measures of effort here.

the concept of "units of measurement" is not so clear cut.[12] Hence even if an effort and a value for e representing it on some ordinal scale were designated, a unique value for x could still not be determined because the scale on which effort is gauged cannot be specified with sufficient particularity.

Matters are further complicated by the fact that even though e has been assumed to vary over non-negative (ordinal) numbers, permissible transformations of scale such as $T(e) = -\lambda^{-e}$, where $\lambda > 1$, result in negative transformed variable values $T(e)$. Thus the domain of f has to be extendable to the entire real line in order for (2) to be meaningful. Moreover, the domain of F clearly depends on the particular admissible transformation invoked. In the previous example, that domain is modified from $\{e : e \geq 0\}$ when T is the identity transformation to $\{e : e < 0\}$. As a further example, the permissible transformation $T(e) = e/(1+e)$ changes $\{e : e \geq 0\}$ to $\{e : 0 \leq e \leq 1\}$. Thus, as an absolute, the earlier assumption that $e \geq 0$ is neither necessary nor appropriate. Confluent with all ordinally measured variables, the range of e is entirely dependent on the scale with respect to which e is gauged.

The equation $x = F(e)$ in (2) is intended to describe a relation between effort and x. The graph of this relation, i.e., the graph of F, is usually drawn in the e-x plane, where values of e appear on the horizontal axis and those for x are identified on the vertical axis. The definition of the x-axis is standard and presents no new problems. But the numbers on the e-axis are determined only up to increasing transformations. To see what is involved, fix one scale for measuring effort and denote the numbers on that scale by e. Then each value of e is uniquely associated with a distinct manifestation of effort that could, in principle, be described verbally. Now suppose a new scale were introduced that squared the numbers on the old scale. For the e-axis to reflect this new scale, the manifestation of effort that was formerly associated with,

---

[12] One way to see this is as follows: With cardinal or ratio measurement, the relationship between different units of measurement is independent of the position on any particular scale. Thus, for example, 1 inch is always 2.54 centimeters regardless of whether 1 inch or 10 inches is under consideration. This property of independence is part of what is accepted as intuitive and correct in typical discussions that involve changes in units of measurement in relation to equations like (2). But the unit length on the original ordinal scale for effort is given by

$$(e+1) - e,$$

and transforming the scale by, say, $T(e) = e^2$, maps that unit length into

$$(e+1)^2 - e^2 = 2e + 1,$$

which depends on the value of e on the original scale. Thus the relation between the units of measurement on the two scales is not the same everywhere and, as a result, ambiguity is introduced into the notion of units of measurement itself.

say 3, must now be associated with 9. Without further adjustment, this means that the e-axis has been redefined, and the graph of the relation between e and x is "stretched" to accommodate the new definition. The old and new relations between e and x cannot be compared because they are particularized in different spaces. Alternatively, if e in (1) is replaced by $T(e) = e^2$ in parallel to the derivation of (2), then the e-axis remains unaltered and the change in scale is reflected in a modified relation between e and x. Under such conditions the old and new relations are defined over the same domain and can, therefore, be compared. To preserve the ability to make such comparisons, subsequent discussion takes the latter approach to transformations of scale.

It could be argued that each alteration of scale in (2) could be accompanied by an appropriate modification of f so as to keep, for each value of e, the value of x under F constant. In that case, the equation $x = F(e)$ would be unchanged by transformations of scale. But the question would remain of how the original scale represented by the symbol e would be selected. Since that choice would still be arbitrary, and since each choice would provide a different functional relationship (with different properties) between effort and x, it would become necessary to examine a relation of the form

$$x = G(e) = F(T(e)),$$

where $T(e)$ would represent alternative possibilities for the original scale. This would bring discussion back to the point at which it began. Thus, since it is not possible to determine an initial production function whose properties are independent of the selection of $T(e)$, the production function with which such an analysis is to begin cannot be specified. The only way to avoid the problem is to take e as a non-quantified variable whose variable values are the verbal descriptions of the different manifestations of effort mentioned above. Then (1) would associate a unique value of x to each verbal description, and f would be independent of any scale on which e might be measured. But the economics literature has not taken this approach, preferring instead to treat e as if it were at least cardinally quantified. Since the present intent is to explore the implications of such practices in the absence of any cardinal measures of effort, the proper focus here is on equations (1) and (2) with e ordinally gauged.

The previously described inability to obtain a unique value of x from a value of e according to (2) is illustrated in the no-shirking condition derived by Shapiro and Stiglitz [19, p. 436, equation (5)]. Their equation expresses the wage above which the employee will not shirk as a function of several variables, including effort. If effort turns out, in fact, to be only ordinally quantified, then by treating effort as if it were a cardinally calibrated variable, one might be led to believe that, given appropriate variable values, this critical wage is uniquely determinate as the critical wage in reality when, as just demonstrated, it is not. Of course, it is always possible to assume that effort is measured on a cardinal scale for the purposes of their model. But without any justification for doing so, the equation still cannot reveal anything about the critical wage in the real world. This dilemma can be resolved only by finding a cardinal measure of effort that is (i) consistent with perceived reality and (ii) acceptable to everyone in the same manner as Fahrenheit, say, is taken as a measure of temperature. And such a measure, at least at the moment, is nowhere in sight.

There is, however, a determination-by-equation context in which the absence of a cardinal gauge for effort does not matter. To describe it, consider, for a moment, one of the standard methods of explaining the observation of a price-quantity pair in an isolated market. To explain what was seen, a model is often constructed by assuming that, at the moment the observation was taken, there was a market demand curve and a market supply curve each passing through the observed point in price-quantity space.[13] The observation is then understood as the outcome of the interaction of demand and supply. No empirical tests are required; no attempt is made to link particular demand and supply curves with what was seen. It is a matter of interpretation. The only necessity is that the model be specified sufficiently so that there are always demand and supply curves intersecting at the relevant points. Although the existence of solutions of simultaneous relations systems with ordinal variables is often scale dependent,[14] for a single equation like (2), say, as long as all values of the dependent variable x that can potentially be observed appear on the left-hand side for some value of the independent variable e regardless of the scale on which e is appraised, then this general kind of explanation of observed values of x based on (2) will work. The same is true in the circumstance of the Shapiro-Stiglitz equation. If the purpose of their model is general explanation, that is, to demonstrate only that an observed wage could be understood as the critical wage, and if it can be shown, under the conditions of the model, that no matter what the effort scale employed, all relevant non-negative numbers can arise as critical wages in their equation with appropriate variation of the independent variables, then there is no problem. But because of the ordinality of

---

[13] Katzner [16, pp. 15-17]. See also Sect. 1 of Essay 3 in this volume.

[14] For example, let $x = e$ and $x = 2 - e$ be a two-equation system in x and e where, as before, e is ordinally measured and x is gauged on a ratio scale. The solution of this system is $x = e = 1$. Now apply the admissible transformation $T(e) = -\lambda^{-e}$, where λ is any positive real number greater than unity. The system becomes $x = -\lambda^{-e}$ and $x = 2 + \lambda^{-e}$, which has no solution since there is no value of e such that $\lambda^{-e} = -1$.

e (assuming it comes to that), there does not, as argued above, exist a unique critical wage determined by their equation that can be identified as the critical wage in the real world. Concrete explanation, that is, is not possible.

Generally, then, there are two situations in which a lack of cardinality in the measurement of a variable is of no consequence. First, if the properties that structure the model, that is, the analytical characteristics used in its manipulation, are qualitatively the same as those conveyed by the ordinal properties of the ordinally numerical variable values, as is the case with, for example, ordinal utility in the traditional theory of demand, then cardinal or ratio measurement is not necessary. Second, if a model is intended only to provide a framework for general explanation with non-specific links to the real world, and if the critical properties of that model such as the ability to determine all appropriate values of the dependent variable in an equation, hold for all scales on which the ordinal variables are gauged, then analysis can proceed on the basis of ordinal calibration alone. It is clear, however, that beyond the boundaries defined by these two situations, the ability of a model containing ordinally measured variables to explain real-world phenomena generally or concretely breaks down. The next section examines the extent to which some of the aforementioned critical properties are scale dependent when, with respect to one variable, viz. effort, only ordinal measurement is possible. Clearly, the presence of scale dependency implies a collapse of the model's explanatory capability.

II

Return now to equation (2). Denote the first- and second-order derivatives of f, which are assumed to exist, by f' and f'', respectively. Were e appraised on a cardinal scale, then applying a permissible transformation of the latter, i.e., switching T from the identity transformation to $T(e) = \alpha e + \beta$ (where $\alpha > 0$) in (2), and differentiating gives

$$\frac{dx}{de} = \alpha f'(\alpha e + \beta),$$

and

$$\frac{d^2x}{de^2} = \alpha^2 f''(\alpha e + \beta).$$

Although, at each e, the magnitudes and sometimes the signs of these derivatives vary with the alteration in scale, although, that is, at each e the steepness and curvature as well as the directions of that steepness and curvature of the graph of F can modify, and although the graph changes its location (since the position of the zero on the e-axis is different with the new scale), the general shape of the graph necessarily remains the same. If $f'(e) > 0$ everywhere, then so is $\alpha f'(\alpha e + \beta)$. And if $f(e)$ rises to a maximum at $\bar{e}$, declining thereafter, then $f(\alpha e + \beta)$ does too, except that the maximizing value of e is different. (Were e measured on a ratio scale so that β would then be zero, the identical conclusions would apply except that the graph would no longer shift its location.)

Because e is actually measured on only an ordinal scale, however, matters are somewhat different. For present purposes, it is only necessary to consider admissible transformations $T(e)$ for which T' exists and is positive everywhere, and for which the second-order derivative T'' also exists. Applying such a permissible transformation T to the ordinal scale on which e is measured and differentiating (2),

$$\frac{dx}{de} = T'(e)f'(T(e)),$$

and

$$\frac{d^2x}{de^2} = [T'(e)]^2 f''(T(e)) + T''(e)f'(T(e)). \tag{3}$$

With the scale change here, at each e both the magnitude and direction of the curvature of the graph of F depend, in part, on the magnitude and sign of T'', and the general shape of the graph can modulate. Thus, for example, applying the transformation $T(e) = e^{1/4}$ to $f(e) = e^2$, where $e \geq 0$, changes F from $F(e) = e^2$ (here T in (2) is the identity transformation) to $F(e) = e^{1/2}$, and alters the graph of F from increasing and strictly convex to increasing and strictly concave. The same phenomenon is also illustrated by the next example below. Regardless, such modification will be significant in subsequent discussion.

Turn now to the problem of maximization. (Analogous arguments could be made in the case of minimization.) Suppose, referring back to equation (1) where e is ordinally calibrated and non-negative, that f has a unique maximum at some interior point $\bar{e}$. Then because application of permissible transformations to the scale on which e is measured (i.e., replacing T as the identity transformation in (2) by any other admissible T) may alter the signs of its derivatives and the shape of its graph, admissible transformations of scale exist for which the resulting F has no maximum at all. As an illustration, the function $f(e) = -e^2$ on $\{e : -\infty \leq e \leq \infty\}$ has a unique maximum at

$e = 0$. And using the transformation $T(e) = -\lambda^{-e}$, where $\lambda > 1$, results in $F(e) = -\lambda^{-2e}$, for which a maximum does not exist.

Although most maximization problems in economics do not concern the unconstrained optimization of functions of the form of (2), a similar conclusion seems to apply quite generally. To consider a highly simplified situation, let

$$\pi(x) = px - wF^{-1}(x), \tag{4}$$

where $p > 0$ and $w > 0$ are parameters, F^{-1} denotes the inverse of F in (2), and T in (2) is the identity transformation. (This clearly could be interpreted as a profit function with p representing output price, w the price per unit of effort, and $wF^{-1}(x)$ the total cost of producing output x.) Suppose a model consisting of the selection of x to maximize $\pi(x)$ in (4) is intended to explain certain observed behavior. Restricting F to be, say, increasing and strictly concave usually ensures that π has a unique interior maximum. But, as has been seen, altering the scale for e changes the shape of F. Such modification can shift the unique maximum, destroy its presence, or even convert it into a unique minimum. For example, suppose $F(e) = e^{1/2}$, for $e > 0$. Then $F^{-1}(x) = x^2$ and a unique maximum of π can be calculated as $x = p/2w$ by solving the appropriate first-order maximization condition derived from (4). Applying the transformation $T(e) = e^{1/2}$ results in $F(e) = e^{1/4}$ and the different maximizing value $x = (p/4w)^{1/3}$. Alternatively, applying $T(e) = e^2$ reduces F to $F(e) = e$ and π to a linear function, in which case, either all values of x maximize (4) or no interior maximum exists. Lastly, applying the transformation $T(e) = e^4$ to the original production function converts F into a strictly convex function, and the first-order condition from (4) identifies a minimum rather than a maximum. Generally, in light of (3), for many $F(e) = f(T(e))$ whose second-order derivative is negative everywhere when $T(e) = e$, a transformation of scale can be found such that, upon its application, the same second-order derivative becomes positive everywhere. And in all circumstances in which a maximum continues to exist, transformations of scale modify the maximizing value. It follows that the intention to explain observed behavior in terms of this model can be subverted by the ordinality of e. Since each scale is as good as the next, since some scales can produce unique maxima while admissible transformations of them do not, and since no two scales that produce unique maxima yield the same maximum (the latter is not an issue if only general explanation is of interest), the maximization of (4) with respect to e often cannot be specified fully enough to sustain meaning and, in that case, the model is unable to provide an explanation of the observed behavior.

A specific example of a well-known model in the economics literature that encounters such obstacles is the efficiency wage model.[15] In that model, f in (1) becomes the appropriately differentiable production function $x = f(eL)$, and (2) is replaced by

$$x = F(eL) = f(T(e)L), \tag{5}$$

where $x \geq 0$ represents output, $e \geq 0$ denotes effort per unit of labor input, $L \geq 0$ is the number of units of labor employed, and T is an admissible differentiable transformation of scale as before. Here e is also a twice-differentiable function of the wage $w > 0$ and is assumed, for purposes of present argument, to be capable of ordinal measurement only. The model further requires that w and L be selected simultaneously to maximize

$$\pi(w, L) = pf(T(e)L) - wL,$$

where π indicates profit and $p > 0$ the output price. Let $T(e)$ first be the identity transformation. Then using subscripts to denote partial derivatives, representing the first-order derivative of e with respect to w by e', and solving the first-order conditions

$$\begin{aligned} \pi_L(w, L) &= pef'(eL) - w = 0, \\ \pi_w(w, L) &= pLe'f'(eL) - L = 0, \end{aligned} \tag{6}$$

leads, under appropriate assumptions, to the determination of unique values for L and w. The latter is called the efficiency wage and is found from (6) as

$$\frac{e}{e'} = w. \tag{7}$$

Since (7) may also be deduced from the minimization of wL/e with respect to w, the efficiency wage is usually characterized as that wage which minimizes labor cost per unit of effort. Two requirements that are part of the sufficient conditions ensuring the existence of unique global maxima of $\pi(w, L)$ are as follows: For all $(w, L) > 0$,

$$\pi_{LL} = pe^2 f'' < 0, \tag{8}$$

and

$$\pi_{ww} = p[e']^2 L^2 f'' + pLe'' f' < 0, \tag{9}$$

---

[15] e.g., Stiglitz [20, p. 27, n. 47].

where subscripts on π again denote partial derivatives, e'' is the second-order derivative of e with respect to w, and functional arguments have been dropped. Clearly, (8) implies that f'', as a function of (w, L), is negative everywhere.

Applying an admissible differentiable transformation to the scale on which e is measured in (5), i.e., removing the supposition that T is the identity transformation, modifies the expressions in (6)-(9), respectively, as indicated below:

$$\begin{aligned} \pi_L(w, L) &= pT(e)f'(T(e)L) - w = 0, \\ \pi_w(w, L) &= pLT'(e)e'f'(T(e)L) - L = 0, \end{aligned} \tag{10}$$

$$\frac{T(e)}{T'(e)e'} = w, \tag{11}$$

$$\pi_{LL} = p[T(e)]^2 f'', \tag{12}$$

$$\pi_{ww} = T' \left\{ p[e']^2 L^2 f'' + pL[e'']f' \right\} + pLT''[e']^2 f'. \tag{13}$$

Evidently, comparing (11), which is derived from (10), with (7) reveals, in confluence with earlier argument, that a unique efficiency wage can never be determined.[16]

Moreover, although $\pi_{LL} < 0$ in (8) ensures $\pi_{LL} < 0$ in (12) (since the former guarantees $f'' < 0$), the inequality in (9) carries no such implication for the sign of π_{ww} in (13). For the latter sign clearly depends, in part, on the magnitude of T' and on the sign and magnitude of T''. (It may also vary with e.) In particular, an appropriate choice of T, could turn (9) into $\pi_{ww} > 0$ everywhere, in which case the necessary conditions for the existence of any maximum at all are violated. To illustrate this last phenomenon, let $e = w^{1/2}$ and $f(eL) = (eL)^{1/2}$. Then the general profit function with arbitrary transformation-of-scale function is

$$\pi(w, L) = [T(w^{1/2})L]^{1/2} - wL. \tag{14}$$

Upon partial differentiation with respect to w, (14) becomes,

$$\pi_w(w, L) = \frac{1}{4} L^{1/2} [T(w^{1/2})]^{-1/2} T'(w^{1/2}) w^{-1/2} - L. \tag{15}$$

[16] A similar point has been made by Currie and Steedman [8, pp. 137-139].

Now on the one hand, if $T(e) = e$, then $T'(e) = 1$, and it can be deduced from (15) that for all $(w, L) > 0$,

$$\pi_{ww}(w, L) = -\frac{3}{16}L^{1/2}w^{-7/4} < 0.$$

On the other, it similarly follows that if $T(e) = e^5$, then $T'(e) = 5e^4$ and

$$\pi_{ww}(w, L) = \frac{5}{16}L^{1/2}w^{-3/4} > 0,$$

for all $(w, L) > 0$. In the latter case, there can be no positive vector (w, L) that maximizes $\pi(w, L)$. Thus, if it turns out that effort is capable of measurement only on an ordinal scale, then since the scale on which e is appraised varies freely with arbitrary, differentiably increasing transformations and without loss of information, some efficiency wage models can never be specified sufficiently to ensure that the same unique maximum always exists independently of the particular scale in use. Therefore, treating e to be cardinally measured when it is not, can lead to the false conclusion that the model is capable of explaining real world behavior.

It might be thought, in this case, that the efficiency wage model could be rescued by replacing $x = f(eL)$ with $x = \zeta(w, L)$, where ζ is a function that relates combinations of wages and labor-unit values to output. Here the inclusion of w as an argument of ζ is meant to roughly capture the part played by effort in production, and the discarding of e eliminates the ordinal measurement problem. Now, of course, there is nothing wrong with using ζ as the basis for constructing a model of the firm. But because, as described earlier in reference to (1), the relation between wages and ordinally gauged effort values cannot be specified with sufficient precision, it is not possible to meaningfully identify the role of effort in such a model. Nor is it possible to characterized the profit-maximizing wage as that which minimizes the labor cost per unit of effort. Hence the efficiency wage model can no longer be said to be a model of the efficiency wage as that wage is normally defined.

Maximization subject to constraint can suffer from similar difficulties. Consider the utility function $u(x, T(e))$, where x, T, and e are defined as before. The fact that utility might decrease with increased effort is of no consequence. Suppose the model to be invoked in explaining behavior consists of choosing x and e to maximize utility subject to the linear budget constraint

$$ax + be = c, \tag{16}$$

where a, b, and c are parameters. When T is the identity transformation, the first-order maximization conditions consist of (16) together with

$$\frac{u_x(x,e)}{u_e(x,e)} = \frac{a}{b},$$

and the curvature of indifference curves depends on the sign (taken to be the same everywhere) of the bordered Hessian determinant

$$|U(x,e)| = \begin{vmatrix} 0 & u_x & u_e \\ u_x & u_{xx} & u_{xe} \\ u_e & u_{ex} & u_{ee} \end{vmatrix},$$

assuming all derivatives exist continuously, where u_x and u_e are the first-order partial derivatives of u with respect to x and e, u_{xx} and u_{ee} are the second-order partial derivatives with respect to the same variables, u_{xe} and u_{ex} are the second-order cross-partial derivatives, and functional arguments of derivatives are omitted where convenient. The same curvature or sign of $|U(x,e)|$ also determines whether the solution-vector of the first-order conditions is unique, and whether it actually identifies a constrained maximum instead of a constrained minimum. However, applying a permissible differentiable transformation of scale (that is, transposing T from the identity to another admissible differentiable transformation) can be shown to result in new first-order conditions

$$\frac{u_x(x,T(e))}{u_e(x,T(e))T'(e)} = \frac{a}{b},$$

$$ax + bT(e) = c,$$

and a new bordered Hessian determinant of the form

$$(T')^2|U| - (u_x)^2 u_e T'',$$

where, in the latter expression, functional arguments have again been dropped to simplify notation. Hence, as argued previously, the interior vector (x,e) that maximizes utility subject to the budget constraint, should one exist, rests on the ordinal scale used to gauge e. In addition, the sign of the new bordered Hessian determinant depends, in part, on the signs and magnitudes of $|U|$ and T''. It follows that if assumptions ensuring the existence of a unique maximum, including appropriate global sign conditions on $|U|$ and u_e, are imposed for the situation in which T is the identity transformation, then applying a permissible differentiable transformation of scale to e could lead to a circumstance in which the solution of the modified first-order conditions, if it still exists, is not associated with a maximum at all. Once again, the model can be rendered meaningless and its explanatory power destroyed by the ordinality of the scale on which effort is measured. Although their constraint is non-linear, the Becker-Lewis constrained maximization with respect to child quality [5] cited at the outset is an example of an analysis in the economics literature that is plagued in this way.

III

Attention now turns to the use of proxy variables. Proxy variables are employed in economics when exact measures of the variables under consideration are not available. Proxies may be (and have been) invoked for variables that are non-quantifiable, or partly or even fully quantified. Return, again, to equation (1) with e ordinally calibrated, where each value of e is uniquely linked to a distinct manifestation of effort that is capable of verbal description. Suppose an appropriate ordinal gauge for e is not available. Let ϵ be a proxy measure for e. Typically, ϵ will measure some, but not all, of that which is measured by e, and it will also measure elements that are not measured by e as well. But if ϵ is to be a proxy, it must in some "fractional" way represent the same thing as e, and this, in turn, means that there has to exist a functional relation mapping the values of e into those of ϵ. Denote the latter relation by $\epsilon = R(e)$. Generally, R is not known. To use ϵ as a proxy for e is to use ϵ in place of e in (1). But upon doing so, $\epsilon = R(e)$ may then be substituted into $x = f(\epsilon)$ to obtain

$$x = F(e) = f(R(e)), \tag{17}$$

where the function F is generally not the same as that of equation (2). If, in addition, the possibility of scale changes were to be accounted for, then (17) would have to be rewritten as

$$x = F(e) = f(R(T(e))), \tag{18}$$

where T is any admissible transformation. But because including T here would lead to considerable repetition of the argument already worked out in Sections I and II, the focus of this section is on equation (17). The same conclusions derived for an ordinally quantified variable e would then apply to circumstances, in different contexts, in which e were redefined as cardinally or ratio quantified. Moreover, when e is, in fact, only ordinally calibrated, these conclusions have to be supplemented by those arising from the introduction of scale transformations permitted in (18).

Actually, however, assuming R is twice differentiable, all of the calculations of derivatives, etc. in Section II apply here anyway with R substituted for T. And the conclusions relating to the use of proxies in these calculations are similar for the viability of economic analysis with proxies to those for the use of ordinal variables in the previous section. Of course, in the case of ordinal variables, the derivative T' is known to be positive and, under appropriate conditions, this fact permits some transfer of assumptions and properties across different ordinal scales. Thus, as long as a transformation is not too drastic, slopes of graphs will not change sign and a maximum of f in (1), should one exist, will be preserved, albeit at a different value of e. However, in the situation with proxies, none of R, R', and R'' are known. Thus, in addition to the inability to properly specify the same kinds of maximization models that could not be specified in the context of Section II, it is not even possible to be sure of the signs of the slopes of graphs and of their curvatures.

Plainly put, without knowing R, there is little sense to the use of proxies in analyses involving the kind of theoretical apparatuses discussed here. Introducing proxies explicitly into the model leaves it vastly under specified. Waiting until after the analysis of the model is completed and then using proxies to "test" or "estimate" the results necessarily implies that the tests or estimates will have little bearing on the model itself. In the latter case, the model cannot imply any knowable restrictions that observations would have to satisfy to be consistent with the model; and the observations can not imply any knowable restrictions that the model would have to satisfy to explain the observations. (The use of occupation and education as proxies for an individual's wage by Fair [10, pp. 52-58] cited earlier falls into such a trap.) All of this, of course, is without even taking into account the ordinality of any ordinal variables present. And the only ways to avoid the problems that arise with proxies is either to discover R or to make the proxy variables the true variables of the model.

In response to this argument, it might be protested that there is often no other method of testing or estimating a model except by using proxies. Why not settle for the best that can be done, imperfect as it is?[17] But without knowing R, testing and estimating cannot provide any information known to be relevant to the model. It would therefore be well to keep Hayek's warning cited at the outset in mind, viz., that there is a significant danger of accepting a false theory, and that such acceptance could have serious consequences. Moreover, as suggested (by citation) in the next section, there are, in fact, legitimate

[17] This is similar to the "some number is better that no number" fallacy identified by Diamond and Hausman [9, p. 58].

means of constructing, testing, and estimating models when measures of the requisite variables are not known or do not exist.

IV

But what if prediction were the only goal? When a variable that is only ordinally measured is present, why not arbitrarily designate some scale as the scale to be employed, take the numbers so obtained to be fully quantified, and then use a model as the basis of prediction with respect to that scale? In the case of a proxy variable, why not estimate the appropriate equations of a model using the proxy and then predict future values of the dependent variables from the estimated equations? Unfortunately, neither of these procedures is entirely satisfactory for the following reasons: In the case of an ordinal variable, say effort, the problem is to construct a suitable ordinal scale. It is not enough just to assume its existence. If prediction of real phenomena is to be undertaken, it is still necessary to have a scale for measuring effort that can be applied in actual circumstances. Since, at present, there is no generally acceptable method of calibrating effort even ordinally, it is hard to see how this could be done. Clearly, it might be possible to come up with proxy variables such as those described in n. 11 on p. 180, but this changes the question from how to handle the ordinal scale to how to deal with proxies. Turning, therefore, to the latter, there is no reason why an equation could not be estimated with proxy variables and used to predict future values of the dependent variable. The difficulty is that, as argued above, without knowledge of R, this equation has nothing knowable to say about the model that generated the equation in the first place. All such prior theoretical considerations have become irrelevant. A new and independent model has been created that consists of only the estimated equation with the proxy variables substituted for the original variables in its expression. And, since the original theoretical structure has no known relation to this equation, a justification for the equation itself has yet to be provided.

This does not seem to be a happy state of affairs. Indeed, the future for the use of ordinal variables and proxies appears to be bleak when the purpose of analysis is to develop theoretical structures and test and estimate them against reality. But there is an alternative. When variables are not fully quantified or when they are fully quantified but numerical measures of them are not available, it is always possible to go back to the verbal manifestations that underlie them. By using verbal descriptions of this sort to characterize variable values, models can be constructed that are quite analogous to those obtained for fully quantified variables. Functions can be defined[18] and maximized. Systems of simultaneous functional relations can be solved, and sufficient conditions ensuring their unique solution can be given. Periodic equations describing dynamic movement over time can also be specified, and these equations may generate both equilibrium time paths and other time paths that converge to or diverge from the equilibrium path. The latter, of course, requires a characterization of what it means for unquantified variable values to become "close" together so that the notion of convergence has meaning. Lastly, such models can even be confronted with reality through statistical tests and estimations. All of this has been established with full mathematical rigor elsewhere (Katzner [15]; see also Essay 4 in this volume). Thus, although some of the convenience and power of numbers is lost, giving up, where necessary, the use of ordinally measured and proxy variables does not destroy the economist's ability to analyze rigorously those phenomena of interest that are not completely amenable to at least cardinal measurement.

References

1. Akerlof, G. A., "The Market for 'Lemons:' Qualitative Uncertainty and the Market Mechanism," *Quarterly Journal of Economics* 84 (1970), pp. 488-500.
2. ________, "A Theory of Social Custom, of which Unemployment May Be One Consequence," *Quarterly Journal of Economics* 94 (1980), pp. 749-775.
3. Azzi, C. and R. Ehrenberg, "Household Allocation of Time and Church Attendance," *Journal of Political Economy* 83 (1975), pp. 27-56.
4. Barro, R. J., "Economic Growth in a Cross Section of Countries," *Quarterly Journal of Economics* 106 (1991), pp. 407-443.
5. Becker, G. S. and H. G. Lewis, "On the Interaction between the Quantity and Quality of Children," *Journal of Political Economy* 81, no. 2, Pt. 1 (March/April, 1973), pp. s279-s288.
6. Bennett, A. and S. Smith-Gavine, "The Percentage Utilisation of Labor Index (PUL)," in *Working Below Capacity*, D. Bosworth and D. F. Heathfield, eds. (London: Macmillan, 1987), pp. 326-363.
7. Boulding, K. E., *Human Betterment* (Beverly Hills: SAGE, 1985).

---

[18] This has already been suggested above in the discussion that considered the possibility of offsetting transformations of scale in (2) with changes in f.

8. Currie, M. and I. Steedman, "Taking Effort Seriously," *Metroeconomica* 44 (1993), pp. 134-145.
9. Diamond, P. A. and J. H. Hausman, "Contingent Valuation: Is Some Number Better Than No Number?" *Journal of Economic Perspectives* 8, no. 4 (1994), pp. 45-64.
10. Fair, R. C., "A Theory of Extramarital Affairs," *Journal of Political Economy* 86 (1978), pp. 45-61.
11. von Hayek, F. A., "The Pretence of Knowledge," Nobel Memorial Lecture, December, 1974. Reprinted in *American Economic Review* 79, no. 6 (December, 1989 - membership survey issue), pp. 3-7.
12. Helliwell, J. F. and R. D. Putnam, "Economic Growth and Social Capital in Italy," *Eastern Economic Journal* 21 (1995), pp. 295-307.
13. Kalt, J. P. and M. A. Zupan, "Capture and Ideology in the Economic Theory of Politics," *American Economic Review* 74 (1984), pp. 279-300.
14. Katzner, D. W., *Choice and the Quality of Life* (Beverly Hills: SAGE, 1979).
15. ________, *Analysis without Measurement* (Cambridge: Cambridge University Press, 1983).
16. ________, *Walrasian Microeconomics* (Reading: Addison-Wesley, 1988).
17. ________, "Our Mad Rush to Measure: How Did We Get into This Mess?" *Methodus* 3, no.2 (December, 1991), pp. 18-26. This volume, Essay 2.
18. Schor, J. B., "Does Work Intensity Respond to Macroeconomic Variables? Evidence from British Manufacturing, 1970-1976," discussion paper 1379 (April, 1988), Harvard Institute of Economic Research, Harvard University, Cambridge.
19. Shapiro, C. and J. E. Stiglitz, "Equilibrium Unemployment as a Worker Discipline Device," *American Economic Review* 74 (1984), pp. 433-444.
20. Stiglitz, J. E., "The Causes and Consequences of the Dependence of Quality on Price," *Journal of Economic Literature* 25 (1987), pp. 1-48.
21. Thomson, Sir W. (Baron Kelvin), "Electrical Units of Measurement," in *Popular Lectures and Addresses* v. 1 (London: Macmillan, 1891), pp. 80-143.
22. Weisskopf, T. E., S. Bowles, and D. M. Gordon, "Hearts and Minds: A Social Model of U.S. Productivity Growth," *Brookings Papers on Economic Activity* 2 (1983), pp. 381-441.

9
Analysis with Ordinal Measurement[1]

Ever since Fisher and Pareto discovered at the end of the nineteenth century that increasing transformations of utility functions have no impact on the consumer demand functions derived from them, and hence that utility could be understood as being ordinal in character, economists have been familiar with ordinal measurement. Today, many other variables like product quality and effort, to name but two, find ordinal expression in economic models. Often, however, these variables have been treated as if they were cardinal variables, and this, in turn, has been shown to create a significant potential for errors and misconceptions (Katzner [5 (this volume, Essay 8)]). Models containing ordinally measured variables really do need to be constructed and manipulated keeping the presence of that ordinality clearly in mind. For such models frequently cannot maintain the same meaning, significance, and explanatory power as those whose variables are all cardinally or ratio calibrated, and the ability to manipulate the ordinal variables in them is often severely limited. Thus it is natural to ask about the kinds of things that can and cannot legitimately be accomplished when constructing and manipulating models with ordinal variables. The purpose of this paper is to examine some of the possibilities.

Generally, there are two situations in which the incorporation of an ordi-

---

[1] *Employment, Economic Growth and the Tyranny of the Market*, v. 2, P. Arestis, ed. (Cheltenham: Elgar, 1996), pp. 37-54. © Edward Elgar Publishing, Ltd. Reprinted with permission.
The author acknowledges with gratitude the help of Douglas Vickers.

nal variable in a model does not hinder the conduct of inquiry with that model. First, if the properties that structure the model, or, that is to say, the analytical characteristics used in its manipulation, are qualitatively the same as those conveyed by the ordinal properties of the ordinally numerical variable values, then the absence of cardinal or ratio gauges is of no consequence. Such is the case, for example, with ordinal utility in the traditional theory of demand. Second, if a model is intended only to provide a framework for general explanation with non-specific links to the real world, and if the critical properties of that model, such as the ability to determine all appropriate values of the dependent variable in an equation, hold for all scales on which the ordinal variable can be appraised, then the analysis can proceed on the basis of ordinal measurement alone. A well-known illustration of general explanation (albeit with ratio-measured variables) is the interpretation of market outcomes generally as arising from the interaction of demand and supply. But beyond the boundaries defined by these two situations, the ability of a model containing an ordinally calibrated variable to explain real-world phenomena breaks down. Among other things, it is often not even possible for the model to determine a unique value of the ordinal variable for all scales on which that variable might be measured (Katzner [5 (this volume, Essay 8)]).

It should also be noted that analysis can be conducted in the absence of any measurement of the variables involved at all (Katzner [3]; see also Essay 4 in this volume). That is, characterizing variable values as verbal description, functions can be defined and maximized. Systems of simultaneous functional equations can be solved and sufficient conditions ensuring their unique solution can be given. Periodic equations describing dynamic movement over time can also be specified, and these equations may generate both equilibrium time paths and other time paths that converge to or diverge from the equilibrium path. The latter, of course, requires a characterization of what it means for unquantified variable values to become "close" together so that the notion of convergence has meaning. But although analysis can be conducted without measurement in this manner, the question arises of how far the presence of a "little" measurement, that is, ordinal measurement, can go towards making argument what it normally could be with respect to numerical expression when all variables and parameters are fully quantifiable in a cardinal or ratio sense. It will be seen that, in many situations, and with the important exception of models like that of traditional demand theory, the answer turns out to be "not very far." After a preliminary discussion of the ordinal character of traditional demand theory, the paper turns to the properties of matrices, sets, and functions, and then moves on to the properties of systems of simultaneous equations, both static and dynamic. In all cases, at issue is whether the property specified is independent of the ordinal scale or scales in terms of which it finds expression. To the extent that it is, analysis with ordinal measurement in terms of that property can contribute to the conduct of inquiry. But properties that are ordinally scale-dependent cannot, as a rule, meaningfully be employed in analytical endeavor.

Traditional Demand Theory

One may begin with the obvious fact that all methods that are sound for analyzing a particular phenomenon in the absence of numerical gauges certainly remain valid if and when ordinal measures become available. Moreover, the benefits derived from the introduction of ordinal calibration into a previously unquantified setting include the ability to use ordinal numbers and all of the analytical techniques that are appropriate with them. Thus, for example, adding an assumption of ordinal measurement of all variables with respect to which a function of unquantified variables achieves a maximum, although not changing the fact of the existence of that maximum, does permit its expression with respect to at least some scales in ordinally numerical terms. But it does not follow that the replacement of non-quantified variable values by ordinally calibrated ones will always permit the derivation of even the same conclusions with numerical techniques as obtained originally without them. For while there are some constructs, such as the economist's model of constrained utility maximization in traditional demand theory, which are able to make good use of the additional properties conferred by the presence of ordinality, there are still many others that are critically dependent on the particular scale or scales on which that ordinality is expressed. The latter turns out to be true of the maximization with respect to ordinally measured variables described above. For in that case, as will be seen below, the existence of the underlying maximum will be recorded on some scales but not on others. Thus, if the maximum were not already known to exist in unquantified terms, and if an analysis of only ordinally calibrated variables were employed, then since the existence of the maximum is scale-dependent, a definitive conclusion concerning that existence cannot be secured. In these kinds of situations, the gains from introducing ordinal scales are minimal. For the same reason, similar conclusions concerning the inability to obtain definitive analytical results with ordinal relationships remain in force generally, even without any prior attempt to analyze in the absence of measurement.

The advantages of introducing ordinal measures where none previously existed depend on the particular discussion in question. An illustration is provided by the traditional theory of demand mentioned above (e.g., Katzner [2, Ch. 3]). This theory employs prices, quantities of goods, and income variables that are numerically gauged in the usual way. But it also contains the variable "utility" that is measured on an ordinal scale. In particular, the theory views the individual as possessing an ordinal utility function that exhibits sufficient properties (often including differentiability) to permit its maximization subject to a linear budget constraint. The budget constraint expresses the idea that once prices and the individual's income have been specified, the amount of each commodity that can be purchased is limited. The individual is assumed to behave as if he always chooses to buy those quantities of goods that maximize his utility subject to such a constraint. This allows the quantities the individual demands of goods (i.e., the quantities that maximize his utility subject to the budget constraint) to be understood as functions of prices and his income. The assumptions imposed on the utility function imply that these demand functions possess certain characteristics as prices and the individual's income hypothetically vary. Neither the demand functions nor their characteristics depends on the particular (differentiable — if the ordinal utility function is itself differentiable) ordinal scale on which utility is expressed.

It turns out that the traditional theory of demand can be recast so as to avoid the requirement that the utility variable be ordinally quantified (e.g., Uzawa [8]). Indeed, such a rearrangement appears to do away with the utility function and its properties altogether. In their place the individual is supposed to be able to order by personal preference all possible combinations of quantities of goods. This ordering is assumed to have its own properties and the argument proceeds by having the individual select the most preferred combination of quantities of commodities from those available, given prices and his income. Thus demand functions are obtained as before. These functions, too, exhibit characteristics as a result of the assumptions made on the preference ordering. However, the same assumptions also ensure the existence of a continuous but not-necessarily-differentiable ordinal utility function (Katzner [2, Sect. 2.1]), so that ordinal utility and its constrained maximization is implicitly, if not explicitly, present in the argument. There are, moreover, only small differences between the characteristics of demand functions derived directly from a preferences ordering and those secured from the ordinal-utility-function route, and neither are worth examining here.

Rather, the question to be asked is, what is there to be gained by formulating the theory in terms of an ordinal utility function when an alternative and similar theory is available in its absence? In the present case, the answer lies in that different mathematical techniques are needed in the arguments of the two approaches and, depending on the mathematical background of the individuals involving themselves with the theory, and depending on the use to which the theory is to be put, one approach may be more convenient and appropriate than the other. For most economists, the assumption that utility is ordinally measured affords more than sufficient ease and convenience to warrant its use, and the ordinal utility theory is, by far, the dominant approach employed today.

But there is a much deeper and more important issue that needs to be addressed. If, as has been noted, ordinal utility is present, at least implicitly, in the derivation of consumer demand functions regardless of whether it is used or not, what role does this ordinality play? What analytical conclusions of the theory of demand would not follow in its absence? To answer these questions, observe that not only is ordinal utility present in the derivation of consumer demand functions, but the presence of a continuous ordinal utility function is also logically equivalent to the presence of a preference ordering (with the standard properties). Hence to eliminate the ordinality it would be necessary either to discard the utility function and the preference ordering entirely, or to weaken the properties of the preference ordering sufficiently so that an ordinal utility function of any form is not implied. In both cases, a construction that makes use of constrained (ordinal) utility maximization or its counterpart in terms of preference orderings would, in general, no longer be possible.[2] There have been attempts to move in these directions (e.g., Katzner [2, Sect. 6.4], Sonnenschein [7]), but the new alternatives are colored in rather different hues than the original. In particular, the idea of maximization or its equivalent with respect to preference orderings as the driving force in the determination of demand has to be articulated in a modified way, and demand functions themselves lose at least one of their fundamental characteristics, namely, the so-called integrability condition. Thus ordinality is a significant part of the traditional derivation of consumer demand functions.

It should also be pointed out that the assumption of ordinality in the traditional theory of demand is capable of pushing analysis within that theory only so far. As suggested earlier, it does introduce a mathematically manipulable ordinal utility function (or preference ordering with appropriate properties)

[2] One exception arises by taking a standard utility function and changing indifference along each indifference to preference. Points on "higher" curves would remain preferred to all points on "lower" ones. But now, in a two-good case, say, moving along what was called an indifference curve by increasing quantities of, for example, good 2 at the expense of good 1 results in more preferred points. If the consumer were always to choose the most preferred point subject to the budget constraint (an assumption quite analogous to constrained utility maximization with "normal" preferences), then the same demand functions would arise as those generated before indifference along the indifference curves was changed to preference. See Katzner [4, pp. 74,75].

that would not otherwise exist, and it does lead to certain analytical conclusions that would not be possible in its absence. But the absence of cardinality of utility does leave gaps. With an ordinal utility function, for example, no economic meaning attaches to the partial derivatives or marginal utilities (assuming they exist) of the utility function. Marginal utilities are dependent on the particular scale on which utility is measured; for them to be economically significant, at least a cardinal utility scale is required. In many circumstances, however, the loss of meaning of marginal utilities is relatively minor. Furthermore, even without cardinality, the ratios of marginal utilities or marginal rates of substitution are still invariant under increasing transformations of scale, and hence economic meaning can be and is imparted to them.

Matrices, Sets and Functions

Before proceeding, it is worth pausing for a moment to recall briefly the nature of different kinds of scales and transformations of them. Ordinal scales (such as ordinal utility scales) are unique up to increasing, continuous transformations. Using the square or logarithm of the numbers, μ, on an ordinal scale[3] is equivalent to, and provides the same information as, the original numbers. Such transformations, often referred to as *permissible* or *admissible* transformations, may be written as $T(\mu)$, where the derivative $T'(\mu)$, if it exists, is positive everywhere except, possibly, for "isolated" points where $T(\mu) = 0$. Cardinal scales (e.g., the Centigrade and Fahrenheit scales) are unique only up to increasing, linear transformations like $T(\mu) = \alpha\mu + \beta$ (where $\alpha > 0$), and ratio scales (e.g., pound and inch scales) are unique up to increasing, linear transformations for which $\beta = 0$. In these latter cases, the admissible transformations of scale are the $T(\mu) = \alpha\mu + \beta$ and $T(\mu) = \alpha\mu$, respectively. To change or transform the numbers μ measured on a given scale into numbers measured on an alternative scale is to replace the original numbers by the transformed numbers $T(\mu)$, where T is an admissible transformation.

In spite of the success of the ordinal utility approach, there are many other situations in which the assumption of ordinality does not contribute much to analysis because the resulting argument decisively rests on the particular ordinal scales introduced. When this happens, analysis of the ordinally measured variables cannot, as has been suggested, proceed very far. In addition to marginal utilities, examples of analytical forms that, in an ordinal context, are

---

3 Squaring and taking the logarithm qualify as increasing, continuous transformations as long as all scale values are positive.

scale-dependent are easy to find. Thus it has been demonstrated elsewhere that both regression and factor analysis fall in this category. Specifically, the application of an increasing transformation to the data can reverse the signs of estimated coefficients in the former, and can change the number of variation-explaining factors that emerge in the latter (Katzner [3, pp. 44-48]). And, in the context of probabilistic uncertainty, the preferential ranking of two portfolios determined from expected utility calculations can be inverted upon application of an increasing transformation to the ordinal utilities of asset returns (Vickers [9, pp. 127-128]).

To obtain further illustrations, begin by considering a simple 2-by-2 matrix, A, in which the entries of each column are measured on separate ordinal scales:

$$A = \begin{bmatrix} 1 & 2 \\ 1/4 & 1 \end{bmatrix}.$$

The determinant of A, namely,

$$|A| = \frac{1}{2} > 0.$$

If the ordinal scale on which the entries of the second column of A are measured is transformed by $\alpha x + \beta$, where x varies over entries, $\alpha > 0$, and β is any real number, then $|A|$ becomes

$$\begin{vmatrix} 1 & 2\alpha + \beta \\ 1/4 & \alpha + \beta \end{vmatrix} = \frac{\alpha}{2} + \frac{3\beta}{4}.$$

Beside its ordinality, were this latter scale also a ratio scale, then β would vanish, in which case, since $\alpha > 0$, the sign of $|A|$ could not be modified by permissible scale transformations. But with only cardinal, and hence, *a fortiori*, ordinal measurement, β can be negative. Hence, given $\alpha > 0$, suitable and permissible choices of β could render $|A| = 0$ or $|A| < 0$. Thus variation of the ordinal (or cardinal) scales on which the ordinal (or cardinal) entries in the columns of a matrix are gauged are capable of altering the sign of the determinant of that matrix or of converting its determinant to or away from zero. The latter implies that the existence of an inverse of a matrix depends on the scales on which its ordinal (or cardinal) entries are measured.

There are many other potential properties of matrices that similarly depend on the ordinal or cardinal scales in use. For example, the matrix A defined above is positive definite,[4] indecomposable,[5] and has positive and distinct eigenvalues,[6] $1 \pm \frac{1}{2}\sqrt{2}$. Applying the admissible transformation $x - 2$ (obtained by letting $\alpha = 1$ and $\beta = -2$ in the previous discussion) to the ordinal (or cardinal) scales underlying both columns of A yields

$$\begin{bmatrix} -1 & 0 \\ -7/4 & -1 \end{bmatrix},$$

which is negative definite, decomposable, and whose eigenvalues, namely -1 and -1, are negative and equal. Therefore definiteness, decomposability, and both the signs (of the real parts) of and the distinctiveness of eigenvalues of ordinal (or cardinal) matrices all turn on the selection of ordinal (or cardinal) scales.

It should also be pointed out that there are operations on and properties of matrices with ordinally calibrated entries that are independent of the scales of measurement. The numbers of rows and columns (which is significant in determining if two matrices can be added or multiplied), commutativity and associativity of matrix addition, associativity of matrix multiplication, and distributivity of matrix addition and multiplication all fall into this category. If significant conclusions can be drawn from the application of such operations and the use of such properties, then the analysis of matrices with ordinally gauged entries is capable of achieving some success.

Similarly, some operations on and properties of sets of ordinally calibrated elements are invariant under scale changes while others are not. Thus, if B, C, and D are such sets, and if the union of the first two is the third, that is, if

$$B \cup C = D,$$

then the same relation between these sets holds when the ordinal scale (or scales) on which the elements of B, C, and D are measured is (or are) altered by permissible transformations. Partial and linear orderings of the elements of sets are also left intact under such modifications. Contrariwise, the open interval of ordinal numbers $(0, 1)$ is a bounded set that becomes unbounded upon application of the admissible transformation $\log x$, where x varies over $(0, 1)$.

---

[4] An n-by-n matrix is *positive definite* whenever $vAv' > 0$, for all 1-by-n row vectors $v \neq 0$, where v' is the transpose of v. It is *negative definite* if the inequality is reversed.

[5] A matrix A is *decomposable* if, by rearranging rows and columns, it is possible to obtain a sub-matrix in the upper-right corner of A in which all entries are zero. Otherwise it is *indecomposable*.

[6] The *eigenvalues* of A are the roots of the polynomial equation $|A - \lambda I| = 0$ in λ, where I is the identity matrix.

Fix attention next on real-valued functions, f, of a scalar or vector variable x, where the elements of (or the components of the elements of) the domain along with the elements of the range are quantified on ordinal scales. On the one hand, there are, of course, numerous scale-dependent properties that these functions may possess, such as strict concavity, strict convexity, linearity, and the existence of maximum or minimum values.[7] To illustrate, over the domain of all positive real numbers, the function

$$f(x) = x^{1/2},$$

where x is a non-negative scalar variable, is strictly concave. It becomes the linear function

$$f(x) = x,$$

if the ordinal scale on which x is measured is squared (that is, x is replaced by x^2 in $f(x) = x^{1/2}$), and a strictly convex function if that scale is raised to the fourth power. Moreover, the function $f(x) = -x^2$, defined for all real numbers, has a unique maximum at $x = 0$. But applying the admissible transformation $T(x) = -e^{-x}$ leads to the function

$$F(x) = f(T(x)) = -e^{-2x},$$

whose first-order derivative is positive everywhere, and which cannot, therefore, have a maximum anywhere. However, if only the function values of f are ordinally measured while its argument values are at least cardinally gauged, and if f has a maximum at $\bar{x}$, then no matter what scale on which the function values are calibrated, that is, for all permissible transformations of scale T, the transformed function $T(f(x))$ has a maximum at $\bar{x}$.[8] And if the cardinal scale on which x is measured were transformed by $T(x) = \alpha x + \beta$ (where $\alpha > 0$), then a maximum would still exist but at a different value of x.

On the other hand, even with both function and argument values ordinally measured, there are still potential properties of f that remain invariant under admissible transformations of scale. Continuity and one-to-oneness illustrate

---

[7] A function $f(x)$ is *strictly concave* provided that

$$f(\theta x' + [1-\theta]x'') > \theta f(x') + [1-\theta]f(x''),$$

for all x' and x'', and all θ between 0 and 1. It is *strictly convex* if the inequality is reversed. And it is *linear* if the inequality is replaced by an equals sign and θ is permitted to take on the values 0 and 1.

[8] This result follows, for example, from Katzner [4, p. 32]. It remains true, of course, even if x is only ordinally quantified. But the next assertion does not.

the point, as does differentiability, provided that only differentiable increasing transformations of scale are permitted.[9] And with these properties in force, standard mathematical results that rest on them, such as the Mean Value Theorem (e.g., Rudin [6, pp. 80,174]), frequently may be applied. Indeed, and in particular, the traditional theory of demand mentioned earlier obtains considerable mileage in the development of its constrained-utility-maximization argument from the assumed continuity and often assumed differentiability of the ordinal utility function. It does so by starting out with, say, an ordinal, differentiable utility function and deriving conclusions from the constrained maximization of that function that do not depend on the scale employed to calibrate utility.[10] The reason why this can be done is that only the function values of the utility function are ordinal in character. With the arguments of the utility function ratio calibrated, their utility-maximizing values, as indicated above, remain invariant under permissible transformations of the scale on which utility is measured. The utility-function value at the maximum, of course, does not.

Observe that in all circumstances described previously in which a property remains in force after application of a permissible transformation of the ordinal scale in use, the ordinal values or value in question still modify. Thus changing scales in a matrix addition leaves commutativity intact but with different numerical matrix entries. And if f has a unique maximum at cardinally-gauged $\bar{x}$, then altering the scale on which the function values $f(x)$ are measured, while changing neither the fact of the existence of that maximum nor the maximizing point $\bar{x}$, nevertheless alters the numerical magnitude of the maximum function value. The use of such properties, then, requires that the purpose of the analysis exclude the determination of specific ordinal variable values for identification with empirical observations. In other words, as long as explanation with respect to the ordinal variables is intended to be general in character, the em-

[9] To require that all admissible transformations of scale, in addition to their increasingness and continuity, also be differentiable with a positive derivative everywhere is to impose additional, unspecified assumptions underlying the constructions of ordinal scales. An example in which everywhere differentiability is destroyed by an increasing, not-everywhere-differentiable transformation of scale is provided below.

[10] Without, in part, the extra assumptions referred to in n. 9 immediately above, increasing continuous functions with zero or non-existent first-order derivatives, or both, at isolated points are permissible transformations of scale for ordinal utility-function values. And since these transformations may render the partial derivatives of the utility function zero-valued or non-existent at interior points of the commodity space, the standard argument requiring non-zero partial derivatives everywhere in the interior has to be altered. But the required modifications are well known. See, for example, Katzner [4, Sect. 3.2].

ployment of ordinally measured variables poses no problems in these cases.[11] But like the analytical possibilities surveyed above, scale independency, and hence the opportunity to engage in meaningful analysis with ordinal variables, also does not turn out to be present very frequently, if at all, with structures that involve simultaneity. It is to these structures that attention now turns.

Systems of Static and Dynamic Simultaneous Equations

The analytic constructions of interest in this section are systems of simultaneous static relations and systems of simultaneous dynamic relations. It is well known, of course, that economists have employed such systems in many different contexts. These include, for example, general equilibrium models, and growth and other models of intertemporal relations. With all variables and parameters calibrated at least on ordinal scales (and with time measured on the usual ratio scale), systems of simultaneous static relations may be expressed as ordinary systems of simultaneous functional equations, and systems of simultaneous dynamic relations become the standard variety of systems of either difference or differential equations. Since the analysis of difference equation systems is perfectly analogous to that of differential equation systems, it is only necessary to examine one, say the latter, here. The relevant questions for systems of simultaneous functional equations have to do with the existence of solutions; those for systems of differential equations relate to the existence of paths, and the existence and stability of stationary paths. However, as indicated above, it will be demonstrated that, in general, these notions of existence and stability cannot be meaningfully expressed in models that contain ordinally calibrated variables or, in other words, that the facts of existence and stability themselves usually depend on the ordinal scales that are employed. It follows that the use of systems of simultaneous static and dynamic relations as modeling techniques cannot be carried over into an environment in which one or more of the variables involved are only ordinally measured.

Focus on systems of simultaneous equations first. Discussion begins by defining the precise nature of the system under consideration. It will then become possible, in light of the structure of the system thus described, to consider the logical problems that arise when ordinal transformations of scale are

[11] It is implicit here that, with respect to the ordinal variables, all numerical values that can be observed in reality are capable of arising, upon suitable parametric and functional adjustment, as ordinal values in the model, for all scales on which the ordinal variables can be measured.

applied.

Let x_i vary over a set of real numbers X_i, where $i = 1, ..., n$, and write the vector and Cartesian product, respectively,

$$x = (x_1, ..., x_n),$$

$$X = X_1 \times \cdots \times X_n,$$

so that x varies over X. A system of simultaneous equations may be written as

$$f^i(x_1, ..., x_n) = 0,$$

for $i = 1, ..., k$, where $k \leq n$ and the f^i are functions defined on X. Using the vector notation $f = (f^1, ..., f^k)$, this may be shortened to

$$f(x) = 0, \tag{1}$$

where f is defined for all x in X. To write (1) is not, in this notation, to say that there actually exist x in X such that $f(x) = 0$. Such existence depends on whether (1) has solutions. Given k, a *solution* of (1) at x^0 is a function $g = (g^1, ..., g^k)$ such that

$$x_i^0 = g^i(x_{k+1}^0, ..., x_n^0),$$

for $i = 1, ..., k$, and

$$f(g(x_{k+1}, ..., x_n), x_{k+1}, ..., x_n) = 0$$

in some (open) neighborhood of $x_{k+1}^0, ..., x_n^0$. Note that the linear system

$$u = Av, \tag{2}$$

where u and v are k-by-1 column vectors with components u_i and v_i, respectively, and A is a k-by-k matrix, is a special case of (1) in which $n = 2k$,

$$x_i = v_i,$$

for $i = 1, ..., k$, and

$$x_{k+j} = u_j,$$

for $j = 1, ..., k$. Assuming all derivatives of f exist continuously, sufficient conditions for (1) to have a continuously differentiable solution at x^0 are that

$f(x^0) = 0$ and the Jacobian determinant

$$\left|J^f(x^0)\right| = \begin{vmatrix} f_1^1(x^0) & \cdots & f_k^1(x^0) \\ \vdots & & \vdots \\ f_1^k(x^0) & \cdots & f_k^k(x^0) \end{vmatrix} \neq 0,$$

where f_j^i is the partial derivative of f^i with respect to its jth argument (e.g., Rudin [6, p. 181]).

For each i, let an admissible transformation of scale, $T^i(x_i)$, be defined on X_i, where the first-order derivative, $T_i^i(x_i)$, if it exists, is positive on X_i except at isolated points where it may vanish. It is not necessary that all n scales be transformed together. If, in a particular instance, no transformation is applied to the scale on which x_j is measured, set $T^j = I^j$, where I^j is the identity transformation. For such j, the function T^j is still an admissible transformation since $T_j^j(x_j) = 1 > 0$. Write

$$y_i = T^i(x_i),$$

for $i = 1, ..., n$,

$$T = (T^1, ..., T^n),$$

and

$$y = (y_1, ..., y_n).$$

Then

$$y = T(x),$$

on $X_1 \times \cdots \times X_n$. Now apply the transformation of scale $T(x)$ to the system of (1). Then (1) becomes

$$f \circ T(x) = 0, \tag{3}$$

defined for all x in X, where

$$f \circ T(x) = f(T(x)) \tag{4}$$

on X. Solutions of (3) are defined analogously to those of (1) and the analogous sufficient conditions for their existence at, say $\bar{x}$, are $f(T(\bar{x})) = 0$ and, from (4),

$$\left|J^{f\circ T}(\bar{x})\right| = \begin{vmatrix} f_1^1(T(\bar{x}))T_1^1(\bar{x}_1) & \cdots & f_k^1(T(\bar{x}))T_k^k(\bar{x}_k) \\ \vdots & & \vdots \\ f_1^k(T(\bar{x}))T_1^1(\bar{x}_1) & \cdots & f_k^k(T(\bar{x}))T_k^k(\bar{x}_k) \end{vmatrix}, \tag{5}$$

$$= |J^f(\bar{y})| \prod_{i=1}^{k} T_i^i(\bar{x}_i) \neq 0,$$

where $\bar{y} = T(\bar{x})$, provided appropriate derivatives exist. In general, of course, $x^0 \neq \bar{x}$.

Against the system of simultaneous equations described to this point, the implications of scale transformations are now considered. Suppose the x_i are ordinally measured so that the admissible transformations are the increasing, continuous transformations, and suppose the sufficient conditions for f to have a solution at x^0 are satisfied. There are good reasons why solutions of $f \circ T(x) = 0$ need not always exist and why the sufficient conditions for them cannot always be satisfied. The former may be illustrated in terms of several examples. Consider the circumstance in which $n = 2$, $k = 1$, $x_1 = z$, $x_2 = a$, where a is a "fixed parameter," and $f = f^1$ is linear with

$$f(z, a) = z - a = 0. \tag{6}$$

Evidently, (6) is also a special instance of (2). Let $T^2 = I^2$, and consider only non-identity transformations of scale $T^1(z)$. To illustrate the broad variety of possibilities, three sub-cases of (6), each with its own transformation T^1, will be presented. First, let $X_1 = \{z : z \geq 0\}$ and $a = 1$. Then the solution of (6) is $z = 1$. Now applying the permissible transformation $T^1(z) = z/(1 + z)$, (6) becomes

$$f(T^1(z), a) = \frac{z}{1+z} - 1 = 0.$$

This results in the contradiction $1 = 0$. Therefore no solution to the transformed equation $f(T^1(z), a) = 0$ can exist. Second, set $X_1 = \{z : -\infty < z < +\infty\}$ and $a \leq 0$. Then $z = a$ is the solution of (6). Application of the admissible transformation $T^1(z) = e^z$ gives

$$f(T^1(z), a) = e^z - a = 0,$$

which has no solution since $a \leq 0$. Finally with $X_1 = \{z : -\infty < z < +\infty\}$ and $a \geq 0$, the equation $z = a$ remains the solution of (6). But once again, application of the permissible transformation $T^1(z) = -e^{-z}$ leads to

$$f(T^1(z), a) = -e^{-z} - a = 0,$$

and no solution can exist, this time because $a \geq 0$. Note that in each of these three examples, the linearity of (6) disappears upon application of the admissible transformation of scale.

In all of the above cases, the Jacobian determinant of (6), namely $|J^f(z, a)|$, is unity, and hence non-zero, throughout X. Also, since T^1 always maps X_1 into itself,[12] the Jacobian of the transformed system reduces, using the formula of (5), to

$$|J^{f \circ T}(z, a)| = T_1^1(z),$$

which is non-zero everywhere because $T_1^1 > 0$ in all situations. Thus the second of the sufficient conditions described above for the existence of solutions is satisfied. But the first, i.e., the existence of a z such that (given a) $f(T(z), a) = 0$, still does not hold. Moreover, the non-vanishing of the Jacobian determinant of the transformed system need not remain in force under other circumstances. Indeed, the determinant itself might not even exist. For as suggested in note 10 on p. 206, the collection of all continuously differentiable functions with everywhere-positive first-order derivatives does not exhaust the possibilities for legitimate transformations of ordinal scales. Increasing, continuous functions that, at isolated points, do not have derivatives, or have zero derivatives, or both, make up the latter. For example, the admissible transformation of scale

$$T(z) = \begin{cases} 2z, & \text{if } z \leq 1, \\ z + 1, & \text{if } z \geq 1, \end{cases}$$

defined for all real z, is not differentiable at $z = 1$. Application of it to the

[12] This need not be true in general. For if $X_1 = \{z : 0 \leq z \leq +\infty\}$, then the permissible transformation $T^1(z) = -e^{-x}$ maps X_1 into the negative real numbers.

everywhere differentiable function

$$f(z, a) = z - a,$$

obliterates the partial derivative with respect to z at $(z, a) = (1, a)$. Note, however, that in this special case, although there is no Jacobian determinant to be non-vanishing at $(1, a)$, the transformed system is still capable of solution everywhere. Regardless, the solvability of systems of simultaneous equations with ordinally calibrated variables fails, as a rule, to be independent of scale changes.

The preceding argument has addressed the logical problems of ordinal transformations of scale in static simultaneous equation systems. It is now time to draw attention to the corresponding implications of scale transformations in dynamic differential equation systems. As before, the starting point is the characterization of the system under investigation, preparatory to the analysis of scale transformations that follows.

Thus consider the system of differential equations

$$\frac{dx_i}{dt} = f^i(x, t), \tag{7}$$

where $i = 1, ..., n$, and f^i is defined on $X \times \{t : t \geq 0\}$ for each i. Often there is a vector of parameters implicit in each equation of (7). Denote them, respectively, by $a_i = (a_{i1}, ..., a_{ik})$, where $i = 1, ..., n$, the a_{ij} are real numbers, and $k \geq 1$. Of course, the linear system

$$\frac{dx_i}{dt} = \sum_{j=1}^{n} a_{ij} x_i, \tag{8}$$

with $i = 1, ..., n$ and $k = n$, is a special instance of (7). A *path* or *solution* of (7) through x^0 in X is a collection of functions

$$x_i = h^i(x^0, t), \tag{9}$$

where $i = 1, ..., n$, such that

$$\frac{dh^i(x^0, t)}{dt} = g^i(h(x^0, t), t),$$

and

$$x_i^0 = h^i(x^0, 0),$$

for each i, where $x^0 = (x_1^0, ..., x_n^0)$, $h = (h^1, ..., h^n)$, and

$$x = h(x^0, t),$$

is an abbreviation of (9). An *equilibrium* path of (7) is a vector $\bar{x}$ in X such that

$$\bar{x} = h(\bar{x}, t), \tag{10}$$

for all $t \geq 0$. The equilibrium path $\bar{x}$ is *locally* stable when there exists a neighborhood N of $\bar{x}$ such that

$$\lim_{t \to \infty} h(x^0, t) = \bar{x}, \tag{11}$$

for all x^o in N. It is *globally* stable if (11) holds for all x^0 in X.

It is common in economics to consider a special case of (7), namely

$$\frac{dx_i}{dt} = f^i(x, a_i), \tag{12}$$

where the parameters implicit in (7) have been made explicit and t is no longer an argument of f. (Clearly (8) is a special instance of (12) too.) Suppose the x_i and a_{ij} are ordinally gauged, and suppose, given the ordinal scales on which these variables and parameters are measured, a globally stable equilibrium path $\bar{x}$ exists for (12). Now according to (10), along an equilibrium path

$$\frac{dx_i}{dt} = f^i(x, a_i) = 0, \tag{13}$$

for each i. That is, each equilibrium path is characterized as a solution of the right-hand equalities of (13). But since, with $i = 1, ..., n$, the right-hand equalities of (13) are identical to (1) except for the obvious change in notation, the conclusions derived above for systems of simultaneous equations apply to the equilibrium paths of (13). In particular, the existence of those paths is dependent on the scales on which the components of x and a_i are measured. Thus the existence of the equilibrium path of (13) could be lost under a suitable transformation of scale. And if, upon transformation of scale it is not certain that an equilibrium path exists, then the question of the post-transformation stability of that path, local or global, cannot even be raised.

It should also be pointed out that even with respect to a single admissible transformation of scale that preserves the existence of equilibrium paths, the stability of the original path, if present, can still be lost in the transformation. This can easily be seen in reference to (8). For it is clear from (13) that $x = 0$ is an equilibrium path of (8). Assume that path is globally stable. Then it is necessary and sufficient that the real parts of the eigenvalues of the matrix of parameters $[a_{ij}]$ be negative (e.g., Bellman, [1, p. 241]). Now, leaving the x_i alone, apply permissible linear transformations of scale to the a_{ij} that force at least one of the signs of the real parts of the eigenvalues of the transformed matrix to be positive. (Earlier discussion indicates that this can always be done.) Then, although the transformed system continues to have an equilibrium path at $x = 0$, it is no longer stable.

Summary and Conclusions

One may conclude, therefore, that there are very few forms of analysis that have the ability to produce results with respect to ordinally measured variables that are independent of all permissible transformations of the ordinal scales in use. In general, then, the introduction of ordinal scales on which to measure previously non-quantified variables cannot add significantly to the investigative techniques available to the researcher. The major exceptions are that first, like ordinal utility analysis, the maximization or constrained maximization of a function whose function values are ordinally measured, but whose functional arguments are ratio gauged, is independent of the scale on which those function values are calibrated. Second, when functional arguments are cardinally quantified, only the location of that maximum, not its existence, can be affected by permissible transformation of scale. For both of these situations, the insertion of ordinal scales is capable of moving the argument one giant step in the direction of the traditional discourse with more fully quantified variables. However, the use of ordinal measurement in these cases, convenient as it may be, need not necessarily contribute anything beyond what already is possible in their absence. Hence the idea that the introduction and use of ordinality is capable of securing still further results can be misleading. Convenience aside, analysis with ordinal measurement is sometimes no better than, and often not as good as, analysis with no measurement at all.

References

1. Bellman, R., *Introduction to Matrix Analysis*, (New York: McGraw-Hill. 1960).
2. Katzner, D. W., *Static Demand Theory*, (New York: Macmillan. 1970).
3. ________, *Analysis without Measurement*, (Cambridge: Cambridge

University Press, 1983).
4. _______, *Walrasian Microeconomics: An Introduction to the Economic Theory of Market Behavior*, (Reading: Addison-Wesley, 1988).
5. _______, "The Misuse of Measurement in Economics", *Metroeconomica* 49 (1998), pp. 1-22. This volume, Essay 8.
6. Rudin, W., *Principles of Mathematical Analysis*, (New York: McGraw-Hill, 1953).
7. Sonnenschein, H. F., "Demand Theory without Transitive Preferences, with Applications to the Theory of Competitive Equilibrium," in *Preferences, Utility, and Demand*, J. S. Chipman, L. Hurwicz, M. K. Richter, and H. F. Sonnenschein, eds. (New York: Harcourt Brace Jovanovich, 1971), pp. 215-223.
8. Uzawa, H., "Preference and Rational Choice in the Theory of Consumption," in *Mathematical Methods in the Social Sciences*, K. J. Arrow, S. Karlin, and P. Suppes, eds. (Stanford: Stanford University Press, 1960), pp. 129-148.
9. Vickers, D., *Money Capital in the Theory of the Firm*, (Cambridge: Cambridge University Press, 1987).

PART II

Applications

10
Effort and Efficiency in the Neoclassical Firm[1]

The neoclassical firm, framed, say, in the context of an Arrow-Debreu, general-equilibrium model, has traditionally been viewed as an institution that combines units of goods and services called inputs, such as raw materials, machines and labor time, into units of another good or service referred to as output. In so doing, the firm is thought of as restrained by both market prices and its production function, and is assumed to hire those quantities of inputs, and produce (and sell) that quantity of output which maximizes its profit. Such a firm is assumed to be technically efficient in that, by definition, its production function associates the maximum possible output with each combination of labor time and non-labor inputs (given technology). Moreover, since its output and all of its inputs flow through perfectly competitive markets, the quantities of output and inputs it achieves at economy-wide, general equilibrium are Pareto efficient.

Recent investigations, however, have introduced new elements into this picture. Two of these are of particular interest here. First, to analyze such things as team production (Alchian and Demsetz [1]), the optimum firm size (Calvo and Wellisz [4]), age-earnings profiles (Lazear [8]), and certain Marxian-type

1 Review of Political Economy 6 (1994), pp. 62-71. © Taylor & Francis, Ltd. (http://www.tandf.co.uk/journals/). Reprinted with permission.

The present paper has benefited greatly from the criticisms and suggestions of Samuel Bowles and Douglas Vickers. The author would like to thank them for their help.

propositions concerning technologies, discrimination, and involuntary unemployment (Bowles [3]), workers have been imagined as supplying "effort" to the firm in addition to their labor time. Bowles [3, p. 20], for example, takes the position that, although labor time must be purchased to obtain effort, it is effort and not labor time that is responsible, along with other non-labor inputs, for producing output.[2] Second, the traditional model of the firm has been expanded and modified so as to permit the examination of organizational forms within its structure (e.g., Williamson [10], Beckmann [2], and Ouchi [9]).

Now with the effort of employees affecting production, it no longer can be supposed that the output obtained from each combination of labor time and non-labor inputs is always maximal. In addition, while labor time is bought and sold in the usual manner, effort supplied cannot be determined by the ordinary market interaction of demand and supply alone. Hence the issue of the technical efficiency of production, which traditionally was assumed away, along with the question of the Pareto efficiency of input allocations within the firm at economy-wide equilibrium, which in the traditional view depended solely on market forces, are reopened in a new context. Moreover, with the same input of goods and services, including the same amount of labor time supplied by each employee, different ways of organizing these inputs in terms of the social interactions that are brought out among individuals in the firm may elicit different kinds of effort. Such variations in effort are likely to have effects on the firm's profitability and efficiency.

The present paper is concerned with these matters. It sets out a model of the firm in which effort, a productive input varying because of organizational differences or for other reasons, is included in the production function. It defines and analyzes two kinds of internal efficiency within the firm that are supplemental to the usual efficiencies imposed by technical imperatives and by markets in a general-equilibrium environment.[3] And it provides conditions under which the model reduces to the standard neoclassical model of the firm in which effort disappears as a productive variable. Of course, even when the conditions reducing the model to the standard neoclassical model are not satisfied, the model itself could still be incorporated into a general-equilibrium model of the microeconomy. But since a market for effort does not exist, doing so leaves the general-equilibrium model with incomplete markets. In this context, the presence of the second kind of inefficiency analyzed below illustrates the well-known fact that incomplete markets support Pareto inferior

[2] Bowles' production function may be regarded as a special case of that employed below.

[3] A more specialized model in which effort is replaced by the activities of workers and the restrictions imposed on these activities by their supervisors, and which permits the efficiencies of particular forms of organization for the firm to be analyzed in greater detail, is given by Katzner [7 (this volume, Essay 11)]. See also the model of Essay 6 above.

competitive equilibria.

I

Consider a firm that employs K workers indexed by $k = 1, ..., K$. Such a firm hires labor time from each worker along with various non-labor inputs. In addition to labor time, employees supply effort of their choosing while on the job. The effort variables are often taken to be cardinally quantified, ranging over a relevant set of real numbers (e.g., Calvo and Wellisz [4]). Such an approach is rather questionable, however, relying, as it does, on the satisfaction of several hard-to-justify conditions.[4] In any case, nothing is gained by imposing these restrictions here. Present purposes are served by leaving effort in its unquantified form and supposing only that (i) for every worker k, the effort variable, e_k, takes on as values any element of a collection, E^k, of distinct and verbally describable efforts appropriate to k,[5] and that (ii) each E^k is linearly ordered by an "extent of effort" relation, $\geq$, which identifies both a unique "maximum" effort $\bar{e}_k$ and a unique "minimum" effort $\hat{e}_k$ in E^k, that is,

$$\bar{e}_k > e_k > \hat{e}_k,$$

for all e_k different from $\bar{e}_k$ and $\hat{e}_k$ in E^k, where $>$ is the "strict" relation derived from $\geq$ in the usual manner.[6] These assumptions by themselves are not enough to ensure that e_k is a cardinally quantifiable variable. Nor are they even sufficient to guarantee ordinal quantifiability unless E^k is, in addition, finite or countably infinite.[7] But they do permit the idea of "greater effort" to be defined in terms of $>$. Thus refer to the effort described by e'_k in E^k as greater than (alternatively, greater than or the same as) that described by e''_k in E^k whenever $e'_k > e''_k$ (or, respectively, $e'_k \geq e''_k$). Let $e = (e_1, ..., e_K)$, $\bar{e} = (\bar{e}_1, ..., \bar{e}_K)$, and $\hat{e} = (\hat{e}_1, ..., \hat{e}_K)$. For all e' and e'', write $e' > e''$ (or $e' \geq e''$) as long as $e'_k > e''_k$ (or $e'_k \geq e''_k$), for all k.

---

4 Cardinal measurement requires that a mathematical operation be defined on the "effort space" that is bisymmetric, continuous in each variable separately, and cancellable. See, for example, Katzner [6, p. 40].

5 As a part of these descriptions, each value of e_k presumably would have a certain quality and intensity identified with it. The technique of defining such non-quantifiable variables in this way has been described by Katzner [6, pp. 53,54]. (See also Essay 4 in this volume.) There is, moreover, no need to assume that E^k is finite or even countably infinite (Katzner [6, Sect. 7.2]).

6 That is, for all e'_k and e''_k in E^k, $e'_k > e''_k$ provided $e'_k \geq e''_k$ and it is not the case that $e''_k \geq e'_k$.

7 Effort may be measured on an ordinal scale if and only if the associated interval topology has a countable base. See, for example, Katzner [6, p. 40].

The effect of effort on output depends on the duration over which that effort is applied. Furthermore, employees working 8 hours, say, require more inputs to heat and light a factory than they would if they worked only 4 hours, regardless of the effort they expend. (The fact that it may be less difficult to sustain a given effort over 4 hours than to dilute it and spread the same effort over 8 hours is not considered.) In general, then, the firm's output is a function of effort, labor time and non-labor inputs, and even with the choice of effort supplied left to the worker, the firm still has to account for trade-offs between labor time and non-labor inputs in calculating its profit-maximizing position. However, to focus attention more sharply on the problem at hand, let quantities of labor time and non-labor inputs be set at profit-maximizing levels for each value of e. The question of how changes in effort affect these profit-maximizing values is not explored. Suffice it to say that an increase in effort by person k, it seems, could be accompanied by either a rise or fall in the firm's (profit-maximizing) demand for that person's labor time. Intuitively speaking, the demand may rise because, with greater effort, person k's labor time is worth more to the firm. But the demand might also fall since the firm can now obtain the same effort upon hiring less labor time. The final result would appear to depend on the specific nature of the firm's production function. In any case, from here on labor time is taken as dependent on e, and non-labor inputs are ignored.

Denote the output of the firm by x, where x varies over non-negative real numbers, and designate the firm's production function by f. Previous assumptions imply that, in equation form, f reduces to

$$x = f(e).$$

Note that the domain of f is the Cartesian product of the sets E^k. Suppose that greater effort (with labor time and all non-labor inputs determined as described above) is both necessary and sufficient for larger output. In other words, for all distinct e' and e'',

$$f(e') > f(e'') \qquad \text{if and only if} \qquad e' \geq e'', \tag{1}$$

where the left-hand inequality, as with all symbols "$>$" (and "$\geq$") subsequently used in reference to real numbers, represents the usual "greater-than" (and "greater-than-or-equal-to") relation.[8] Thus output is maximized at $\bar{e}$ and minimized at $\hat{e}$.

[8] Note $e' \geq e''$ together with the condition that e' be distinct from e'' means $e'_k \geq e''_k$ for every k and $e'_k > e''_k$ for at least one k.

As suggested earlier, effort does not flow through the usual kind of market, and hence the vector e is not subject to the standard market restraints. Each component e_k is selected by worker k. Although the actual efforts chosen may depend on many factors, the factor identified for subsequent analysis here is the way in which the firm is organized with respect to the social interactions that are brought forth among the firm's employees. Two examples of firm organization are the bureaucracy and the clan. A *bureaucracy* is an hierarchical organizational form in which those higher up, in addition to providing direction, also monitor and evaluate the performances of those below (Ouchi [9, p. 134]). The performance of each employee, as indicated by these evaluations, determines his pay increases and promotions. Wage incentives, then, are an important part of a bureaucracy. In a *clan*, which is also an hierarchical form, workers are subjected to a continual socialization process that tends to reshape and maintain their goals so as to be identical to those of the firm (Ouchi [9, p. 132]). Thus individuals naturally behave in the best interests of the firm and wage incentives are not needed. The details of how the organization of the firm influences the selection of e will be clarified momentarily.

To allow for the possibly, present in a bureaucracy, of encouraging employees through monetary incentives to put forth greater effort, let the firm use an incentive function in determining workers' wages. For notational simplicity, suppose this function, W, is the same for all workers. With w_k denoting the wage of employee k per unit of time, write

$$w_k = W(e_k),$$

on E^k, where $k = 1, ..., K$, and set

$$W(e) = (W(e_1), ..., W(e_K)).$$

Sometimes W could, as it would for a clan, be a constant function, assigning the same wages regardless of effort. At other times W could have the property, relevant for a bureaucracy, that

$$W(e'_k) > W(e''_k) \qquad \text{if and only if} \qquad e'_k > e''_k, \tag{2}$$

for all distinct e'_k and e''_k in E^k, and every k, in which case, greater effort is rewarded with a larger wage.

Let y^0_k be the (profit-maximizing) quantity of time that employee k spends working in the firm. Set $y^0 = (y^0_1, ..., y^0_K)$. Then, as indicated earlier, y^0 depends on e. Further, the cost to the firm of hiring labor time, which is the same as the cost of securing effort, is the inner product $W(e) \cdot y^0$.

Production costs are the costs of hiring labor time and all non-labor inputs that appear in the production function. Included in these costs are the costs of whatever wage incentives are present. Beyond production costs are "administrative costs" that the firm incurs as part of the attempt to induce workers to supply maximum effort. In a bureaucracy, for example, these costs would include the cost of monitoring and evaluating worker performance. In a clan, they arise from the costs of socializing new recruits and programs to maintain a sense of community and commitment. In any case, assume that the farther worker performance is from maximum effort, the greater the administrative cost required to attain it. Generally, administrative costs are incurred by hiring extra labor and non-labor resources, but it is not necessary to identify the nature and quantity of these resources explicitly here. Instead, the salient features of administrative costs as described above can be accounted for by introducing a function, A, indicating the administrative cost associated with each vector e. This function is intended to reflect the fact that as workers vary their effort, the firm responds by altering its expenditure on administration. Previous assumptions imply that $A(\bar{e}) = 0$, $A(\hat{e}) > 0$, and that

$$A(e') < A(e'') \qquad \text{if and only if} \qquad e' \geq e'', \tag{3}$$

for all distinct e' and e''. That is, if workers choose to increase their effort, then firms do not have to spend as much on administration.[9] Greater effort, in other words, reduces administrative cost until, at maximum effort $\bar{e}$, it vanishes. Clearly, each distinct organizational form may have its own unique function A.

Take the price of the firm's output to rely on market forces and denote it by p. Then the profit function of the firm, $\pi(e)$, defined for all vectors e, is given by

$$\pi(e) = pf(e) - A(e) - W(e) \cdot y^0,$$

where, recall, the dot denotes inner product and y^0 depends on e. Suppose the firm is *profit-efficient* in the sense that increases in output due to changing efforts always raise profit (see Gintis and Katzner [5, p. 282, or p. 217 in the

---

[9] An alternative possibility would be to suppose that the firm sets its administrative cost, a, and workers then choose the effort they supply in return. Such an approach would provide a substitute function for A, say $e = A^*(a)$, which would be separate from and independent of A as described in the text. In addition, something like

$$A^*(a') < A^*(a'') \quad \text{if and only if} \quad a' < a'',$$

might be assumed in place of (3). This construction, however, would not only necessitate different notions of efficiency from those used below, but would also require a different perspective for determining the workers' choice of e.

reprinted version]). Mathematically,[10]

$$f(e') > f(e'') \qquad \text{if and only if} \qquad \pi(e') > \pi(e''), \tag{4}$$

for all distinct e' and e''. From (1) and (4),

$$\pi(e') > \pi(e'') \qquad \text{if and only if} \qquad e' \geq e'',$$

again, for all distinct e' and e''. Observe, in the present context, that profit efficiency forces the incentive function W to be set in such a way that greater effort generates sufficient increases in revenue and savings in administrative cost (the latter savings derives from (3)) to more than offset whatever raises in wages that have to be paid, thus ensuring a larger profit. Such is always the case when W is a constant function as in a clan.

It has already been indicated that the value of e actually present in the firm is chosen by the firm's employees. Let each worker k have a utility function, u^k, defined on the Cartesian product of E^k with the collection of all relevant wages appearing in the range of the incentive function W. In equation form it is written as

$$\mu_k = u^k(e_k, w_k), \tag{5}$$

where μ_k varies over utility values obtained by worker k. To keep matters simple, it has been assumed that the worker's consumption and labor time decisions are made independently of the effort decision. Because w_k depends on e_k according to the incentive function W, w_k may be eliminated from (5) by substitution. Thus utility is reduced to a function, $U^k(e_k)$, of e_k alone, where

$$U^k(e_k) = u^k(e_k, W(e_k)), \tag{6}$$

for all e_k in E^k. Assume that worker k selects e_k so as to maximize $U^k(e_k)$ over E^k, and suppose that U^k has sufficient properties to guarantee that such a maximum always exists (see Katzner [6, Sect 5.4]). Specification of $e = (e_1, ..., e_K)$ in this manner characterizes "internal" equilibrium in the firm.

II

The model just described clearly applies to a variety of firms having, among other things, many possible kinds of organization. One way to compare the technical efficiency of all such firms with the same production function, the

[10] A similar definition with a different notion of profit and with the strong inequalities replaced by weak inequalities appears in Essays 6 and 11 on, respectively, pp. 136 and 137, and 239.

same labor time hired and the same non-labor input values, is to compare their administrative costs at internal equilibrium. Thus one firm may be said to be technically or administratively more efficient than another (having identical labor times and non-labor inputs, and the same production function) provided that its administrative cost, $A(e)$, at internal equilibrium, is lower.[11] Moreover, conditions on worker utility functions may be specified under which workers arrive at the internal equilibrium $\bar{e}$ and all administrative costs disappear. Two illustrations are provided momentarily.

A second kind of efficiency that arises within the firm parallels the Pareto efficiency imposed by markets. Refer to the vector $\tilde{e} = (\tilde{e}_1, ..., \tilde{e}_K)$ as internally Pareto optimal in production whenever there is no other vector e such that

$$U^k(e_k) \geq U^k(\tilde{e}_k),$$

for all $k = 1, ..., K$,

$$U^k(e_k) > U^k(\tilde{e}_k),$$

for at least one k,

$$f(e) \geq f(\tilde{e}),$$

and

$$A(e) \leq A(\tilde{e}).$$

The vector e' may be said to be internally Pareto superior in production to another vector e'' if the above four inequalities hold with e replaced by e' and $\tilde{e}$ by e''. (Thus $\tilde{e}$ is internally Pareto optimal in production as long as there is no other e Pareto superior in production to it.) As is the case with the standard notion of Pareto superiority, internal Pareto superiority defines a partial ordering among comparable firms (i.e., firms with the same production functions and the same labor times and non-labor input values) in which the firm that is internally Pareto superior in production may be called more Pareto efficient. And it is possible to give conditions on incentive functions and worker utility functions ensuring that internal equilibrium is, indeed, internally Pareto optimal in production. Such constraints are the present analogue of the forces that impose Pareto efficiency with respect to variables that flow through markets.

These ideas may be illustrated first in terms of a firm that is organized as a bureaucracy. Bureaucracies work on the basis of monetary incentives designed to bring out the greatest effort from workers. To the extent that workers

[11] Instead of pure administrative cost, administrative cost per unit of output or administrative cost per dollar of profit could also be used as measures of technical efficiency.

are motivated by elements other than financial reward, and hence utility maximization on the part of workers calls forth an effort vector other (i.e., "less") than $\bar{e}$, workers' performances have to be monitored and administrative costs incurred. In an ideal bureaucratic situation, workers respond only to wage incentives and in such a manner that administrative costs vanish.

More precisely, call the firm an *ideal bureaucracy* when (2) is in force and (using the form for worker utility functions on the right-hand side of the equality in (6))

$$u^k(e'_k, W(e'_k)) > u^k(e''_k, W(e''_k)) \quad \text{if and only if} \quad W(e'_k) > W(e''_k), \tag{7}$$

for all distinct e'_k and e''_k in E^k, where $k = 1, ..., K$. Note condition (7) implies that the higher wages secured from greater effort always overcome, in terms of workers' preferences, the disutility associated with that greater effort. Combining (7) and (2),

$$u^k(e'_k, W(e'_k)) > u^k(e''_k, W(e''_k)) \qquad \text{if and only if} \qquad e'_k > e''_k, \tag{8}$$

for all distinct e'_k and e''_k in E^k, and $k = 1, ..., K$. Thus, in an ideal bureaucracy, workers always choose $\bar{e}$, thereby eliminating all administrative costs and causing both profit and output to be maximized. Moreover, this internal equilibrium is internally Pareto optimal in production. For if $\tilde{e} = (\tilde{e}_1, ..., \tilde{e}_K)$ were internally Pareto superior in production to $\bar{e} = (\bar{e}_1, ..., \bar{e}_K)$, where $\tilde{e}_k$ is in E^k for all k, then from (8) in conjunction with the definition of Pareto superiority, $\tilde{e}_k > \bar{e}_k$ for at least one k. Hence the assumption that $\bar{e}_k$ represents maximum effort over E^k, for every k, would be contradicted. Just as the usual market constraints are enough to ensure the ordinary (external) Pareto optimality with respect to labor and non-labor inputs, the characteristics of ideal bureaucracies impose sufficient restrictions on workers' supplies of effort to yield internal Pareto optimality within the firm.

As a second illustration, consider the clan. In this case, it is the presence of community and commitment that elicits effort from employees. To the extent that employee goals are not coincident with those of the firm, and utility maximization by them does not yield maximum effort on their part, the firm has to devote resources to the socialization process. In an *ideal clan* workers identify with the firm to such a degree that the incurrence of such administrative cost is not necessary. Formally, the firm is an ideal clan if W is a constant function and (8) holds for all for all distinct e'_k and e''_k in E^k, and $k = 1, ..., K$. As before, then, in an ideal clan, workers automatically choose $\bar{e}$, and the internal equilibrium $\bar{e}$ is internally Pareto optimal in production.

In general, of course, there is no reason why employees in a firm of any organizational form should give that firm their maximum effort. When they do not, internal equilibrium is not internally Pareto optimal in production and, in addition, since the output associated with vectors of labor time and non-labor inputs critically depends on the effort supplied by workers, the firm's production function cannot be said to always indicate the maximum output attainable from those vectors. Under these conditions, then, the production function becomes an institutionally specific concept whose effort parameters depend on the organizational form in question, and this is so regardless of whether the firm is part of a larger model in which market quantities and prices have settled at a competitive equilibrium. But for both ideal bureaucracies and clans, in which each worker always supplies maximum effort and administrative costs always vanish, nothing is lost by reverting to tradition and writing the production function as dependent on labor time and non-labor inputs with all reference to effort eliminated. Indeed, under such ideal organizational circumstances, the traditional theory of the firm is quite adequate for explaining firm behavior. Effort may be translated into labor time without discarding relevant analytical substance. Alternative organizational forms, each associated with their own effort vectors e, need not be distinguished because, regardless of the particular form the organization of the firm takes, effort always settles at the maximum level $\bar{e}$, and the firm is always as technically efficient as it can be. In other words, $\bar{e}$ becomes a fixed parameter in the production function which now, as in the traditional analysis, associates maximum output with each combination of labor time and non-labor inputs. Thus the assumption of an ideal form of organization is an implicit part of the intellectual baggage that accompanies the economist's model of the neoclassical firm and, as a result, the production function it contains is necessarily relevant only under special conditions.

References

1. Alchian, A. A., and H. Demsetz, "Production, Information Costs and Economic Organization," *American Economic Review* 62 (1972), pp. 777-795.
2. Beckmann, M. J., *Rank in Organizations* (Berlin: Springer-Verlag, 1978).
3. Bowles, S., "The Production Process in a Competitive Economy: Walrasian, Neo-Hobbesian, and Marxian Models," *American Economic Review* 75 (1985), pp. 16-36.

4. Calvo, G. A., and S. Wellisz, "Supervision, Loss of Control, and the Optimum Size of the Firm," *Journal of Political Economy* 86 (1978), pp. 943-952.
5. Gintis, H., and D. W. Katzner, "Profits, Optimality, and the Social Division of Labor in the Firm," in *Sociological Economics*, L. Lévy-Garboua, ed. (London: SAGE, 1979), pp. 269-297. Reprinted in D. W. Katzner, *Analysis without Measurement* (Cambridge: Cambridge University Press, 1983), Ch. 11.
6. Katzner, D. W., *Analysis without Measurement* (Cambridge: Cambridge University Press, 1983).
7. ________, "The Efficiency of Organizational Forms," *Économie Appliquée* 40 (1987), pp. 539-564. This volume, Essay 11.
8. Lazear, E. P., "Agency, Earnings Profiles, Productivity and Hours Restrictions," *American Economic Review* 71 (1981), pp. 606-620.
9. Ouchi, W. G., "Markets, Bureaucracies and Clans," *Administrative Science Quarterly* 25 (1980), pp. 129-141.
10. Williamson, O. E., *Markets and Hierarchies: Analysis and Antitrust Implications* (New York: Free Press, 1975).

11
The Efficiency of Organizational Forms[1]

For a long time economists have been aware of the fact that certain ways of organizing firms are more efficient than others. Adam Smith, for example, knew that a firm producing pins in which employees specialized in straightening wire, cutting wire, making points, etc. would be more efficient than one in which each worker produced complete pins by himself alone.[2] However, recent approaches to this problem (e.g., Beckmann [1], Calvo and Wellisz [2], Sah and Stiglitz [12], and Willamson [14], [15]) have tended to de-emphasize the technological aspects of production and centered instead on certain social relations among individuals in the firm. These social relations arise in that some workers are "above" other workers in the firm's authority structure; they are significant because it is the social interactions between those above and those below which seem to be responsible for coordinating effort and seeing production through.[3]

The ways in which a supervisor and subordinate interact socially on the

[1] *Économie Appliquée* 40 (1987), pp. 539-564. Reprinted with permission of the publisher: Institut de Sciences Mathématiques et Economiques Appliquées, Paris.

The author would like to thank S. Bowles, R. W. Drago, H. Gintis, C. Menard, W. G. Shephard, and D. Vickers for helping to clarify a number of important issues.

[2] Smith [13, pp. 4, 5].

[3] It is the coordination and accomplishment of the activities of production alone, without direct reliance on a price mechanism for guidance, that Coase regards as the distinguishing feature in the economist's notion of a firm [3, pp. 388, 389].

job depend in part on such organizational matters as whether the two arrive at work decisions through mutual discussion or whether the supervisor makes all relevant decisions and tells the subordinate what to do. In other words, they depend on the specific activities of production in which the supervisor and subordinate engage. Each circumstance is accompanied by its own range of possible social interactions between them. The particular collection of social interactions which obtain in any one case are an indicator of how well the supervisor and subordinate are "getting along." When the two have difficulty in getting along, their social interactions tend to impede the smooth functioning of the firm and lower its productivity. Thus the pattern of lines of authority and the social interactions and productive activities that go with it makes for efficiency or inefficiency of an organizational form.

The present paper discusses two kinds of organizational efficiency, each founded on a distinct approach to dealing with conflicts among employees arising along hierarchical lines. Either the firm takes these conflicts as given and tries to overcome their effects by incurring administrative costs, or it attempts to cause the conflicts to disappear by hiring only certain kinds of individuals. The notion of efficiency emerging from the former is based on the idea that different forms of organization require different social interactions and different productive activities. Hence different sorts of conflicts come up and different costs of administration are needed to surmount them. This kind of organizational efficiency is the better known of the two and leads to comparative statements indicating that under certain conditions, organization of form α is more efficient than organization of form β. The concept of efficiency arising from the latter also derives from the fact that the different patterns of social interactions occurring in different organizational forms spring from different allocations of productive activities among employees. But here, putting people with the right characteristics in the right jobs eliminates the conflicts that impede the smooth functioning of the firm. Taking such an approach to efficiency, the allocation of activities accompanying "internal" equilibria in certain ideal organizational forms (ideal, that is, with respect to the nature of the people employed) turns out to be "internally" Pareto optimal. Thus the development of the complex mesh of activities and social interactions which support the organizational structure of the modern business enterprise does not, by itself, necessarily lead to allocative waste.

The paper begins with an informal discussion of various organizational forms. Next a model is introduced which lends itself to the analysis of the two kinds of efficiency described above. The efficiency of organizational forms is then considered from both points of view. Although many of the ideas presented have significance that extends beyond the normal limits imposed in an analysis of the firm, no effort is made here to cross over these boundaries and expand discussion into more general territory.

I

According to Ouchi, an organization is "any stable pattern of transactions between individuals or aggregations of individuals" [10, p. 132n]. Implicit in this conceptualization is a configuration of information flows among participants that supports the pattern of transactions and permits the organization to function. Ouchi's definition is very broad; yet it is useful for present purposes. Clearly, collections of markets may be understood as organizations. Firms, too, are organizations since they may be viewed as consisting of implicit transactions among individuals or groups.[4] Similarly, governments, universities, hospitals, etc., are also organizations. Although only organizations which may be conceived of as firms are considered subsequently, these still may take on a variety of forms. A sampling appropriate for subsequent discussion is as follows:

Imagine a "firm" producing output from given inputs in which all implicit transactions are made explicit through markets. Each "employee" is a "sub-firm:" he buys the things he uses in markets, does his "job," and sells what he has done in another market to another employee. The difference between his receipts and costs is his pay. The firm consists of all of its sub-firms (employees) and the market relations among them. Together they convert those items taken to be the firm's "inputs" into that identified as its "output." There is no authority structure and no social interaction among employees beyond what is necessary to complete transactions. The market network serves as the coordinating instrument which, in the firm, ensures that production is accomplished. The human characteristics of the individuals involved, together with the environmental factors of the markets defining the firm, require that all transactions be based on complex contingent claims contracts which are costly to write, execute and enforce.[5] These contract costs (which include the costs of gathering sufficient information to be able to write, execute and enforce the contracts) are the coordination or organizational costs of production. Such an arrangement is referred to here as the *market* organizational form for the firm.

All other forms of organization introduced subsequently are hierarchical in that most of the market transactions are absorbed into an authority structure

[4] Williamson [15, pp. 8,9].

[5] Williamson [15, p. 9].

with individuals higher up having status and jurisdiction over persons below. Hence the Smithian invisible hand, or the market process that in the market form of organization coordinates employee behavior based on self interest, is replaced by other "invisible hands," now non-market processes, that coordinate self-interest-motivated behavior within the internal organizational structure of the firm. The only explicit market transactions remaining are those linking the firm to the markets in which it buys its inputs (such as labor) and sells its output. The cost of market transactions (i.e., the cost of contracts) is replaced by the cost of administering the organizational form. Thus the cost of organization or coordination arises from a different source. The instrument of the non-market invisible hand which coordinates social interactions so that production gets done is an important factor in determining the nature of the organizational form in question along with the administrative cost incurred.

Three non-market forms of organization are described below: the bureaucracy, the clan, and the military. Following convention, the class of all bureaucratic forms is subdivided into its own distinct categories. The U-form and M-form bureaucracies are examples of the latter.

A *bureaucracy* is an hierarchical organizational form in which those higher up, in addition to providing direction, also monitor and evaluate the performance of those below.[6] Upon leaving the labor market and joining the firm, the employee's pay increases and promotions depend on his performance. Good performance is rewarded; poor performance is punished. Of course, the presumption is that all employees respond to these incentives, which constitute the coordinating instrument of the bureaucracy. The cost of administering a bureaucracy includes the costs of monitoring and evaluating individuals below by individuals above. For convenience, the cost of the incentives themselves (i.e., the incentive payments to employees) are included as a part of production, not administrative costs.

Two kinds of bureaucracies may be identified.[7] The *unitary* or *U-form* bureaucracy is organized in the traditionally functional manner. Thus sales, manufacturing, finance and other functional units all lie directly under a chief executive or director. The units directly beneath the director in the *multidivisional* or *M-form* bureaucracy are themselves U-form divisions each responsible for their own routine operations. In the M-form structure, the director is concerned only with strategic decision-making for the entire firm and is not involved with day-to-day problems. Observe that these two types of bureaucracies are defined solely in terms of their pattern of lines of authority. In both

---

6 Ouchi [10, p. 134].

7 See, for example, Williamson [15. Ch. 8].

cases, the instrument which coordinates social interactions is the same as that for the bureaucracy in general, namely a system of monetary and promotional incentives.

Unlike market forms and bureaucracies, a *clan* is a hierarchical form in which all individuals are socialized into the firm in such a way that their goals become identical to those of the firm.[8] When the goals of the firm and of all employees are the same, individuals naturally act in the best interests of the firm. Hence it is no longer necessary to monitor and evaluate the performance of each person. Moreover, rewards based on performance become irrelevant. Wages and promotions can be distributed according to non-performance criteria such as numbers of years of service and numbers of dependents. And, of course, the administrative costs of monitoring and evaluating performances disappears. In place of these expenses are substituted the costs of socializing new recruits and of maintaining the sense of community and commitment on the part of employees. Thus conformity of goals is the instrument coordinating social interactions in a clan. The clan form of organization is often considered to be a trait of some Japanese firms.[9]

In addition to monitoring and evaluating performances, and socialization so that goals conform to those of the firm, individuals may also be induced to cooperate by other means. The exercise of personal persuasion and leadership is one possibility. The use of dominance and manipulation as in the armed forces is another.[10] Thus with little in the way of monetary or promotional incentives, and with little similarity between his goals and that of thc organization, an employee may still be willing to carry out tasks as directed from above. An hierarchical form in which all individuals follow instructions in this way will be called a *military*. The coordinating instrument here is the exercise of "influence," in one form or another over employees. As with the clan, the military form of organization does not incur the administrative costs of monitoring and evaluating performances, but it must expend funds to enforce and enhance the legal codes, customs, and traditions from which its ability to influence the behavior of individuals derives.[11] Although few organizations in the free world (except armies) have such characteristics, it is nevertheless instructive to consider the military as a distinct organizational form.

---

8 Ouchi [10, p. 132].

9 *Ibid.*

10 Janowitz [5, p. 43].

11 It is not necessary to monitor performances in a military because employees believe that the cost to them of not cooperating is so high (e.g., the sacrifice of ones entire career) that they do not consider non-cooperation as a viable alternative. A professional football or other sports team is an example.

The information flows required to run non-market organizational forms have both production and administrative components. To illustrate the origins of the former, imagine that the process of making decisions differs across non-market organizational forms as follows: In a bureaucracy the department head, division manager, and president have the responsibility for decision-making.[12] Sometimes, to arrive at decisions, they may consult with subordinates, perhaps achieving a partial or complete consensus, and sometimes no consultation is initiated. For clans, everyone throughout the pyramid of authority who will feel the impact of a decision is directly involved in making it. Discussions continue until a consensus about the correct decision to take is achieved.[13] In militaries, the primary responsibility for decision-making rests with those at the top of the pyramid. Discretionary decision-making at lower levels is strictly and progressively limited.[14] Consultation with subordinates is unlikely in arriving at decisions. Although in all three cases information flows from the bottom to the top of the pyramid and directives flow in the opposite direction from the top to the bottom, the content and pattern of these flows has to vary across organizational forms because the decision-making processes in each clearly have different informational requirements.

The information flows needed to conduct administration also vary over non-market forms of organization. In bureaucracies they arise because supervisors have to monitor and evaluate the performances of their subordinates. In clans they come about through the socialization of new recruits and the maintenance of a sense of community and commitment. And in militaries they derive from the enforcement of legal codes, customs, and traditions.

In an idealized, certain world the imperative to collect information for organizational and administrative purposes disappears and the cost associated with organization and administration in each organizational form drops to zero. Without uncertainty, the only information needed by the market form of organization is the values of prices that are supplied by the markets free of charge. The necessity of contingent claims contracts evaporates and, along with it, all costs of organization. For bureaucracies, clans, and militaries, "ideal" individual participants react in perfect confluence with the organizational structure so that monitoring and evaluating performances, socialization and maintaining a sense of commitment, and enhancing legal codes, customs, and traditions, respectively, are no longer necessary. Thus information for administration, indeed, administration itself is not required, and all administrative costs are

---

12 See Ouchi [11, p. 43].
13 See Ouchi [11, p. 44].
14 See Lang [8, p. 852].

eliminated. Discussion will return to this point in Section IV.

II

Clearly, in developing a model of the firm within which the efficiency of the organizational forms of the previous section can be analyzed, it is necessary to account for the possibility of social interactions among employees. But to do so requires the inclusion of variables which appear to be incapable of measurement and hence the question of how to deal with them arises. It turns out, however, that techniques for handling such variables have recently become available.[15] These methods permit the construction of models which are similar in many respects to those obtained when all variables are quantified. Subsequent discussion is based upon them. More formal presentations and more extended analyses of a similar model may be found in Katzner [7 (this volume, Essay 6)] and Gintis and Katzner [4].

Assume lines of authority in the firm are pyramidal so that every employee k (where $k = 1, ..., K$) has exactly one immediate superior or supervisor. All employees except those at the bottom end of a line of authority in the pyramid have at least one subordinate. Two or more employees with the same supervisor are co-workers. Situated at the top of the pyramid is the director who is designated by the symbol $k = 0$. The director may also be thought of as a chief executive, board of directors, or as a combination of both.

Each employee k supplies labor time z_k to the firm. During time supplied the employee performs activities a_k which fall within the terms of his work contract.[16] These activities involve social interactions among employees and are limited by the technological imperatives of production. It is not required that the a_k be quantifiable: The only restrictions are that each "value" of a_k be capable of distinct, discrete, verbal description, and that the set of activities, A_k, over which a_k may range also be subject to similarly precise definition. In addition to performing activities, each employee provides rules which constrain the activities (i.e., limit the activity sets) of all workers (not only immediate subordinates) below him in authority. These rules are completely characterized in terms of the constraints they impose. Thus, if k is above k' in authority and if $R_{kk'}$ is a set of rules prescribed by k for k', then $R_{kk'}$, is

[15] See Katzner [6] and Essay 4 in this volume..

[16] The definition of an activity would normally include a statement or an implication regarding the length of time necessary to perform the activity. This, in turn, suggests a relation between z_k and a_k. The latter relation, however, is beyond the scope of present discussion and will be ignored.

defined as a subset of $A_{k'}$, or $R_{kk'} \subseteq A_{k'}$. The furnishing of rules may be thought of as an activity which is independent of all other activities and singled out for special attention. Rules may be so restrictive as to dictate exactly what must be done (i.e., select a single element from the employee's activity set) or they may allow for considerable flexibility and choice. Rules also have to be adapted to the technology of production and the capabilities of the individuals for whom they are intended. Moreover, the collection of rules imposed on any employee k' by all persons above him have to be consistent, that is, $\cap_k R_{kk'}$ must be non-empty, where the intersection is taken over all k above k' in authority. Let r_k denote the collection of sets of rules — one set $R_{kk'}$ for each person k' below him — issued by person k. As with a_k, each value of r_k is verbally defined. When k has no subordinates, the symbol r_k has no meaning. Write $a = (a_1, ..., a_K)$ and $r = (r_1, ..., r_K)$. The director's rules, r_0, are presumed given.

The output of the firm, x, depends on quantities of labor time and non-labor inputs purchased by the firm, as well as on rules for subordinates and activities (consistent with rules received from above) supplied by employees. This production function may be written mathematically as

$$x = f(y, z, a, r), \tag{1}$$

where $z = (z_1, ..., z_K)$ and $y = (y_1, ..., y_I)$ is an I-vector of quantities of non-labor inputs. Actually, since it only serves to limit the values that a can take on and does not affect output directly, r need not be listed as an argument of f. But retaining r in the production function introduces no difficulties and at the same time provides convenience that is useful below. In the currently standard textbook treatment, y and z are picked by the firm on the basis of profit maximization and a and r are ignored. The present approach maintains the criterion of profit maximization on the part of the firm as the basis for selection of y and z given values for a and r, and, in addition, a and r are thought of as determined by employees through the (constrained) maximization of their individual utility functions.[17] Of course, the choice of a and r reflects and describes the relevant social interactions among the employees of the firm.

Let the firm pay each employee k a wage w_k according to the incentive

[17] The presence of real capital assets among the components of y could be taken to imply that the model, in making y a decision variable, is determining an instantaneous, optimum capital structure for the firm. Analytically, that raises the question as to whether employees' choices of activities and rules (a, r) can be exceped to remain constant throughout the lives of the assets. But this problem is set aside and disregarded in subsequent discussion.

function[18]

$$w_k = W^k(a_k, r_k), \tag{2}$$

where $k = 1, ..., K$. Non-monetary incentives, such as the possibility of promotion and guaranteed long-term employment, are not considered. The firm's profit function which, given a and r, it maximizes to secure values for y and z is

$$\pi(y, z, a, r) = p_x f(y, z, a, r) - \sum_{i=1}^{I} p_i y_i - \sum_{k=1}^{K} w_k z_k, \tag{3}$$

where p_x denotes output price, and p_i the price of non-labor input i. To keep matters simple, p_x and the p_i are taken to be determined in perfectly competitive markets and the director is assumed to be paid out of profit rather than provided a wage.

The nature of the incentive functions W^k selected by the firm (or its director) deserves comment. On one hand, the W^k may be constant functions associating the same wage to all (a_k, r_k). Alternatively, those values of $(a, r) = (a_1, ..., a_K, r_1, ..., r_K)$ which enhance the productivity or profitability of the firm may be assigned a higher wage by the W_k. In the latter case, however, suppose that for fixed values of p_x, $p_1, ..., p_I$, y, and z, output is higher at (a', r') than at (a'', r''). If profit is also to be higher at (a', r'), then it is necessary that the firm set the W^k so that the additional wages paid employees at (a', r') over those paid at (a'', r'') is less than the additional revenue received at (a', r'). Were this not the case, then the most productive (a, r) need not be the most profitable, and hence moving to increase productivity might reduce profitability. Formally, the collection of incentive functions $\{W^k\}$, one for each employee $k = 1, ..., K$, is said to be *profit-efficient*[19] whenever

$$f(y, z, a', r') \geq f(y, z, a'', r'')$$

if and only if

$$\pi(y, z, a', r') \geq \pi(y, z, a'', r''),$$

for all y, z, a', a'', r', and r''. Profit-efficient incentives, then, have the property that productivity increases due to changes in (a, r) always are translated into larger profit. Note that in addition to incentives which provide wage raises

---

18 The determination of W^k and its relation to the labor market is not considered.

19 This definition of profit efficiency, although identical to the one appearing in Katzner [7 (this volume, Essay 6, pp. 136,137)] is not quite the same as that employed by Gintis and Katzner [4].

that are smaller than resulting revenue increments, all collections of constant incentive functions are also profit-efficient.

To capture the idea that leadership and influence may be exercised by supervisors in their provision of information, training, encouragement, and advice to subordinates, suppose each employee k senses a goals and premise (g-p) function

$$g_k = G^k(a_k, r_k), \tag{4}$$

in which g_k varies over ordinal numbers that express the preferences of his immediate supervisor among vectors (a_k, r_k) as perceived by k. The G^k are taken to be given and the characteristics they might be expected to possess are not discussed. G-p functions are independent of incentive functions. They rely on social rather than economic pressures for their effect.

Assume employees choose values of the a_k and r_k independently from their selection of leisure time and consumption. Ignoring the latter, let the utility function of employee k be written as

$$\mu_k = u^k(a_k, r_k, w_k, g_k), \tag{5}$$

so that the roles of incentives and influences are explicit. However, substitution of (2) and (4) into (5) eliminates w_k and g_k from the latter and reduces it to

$$\mu_k = U^k(a_k, r_k).$$

Suppose $(a, r) = (a_1, ..., a_K, r_1, ..., r_K)$ emerges uniquely from the simultaneous maximization of $U^k(a_k, r_k)$ by each employee $k \neq 0$, subject to the constraints that every a_k is consistent with all rules imposed on k from above or, in other words, that a_k is in $\bigcap_{k'} R_{k'k}$ for each k, where the intersection is taken over all k' above k in authority. Such an (a, r) is called an *internal equilibrium* for the firm. Thus given the director's rules r_0, (a, r) is obtained from utility maximization, (y, z) is secured from profit maximization as described earlier, and the firm's output and profit are determined from (1) and (3). The collection of all internal equilibria generated as the director's rules vary and (y, z) remains fixed is denoted by $\mathcal{E}$. Note that $\mathcal{E}$ contains the internal equilibria arising when the director's rules are such that they impose no effective constraints on the activities of any worker.

The preceding model is sufficiently rich to encompass all of the organizational forms described in Section I except the market form. (Of course the market form does not have a hierarchical authority structure and can not, therefore, fit in.) The instruments required to coordinate social interactions and hence production in bureaucracies, clans, and militaries are all present in that incentive, utility, and g-p functions have been included. In an idealized or perfect environment, differences among these organizational forms are accounted for by differences in the characteristics of the incentive, utility, and g-p functions pertaining to the individuals employed in each case. Indeed, the notions of (ideal) bureaucracy, clan, and military will be defined abstractly by imposing certain restrictions on these functions later on (Section IV) so that their allocative efficiency properties can be studied. But before following this route, attention is focused first on administrative efficiency.

III

Fix y and z and suppose there exists a unique internal equilibrium $(\hat{a}, \hat{r}) = (\hat{a}_1, ..., \hat{a}_K, \hat{r}_1, ..., \hat{r}_K)$ which maximizes $\pi(y, z, a, r)$ over $\mathcal{E}$. Then the utility-maximizing selection by workers of any other (a, r) in $\mathcal{E}$ is not profit-maximizing. Of course, if the director believes that workers, when left alone, are likely choose $(a, r) \neq (\hat{a}, \hat{r})$, he can always issue rules that confine individual choice options in such a way so as to increase profit beyond $\pi(y, z, a, r)$. At the extreme, he could even force workers to choose from the single-element sets $\{(\hat{a}_k, \hat{r}_k)\}$, thereby ensuring compliance with profit-maximizing behavior. However, the more confining the directors rules, the more workers have to gain (in terms of their own utility) by violating them. Hence, for the director to proceed in this way, he must establish an administrative mechanism to ensure that his rules are carried out. (A similar problem arises in the relationship between any supervisor and his subordinates, but this complication is not pursued here.)

Suppose the director does not want to post rules which, in the absence of violations, would lead workers to the profit-maximizing internal equilibrium $(\hat{a}, \hat{r})$.[20] Assume, however, that he nevertheless hires the extra administrative resources required to achieve $(\hat{a}, \hat{r})$. The actual resources needed would depend on the choice (a, r) in $\mathcal{E}$ that workers would make when the director's rules by themselves do not bring forth $(\hat{a}, \hat{r})$. The cost of these resources is called the *administrative* cost of the firm and is described symbolically by the function $C(a, r)$. Clearly, $C(\hat{a}, \hat{r}) = 0$ and $C(a, r) > 0$ for all other (a, r) in $\mathcal{E}$. It is assumed that $C(a, r)$ is sufficient to ensure that workers perform $(\hat{a}, \hat{r})$ for each (a, r).

The net profit accruing to the firm if the director were to ensure indirectly

20 For example, there may be personal or cultural constraints that make him reluctant to force workers to choose from the single-element sets $\{(\hat{a}_k, \hat{r}_k)\}$.

the selection of $(\hat{a}, \hat{r})$ as described above is

$$\pi(y, z, \hat{a}, \hat{r}) - C(a, r), \quad (6)$$

where y and z are given and (a, r) is the internal equilibrium that would arise given the director's rules. Only when

$$\pi(y, z, \hat{a}, \hat{r}) - C(a, r) > \pi(y, z, a, r)$$

will it pay to incur the administrative cost necessary to pressure workers into maintaining profit-maximizing behavior. In general, net profit need not be maximized by pushing workers to $(\hat{a}, \hat{r})$. The director may be able to do better than (6) by, for example, allowing workers some flexibility in their choices (i.e., by not insisting on $(\hat{a}, \hat{r})$) and also by not hiring the full complement of resources $C(a, r)$. Net profit would be larger than (6) in this case if the loss from not achieving $\pi(y, z, \hat{a}, \hat{r})$ were smaller than the savings in $C(a, r)$. Let $(\tilde{a}, \tilde{r})$ denote the internal equilibrium in $\mathcal{E}$ that arises when the director imposes no rules at all and workers are relieved of directorial constraints in the selection of their own activities and the rules they designate for their subordinates. The imposition of no rules by the director is one element in the collection of all sets of rules the director may issue that impose no effective constraints on the selection of activities and rules by any worker.

The administrative mechanisms implemented to enforce the director's rules differ for bureaucracies, clans, and militaries. In bureaucracies they take the form of an arrangement to monitor (and evaluate) worker performance.[21] Workers are said to "shirk" whenever $(a, r) \neq (\hat{a}, \hat{r})$. The purpose of monitoring is to reduce or eliminate shirking and thus increase profit. In clans, administrative mechanisms are concerned with establishing and maintaining the sense of community and commitment; and in militaries they attempt to build and preserve the ability of supervisors to influence subordinates. As indicated in Section I, all of these administrative mechanisms have informational requirements that are costly to meet. The appropriate costs of information are a part of $C(a, r)$ in each case.

Recall that in all non-market forms of organization, administrative cost replaces the transactions costs which must be present and explicit if the same firm were reorganized as a collection of sub-firms each consisting of a single employee. The administrative cost of the market form, written c_m, is the sum of all market transactions costs (i.e., all contingent claims contract costs) necessary for its operation. Note that c_m is determined by the structure and pattern

21 See, for example, Calvo and Wellisz [2].

of the contingent claims contracts required. The selection of (a_k, r_k) by each employee (sub-firm) k is inconsequential since no employee has supervisors to constrain his activities with rules, and there is no social interaction among workers beyond that arising from the participation in market transactions.

One way to think of the efficiency of organizational forms is with reference to the $C(\tilde{a}, \tilde{r})$ and c_m. Given a firm as described in Section II having fixed quantities of inputs y and z, and a number of potential organizational forms, one form may be said to be more *administratively efficient* than another if its administrative cost when all workers are free of directorial constraints is lower.[22] Thus the market form is relatively inefficient when the transactions costs it requires, namely c_m rise above the values of $C(\tilde{a}, \tilde{r})$ from other forms. The bureaucratic form is relatively inefficient when it becomes prohibitively expensive to monitor performances. Similarly, the clan and military forms are relatively inefficient if the costs, respectively, of maintaining the sense of community and commitment, and of preserving the ability to influence are very high. The exact manner in which, for a given firm, these four organizational forms are ordered by this notion of administrative efficiency depends on the relative values of $C(\tilde{a}, \tilde{r})$ and c_m where in each case once again, $(\tilde{a}, \tilde{r})$ is selected by the firm's workers in the absence of rules imposed by the director.

Suppose $C'(\tilde{a}', \tilde{r}')$ represents the administrative cost of one non-market form of organization, say, where $(\tilde{a}', \tilde{r}')$ is the internal equilibrium chosen within this organizational form without directoral constraints, and let $C''(\tilde{a}'', \tilde{r}'')$ denote the administrative cost of another. Then

$$C'(\tilde{a}', \tilde{r}') < C''(\tilde{a}'', \tilde{r}'') \tag{7}$$

does not necessarily imply

$$\pi'(y, z, \hat{a}, \hat{r}) - C'(\tilde{a}', \tilde{r}') > \pi''(y, z, \hat{a}, \hat{r}) - C''(\tilde{a}'', \tilde{r}''), \tag{8}$$

where π' and π'' are the profit functions defined in (3) for the two forms, respectively, and $(\hat{a}, \hat{r})$ indicates generally different profit-maximizing activities and rules in each case. That is, lower administrative cost may be accompanied by lower net profit. Thus, depending on the intended purpose, (6) evaluated at $(\tilde{a}, \tilde{r})$ may be a more appropriate measure of administrative efficiency than $C(\tilde{a}, \tilde{r})$. An obvious sufficient condition for (7) to imply (8) is that

$$\pi'(y, z, \hat{a}, \hat{r}) \geq \pi''(y, z, \hat{a}, \hat{r}), \tag{9}$$

[22] See Ouchi [10, pp. 132-137]. Note this definition of comparative administrative efficiency implicitly requires that administrative and production costs be separable and that the production function (1) be the same for all organizational forms under consideration. Use of the latter precludes examination of the ability of an organizational form to adapt to technological change.

and such will obtain if the level of maximum (gross) profit is the same over the relevant sets $\mathcal{E}$ for both forms. With (9) in force, lower administrative cost or greater administrative efficiency always corresponds to higher net profit.

These ideas may be applied to compare administrative efficiencies as the firm's pyramidal structure expands and changes. To do so requires that administrative cost be expressed as a function of hierarchical levels. Two employees in the firm's pyramid of authority are said to be on the same hierarchical level if there are an equal number of persons above each. Let a pyramid of authority for a large number of levels be given which depicts the authority structure of the firm as it expands by adding hierarchical levels. Take the number of hierarchical levels to indicate the size of the firm. Then once the firm has decided to go down to a particular level, n, the optimal quantity of labor and non-labor inputs to be employed along with the size of the firm is determined. Also determined at n are the utility-maximizing $(\tilde{a}, \tilde{r})$ and profit-maximizing $(\hat{a}, \hat{r})$, as well as the corresponding function values $\pi(y, z, \hat{a}, \hat{r})$ and $C(\tilde{a}, \tilde{r})$. The latter, in particular, may be expressed as functions of n. Thus write $\hat{\pi}(n)$ and $C(n)$ as, respectively, the maximum profit and the administrative cost associated with level n. Since the number of employees usually increases at an increasing rate with n, one would expect the same to be true of $C(n)$. Hence administrative efficiency declines as n rises.[23] Moreover, the optimal firm size can be defined as that which maximizes

$$\hat{\pi}(n) - C(n),$$

provided such an optimum exists.[24]

The replacement of the market form of organization by the bureaucratic U-form in many late nineteenth century American industries has been explained in part by arguing that the latter had become relatively more administratively efficient than the former.[25] The subsequent switch (beginning in the early 1920s) from the U-form to the M-form as the number of hierarchical levels of the U-form grew has been interpreted similarly.[26] The rational for the latter abandonment of the U-form in favor of the M-form as n rises is especially easy to illustrate in the present scheme. As many such explanations do, the one given here abstracts from practical considerations in order to focus all attention on the pure logic of what is involved. Consider a hierarchical firm organized as a U-form bureaucracy with administrative cost $C(n)$. Suppose the firm has

23 See Coase [3, pp. 394-395].

24 See, for example, Williamson [14].

25 See, for example, Williamson [15, p. 133], [16].

26 See, for example, Williamson [15, Ch. 8], [16].

the option of expanding by either adding θ hierarchical levels to its U-form or replicating itself θ times in an M-form multidivisional structure, and that in either case it is the same for each n. The administrative cost of the first option is $C(n+\theta)$; that of the second is $\theta C(n)$. In both instances the firm expands by enlarging θ for fixed n. Hence administrative cost expands (as indicated earlier) at an increasing rate with θ for the U-form, but only proportionately for the M-form. Thus it is possible for the M-form to eventually become (if it is not already) more efficient than the U-form. To the extent that the M-form equivalent of adding θ levels to the U-form is smaller than θ replications of the original firm, the M-form will become more efficient than the U-form that much sooner.

As an example suppose $C(n) = n^2$ so that

$$\theta C(n) = \theta n^2$$

and

$$C(n+\theta) = (n+\theta)^2.$$

In this case it can be shown that if $n > 4$, then for all θ where

$$\theta > \frac{n^2 - 2n}{2} + \frac{n\sqrt{n^2 - 4}}{2}, \tag{10}$$

one necessarily has

$$\theta C(n) < C(n+\theta).$$

Thus the M-form will be more efficient than the U-form whenever $n > 4$ and θ grows large enough to satisfy (10).

Precise mathematical propositions describing the formal conditions under which a bureaucracy, say, is more administratively efficient than a market form, clan, or military are not possible without much more detailed analysis of the structure of the costs that determine $C(n)$. Rather than proceed along this path, however, the next section examines the allocative efficiency of the distribution of activities among employees occurring within these organizational forms.

IV

The first step in the development of allocative efficiency propositions is to provide idealized characterizations of the organizational forms under consideration — i.e., the bureaucracy, clan, military, and market form — in the context of the model of Section II. Now it has already been pointed out that the instruments of the non-market invisible hands which coordinate social interactions among employees in bureaucracies, clans, and militaries (namely incentive, utility, and g-p functions, respectively) are all present in the model. But rigorous definitions of these organizational forms are not provided by merely noting the presence of such functions. One must still specify how individuals respond to them, or in other words, how the coordination of social interactions actually works in an ideal environment. The relevant concepts for doing so are presented next.

An employee $k \neq 0$ is called *incentive motivated* if for all pairs of values (a'_k, r'_k) and (a''_k, r''_k) the numerical inequality

$$W^k(a'_k, r'_k) \geq W^k(a''_k, r''_k)$$

implies

$$U^k(a'_k, r'_k) \geq U^k(a''_k, r''_k).$$

He is *vertically influenced* when

$$G^k(a'_k, r'_k) \geq G^k(a''_k, r''_k)$$

forces

$$U^k(a'_k, r'_k) \geq U^k(a''_k, r''_k).$$

Incentive motivation and vertical influence mean, respectively, that individual preferences are such that employees respond in the "same direction" as that of incentives and influence.

Now recall production function (1). For employee $k \neq 0$ consider any two vectors (a'_k, r'_k) and (a''_k, r''_k) such that (i) output is at least as high using a'_k in (1) instead of a''_k , and (ii) r'_k restricts all subordinates of k to subsets of their respective activity sets obtained under r''_k on which output is at least as large as it is anywhere else in the r''_k sets. Other things being equal, then, the output associated with (a'_k, r'_k) can not be less than that associated with (a''_k, r''_k). Assume that (i) and (ii) hold regardless of the activities performed by the remaining employees, and regardless of the quantities of labor time and non-labor inputs hired by the firm.[27] Under these conditions, if

$$W^k(a'_k, r'_k) \geq W^k(a''_k, r''_k),$$

[27] The idea that in these circumstances the output associated with (a'_k, r'_k) is larger than that identified with (a''_k, r''_k) furnishes a way of ordering the collection of all vectors (a_k, r_k). The "weak" version of this ordering is assumed to be reflexive, transitive, antisymmetric, and total. See Katzner [7 (this volume, Essay 6)] and Gintis and Katzner [4].

or if

$$G^k(a'_k, r'_k) \geq G^k(a''_k, r''_k),$$

then W^k and G^k, respectively, are referred to as *non-decreasing*. In other words, incentive or *g-p* functions are non-decreasing provided they are set so as to reward or influence employees toward activities which do not decrease output. Similarly, employee k is said to *internalize the values of the firm* when, under the same conditions,

$$U^k(a'_k, r'_k) \geq U^k(a''_k, r''_k).$$

Thus, a socialization process has taken place leaving the employee's preferences among activities and rules coincident with the interests of the firm.

It is now possible to give abstract definitions of the notions of bureaucracy, clan, and military in idealized form. Like the standard characterization of perfect competition, these may be thought of as "ideal types" which do not usually appear in reality exactly as pictured, but which are useful for study nonetheless. The firm described in Section II is called an *idea bureaucracy* provided that all incentive functions W^k (where $k \neq 0$) are non-decreasing and (as a group) profit-efficient, and all employees ($k \neq 0$) are incentive motivated. It is referred to as an *ideal clan* whenever all incentive functions are constant functions (and hence profit-efficient) and all employees ($k \neq 0$) internalize the values of the firm. And it is said to be an *ideal military* if all incentive functions are constant functions (and hence profit-efficient), all *g-p* functions G^k (where $k \neq 0$) are non-decreasing, and all employees ($k \neq 0$) are vertically influenced.[28] These definitions capture and formalize the essence of the concepts of bureaucracy, clan, and military discussed in Section I. The *ideal market* form of organization of the firm is the market form described in Section I for the case in which all contingent claims contract costs, i.e., the administrative cost, $c_m = 0$.

Consider now a distinct internal equilibrium (a, r) in different sets $\mathcal{E}$ for each of the idealized organizational forms described above. Such equilibria have been defined in general in Section II and hence apply directly to bureaucracies, clans, and militaries. With respect to the market form, rules do not constrain individual choices, and the selection of activities, which defines internal equilibrium here, has no impact on output and profit. All that matters

[28] According to these definitions, it is technically possible for the firm to be, say, both an ideal clan and an ideal bureaucracy at the same time. But such combinations of organizational forms are irrelevant for present purposes. In a clan, the emphasis is on internalization of values, regardless of how individuals might react to incentives. A bureaucracy, on the other hand, focuses on incentive motivation independently of the extent to which values happen to be internalized.

is that certain quantities of goods are exchanged in the relevant markets according to the contingent claims contracts. Hence the profit of the firm, that is, the sum of the "profits" of the individual sub-firms (employees), is constant over all vectors (a, r) or, what in this case is the set of all internal equilibria, also denoted by $\mathcal{E}$. The following proposition, then, follows immediately from previous definitions.

Theorem 1. Let fixed values of y and z be given and suppose the director's rules impose no effective constraints on the selection of activities and rules by any worker. Then in an ideal bureaucracy, clan, military, or market form, internal equilibrium always maximizes profit over the set of all consistent vectors (a, r), that is, over the relevant $\mathcal{E}$.

Theorem 1 has several implications. First, every (a, r) in $\mathcal{E}$ that is not profit maximizing must arise because the director's rules exclude the profit-maximizing (a, r) from the options opened to employees. Although logically possible, one would not expect the director's rules to be so constituted. Second, assuming that the director's rules do not effectively constrain workers choices, at internal equilibria in ideal bureaucracies, clans, and militaries, administrative cost $C(a, r) = 0$. (Recall that c_m has already been defined to be zero in the idealized market form.) Hence, according to the criteria of Section III, the administrative efficiencies of (ideal) bureaucracies, clans, militaries, and market forms are all equal. In each case, individuals pursue profit maximization automatically without needing the director to dictate rules and incur administrative costs. Third, these conclusions apply regardless of whether the pyramidal structure of the firm is of the U-form or M-form variety.

Another way to study the efficiency properties of idealized organizational forms is in terms of internal Pareto optimality. Economists are quite familiar with the proposition that, under certain well-known conditions, in a perfectly competitive economy, equilibrium is Pareto optimal. That is, given endowments, tastes, and technology, and with consumers buying output quantities and supplying factor quantities so as to maximize utility subject to their budget constraints, with firms selling output quantities and buying input quantities so as to maximize profits, and with supply equal to demand in all markets, quantities of outputs and inputs can not be redistributed among consumers and firms without lowering some output or making at least one person worse off. In this sense, the market form of organization is allocatively efficient: having perfectly competitive equilibrium inputs and outputs in all sub-firms, it is part of an economy-wide Pareto optimum. Of course the same thing is true for any organizational form whose input and output quantities are consistent with perfect competition. But as soon as the market form is discarded in favor of bureaucracies, clans, or militaries, the possibility of waste in the "improper" allocation of the activities of production within the firm arises.[29] And such is the case regardless of whether the distribution of input and output quantities across the economy is Pareto optimal. For even at an economy-wide competitive equilibrium, it might be possible (without any change in input quantities and without lowering anyone's utility) to expand output in a bureaucracy, say, by reallocating activities inside the firm. Hence it becomes necessary to ask if the coordination of social interaction in bureaucracies, clans, and militaries, which replaces coordination by markets in these non-market organizational forms, is sufficient to ensure the allocative efficiency of internal equilibrium.

Let y and z in the production function (1) be given. A vector $(a^0, r^0) = (a_1^0, ..., a_K^0, r_1^0, ..., r_K^0)$ is called *internally Pareto optimal in production* as long as there is no other (a, r) in the relevant $\mathcal{E}$ such that

$$U^k(a_k, r_k) \geq U^k(a_k^0, r_k^0)$$

for all $k = l, ..., K$,

$$U^k(a_k, r_k) > U^k(a_k^0, r_k^0)$$

for at least one $k = 1, ..., K$,

$$f(y, z, a, r) \geq f(y, z, a^0, r^0),$$

and

$$C(a, r) \leq C(a^0, r^0).$$

Thus at an internal Pareto optimum, no reorganization of production in terms of activities and rules can make one employee better off, and no one else worse off, without lowering output or raising the administrative cost that pushes the firm to maximum profit. If, for example, through the imposition of rules, workers are not permitted to perform their jobs in ways in which they prefer, even though their preferred ways leads to the same output and administrative cost, then the (a, r) obtained is not Pareto optimal. Note that the director is not included in this notion of Pareto optimality and that the functions U^k, f and C are all taken to be given.

Propositions asserting the allocative efficiency of ideal bureaucracies, clans, and militaries are presented below. In all cases y and z are assumed fixed and, as in the perfectly competitive economy, a non-market invisible hand allocates activities and rules so as to achieve optimality. Only the proof of Theorem 2 is

[29] Leibenstein refers to this waste as "X-inefficiency" [9, p. 95].

outlined here; those of Theorems 3 and 4 are similar.[30]

Theorem 2. Let the firm described in Section II be an ideal bureaucracy and suppose the director's rules impose no effective constraints on the selection of activities and rules by any worker. If $(\bar{a}, \bar{r})$ is an internal equilibrium for the firm, then it is also internally Pareto optimal in production.

Proof:

Suppose $(\bar{a}, \bar{r}) = (\bar{a}_1, ..., \bar{a}_K, \bar{r}_1, ..., \bar{r}_K)$ is an internal equilibrium (given y and z). Invoking Theorem 1 and the profit efficiency property that characterizes (in part) ideal bureaucracies, $(\bar{a}, \bar{r})$ also maximizes both profit and output. If $(\bar{a}, \bar{r})$ were not internally Pareto optimal, then there would exist a reorganization of production $(a, r) = (a_1, ..., a_K, r_1, ..., r_K)$ in the relevant $\mathcal{E}$ such that

$$U^k(a_k, r_k) > U^k(\bar{a}_k, \bar{r}_k), \tag{11}$$

for some employee k, and the levels of output and of utility of all other employees are no lower, and administrative cost is no higher at (a, r) than at $(\bar{a}, \bar{r})$. Now because the firm is an ideal bureaucracy, all employees are incentive motivated and all incentive functions are non-decreasing. But incentive motivation for the employee k in (11) implies

$$W^k(a_k, r_k) > W^k(\bar{a}_k, \bar{r}_k) \tag{12}$$

and hence by the non-decreasingness of W^k, output must be larger at (a, r) than at $(\bar{a}, \bar{r})$.[31] This contradicts the maximality of output at $(\bar{a}, \bar{r})$. Therefore $(\bar{a}, \bar{r})$ is internally Pareto optimal in production.

Q.E.D.

Theorem 3. Let the firm described in Section II be an ideal clan and suppose the director's rules impose no effective constraints on the selection of activities and rules by any worker. If $(\bar{a}, \bar{r})$ is an internal equilibrium for the firm, then it is also internally Pareto optimal in production.

Theorem 4. Let the firm described in Section II be an ideal military and suppose the director's rules impose no effective constraints on the selection of

[30] The proof of Theorem 3 is the same as that of Theorem 5 (or Theorem 11.2-5 in the reprinted version) in Gintis and Katzner [4]. See also Theorems 9, 7, and 8, respectively, in Katzner [7 (this volume, Essay 6)].

[31] The last step depends on the totality of the ordering described in n. 27 on p. 246 above. For the uninteresting special case in which W^k is a constant function, equation (12) by itself provides a more immediate contradiction. An alternative proof which does not use the non-decreasingness property of incentive functions can be found in Gintis and Katzner [4] as the proof of Theorem 3 in the original or of Theorem 11.2-3 in the reprinted version.

activities and rules by any worker. If $(\bar{a}, \bar{r})$ is an internal equilibrium for the firm, then it is also internally Pareto optimal in production.

An analogous theorem for the ideal market form of organization is easily established since (a) in this case employees (sub-firms) choose, without being subject to rule constraints, the highest level of utility that they can achieve; (b) output and profit are independent of these choices and hence automatically "rnaximized" over them; and (c) administrative cost is defined to be zero.

Thus, although trading the coordination of production within a firm by markets for the non-market coordination of social interactions among employees present in bureaucracies, clans, and militaries necessarily introduces social interactions where none formerly existed, it still does not force allocative inefficiencies of the activities and rules of production to which these social interactions relate. Internal Pareto optimality is a characteristic of internal equilibrium, at least theoretically, in all four idealized organizational forms. Therefore, the insertion or emergence of such organizational forms into an economy need not, as a matter of course, create new allocative waste which was not already there.

References

1. Beckmann, M. J., *Rank in Organizations* (Berlin: Springer-Verlag, 1978).
2. Calvo, G. A., and S. Wellisz, "Hierarchy, Ability and Income Distribution," *Journal of Political Economy* 87 (1979), pp. 991-1010.
3. Coase, R. H., "The Nature of the Firm," *Economica*, n.s. 4 (1937), pp. 386-405.
4. Gintis, H., and D. W. Katzner, "Profits, Optimality and the Social Division of Labor in the Firm," in *Sociological Economics*, L. Lévy-Garboua, ed. (London: SAGE, 1979), pp. 269-297. Reprinted as Ch. 11 in D. W. Katzner, *Analysis without Measurement* (Cambridge: Cambridge University Press, 1983).
5. Janowitz, M., *Sociology and the Military Establishment*, rev. ed. (New York: Russell Sage Foundation, 1965).
6. Katzner, D. W., *Analysis without Measurement* (Cambridge: Cambridge University Press, 1983).
7. ________, "The Role of Formalism in Economic Thought, with Illustration Drawn from the Analysis of Social Interaction in the Firm," in *The Reconstruction of Economic Theory*, P. Mirowski, ed. (Boston:

Kluwer-Nijhoff, 1986), pp. 137-177. This volume, Essay 6.

8. Lang, K., "Military Organizations," in *Handbook of Organizations*, J. C. March, ed. (Chicago: Rand McNally, 1965), Ch. 20.
9. Leibenstein, H., *Beyond Economic Man* (Cambridge: Harvard University Press, 1976).
10. Ouchi, W. G., "Markets, Bureaucracies, and Clans," *Administrative Science Quarterly* 25 (1980), pp. 129-141.
11. ________, *Theory Z* (Reading: Addison-Wesley, 1981).
12. Sah, R. K., and J. E. Stiglitz, "The Architecture of Economic Systems: Hierarchies and Polyarchies," *American Economic Review* 76 (1986), pp. 716-727.
13. Smith, A., *An Inquiry into the Nature and Causes of the Wealth of Nations* (New York: Random House, 1937).
14. Williamson, O. E., "Hierarchical Control and Optimum Firm Size," *Journal of Political Economy* 75 (1967), pp. 123-138.
15. ________, *Markets and Hierarchies: Analysis and Antitrust Implications* (New York: Free Press, (1975).
16. ________, "The Modern Corporation: Origins, Evolution, Attributes," *Journal of Economic Literature* 19 (1981), pp. 1537-1568.

12
Attitudes, Rationality, and Consumer Demand[1]

Ever since the marginalist revolution, the analysis of consumer behavior has occupied a central place in economic thought. Indeed, its development has moulded much of the apparatus and technique that forms today's economic tool kit. In the heyday of nineteenth century neoclassicism, preoccupation with this subject substantially absorbed the economic landscape. The notion of maximization and its counterpart of equality at the margin carried thinking about the consumer, along with the science of economics itself, to new intellectual heights.

In the process, rationality became embodied in the notion of maximization, and maximization was anointed as the implication and hallmark of rationality. The consumer, it came to be supposed, confronted the problem of choosing among baskets of commodities against a preference ordering that exhibited certain properties. One such property was representability in terms of utility. Upon specification of commodity prices and income, rational choice arose as the selection, from baskets the consumer could afford, of that basket providing maximum utility. As prices and incomes hypothetically varied, repeated maximization picked out a unique basket in each case or, in other words, a demand

---

[1] *Inflation and Income Distribution in Capitalist Crisis*, J. A. Kregel, ed. (London: Macmillan, 1989), pp. 133-153.

The author gratefully acknowledges the insightful aid of Thomas J. Madden and Douglas Vickers in developing the argument of this paper.

function was defined over the set of all relevant price-income vectors. Thus rationality found expression in terms of demand functions and their characteristics (e.g., Katzner [8]).

In this view of things no accommodation is given to the uncertainties that exist in real-world decision environments. Ignorance and unsureness about both present and future outcomes and the potential satisfactions arising from choices are set aside. The analysis focuses, instead, on the notions and mechanics of maximization in a deterministic framework, though the stochastic properties of situations and decisions have, of course, attracted and continue to attract considerable attention.

There is, however, an alternative explanation of consumer behavior having nothing to do with utility maximization and rationality. It is located in the marketing literature and is interdisciplinary in character. Its primary thrust focuses on such considerations as personalities, attitudes, cultural influences, and social class as the determinants of consumer demand (e.g., Engel, Blackwell and Kollat [5]). Probabilistic uncertainty is frequently taken into account. Although the approach often is concerned more with an individual's (or group's) selection of a particular brand of a given good rather than with the total amount (regardless of brand) of the good chosen, the suggestion remains that things such as attitudes might also have a useful role to play in the rationality explanation of demand.

The purpose of the present paper is to begin an exploration of this terrain by concentrating only on attitudes and by analyzing the relevance of attitudes and attitude change for the utility-maximization perspective on consumer behavior. Attitudes may be introduced into the rationality vision in a variety of ways. These include permitting attitudes to restrict the sets out of which choices are made, or to influence preferences by inserting them as parameters in the utility function. Only the latter is considered below. It is also reasonable to think of attitudes as being determined, in part, by prices and incomes as the market presents them to the consumer. When the relation between these variables (attitudes, prices, and incomes) is known, then upon substituting for the attitude variables in the utility function, analysis can proceed as if prices and incomes were the parametric arguments of the utility function.[2] Alternatively, when this relation is uncertain, an entirely different collection of problems arises. As interesting as these possibilities are, however, the present discussion excludes them both. Instead, attention focuses on the special cases in which attitudes, prices and incomes are all independent of each other.

One of the reasons why those explaining demand on the basis of rationality may previously have ignored personalities, attitudes, social class, etc., is

2 Kalman [7] has considered the case in which prices enter the utility function.

that these facets of the individual appear to be incapable of numerical calibration. Investigators may therefore have felt that their inclusion in the logic of utility maximization could have led to indeterminacy, fuzziness, and error. But it has recently been demonstrated that formal, deterministic models analogous to those of the rationality theory of demand can be constructed even in the absence of measurement (Katzner [9]; see also Essay 4 in this volume). Exactness and quantification, then, are not synonymous, nor does a lack of numerical gauges impose barriers to the conduct of rigorous, scientific inquiry. At the same time, psychologists and marketers have made progress in constructing scales on which certain limited aspects of things like attitudes may be measured (e.g., Fishbein and Ajzen [6]). Subsequent discussion draws on both developments.

The paper begins with a discussion of the marketing explanation of consumer behavior by developing demand as a function of attitude, prices, and income from a general relation between attitude and behavior that is sometimes employed by psychologists. This is then contrasted with a rationality explanation of the same demand function. Since uncertainty is not present in the vision of rationality employed, it is obviously necessary, in order to have the marketing approach arrive at the same result as that generated by utility maximization, to assume away all uncertainty permitted in the general marketing context. Next, the attitude properties of demand are investigated from both points of view. Along the way, a basis for a general analysis of the impact on demand of changes in any non-quantifiable (exogenous) parameter in the utility function (not only attitudes) is obtained. For comparative purposes, the attitude properties of demand are examined further in the special case in which ratio quantifiability of attitudes is assumed. Examples are presented to illustrate the main results. It should be emphasized that the primary intent of the paper is to throw new light on the potential integration of two different explanations of consumer behavior and, as a result, a large amount of the highly valuable literature that takes the marketing perspective is left unexplored.

I

In general, an attitude may be described as "... a learned predisposition to respond in a consistently favorable or unfavorable manner with respect to a given object" (Fishbein and Ajzen [6, p. 6]). Although the notions that an attitude is learned, that it predisposes action, and that actions are consistently favorable or unfavorable may all be interpreted in a variety of ways (*Ibid.*, pp. 6-10), this definition will suffice for present purposes. In the context of consumer behavior, one might want to require that instead of responding to the "given object" itself, the individual actually reacts to the perceived or imagined want-satisfying capacity inherent in that object. One might also wish to permit the "predisposition to respond" to arise as the result of the acquisition of costly information. But neither of these directions is pursued here. Moreover, the term object may refer either to things or to behavior relative to things. Thus a persons attitude toward dogs may be different from his attitude toward the act of bringing a dog home for a pet. Regardless of interpretation, however, this definition of attitude implicitly requires that some kind of evaluation — favorable or unfavorable — be a part of the response.

A conceptual framework for thinking about attitudes in relation to beliefs, evaluations, intentions, and behavior has been proposed by Fishbein and Ajzen [6, pp. 13-16]. Briefly their scheme is as follows: From direct observation, other sources of information, and inference, a person forms beliefs about the attributes of an object. Beliefs are thus statements about whether or not, or in what ways, the object possesses certain attributes. Attributes are evaluated independently in terms of their "favorableness" or "unfavorableness". Both beliefs and evaluations are taken to be exogenously and independently determined. The person's attitude toward an object then depends on his beliefs about the attributes of that object together with his evaluations of those attributes. Attitudes, in turn, generate intentions, and intentions determine behavior.[3] Formally, let there be L attributes (of the object in question) about which the individual has beliefs, and index them by $\ell = 1, ..., L$. Suppose b_ℓ is a variable[4] ranging over possible (verbally described) beliefs about attribute ℓ. Write $b = (b_1, ..., b_L)$. Similarly, denote the (verbal) evaluation of ℓ by e_ℓ and set $e = (e_1, ..., e_L)$. Represent the scalar variable "attitude" as a, the scalar variable "intention" as z, and the scalar variable "behavior" as x. These also are expressed in qualitative rather than numerical terms. Clearly the Fishbein-Ajzen conceptual framework defines three functional relations among these variables:[5]

$$a = f^1(b, e), \tag{1}$$

$$z = f^2(a), \tag{2}$$

[3] In another context, Bausor [3] has also considered the relation between intentions and behaviour.

[4] The problems relating to defining qualitative variables in this way have been discussed by Katzner [9]. See also Essay 4 in this volume.

[5] The ordinary mathematical definition of function carries over here. See Katzner [9, p. 56] and Essay 4 in this volume.

$$x = f^3(z), \tag{3}$$

where f, f^2, and f^3 are the symbolic names of the relations, respectively. Thus, for example, equation (1) is meant to be read as saying that to each vector of beliefs and evaluations, the individual assigns a unique attitude.

Two implications of equations (1)-(3) deserve mention. First, knowledge of attitudes by itself is evidently not enough to predict behavior: It is also necessary to know how attitudes translate into intentions (f^2) and how intentions give rise to behavior (f^3). The latter functions, of course, may be combined into a single composite function relating behavior to attitudes:

$$x = f^3(f^2(a)). \tag{4}$$

Second, it is obvious that attitudes (and the resulting behavior implied by (4)) can only be modified by changing beliefs and/or evaluations. This may be inspired, say, from information secured upon exposure to advertising (Aaker and Myers [1, Ch. 10]) or through the personal influence exerted by someone else (Robertson [11, Chs. 7,8]).

An example will serve to clarify these ideas. Consider an individual who believes that a residue of insecticide sprayed on apple trees always remains with the apples and that this residue is potentially injurious to one's health. Assume that, in assessing his attitude toward purchasing apples, this belief is evaluated "negatively" to such an extent that his overall attitude toward them is also "negative." It does not follow that our person will not consume any apples, since he may be masochistic or like their taste enough to overcome, in part, his negative attitude. Such an effect would be recorded in (2) and (3), or (4). Now suppose that the use of insecticides on apple trees is dropped in favor of safer (so the individual believes) procedures and that, as a result, his attitude toward buying apples becomes more "positive." Then his behavior could respond through (2)-(4) in one of three ways: First, other things being equal, the individual might consume more apples. Second, he might just be content to feel more comfortable eating the same number of apples as before. And third, there is nothing to rule out the possibility that he might actually consume less.

By imposing assumptions and redefining variables so as to narrow their meaning significantly, the attitude function f^1 can be formulated quantitatively (Fishbein and Ajzen [6, p. 29]). Suppose each attribute arises in only one way and is either present or absent in the object under discussion. Redefine the idea of belief to be the likelihood, as perceived by the individual, that a relevant attribute is present. Thus b_ℓ becomes the subjective probability (sometimes referred to as the "strength of belief") that the object has attribute ℓ. Let evaluations of ℓ be recorded on ordinal, cardinal (interval), or ratio scales and take the e_ℓ to reflect these evaluations numerically. Lastly assume f^1 to be linear and rewrite (1) as

$$a = \sum_{\ell=1}^{L} b_\ell e_\ell. \tag{5}$$

Evidently a is now a quantitative variable which is, say, cardinally measured whenever all e_ℓ are finite values on cardinal scales. Even if only one e_ℓ is ordinal, then a has to be viewed as measured ordinally rather than cardinally. Although this formulation focuses on certain rather limited dimensions and drops important substance from the concepts of attitude and belief as described earlier, it is still useful and will be employed later on. Various procedures for measuring attitudes based on (5) have been surveyed by Fishbein and Ajzen [6, Ch. 3].

Marketers have introduced attitudes into their explanations of consumer behavior in a variety of ways. In one approach (Engel, Blackwell, and Kollat [5, esp. p. 557]), equations (2) and (3) are first revised and extended, and then supplemented with additional equations to fit the marketing context. Thus behavior (x) is now limited to making a choice among goods, brands of goods, quantities of goods, and so on, and only those aspects of intention (z) and attitude (a) relevant for such choice behavior are considered. In recognition of the latter, the phrase "attitude toward a good" is hereafter interpreted to mean "attitude toward the purchase of that good." The choice itself is assumed to depend on intentions and on a variable (verbally defined) called "unanticipated circumstances,"[6] which shall be denoted by c_1. Mathematically,

$$x = g^1(z, c_1). \tag{6}$$

The difference between g^1 and f^3 is the restriction of the setting in which behavior occurs and the addition of uncertainty through the variable c_1. Similarly intention is determined by attitude, "compliance with social pressures to conform," and "anticipated circumstances." Writing the latter two variables as c_2 and c_3, respectively,

$$z = g^2(a, c_2, c_3). \tag{7}$$

[6] This variable, employed by Engel, Blackwell and Kollat [5, p. 557], incorporates part of the situational effects variable studied by Belk [4]. Other aspects of situational effects are contained in the variable "anticipated circumstances" (c_3) introduced momentarily.

Observe that g^2 is an expansion of f^2 with the meaning of its variables restricted to the realm of choice. Specification of the equations of this approach supplemental to (6) and (7) is unnecessary except to note that, although independent of c_1, c_3, and each other, both compliance with social pressures to conform and attitudes are further determined by other variables and are not viewed exogenously as they are here.

Substituting (7) into (6),

$$x = g^3(a, c_3), \tag{8}$$

where c_1 and c_2 are now taken to be fixed parameters subsumed in the functional symbol g^3 (thus the uncertainty in equation (6) is dropped) and

$$g^3(a, c_3) = g^1(g^2(a, c_2, c_3), c_1).$$

Note that (8) is the marketing-context counterpart to (4). It says that choice is determined by attitude and anticipated circumstances.

To become still more restrictive and concrete, and thereby to transpose the above marketing approach into the language of economic demand functions, suppose that the choices the individual makes in (8) are among quantities of goods. With I goods indexed by $I = 1, ..., I$, let x_i vary over possible quantities of good i chosen by this person, a_i vary over possible (and typically unmeasured) attitudes toward good i assumed by him, and p_i vary over possible prices for good i. Denote the variable representing his income, that is, the amount of money he has to spend, by m, and write $p = (p_1, ..., p_I)$. Now take the choice variable x to be the vector $x = (x_1, ..., x_I)$, the attitude variable a to be the vector $a = (a_1, ..., a_I)$, and the anticipated circumstances variable c_3 to be the vector $c_3 = (p, m)$. Confine attention to anticipated circumstances such that $(p, m) > 0$, where p and m are known with certainty, and permit x to range over the commodity space $X = \{x : x > 0\}$ and a to range over some appropriate, not-necessarily-quantifiable, and possibly uncountable[7] set A. Then, using d to denote the special case of g^3 defined by the above interpretations of x, a, and c_3, equation (8) may be written as

$$x = d(a, p, m). \tag{9}$$

Thus the relation between attitude, anticipated circumstances, and behavior of (8) has been reduced to the individual's demand function which identifies to each appropriate collection of attitudes, prices, and income, a unique basket of

[7] Uncountable sets of non-quantifiable elements are legitimate analytical constructs. See Katzner [9, Section 7.2].

goods demanded. Note that although x, p and m are numerical variables, it is not required that the components of a be scaleable. Also, d is really short for a vector of functions $d = (d_1, ..., d_I)$, where

$$x_i = d^i(a, p, m), \tag{10}$$

for $i = 1, ..., I$. Without attempting to provide deeper insight into the source of d, the marketing explanation of consumer behavior stops here. The rationality explanation, on the other hand, begins with d in the form of (9) or (10) and attempts to understand it as the outcome of utility maximization.

II

To explain the demand function (9) or (10) in the thought form of rationality (utility maximization), let the individual have preferences among baskets of goods in the commodity space X which depend on his unquantified attitudes in A. Assume his preferences are represented by a utility function u, written

$$\mu = u(a, x), \tag{11}$$

where u is defined on the Cartesian product $A \times X$ and μ denotes the ordinal utility values identified with (a, x) by u. For each a in A (recall that the components a_i of these attitude variables are verbally described variable values and generally not associated with numbers on either ordinal or cardinal scales), suppose u to be (i) continuous on X and twice continuously differentiable in the interior of X; (ii) increasing in the sense that the marginal utilities or first-order partial derivatives with respect to the x_i, namely

$$u_{x_i}(a, x) = \frac{\partial u(a, x)}{\partial x_i},$$

are everywhere positive for $i = 1, ..., I$; and (iii) strictly quasi-concave. It is also convenient to require, again for each a in A, that indifference surfaces do not touch the boundaries of X. Under these conditions, it can be shown (Katzner [8, p. 42]) that for every (a, p, m), with verbally described vector a in A and numerical vector $(p, m) > 0$, there exists a unique basket x in the interior of X which maximizes u subject to the budget constraint

$$p \cdot x = m,$$

where the dot "·" denotes inner product. Hence each (a, p, m) is associated with a unique x or, in other words, a function

$$x = h(a, p, m), \tag{12}$$

is defined. As in (9), h is an abbreviation for a vector of functions $h = (h^1, ..., h^I)$ such that

$$x_i = h^i(a, p, m),$$

for $i = 1, ..., I$.

Thinking of $h(a, p, m)$ as a function of (p, m) alone for each value of a, the properties imposed on it by dint of the fact that h comes from the constrained maximization of a utility function with the previously described characteristics, are well known. Thus given any verbal vector a in A, h must be positive, homogeneous of degree zero, continuous everywhere, and differentiable except possibly at certain isolated points, and must satisfy the budget constraint and, where differentiable, the symmetry and negative definiteness restrictions (Katzner [8, pp. 42-51]). Clearly, as long as d, whose domain and range coincide with those of h, exhibits the same properties as h, then (9) or (10) may be explained as the outcome of constrained utility maximization. Taking this perspective here, from now on h and d are regarded as identical and the symbol d is dropped. Thus there are two independent explanations or ways to derive h: either as a special case of the Fishbein-Ajzen attitude model or from the maximization of utility (which depends on both unquantified attitudes and quantified commodity baskets) subject to the budget constraint.

The main issues of this paper are concerned with the relation between attitudes and demand, that is with $h(a, p, m)$ as a function of a alone for fixed values of (p, m). It was pointed out in conjunction with equation (4) (of which (12) may be viewed as a special case) and the apple example already presented that, in the marketing vision of demand, behavior is not determined only by attitude, but also by the ways in which attitude affects intention and intention influences behavior. Thus a "positive" or "favorable" attitude toward a good does not imply that the individual would buy more of it than would otherwise be the case. Nor does a change to an even "more positive" attitude necessarily mean greater consumption. These conclusions are not mitigated by imposing an explanation of rationality on h. But it is reasonable to ask if there are conditions on the composites making up h (as in (4) and (8)) or on utility functions which, if satisfied, will ensure that more positive attitudes imply increased (or, perhaps, decreased or no change in) demand. Providing an answer will furnish insight into the role attitudes play in determining consumer behavior. Before dealing with the issue itself, however, it is first necessary to develop an analytic structure within which the problem can be clearly and precisely described.

To keep things simple, only the attitude of the individual toward a single good, say good 1, is considered for now. Let his attitudes toward all other goods be given and subsume the resulting fixed values of $a_2, ..., a_I$ in the utility-function symbol u. Denote the set of values over which a_1 ranges by A_1. Thus (11) becomes

$$\mu = u(a_1, x), \tag{13}$$

defined on $A_1 \times X$. Similarly the demand function h from (12) may be written as

$$x = h(a_1, p, m),$$

for all $(p, m) > 0$ and a_1 in A_1, where the fixed values of $a_2, ..., a_I$ here are subsumed in h.

Now define an ordering relation "$\geq$"on A_1 according to the "favorableness" or "positiveness" of the verbally described attitudes in A_1 toward good 1. Since attitudes are not yet assumed to be quantifiable, $\geq$ cannot yet be read as "greater than or equal to." Rather, $a_1' \geq a_1''$ is intended to mean that a_1' is at least as positive toward good 1 as a_1''. Suppose that $\geq$ on A_1 is reflexive, transitive, and total. (Since A_1 may be uncountable, this is still not enough to ensure that ordinal measurement is possible. See Pfanzagl [10, pp. 75,79].) Then "$>$" and "$=$" may be separated out from $\geq$ in the usual way, where $a_1' > a_1''$ asserts that a_1' is more positive toward good 1 than a_1'', and $a_1' = a_1''$ means that a_1' and a_1'' are equivalent in positiveness toward good 1. Note that $a_1' > a_1''$ may also be read as a_1'' is more negative toward good 1 than a_1'. Evidently $>$ is irreflexive, transitive, and asymmetric, and $=$ is an equivalence relation on A_1.

Call the demand function h *attitude consistent* with respect to good 1 if for all a_1' and a_1'' in A_1 and all $(p, m) > 0$,

$$a_1' > a_1'' \quad \text{implies} \quad h^1(a_1', p, m) > h^1(a_1'', p, m),$$

where the right hand $>$ reflects "greater than" among real numbers. Thus h is attitude consistent with respect to good 1 whenever a more positive (or negative) attitude toward good 1 increases (or decreases) demand for it. Similarly, refer to h as *attitude neutral* or *attitude perverse* with respect to good 1 provided that for all a_1' and a_1'' in A_1 and all $(p, m) > 0$,

$$a_1' > a_1'' \quad \text{implies} \quad h^1(a_1', p, m) = h^1(a_1'', p, m),$$

or, respectively,

$$a_1' > a_1'' \quad \text{implies} \quad h^1(a_1', p, m) < h^1(a_1'', p, m).$$

Attitude neutrality with, respect to good 1 means that a change in attitude toward good 1 has no impact on the demand for it while attitude perversity captures the idea that a more positive (or negative) attitude toward good 1 results in less (or more) demand.

Represent the set of all intentions (i.e., all verbally described values the variable z may take on) by the symbol Z. Define orderings similar to $\geq$, $>$, and $=$ on A_1 among the elements of Z. (As was the case with A_1, the existence of an ordinal scale on which the values of z may be measured is not implied.) Write the decomposition of h in (4) and (8) as

$$z = \phi(a_1, p, m),$$

$$x = \psi(z),$$

so that h appears as

$$h(a_1, p, m) = \psi(\phi(a_1, p, m)).$$

Sufficient conditions on ϕ and ψ for attitude consistency, neutrality, and perversity of h are described in the following propositions. Proofs are simple and left to the reader.

Theorem 1. If ϕ, as a function of a_1 for each $(p, m) > 0$, and ψ are either both order preserving[8] or both order reversing,[9] then h is attitude consistent with respect to good 1.

Theorem 2. If one of ϕ, as a function of a_1 for each $(p, m) > 0$, and ψ is a constant function,[10] then h is attitude neutral with respect to good 1.

Theorem 3. If one of ϕ, as a function of a_1 for each $(p, m) > 0$, and ψ is

8 For example, the function ψ is *order preserving* if for all z' and z'' in Z,

$$z' \geq z'' \quad \text{implies} \quad \psi(z') \geq \psi(z''),$$

where the left-hand $\geq$ is the ordering defined on Z and the right-hand $\geq$ is "greater than or equal to" among real numbers.

9 For example, ψ in n. 8 immediately above is *order reversing* when

$$z' \geq z'' \quad \text{implies} \quad \psi(z') \leq \psi(z'').$$

10 For example, ψ is a *constant function* if there is an x^0 in X such that

$$x^0 = \psi(z),$$

for all z in Z.

order preserving while the other is order reversing, then h is attitude perverse with respect to good 1.

Not surprisingly, from the perspective of the marketing explanation of consumer behavior, the attitude properties of $h(a_1, p, m)$ turn on what ϕ and ψ do to the relevant orderings of their respective domains. The corresponding theorems based on the utility-maximization explanation are more complicated and require some further definitions. The utility function of (13) is said to *reflect attitudes* toward good 1 if for all a_1' and a_1'' in A_1,

$$a_1' > a_1'' \qquad \text{implies} \qquad u_{x_1}(a_1', x) > u_{x_1}(a_1'', x),$$

for every x in X. In words, attitude reflection means that marginal utilities rise with more positive attitudes. (Were a_1 capable of measurement on a cardinal scale, then attitude reflection could be characterized by requiring the partial derivative of the marginal utility function u_{x_1} with respect to a_1 to exist and be positive everywhere. Indeed, this is the definition employed in Section III subsequently.) Likewise, when

$$a_1' > a_1'' \qquad \text{implies} \qquad u_{x_1}(a_1', x) = u_{x_1}(a_1'', x),$$

or

$$a_1' > a_1'' \qquad \text{implies} \qquad u_{x_1}(a_1', x) < u_{x_1}(a_1'', x),$$

for all a_1' and a_1'' in A_1 and x in X, then u is *independent of attitudes* or *reverses attitudes* toward good 1, respectively. Lastly, the utility function u is called *attitude additive* with respect to good 1 as long as there exist functions v^1 and v^2 such that

$$u(a_1, x) = v^1(a_1, x_1) + v^2(x_{(2)}), \tag{14}$$

for all (a_1, x) in $A_1 \times X$, where $x_{(2)} = (x_2, ..., x_I)$. The following lemma is needed to derive the attitude properties of demand from the perspective of the rationality explanation of consumer behavior:

Lemma 1. Let verbally described a_1' and a_1'' in A_1 be fixed and

$$u_{x_1}(a_1', x) > u_{x_1}(a_1'', x), \tag{15}$$

for all x in X. Suppose u is attitude additive with respect to good 1. If, as functions of x alone, $x' = (x_1', ..., x_I')$ uniquely maximizes $u(a_1', x)$ and $x'' = (x_1'', ..., .x_I'')$ uniquely maximizes $u(a_1'', x)$, each subject to the same budget constraint $p \cdot x = m$, then $x_1' > x_1''$.

Proof:

Observe first that if $x' = x''$, then Lagrange's constrained maximization theorem, in conjunction with attitude additivity, implies

$$u_{x_1}(a_1', x') = u_{x_1}(a_1'', x'),$$

contrary to (15). Hence $x' \neq x''$.

Now, from attitude additivity and application of the fundamental theorem of the integral calculus to both sides of (15), it follows that

$$\hat{x}_1 > \check{x}_1 \qquad \text{if and only if} \qquad \begin{cases} v^1(a_1', \hat{x}_1) - v^1(a_1'', \hat{x}_1) \\ \qquad > v^1(a_1', \check{x}_1) - v^1(a_1'', \check{x}_1), \end{cases} \tag{16}$$

for all $\hat{x}_1$ and $\check{x}_1$, where v^1 is one of the functions characterizing u in (14). Set $x' = (x_1', x_{(2)}')$ and $x'' = (x_1'', x_{(2)}'')$. Using (14) and the facts that x' is the unique constrained maximizer of $u(a_1', x)$ and that both x' and x'' lie in the budget set determined by $p \cdot x = m$,

$$\begin{aligned} 0 &< u(a_1', x') - u(a_1', x''), \\ &= v^1(a_1', x_1') + v^2(x_{(2)}') - [v^1(a_1', x_1'') + v^2(x_{(2)}'')], \\ &= v^1(a_1', x_1') - v^1(a_1'', x_1') + v^1(a_1'', x_1') + v^2(x_{(2)}') \\ &\qquad - v^1(a_1', x_1'') + v^1(a_1'', x_1'') - v^1(a_1'', x_1'') - v^2(x_{(2)}''), \\ &= [v^1(a_1', x_1') - v^1(a_1'', x_1')] - [u(a_1'', x_1'') - u(a_1'', x_1')] \\ &\qquad - [v^1(a_1', x_1'') + v^1(a_1'', x_1'')]. \end{aligned}$$

Since x'' uniquely maximizes $u(a_1'', x)$ subject to $p \cdot x = m$,

$$v^1(a_1', x_1') - v^1(a_1'', x_1') > v^1(a_1', x_1'') - v^1(a_1'', x_1'').$$

By (16), $x_1' > x_1''$.

Q.E.D.

Clearly Lemma 1 may be viewed as a general result which applies regardless of the specific interpretation of the unmeasured variable a_1. In addition to attitudes, a_1 could represent any "parameter" in the utility function which is independent of prices, incomes, and commodity baskets, and which is not necessarily quantifiable. Thus, for example, a_1 might vary over possible "qualities" of good 1 or possible "influences" from the outside exerted on the individual's preference toward good 1, or a_1 might just be a general parameter reflecting various modulations in tastes with respect to good 1. In all cases, the lemma provides a way of analyzing the impact on demand (i.e., on utility-maximizing baskets of commodities) of changes in a_1. The latter is accomplished for attitudes momentarily by using (in part) Lemma 1 in conjunction with the favorableness ordering $\geq$ previously defined on A_1. Similar comments are also relevant for Lemma 2 which appears in Section III. That lemma provides additional machinery for dealing with the same problem in the special case in which a_1 has been ratio quantified.

Sufficient conditions on utility functions for attitude consistency, neutrality, and perversity of demand functions when attitudes are not required to be numerically scaleable, are presented in the next three propositions. Proofs are straightforward and omitted. The arguments establishing Theorems 4 and 6 are based on Lemma 1.

Theorem 4. If there exists a utility representation of preferences which reflects attitudes toward good 1 and is attitude additive with respect to good 1, then h is attitude consistent with respect to good 1.

Theorem 5. If there exists a utility representation of preferences which is independent of attitudes toward good 1 and is attitude additive with respect to good 1, then h is attitude neutral with respect to good 1.

Theorem 6. If there exists a utility representation of preferences which reverses attitudes toward good 1 and is attitude additive with respect to good 1, then h is attitude perverse with respect to good 1.

Observe that if the property of attitude independence toward good 1 held for all marginal utilities $u_{x_i}(a_1, x)$, where $i = 1, ..., I$, then the attitude additivity of the utility function would not be needed in the hypothesis of Theorem 5. Note also the parallel between Theorems 1-3 and 4-6. Illustrations of Theorems 4-6 are provided in Table 1 which shows the demand functions derived from specific utility functions assuming $A_1 = \{a_1', a_1''\}$ and $a_1' > a_1''$.

III

Because the standard rationality explanation of consumer behavior is almost always stated entirely in quantitative terms, and hence scholars are naturally more comfortable thinking about it in numerical language, and also because some rather sharp conclusions (e.g., Lemma 2 below) and examples can be obtained, the special case in which attitudes are assumed to be measured (per-

Table 1. Illustrations of Theorems 4-6

Utility function $\mu = u(a_1, x)$ defined on $\{a'_1, a''_1\} \times X$	With $a'_1 > a''_1$, the utility function	Derived demand function $x_1 = h^1(a_1, p, m)$ defined on $\{a'_1, a''_1\} \times \{(p, m) : p > 0, m > 0\}$	With $a'_1 > a''_1$, the demand function is
$u(a_1, x) = \begin{cases} 2 \log x_1 + \log x_2, & \text{if } a_1 = a'_1 \\ \log x_1 + \log x_2, & \text{if } a_1 = a''_1 \end{cases}$	reflects attitudes	$h^1(a_1, p, m) = \begin{cases} 2m/3p_1, & \text{if } a_1 = a'_1 \\ m/2p_1, & \text{if } a_1 = a''_1 \end{cases}$	attitude consistent
$u(a_1, x) = \log x_1 + \log x_2$	is independent of attitudes	$h^1(a_1, p, m) = m/2p_1$	attitude neutral
$u(a_1, x) = \begin{cases} \frac{1}{2} \log x_1 + \log x_2, & \text{if } a_1 = a'_1 \\ \log x_1 + \log x_2, & \text{if } a_1 = a''_1 \end{cases}$	reverses attitudes	$h^1(a_1, p, m) = \begin{cases} m/3p_1, & \text{if } a_1 = a'_1 \\ m/2p_1, & \text{if } a_1 = a''_1 \end{cases}$	attitude perverse

haps as in (5)) on ratio scales deserves, for comparative purposes, brief mention. Thus the symbol a_i now refers to a real number rather than a verbal description, for $i = 1, ..., I$. It is also convenient to revert to the more general formulation of the utility and demand functions of (11) and (12), to require that $a = (a_1, ..., a_I)$ now range over the set of real vectors $A = \{a : a > 0\}$, and to suppose that the ratio numbers over which a_i ranges, as ordered by "greater than or equal to" for real numbers, reflect the favorableness ordering of the individual's attitudes toward good i as defined for good 1 in Section II. Parallel to the marginal utility notation $u_{x_i}(a, x)$, the first-order partial derivative of u with respect to a_i is written $u_{a_i}(a, x)$, for $i = 1, ..., I$. Second-order cross-partial derivatives appear as $u_{x_i x_j}(a, x)$, $u_{x_i a_j}(a, x)$, etc., for all i and j. Similarly $h^i_{a_j}(a, p, m)$, $h^i_{p_j}(a, p, m)$, and $h^i_m(a, p, m)$ are the first-order partial derivatives of h with respect to a_j, p_j, and m, respectively.

To those properties of the utility function set out at the start of Section II, add the restriction that u is twice continuously differentiable everywhere on the Cartesian product of A with the interior of X, that is, on $A \times \{x : x > 0\}$. Define the boarded Hessian matrix

$$U(a,x) = \begin{bmatrix} 0 & u_{x_1}(a,x) & \cdot \cdot \cdot & u_{x_I}(a,x) \\ u_{x_1}(a,x) & u_{x_1 x_1}(a,x) & \cdot \cdot \cdot & u_{x_1 x_I}(a,x) \\ \cdot & \cdot & & \cdot \\ \cdot & \cdot & & \cdot \\ \cdot & \cdot & & \cdot \\ u_{x_I}(a,x) & u_{x_I x_1}(a,x) & \cdot \cdot \cdot & u_{x_I x_I}(a,x) \end{bmatrix}$$

on this set. When the determinant $|U(a, x)| \neq 0$, for all (a, x) in $A \times \{x : x > 0\}$, an equivalent characterization of $h(a, p, m)$ is as the solution of the first-order Lagrangean conditions for constrained maximization:

$$\begin{aligned} \lambda(a,x)p_n - u_{x_n}(a,x) = 0, \qquad n = 1, ..., I, \\ p \cdot x = m, \end{aligned} \tag{17}$$

where λ is an appropriate functional multiplier. Moreover h is now continuously differentiable on $A \times \{(p, m) : p > 0, m > 0\}$ (Katzner [8, p. 46]). It is convenient to maintain the assumption that $|U(a, x)| \neq 0$ everywhere from here on. Define the Slutsky functions over the latter set by

$$s^{ij}(a,p,m) = h^i_{p_j}(a,p,m) + h^j(a,p,m)h^i_m(a,p,m),$$

for all i and j. The next lemma and its corollary play the same role here as Lemma 1 did in the development of the attitude properties of demand when a was not necessarily quantifiable. These propositions apply in general to any utility function containing as arguments a vector of numerical parameters which are independent of p, m, and x, regardless of the particular interpretation assigned to the components of a.[11]

Lemma 2. For all (a, p, m) in $A \times \{(p, m) : p > 0, m > 0\}$,

$$h^i_{a_j}(a, p, m) = -\frac{1}{\lambda(a, p, m)} \sum_{n=1}^{I} u_{x_n a_j}(a, h(a, p, m)) s^{ni}(a, p, m),$$

where $i, j = 1, ..., I$.

Proof:

Let appropriate i, j, and (a, p, m) be given. Substitution of $x = h(a, p, m)$ for x in (17) and differentiating with respect to a_j gives

$$\lambda_{a_j} p_n - \sum_{i=1}^{I} u_{x_n x_i} h^i_{a_j} = u_{x_n a_j}, \qquad n = 1, ..., I,$$

$$\sum_{i-1}^{I} p_i h^i_{a_j} = 0,$$

where functional arguments have been dropped to simplify notation. Using (17) to replace p_n (and p_i) with $\frac{1}{\lambda} u_{x_n}$ and solving for $h^i_{a_j}$ by Cramer's rule,

$$h^i_{a_j} = -\sum_{n=1}^{I} u_{x_n a_j} \frac{|U^{ni}|}{|U|},$$

where $|U^{ni}|$ is the cofactor of $u_{x_n x_i}$ in U. By a well-known formula (e.g., Katzner [8, p. 47]),

$$h^i_{a_j} = -\frac{1}{\lambda} \sum_{n=1}^{I} u_{x_n a_j} s^{in}.$$

Q.E.D.

---

[11] Similar results have already been derived from analyzing the impact of changes in numerical indicators of "tastes" and "product quality" on demand. See the discussion in Katzner [9, pp. 137-138].

Corollary. Let i be fixed. Assume $u_{x_n a_i} = 0$ on $A \times \{x : x > 0\}$, for all $n \neq i$. Then

$$h^i_{a_i}(a,p,m) = -\frac{1}{\lambda(a,p,m)} u_{x_n a_i}(a, h(a,p,m)) s^{ii}(a,p,m),$$

for every (a,p,m) in $A \times \{p,m) : p > 0, m > 0\}$.

Transference of the attitude concepts of Section II to the present numerical setting is straightforward. As indicated earlier, $a'_i > a''_i$ here is read "a'_i is greater than or equal to a''_i" and means that the attitude represented by a'_i is more favorable toward good i than that represented by a''_i. Hence the appropriate counterparts to attitude consistency, neutrality, and perversity are expressed in terms of the partial derivatives $h^i_{a_i}$. Thus the demand function h is attitude consistent, neutral, or perverse with respect to good i according as $h^i_{a_i}(a,p,m) \gtreqless 0$, for all (a,p,m). Similarly, the utility function u reflects, is independent of, or reverses attitudes toward good i according as $u_{x_i a_i}(a,x) \gtreqless 0$, for all (a,x) in $A \times \{x : x > 0\}$. The following analogues of Theorems 4-6 replace the notion of attitude additivity by the vanishing of suitable second-order, cross-partial derivatives of the utility function:

Theorem 7. If there exists a utility representation (u) of preferences which reflects attitudes toward good i, and if $u_{x_n a_i}(a,x) = 0$ on $A \times \{x : x > 0\}$, for all $n \neq i$, then h is attitude consistent with respect to good i.

Theorem 8. If there exists a utility representation (u) of preferences which is independent of attitudes toward good i, and if $u_{x_n a_i}(a,x) = 0$ on $A \times \{x : x > 0\}$, for all $n \neq i$, then h is attitude neutral with respect to good i.

Theorem 9. If there exists a utility representation (u) of preferences which reverses attitudes toward good i, and if $u_{x_n a_i}(a,x) = 0$ on $A \times \{x : x > 0\}$, for all $n \neq i$, then h is attitude perverse with respect to good i.

The proofs of these theorems are based on the corollary of Lemma 2 and the facts that $\lambda(a,p,m) > 0$ and $s^{ii}(a,p,m) < 0$, for all (a,p,m) in $A \times \{(,p,m) : p > 0, m > 0\}$ and $i = 1, ..., I$. Observe that although the context and the reasoning establishing them are different, Theorems 4-6 are similar in statement to Theorems 7-9. Examples illustrating the latter appear in Table 2. In each case there are two goods and only the attitude toward good 1 appears as an argument of the utility function. The examples of Table 2 may be seen as the "attitude-quantified" counterparts to those of Table 1.

Note also that the additional assumption of quantifiability does not add significantly to either the statements or the proofs of Theorems 1-3, except for

Table 2. Illustrations of Theorems 7-9

Utility function $\mu = u(a_1, x)$ defined for all $(a_1, x) > 0$	Sign of $u_{x_1 a_1}(a_1, x)$ at all $(a_1, x) > 0$	Derived demand function $x_1 = h^1(a_1, p, m)$ defined for all $(a_1, p, m) > 0$	Sign of $h^1_{a_1}(a_1, p, m)$ at all $(a_1, p, m) > 0$
$u(a_1, x) = a_1 \log x_1 + \log x_2$	positive (reflects attitudes)	$h^1(a_1, p, m) = \left(\frac{a_1}{1+a_1}\right)(m/2p_1)$	positive (attitude consistent)
$u(a_1, x) = \log a_1 x_1 + \log x_2$	zero (independent of attitudes)	$h^1(a_1, p, m) = m/2p_1$	zero (attitude neutral)
$u(a_1, x) = \frac{1}{a_1} \log x_1 + \log x_2$	negative (reverses attitudes)	$h^1(a_1, p, m) = \left(\frac{1}{1+a_1}\right)(m/2p_1)$	negative (attitude perverse)

the obvious fact that the concepts of order preserving and order reversing can be expressed as a positive or, respectively, negative derivative (or appropriate partial derivative) of ϕ and ψ.

IV

It is clear that in the absence of very special assumptions (such as, for example, order preservation or attitude reflection and additivity), attitude consistency, neutrality, or perversity of h cannot be deduced from either the marketing or rationality perspectives on demand behavior. A more favorable attitude toward any good could result in greater demand; on the other hand, the consumer might be satisfied with less because, having a more favorable attitude (and taking the rationality approach to demand), he now likes it more. To find out which, if any, of these cases apply to a given individual requires investigation of the empirical relationship between that person's attitudes and his actual purchases.

Empirical studies to date, however, do not seem to have focused on this particular issue. Although considerable energy has been expended on the problem of predicting behavior from attitude, these efforts have not dealt specifically with demand functions. Thus, for example, researchers have investigated how a person's attitude toward his job might affect his job performance, and how a student's attitude toward cheating might affect actual cheating on a self-graded examination (see Fishbein and Ajzen [6, pp. 337-339]). Even when centering on consumer attitudes and buying behavior, little interest is shown in how quantities of a single good purchased by a person vary with his attitude toward that good.[12] Thus the empirical viability of many of the ideas developed above, including attitude consistency, neutrality, and perversity, remains an open question.

References

1. Aaker, D. A., and J. G. Myers, *Advertising Management* (Englewood Cliffs: Prentice Hall, 1975).
2. Achenbaum, A. A., "Knowledge is a Thing Called Measurement," in

[12] Thus, for example, Achenbaum [2, p. 113] calculates the percentages of individuals using a particular brand of a good in groups of people all having attitudes which are "similar" in terms of their favorableness toward that brand.

Attitude Research at Sea, L. Adler and I. Crespi, eds. (American Marketing Association, 1966), pp. 111-126.

3. Bausor, R., "Time and the Structure of Economic Analysis," *Journal of Post Keynesian Economics* 5 (1982-82), pp. 163-179.
4. Belk, R. W., "An Exploratory Assessment of Situational Effects in Buyer Behavior," *Journal of Marketing Research*, 11 (1974), pp. 156-163.
5. Engel, J. F., R. D. Blackwell, and D. T. Kollat, *Consumer Behavior*, 3rd ed. (Hinsdale: Dryden, 1978).
6. Fishbein, M., and I. Ajzen, *Belief, Attitude, Intention and Behavior: An Introduction to Theory and Research* (Reading: Addison-Wesley, 1975).
7. Kalman, P. J., "The Theory of Consumer Behavior when Prices Enter the Utility Function," *Econometrica*, 36 (1968), pp. 497-510.
8. Katzner, D. W., *Static Demand Theory* (New York: Macmillan, 1970).
9. ________, *Analysis Without Measurement* (New York: Cambridge University Press, 1983).
10. Pfanzagl, J., *Theory of Measurement*, 2nd ed. (Würtzburg-Vienna: Physica-Verlag, 1971).
11. Robertson, T. S., *Innovative Behavior and Communication* (New York: Holt, Rinehart and Winston, 1971).

13
Political Structure and System and the Notion of Logical Completeness[1]

The purpose of this note is to provide a technique which may be used to define the concepts of political structure and political system. As suggested by Almond [1], such definitions should be capable of distinguishing between those political elements which may be common to all societies and those which are particular to each. Indeed, the point of view taken here will be essentially to think of the former as comprising the political structure and the latter as determining the particular political system within that structure. This distinction will permit more rigorous and formal definitions than those already familiar to political scientists.[2] It will also provide tests for determining the logical completeness of models and suggest a way of organizing future research.

I

Perhaps it is best to begin with an analogy drawn from elementary algebra.

---

[1] *General Systems* 14 (1969), pp. 169-171.

The author would like to acknowledge his debt to Clifford Kaufman and Lucy Behrman for many helpful comments and suggestions.

[2] The existing literature on this subject is summarized by Almond [1, pp. 5-7].

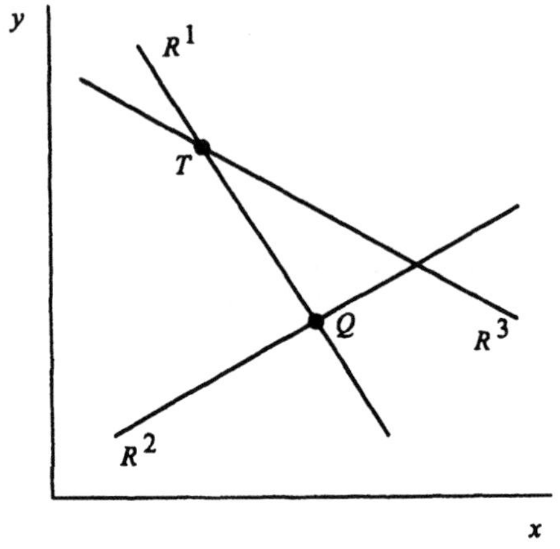

Figure 1

Consider for the moment two variables, say x and y. Let R^1 denote one relationship between them and R^2 another. For example, R^1 and R^2 may be linear as pictured in Figure 1. In that diagram R^1 determines a line in the x-y plane, R^2 determines another line in that plane, and both relationships taken simultaneously determine the unique point of intersection Q. If there were a third relationship R^3, then there would be no point simultaneously satisfying R^1, R^2, and R^3 and the set of relationships would be overdetermined. If there were only one relationship R^1 then the model would be underdetermined and a unique point on the line R^1 could not be specified. Thus, in order to have a determinate model (i.e., one which resolves itself into a unique point), it is necessary that the number of relationships be exactly equal to the number of variables. If the number of relationships and variables of a model are equal, the model will be said to pass the *primary test* for logical completeness.

Of course the fact that the number of relationships equals the number of variables does not guarantee that the model is determinate. R^1 and R^2 could turn out to be two ways of writing the same thing;[3] they could describe two parallel lines which do not intersect; or they could be non-linear curves in the plane which twist and turn but never cross. There are well-known mathematical conditions which, if met, ensure the existence of unique intersection points. The model will be said to satisfy the *secondary test* for completeness whenever

[3] For example, let R^1 be the equation $3x + 4y = 1$ and R^2 be $6x + 8y = 2$. Then R^1 and R^2 describe the same line in the x-y plane.

such conditions are met.

One more comment about this analogy: R^1 and R^2 may themselves depend on parameters.[4] Each time a parameter changes, a relationship will "shift." Thus, for example, a change in parameters could cause R^2 in Figure 1 to change into R^3. In this case the intersection point would move from Q to T. Hence the intersection point depends on the values of the parameters as well as on the nature of R^1 and R^2. Specifying R^1 and R^2 in general, then, determines a new relationship which relates each set of parameter values to a point of intersection.

In what follows an attempt is made to apply this technique to the problem at hand. Political variables and relationships between them are specified. It makes no difference that the variables cannot be quantified as in the above analogy because the property of "capability of quantification" is never used in the analysis. Political structure is defined as the set of relationships between the variables while a political system is thought of as an "intersection point" which depends on parameter values.

II

It is axiomatic that there is no general agreement among political scientists as to which variables and relationships should be used to define political structure. Nor is this the place to resolve any such arguments. The variables and relationships presented below are intended only as an illustration of the technique of definition proposed. Many of them have been taken from Apter [2]. In order to simplify the discussion they will be presented in symbolic form. The variables are:

v – values and goals of society.

c – coercion used by government to maintain authority and operate efficiently.

z – types and quantities of information flowing between government and those governed.

d – patterns and processes for making authoritative decisions.

---

4 The values of the three parameters of R^1 in n. 3 on p. 276 are 3, 4, and 1.

a – ways in which government may be held accountable to a group or groups outside itself.

I – ideology.

P – government policy in all situations.

There is one parameter, n, which denotes the needs, values, and perceptions of reality of all individuals in society.

Seven relationships are assumed to hold. The first states that authoritative decision making is related to the values of society, coercion, and information. This may be written as

$$d = f^1(v, c, z),$$

where f^1 is a symbolic representation of the relationship itself. For the moment it is not necessary to specify the precise nature of f^1; the important fact is that it exists. The remaining six relationships, which may be read verbally as the first, are:

$$a = f^2(v, c, z),$$

$$c = f^3(z),$$

$$P = f^4(v, c, z, I),$$

$$v = f^5(P, I),$$

$$z = f^6(P, I, v),$$

$$I = f^7(n; v).$$

Note that the semicolon in the last relationship is used only to separate the parameter n from the variable v.

This is a system of seven relationships in seven variables and one parameter. The political structure consists of $f^1, ..., f^7$. For each value of the parameter n, unique values of the variables frequently may be determined. The latter constitute the political system which, to use Apter's terminology [2], may range anywhere from the "reconciliation" to the "mobilization" type. The model passes the primary test for logical completeness since the number of relationships and variables are the same.

This technique of definition and the tests for completeness have been known to economists for some time. Although there were precursors, Léon Walras [3] is usually given credit for being the first to apply them to economic analysis. He defined the "perfectly competitive economic model" as a system of simultaneous demand and supply relationships which reflect respectively the assumptions that for every set of input and output prices, (a) the rational consumer buys those commodities and sells those resources which maximize his satisfaction within the limitations of his budget, and (b) the rational firm produces those outputs and hires those inputs which maximize its profits. The concept of general equilibrium was then defined as a point which satisfies all relationships simultaneously (thus demand equals supply in every market). Economists have spent considerable time and effort studying the properties of this model. When stated in terms of simultaneous relationships it becomes immediately clear, for example, that due to the presence of budget constraints, in an economy with n markets if $n-1$ of them are in equilibrium, then the last must, of necessity, also be in equilibrium. Therefore the logically complete formulation consists of the relationships and variables in $n - 1$ markets only. This is, indeed, a valuable lesson concerning the advantages and power of the technique proposed here.

Further investigations into the secondary tests of completeness have led economists into fruitful studies of the conditions under which general equilibrium exists and is unique. Thus restrictions are now known which must be placed on the parameters and relationships in order to guarantee that equilibrium is possible in the model. This is crucially important since observations of economic phenomenon in the real world are thought of as either being equilibrium points or located on a dynamic time path which approaches equilibrium. It follows that if these restrictions are not assumed, then the model may have no bearing on reality since equilibrium may not exist within it. Finally, aside from the secondary tests, economists have also pursued inquiries into the stability and optimality (welfare aspects) of equilibria. The importance of these investigations is again obvious.

There is no reason why research in political science cannot be organized along similar lines. Political structure may be defined as a set of simultaneous relationships and political system as an equilibrium point. Questions concerning the existence, uniqueness, stability, and optimality of the system may now be posed within the context of a fixed postulated structure. As such they are relevant and important for, among other things, they help determine the logical completeness and usefulness of the model.

In conclusion, it may be useful to provide specific examples of the kinds of questions this approach raises. First, what are the principal variables and relationships determining political structure out of which observable political systems may be derived as intersection points? How do political structures (i.e., the relationships) vary among societies and how do these variations affect intersection points? Is there one political structure out of which all observable political systems can be derived? What is the precise nature of the relationships and what restrictions must be placed on them in order that they be complete and useful? Finally, which values of the parameters in a given model determine which political system? Once the answer to the last is known it may become possible by observing changes in parameter values to predict the direction in which a political system is going to change.

References

1. Almond, G. A., "Introduction: A Functional Approach to Comparative Politics," in *The Politics of the Developing Areas*, G. A. Almond and J. S. Coleman, eds. (Princeton: Princeton University Press, 1960), pp. 3-64.
2. Apter, D. E., *The Politics of Modernization* (Chicago: University of Chicago Press, 1965).
3. Walras, L., *Elements of Pure Economics*, W. Jaffé, trans. (Homewood: Irwin, 1954).

14
The Formal Structure of Argument in Professor Apter's *Choice and the Politics of Allocation*[1]

Science in general, and social science in particular, seem to be divided according to the use of mathematical technique. In many areas elegant and sophisticated mathematical reasoning has found an important place, but in many others, there has been hardly any attempt to introduce mathematics at all. This is a pity, for the advantages of employing mathematical methods are many: concepts and propositions are forced to be described more precisely; the logic and consistency of argument is exposed more openly; and the role of each assumption must be identified more clearly. The upshot is deeper understanding. Furthermore, errors are easier to prevent and discover, and unforeseen extensions may become apparent.

One of the reasons for failure to employ mathematical reasoning may lie in the difficulty of quantifying the significant variables involved. Indeed, most common applications of mathematics in scientific inquiry are based on the presence of numbers. Thus, for example, use of the calculus requires that relevant variables be measured on some subset of the real line. But it is not

---

[1] *Political Methodology* 6 (1979), pp. 217-235.

widely recognized that mathematics may still be employed to obtain the same precision of meaning and logical tightness of argument in the absence of measurement. Although addition, multiplication, the calculus, etc. are no longer applicable, relevant and useful techniques remain. And the results so obtained often parallel those derived with quantifiable methods. One purpose of the following is to illustrate how this can be done.

Since more complete discussions of the methodological issues are available elsewhere (Katzner [5], [6 (this volume, Essay 4)], [7]), attention here focuses on a completed non-mathematical study, chosen because the benefits of employing mathematical reasoning, even *ex post*, are striking. In the first place, various aspects of the original discussion are illuminated. Secondly, weaknesses in argument are located and the steps required to remedy the defects are identified. Lastly, it becomes obvious that, in general, a similar methodology could have been employed initially to enhance clarity and depth, and to avoid error.

The specific example is Professor Apter's *Choice and the Politics of Allocation*. Although praised for its many virtues, this work has also been criticized for its murky presentation (Clark [3], Jessop [4], Pennock [8]) — its argument having been called "dense," "opaque," and "impossible." There is little doubt that part of Apter's problem lies in the intricacy of the matters he considers. Tangled interrelationships are hard to describe simply. Nevertheless, if the analysis is to progress at all, his relatively loose verbal theorizing must be replaced by a fully specified model.

At the outset, I note that I do not wish to detract from the importance and significance of Apter's effort, nor to deny the logic of his overall result. At issue is the formal structure of his argument: What are the pieces and how do they fit together? Are there gaps? Inconsistencies? Moreover, I do not claim completeness for the following presentation. In fact, to keep things as brief and simple as possible, relatively inessential elements are omitted. And, although weaknesses are pointed out, no serious effort is made to rectify them. Transformation (Carnap [2, p. 3] would call it explication) of inexact ideas into precise, rigorous ones is my central concern.

Apter's Basic Model

To set out the formal structure of Apter's argument precisely requires that: (a) all variables be defined, (b) all relations between the variables be identified, (c) the properties of both the individual relations and the entire system of relations as a whole be examined, and (d) variable values consistent with individual relations and time paths generated by the entire system be described. Obviously, in a short paper, a complete analysis of these four elements is impossible. But fragmentary as it is, the analysis should permit a better understanding of the argument's strengths and weaknesses and should suggest steps to take next.

All relations are abbreviated symbolically in mathematical form.[2] They are usually denoted by f^1, f^2, ... where the numerical superscript identifies them as relation one, two, and so on. The subscript t on a variable indicates the time period in which the relevant variable value appears. Thus the abbreviation, $x_t = f^3(y_t, w_{t-1})$, is to be read as "relation f^3 links values of variable y in period t and variable w in period $t-1$ to values of variable x in t." Actually, the variables themselves are written symbolically and described with short, suggestive words and phrases, hopefully permitting a more rapid identification of the relations and variables under discussion. Page numbers, in parentheses, follow quotations from Apter's text.

Apter's first chapter provides a theoretical model of development that serves as the basis for the rest of the book. The ten major variables introduced there, with their describing words and phrases in parentheses and with the subscript t dropped, are:

N^S (societal norms) – general preferences prevailing in society (p. 10).

N^P (political norms) – specific preferences about the way government is to function in light of societal norms (p. 12).

A^R (role allocation) – the way non-political roles are distributed across society (p. 11).

P (participation) – the way political roles are distributed across society (p. 12).

A^E (equity of allocation) – distribution of specific equity beliefs about the allocation of roles (p. 11).

M (state of development or maturation) – the choice opportunities open to individuals in society (p. 10).

D (disorder) – a state of social unrest. A state of no disorder is a state of *complete* order (p. 6).

[2] Definitions of the notions of variable, variable value, and function appear in Katzner ([5], [6 (this volume, Essay 4)], [7]).

I (information) – information about discrepancies between role allocation and equity of allocation (i.e., the differences between the way roles are actually distributed and the way different groups of people think they ought to be distributed (p. 13)).

C (coercion) – punitive action or the threat of action by government (p. 14).

N^G (permissible norms) – societal norms defined as permissible by the government (p. 14).

Each of these ten variables is assumed to be independent of the others. The main relations among them, as described in Apter's first chapter, are now considered.

The *political system* in existence at time t (denoted by π^t) is defined as the relation between political norms at t and participation at t (p. 12). This may be written as

$$P_t = \pi^t(N_t^P). \tag{1}$$

Furthermore, the statement (pp. 12, 20) that persistent failure to maintain balance between equity of allocation and role allocation will lead to a new political system, suggests that π^t is determined at time t by the previous sequences of equities of allocation and role allocations, or

$$\pi^t = f^1(A_{t-1}^E, A_{t-1}^R, A_{t-2}^E, A_{t-2}^R, ..., A_0^E, A_0^R). \tag{2}$$

Here equity of allocation, A_0^E, and role allocation, A_0^R, refer to the values of these variables in the initial period under consideration. No indication is given as to whether f^1 or the remaining relations introduced below are subject to change over time. For simplicity, it is assumed here that they are not.

Apter identifies four general kinds of political systems (realizations of π^t): "mobilization," "bureaucratic," "theocratic," and "reconciliation" (p. 32).

Disorder is determined "by the way people think allocation should occur and by the way it does occur. If these are in good fit ... then order prevails" (p. 11). Disorder also depends on coercion (p. 14). Thus,

$$D_t = f^2(A_t^E, A_t^R, C_t). \tag{3}$$

The state of development (or maturation), in turn, is related to disorder (p. 6):

$$M_t = f^3(D_t). \tag{4}$$

Of course at any time t, equity of allocation depends on societal norms.

But the former can also be influenced by development occurring during the previous period (p. 11). That is,

$$A_t^E = f^4(N_t^S, M_{t-1}). \tag{5}$$

The incomplete model described thus far permits several interesting inferences to be drawn. First, substitution of relation (5) into (3) gives[3]

$$D_t = f^2(f^4(N_t^S, M_{t-1}), A_t^R, C_t). \tag{6}$$

Thus state of development can have an impact on disorder as well as the other way around (as indicated by (4)). This may resolve Apter's seemingly contradictory statement, "Disorder may make development more difficult to achieve ... development may generate disorder" (p. 6). The only way that "more" disorder can go with both "less" and "more" development (i.e., higher and lower states of development or maturation) at the same time, as this citation implies, is if these two conflicting effects are separated from each other. The association between more disorder and less development is described in (4). The association between more disorder and more development arises with development lagged one period in (6), the relation obtained by combining (3) and (5) and fixing the other variables.

Further inferences are obtained upon substituting (6) into (4):

$$M_t = f^3(D_t = f^2(f^4(N_t^S, M_{t-1}), A_t^R, C_t)). \tag{7}$$

Alternatively, substituting (4) for period $t - 1$ into (6) yields

$$D_t = f^2(f^4(N_t^S, f^3(D_{t-1})), A_t^R, C_t). \tag{8}$$

If societal norms, role allocation, and coercion, are assumed to be fixed over time, (7) and (8) are each periodic relations in a single variable. These are not independent since knowledge of either state of development or disorder permits determination of the other from (4). Relation (8) can be thought of as having an equilibrium or stationary time path when disorder assumes as its value the state in which there is no disorder (i.e., complete order).[4] There is a corresponding stationary time path for state of development. The actual time paths followed by disorder, D_t, and state of development, M_t, are unlikely to be the stationary ones. In principle they may converge to, diverge from, or oscillate around the stationary paths. Apter suggests that, in fact, actual time paths are cyclic in nature (pp. 11, 20). But to have stationary and cyclical

[3] Substitution among relations does not require measurement.

[4] An equilibrium time path is one along which variable values do not change over time.

paths in the model requires additional hypotheses about the properties of the relations in (7) or (8). These are discussed by Katzner ([5], [6 (this volume, Essay 4)], [7]) and are not treated here. Assuming the additional hypotheses are in force, as the values of the variables state of development and disorder change over time, the disparity between role allocation (here taken as given) and equity of allocation (as determined by (5) since the value of societal norms, N^S, is also taken as given) emerges, yielding the same conclusion as Apter: "By examining any development sequence as a departure from any point of order [stationarity], we can determine the pattern of discrepancy between equity norms about allocation and role stratification in society as a whole" (p. 12).

Apter next describes the processes whereby information and coercion flow between government and those governed. Information arises from combinations of equities of allocation and role allocations (p. 13) and is restricted by coercion (p. 14). Information, in turn, has its impact on political norms (p. 13), as do societal norms (p. 10). Thus,

$$I_t = f^5(A_t^E, A_t^R, C_t), \tag{9}$$

and

$$N^P = f^6(I_t, N_t^S). \tag{10}$$

On the other hand, coercion is determined by political norms and defines social norms permitted by the government[5] (p. 14):

$$C_t = f^7(N_t^P), \tag{11}$$

$$N_t^G = f^8(C_t). \tag{12}$$

Finally, Apter asserts (p. 16) that both societal norms and role allocations change with development. Independently of development, the former also changes dialectically and the latter functionally. Since dialectical and functional change are each taken as given parameters, changes in societal norms and role allocation may be described by

$$N_t^S = f^9(N_{t-1}^S, M_{t-1}), \tag{13}$$

and

$$A_t^R = f^{10}(A_{t-1}^R, M_{t-1}). \tag{14}$$

[5] At this point, government does not seem to play a very important role in Apter's model. It does, however, become significant later.

The model as a whole consists of ten variables and the eleven relations π^t, $f^1, ..., f^{10}$, as indicated in (1)-(5) and (9)-(14). In any given period, the political system π^t, societal norms N_t^S, and role allocation A_t^R, are all determined by what has gone before from, respectively, the relations of (2), (13), and (14). This leaves eight variables in period t to be determined by the simultaneous interaction of the remaining eight relations. But without further assumptions there is no guarantee that the system can, in fact, determine the values of these eight variables. The extra requirements are unimportant for present purposes and may be found in Katzner ([5], [6 (this volume, Essay 4)], [7]). They are statements about properties of the relations of the model and there does not seem to be anything in *Choice and the Politics of Allocation* to suggest either that they are or are not satisfied. But it is absolutely essential both for the internal consistency of Apter's model and for his subsequent discussion that these conditions hold. And so henceforth they are assumed. Thus the entire system is solved at any point in time by knowing $f^1, ..., f^{10}$, and the four initial values: A_0^E, A_0^R, N_0^S, and M_0. Apter's next four chapters amplify, refine, and analyze time paths generated by his model.

Before proceeding, it should be pointed out that nowhere does Apter characterize any of the above relations with the detail and precision necessary to avoid confusion about their meaning. In particular, he neither describes the specific values his variables may take on, nor indicates which values of the independent variables in a relation are assigned to which values of the dependent variable. This leads to a certain fuzziness and a tendency towards obscurity. For example, what does it mean to say that if equity of allocation and role allocation "... are in good fit, if there are not many discrepancies between them, then a condition of order prevails" (p. 11)? In the present context, Apter is talking about relation (3) with coercion held fixed. But he never discusses what constitutes a good fit, nor does he reveal the kinds of order or disorder resulting from specific discrepancies. Thus, if one observes a particular equity of allocation along with a particular role allocation in a society, how does one determine just how good the fit is and the nature of the state of order that should arise from it? These questions can only be answered by knowing which values of disorder f^3 assigns to values of equity and role allocation for given values of coercion.

To illustrate further, consider Apter's assertion that "... there is an inverse relationship between coercion and information..." (p. 32). It is not clear from the context whether Apter is referring to a sequence of variable values solving his system of relations along a specific time path (see below), or to a relation obtained by substituting (10) into (11). But in either case, because the phrase "inverse relationship" itself is a precise term, more exactitude is needed before the meaning of this statement can be understood. First, it is necessary to identify clearly the relevant values that the variables coercion and information may assume. Second, a meaningful way to order the values of coercion must be found. Among other things, this may permit the specification of unquantified "degrees" of coercion by defining which values exhibit "more" coercion and which exhibit "less." Lastly, Apter needs to provide an ordering for the values of information. Given these particulars, Apter's inverse relationship means that values of coercion "rising" in the coercion ordering always correspond to or go with values of information that "fall" in the information ordering.

Similar considerations apply to the earlier discussion of "more" disorder seemingly corresponding to both "more" and "less" development at the same time, as well as to concepts like "high [in the sense of unquantified degree of] participation" (p. 15), "maximize development and order" (p. 15), and "maximize information" (p. 32). The notions of "more" and "less" are central in all of these cases. One must know how the value of a variable when it is more differs from that when it is less.

Time Paths

Apter's model generates sequences of vectors of variable values over time. Each sequence is the outcome of a particular specification of the system's ten relations $f^1, ..., f^{10}$, and four initial values. Each vector has ten components — one variable value for each of the ten variables in the system. A vector of variable values at time t defines the state of society at t. Thus the system produces sequences of social states over time, expressed in terms of variable values. The special sequence relevant for a given real experience depends on the actual relations and initial values in that experience. If Apter had described his relations by indicating that certain values of the independent variables correspond to particular values of the dependent variables, then it would be possible to solve the system for each specification of the initial values and to line up the variable values that go together in sequences over time. It would also be possible to make clear and precise statements about the nature of these sequences and their properties. But such precise statements can not be achieved when only vague characterization of $f^1, ..., f^{10}$ are provided. Apter's assertions about sequences of variable values over time reflect this vagueness. Several of them are presented in different contexts below.

Some of Apter's statements apply only to isolated relations with specific variable values held fixed. To illustrate, one of the components of the state of society vector (i.e., one of the variables of the model) is the state of development (M) or choice opportunities open to individuals in society. Vectors of variable values whose state-of-development component provides the highest number of choice alternatives are called *industrial* social states. Those with the lowest are *traditional* states. The various stages in between are *modernizing* states (p. 43). Fixing, for the moment, societal norms N^S, prior state of development M_{t-1}, and coercion C_t, the pair wise relation between current state of development M_t, and role allocations A_t^R, is given by the substitution of (14) into (7):

$$M_t = f^3(f^2(f^4(N_t^S, M_{t-1}), f^{10}(A_{t-1}^R, M_{t-1}), C_t)). \tag{15}$$

Apter (p. 49) posits part of the nature of this composite of f^2, f^3, f^4, and f^{10} as follows: Each role in any role allocation is identified with a certain kind of behavior by the individual in it. Role allocations resulting in behavior that (a) increases the dependence of society on industrial countries for advanced technology, or (b) overemphasizes consumption at the expense of investment, tend to limit future choice alternatives and hence to impede development (i.e., induce a "lower" state of development).

Other statements about sequences of variable values focus on subsets of relations and variables. These could apply to any time path since other variable values are not necessarily fixed. For example, two of the variables defining social states are role allocations and societal norms. Apter uses these to characterize four stratification types: "segmentary," "fused," "differentiated," and "functional" (pp. 51-54). Each type is identified by a particular pair of values, namely, a value of the variable role allocation and a value of the variable societal norms. Moving from the first type to the last involves changes in the distribution of roles. These changes are based on "the adoption of function as the principle of role allocation at the expense of reciprocal obligation" (p. 66). In addition to variation in role allocation across types, changes occur in societal norms requiring "secularization at the expense of the sacred" (p. 66). Apter argues that as society develops, it progresses through the four types in the order listed above (p. 55). He is therefore describing the nature of f^9 and f^{10} from, respectively, (13) and (14). In other words, he is saying (without precise specification) that certain values of the variables prior societal norms N_{t-1}^S, prior role allocation A_{t-1}^R, and state of development M_{t-1}, are associated with certain other values of current societal norms N_t^S, and current role allocation A_t^R. Apter's assertion that, "As a general tendency ... the greater the degree of development, the more the differentiation phenomenon becomes a function of the upper levels of society rather than the lower" (pp. 56, 57), can be understood similarly.

As a further example, consider a sequence of variable values for role allocation and societal norms over time. It may be possible to identify some sequences as the outcome of behavior that (a) implies an acceptance of the existing collection of roles (but not necessarily an acceptance of their allocation among individuals), and (b) is directed towards increasing the social mobility of individuals among them. Such a pattern over time is called *embourgeoisement* (p. 36). On the other hand, a pattern emerging from rejecting the existing collection of roles and the creation of new ones from new norms is called *radicalization* (p. 36). Embourgeoisement and radicalization are two outcomes consistent with modernization[6] (p. 62). Whenever one or the other occurs, it must go hand in hand with the movement across the stratification types described above. Radicalization, it has been noted, always accompanies the expansion of choice opportunities. Both embourgeoisement and radicalization emerge from equity-of-allocation-role-allocation imbalances that arise on the non-stationary time paths described in the discussion following (8).

In addition to dealing with subsets of relations and subsets of variable values, Apter also makes assertions about the nature of time paths or sequences of all variable values generated through the interaction of all relations in the model. Suppose that $f^1, ..., f^{10}$ and the four initial values, equity of allocation A_0^E, role allocation A_0^R, societal norms N_0^S, and state of development M_0, are given. Then at each point in time, t, all variable values are determined as indicated above. The political system at each t is determined from (2). Now in the late stages of modernization, says Apter (p. 66), if a pattern of embourgeoisement emerges in the sequence of variable values generated by the model, it will be accompanied by a movement in the political system, through (2), towards the reconciliation type. But because the impact on the time path of emerging variable values associated with embourgeoisement is to limit development, subsequent variable values generated by the interaction of all relations of the model tend, again through (2), to change the political system once more — this time in the direction of the bureaucratic type. This is clearly a proposition (however imprecise) about the nature of the output of the model under certain requisite conditions, It also gives a glimpse of (2) by indicating the kinds of independent variable values associated with political systems under f^1.

A second proposition provides similar kinds of information about the early stages of modernization. "Systems originating in the mobilization ... or reconciliation form ... show periodic tendencies in the early stages of modernization

[6] Recall, a country is in a "modernizing state" if its state of development is between that of traditional and industrial societies. (Apter [1, p. 43].)

towards bureaucratic systems, in a military or some other form. Bureaucratic systems show a continual tendency toward the reconciliation type ..." (p. 71). The last proposition of this sort mentioned here is that in all stages of modernization oscillations between bureaucratic and reconciliation systems tend to occur, while in the late stages there may also be oscillations between bureaucratic and mobilization systems.

Another illustration of the analysis of time paths generated by the complete model is based on the notion of industrialization. According to Apter, *industrialization* (as distinct from the notion of industrial society introduced earlier) is a sequence of social states over time in which variable values are consistent with (a) rapid generation of new knowledge (p. 72), (b) application of this knowledge to all aspects of social life (p. 72), (c) production of exportable industrial surpluses (p. 72), and (d) role allocation based on competition between functional claims (p. 83). How the values of variables in the model can reflect these elements is not made clear. As indicated above, the stratification type of industrial society is functional. Apter classifies groups of individuals in industrial society according to their roles: "functionally superfluous" caste and ethnic groups, "residual fused" groups, "differentiated" groups, the "functional status elite," and the "bourgeois radicals" (pp. 87-95). Each group has peculiar characteristics resulting from the roles that define it (pp. 95, 96). There are also multiple coalitions and relationships among roles and complicated networks of cliques and friendships (p. 100).

Apter now describes a part of (8): As society moves through states of industrialization, instrumental norms are clarified (p. 76) while consumatory norms become confused (p. 76) and are subsequently redefined (p. 73). This arises from an equity-of-allocation-role-allocation imbalance (73). Apter's assertion here that in industrial societies " ... except for moments of equilibrium the functional needs of society based on industrial life [role allocation] remain in conflict with the normative needs of society based on consumatory principles of equity" (pp. 86, 87) is a restatement of the cyclical property of time paths mentioned in the discussion following (8).

Furthermore, as industrialized society progresses over time, the variable values along society's time path reflect certain facts. To begin with, "the expansion of choice occurs at the top of the stratification system" (p. 100). This is what precipitates the equity-of-allocation-role-allocation imbalance that, in turn, causes the redefinition of consumatory values (pp. 100, 101). Thus the process of radicalization originates in the upper echelons of industrial society. As radicalization expands, "the result is growing conflict between representatives of various stratification groups" (p. 103). If disorder is to be minimized, the government will need considerably more information (p. 104). Hence the proposition that the value of the information variable tends to be associated with "large" quantities of information in industrial states.

Some Gaps and Pitfalls

Previous sections have concentrated, in part, on problems arising from a lack of precision in Apter's description of the variables and relations of his model. In continuing to work through the formal structure of his argument, this section identifies some logical gaps and pitfalls in relating several amplifications and refinements back to the basic model itself.

Recall that the participation variable, P, ranges over ways in which political roles are distributed in society. Political roles are those with access to political decision making; their occupants are "political elites" (p. 106). Representatives of the various groups of society compete to occupy the political roles and, if successful, become political elites. The competition reflects group claims to representation. These claims fall into one of three categories: "populist," "interest," and "professional" claims (p. 109). The pressing of claims is, in the context of Apter's study, the same thing as the transmission of information (pp. 188-124). Hence, this formulation describes how, given the variable value for coercion C_t, equity of allocation A_t^E, and role allocation A_t^R, are translated by f^5 into information in (9). Note that the formulation does not describe the relation itself, but rather shows how the relation arises.

Occupants of political roles (political elites) perform two functions: goal specification and central control. The former involves determining society's goals based on the perceptions of the particular individuals in the political roles; the latter has to do with "coordinating the work of government and translating governmental decisions into practice" (p. 109).

To identify the values of the information variable arising along a modernizing time path for a society, Apter supposes that the representatives of each of society's groups behave so as to maximize their claims to access to governmental decision making. "As modernization proceeds, these claims shift from the primordial to the functional, from the populist to the professional. At the same time, stratification types move away from caste toward functional status." Information corresponding to these phenomena is transmitted by the political elites (p. 117).

Apter hypothesizes that in industrial societies stratification according to functional status and differentiated groups is "high," according to segmentary groups is "moderate," and according to fused groups is "low" (p. 118). He goes on to describe the properties of reconciliation and mobilization systems in terms of the extent of kinds of access claims and kinds of elite involvement (p. 118) as summarized in Table 1. Here Apter is, in effect, adding ten new variables to the model: four stratification types, three access claim types, and three forms of political elite activity. New relations are added too. But the relations between these variables and those originally considered are not explicitly identified. Nor are the properties of the new relations. Thus it is hard to tell if the new relations are logically consistent with (1)-(15).

In fact, if (1)-(15) accurately reflect Apter's model, then some of his statements at this point become problematic. For example, he states, "Participation affects the type of political system ... [which, after eliminating an intermediate variable] determines coercion and information" (p. 110). Three aspects of this statement raise difficulties. First, according to (2), previous sequences of equity of allocation A_t^E, and role allocation A_t^R, affect the type of political system π^t; participation P_t, does not. Note, however, that participation can also be seen to depend on equity of allocation and role allocation through a combination of (1), (10), and (9). Hence, as equity of allocation and role allocation change, both the political system and participation change. Thus it may still be possible to observe the correlations between political systems and participation that Apter has in mind. But as long as (1), (2), (10), and (9) are correct, the explanation for those changes cannot be that "participation affects the type of political system."

Next, this difficulty could be eliminated by modifying (2) and other appropriate relations of the original model — an issue not pursued here except to mention the following: First, additional independent relations cannot be added without expanding the number of variables, modifying existing relations, or both. Otherwise the model would be overdetermined and internally inconsistent. It would be impossible for all relations to be realized simultaneously. Second, if (2) were modified to include, say, participation, then all statements previously made about this relation could be valid (if, indeed, they remained so) only for fixed values of the variable P_t. Furthermore, the model is now underdetermined. The political system π^t, cannot be found without knowing P_t and, from (1), the converse assertion is also true. Even knowing the values of all other variables in (1) and (2) (which are now obtained anyway either as parameters from previous time periods or by solving the remaining relations concomitantly) will still not permit P_t and π^t to be inferred from the simultaneous solution of (1) and (2). This is so because, in terms of the logical structure of the argument, the "variable" political system does not play the same role in each relation. In (1) it is the relation itself while in (2) it is a true variable. The

Table 1. Properties of political systems in industrialized societies

Type of System	Access claims			Involvement of elite in		
	Populist	Interest	Professional	Goal specification	Central control	Coercion
Reconciliation	"High"	"High"	"High"	"High"	"High"	"Low"
Mobilization	"Low"	"Moderate"	"High"	"Low"	"Low"	"High"

Source: Apter [1, p. 118]

dilemma could be resolved, for example, by adding an extra relation involving both the political system and participation as variables. Then the values of these variables would be obtained from the solution of the modified (2) and the new relation. But since the value of the variable political norms N_t^P, still would be determined independently in the remainder of the system, (1) would become untenable and would have to be discarded.

The third and last aspect of the statement quoted above to be discussed, namely, the implication that "participation ... determines coercion and information," can only be "justified" if the relation π^t in (1) has an inverse.[7] For then it would be possible to write

$$N_t^P = [\pi^t]^{-1}(P_t), \tag{16}$$

where $[\pi^t]^{-1}$ denotes the inverse of π^t. Now substituting (16) into (11) gives

$$C_t = f^7([\pi^t]^{-1}(P_t)), \tag{17}$$

and using (17) in (9),

$$I_t = f^5(A_t^E, A_t^R, f^7([\pi^t]^{-1}(P_t))). \tag{18}$$

Relations (17) and (18) express information I_t, and coercion C_t, as dependent on participation P_t, (given fixed values for equity of allocation A_t^E, and role allocation A_t^R). It is important to note, however, that at any time t, P_t, I_t, and C_t are all determined simultaneously through the interaction of the relations of the model. This is true for the entire collection of ten variables listed at the outset. Therefore the intended meaning of the phrase "participation determines coercion and information" is still not clear.

Picking up the last few threads of Apter's argument, interactions among the political system, information, and coercion are analyzed by introducing further relations and variables, including government (p. 132), accountability and consent (p. 136), authoritative decision making (p. 136), and hierarchical and pyramidal authority (p. 133). Examples of Apter's assumptions about these relations and those originally introduced include: "increased" coercion accompanies "greater" hierarchical authority; "increased" information accompanies "greater" pyramidal authority; and, in societies tending towards mobilization or bureaucratic systems, government policy depends "more" on coercion and "less" on information (pp. 138, 139). Once again the relations are not set out as explicitly as those in the original system and the logical connection between the two is difficult to identify.

---

[7] If $y = f(x)$ has an inverse, then f may be "inverted" to obtain the relation $x = f^{-1}(y)$.

Apter also proposes hypotheses about the way in which political systems change over time in terms of variable values along time paths generated by this expanded model: As modernization progresses, governments show a tendency to "increase" coercion. This results in "greater and greater" losses of information until government effectiveness in decision making is reduced to the point where development "declines" and disorder "magnifies." These changes in information and coercion produce changes in the political system (p. 144). As before, the latter relation between the political system and information and coercion is not in the original formulation of Apter's model.

The final two chapters of *Choice and the Politics of Allocation* do not elaborate further on the model and are therefore irrelevant for present purposes.

Conclusion

I would now like to draw together some of the loose ends in this discussion of the formal structure of Apter's argument.

First of all, it is clear that the main thrust of the five chapters of *Choice and the Politics of Allocation* considered here is to elucidate a very complex model of the development process. The following elements are all included in Apter's presentation: Variables are introduced and relations among them identified. Development is explained as the outcome of the simultaneous interaction of all of the models relations. This interaction produces cyclical behavior oscillating about an equilibrium or stationary time path. Theoretical and empirical statements about the nature of the relations, and combinations thereof, consist of assertions that specific values of certain variables are associated with specific values of certain other variables. Further theoretical and empirical statements are made about time paths (i.e., sequences of variable values over time) emerging from the interaction of the model's relations.

But there are gaps. Precision and detail are lacking in describing the values variables may take on, in characterizing the order properties among these variable values, and in defining the relations of the model. In consequence, Apter's assertions are difficult to comprehend. Furthermore, some relations are less completely specified than others in that the possible combinations of values of independent variables, as they relate to values of the dependent variable, are not considered. This occurs, for example, when a relation is described under the implicit assumption that one or more of the independent variables in the relation is fixed; it ignores what happens when all variables in the relation are permitted to vary at once. Also serious is the apparent lack of integration of variables and relations, introduced in the later chapters, with the model as initially set out. Lastly, Apter neglects to consider the restrictions that must be imposed on his relations to ensure that (a) the system is neither overdetermined (inconsistent) nor underdetermined, and thus capable of generating the cyclical behavior so important to his discussion, and (b) the system actually does produce the cyclical activity he describes.

The present attempt to recast Apter's argument in terms of a fully specified, mathematical model has revealed the existence of these weaknesses and has suggested improvements. Eliminating the former should expose more clearly the generality and depth of Apter's propositions, and should suggest avenues along which to extend his basic results.

References

1. Apter, D. E., *Choice and the Politics of Allocation: A Developmental Theory* (New Haven: Yale University Press, 1971).
2. Carnap, R., *Logical Foundations of Probability*, 2nd ed. (Chicago: University of Chicago Press, 1962).
3. Clark, T. N., "Review of *Choice and the Politics of Allocation*," *American Journal of Sociology* 70 (1973), pp. 472-473.
4. Jessop, B., "Review of *Choice and the Politics of Allocation*," *Political Studies* 21 (1973), pp.101-103.
5. Katzner, D. W., "On the Analysis of Systems Containing Non-Quantifiable Elements," *Kybernetes* 2 (1973), pp. 147-155.
6. ________, "On Not Quantifying the Nonquantifiable," *Journal of Post Keynesian Economics* 1, no. 2 (Winter, 1978-79), pp. 113-128. This volume, Essay 4.
7. ________, *Analysis without Measurement* (Cambridge: Cambridge University Press, 1983).
8. Pennock, J. R., "Review of *Choice and the Politics of Allocation*," *American Political Science Review* 67 (1973), pp. 3348-3349.

Index

Aaker, D.A., 257, 272
accountability, 278
Achenbaum, A.A., 272
Ackermann, R.J., 39n, 43
activities, 132-133, 237
  ordering of, 141, 246n
Adelman, I., 84, 103, 111
administration, 236, 241
  efficiency of, 243-245
administrative costs, 224, 236, 241-245
Ajzen, I., 255, 256, 257, 258, 261, 273
Akerlof, G.A., 176, 194
Alchian, A.A., 219, 228
Alker, H.R., 10n, 23
Allen, R.G.D., 71, 74
Almond, G.A., 257, 280
analysis, 29
  and ordinal variables, 198-202
  by example, 49
  measured, 30
  numerical, quantified, quantitative, 30
  objective, 39-40
  purpose of, 49, 177
  qualitative, 30
  with measurement, 30
  without measurement, 30
Anderson, A.B., 1n, 27n, 83n
Andreski, S., 6n, 23
angle of vision, 56
Apter, D.E., 22, 62n, 68, 78, 79, 277, 278, 280, 281, 282, 283, 284, 285, 286, 287, 288, 289, 290, 291, 292, 293, 294, 295, 296, 297
arithmorphic concepts, 118
arithmorphic description of process, 128
arithmorphic functions, 129-130
arithmorphic metaphors, 151-152
arithmorphic relations, 123
arithmorphic similies, 119,151
arithmorphic variables, 120-121
Arrow, K.J., 68, 74, 215, 219
attitude, 255-258
  additive, 264, 266
  and behavior, 256-258
  consistent, 262-263, 266-267, 270-271
  favorable. *See* attitude, positive

independent of, 264, 266-267, 270-271
measurement of, 257-258
more favorable. *See* attitude, more positive
more positive, 257, 261, 270
neutral, 262-263, 266-267, 270-271
perverse, 262-263, 266-267, 270-271
positive, 257-261
reflects, 264, 266-267, 270-271
reverses, 264, 266-267, 270-271
Augustine, 28n, 31
authoritative decisions, 277
authority, 132, 237
number of levels of, 244-245
pyramidal, 132, 237
Azzi, C., 176, 194
balance point, 166-167
Baritz, L., 41n, 43
Barrett, J., 1n
Barro, R.J., 176, 194
Bausor, R., 47n, 83n, 120n, 153, 256n, 273
Becker, G.S., 148, 153, 176, 191, 194
Beckmann, M.J., 220, 228, 231, 251
Behrman, L., 275n
beliefs, 256-258
as subjective probability, 258
Belk, R.W., 258n, 273
Bell, D., 47n, 58
Bellman, R., 214
Bennett, A., 180n, 194
Bentham, J., 10n
Binet, A., 38
Birnberg, T.B., 83, 111
Blackwell, R.D., 254, 258, 273
Blau, P.M., 78, 79
Boland, L.A., 164, 172
Boole, G., 35n, 43
Boorstin, D.J., 41, 43
Booth, C., 42n, 43
Boring, E.G., 39n, 43
Bosworth, D., 194
Boulding, K.E., 176, 194
Bowles, S., 157n, 158n, 159, 168, 169, 173, 175n, 180n, 195, 219n, 220, 228, 231n
Boyle-Lock-Leibniz, vision of, 34
Boyle's Law, 36
break point, 166-167
Brennan, T.J., 77, 78, 79
Brown, L., 164, 172
Brzezinski, Z., 84, 111
bureaucracy, 223, 226-227, 234, 236, 242-243
ideal, 227, 236, 247-250
multidivisional, 234, 244-245
unitary., 234, 244-245
Burtt, E.A., 32, 33n, 34n, 35n, 43
Caldwell, B.J., 49n, 58
Calvo, G.A., 148, 153, 219, 221, 229, 231, 242n, 251
Campbell, D.T., 6n, 23
Cantor, G., 35
cardinal measurement, 178, 202
career-living alternatives, 73
Carnap, R., 282, 297
change, 125
and balance points, 166-167
and breakpoints, 166-167
and institutions, 169
of scale of measurement, 179-182, 184-191, 199, 203-214
Cherry, R., 173
Chipman, J.S., 215
clan, 223, 227, 235, 236, 242-243

ideal, 227, 236, 247-250
Clark, T.N., 282, 297
closeness among countries, 105-111
closeness and taxanomic resemblance, 85
closeness, measures of. *See* measures of closeness
closeness of closeness measures, 91, 109-111
Coase, R.H., 132, 138, 153, 231n, 244n, 251
coercion, 277, 284
more and less of, 288, 295, 296
Cohen, P.C., 37, 43
Coleman, J.S., 280
complete order, state of, 283
convergence, 69, 70
among countries, 84
Coopersmith, S., 78, 80
corroboration, 8-9, 12
Cournot, A., 54, 58, 116, 153
co-workers, 132, 237
Cramer's rule, 269
crisis of abstraction, 55
Crombie, A.C., 32, 33, 43
Curie, M., 176n, 179n, 188n, 195
cycles, 159
amplitude of, 160
and balance points, 167
and break points, 167
long-term. *See* long-term cycles
period of, 160
phase of, 160
short-term, 159-162
trend of, 161
Dalkey, N.C., 73, 74
Danziger, K., 36n, 43
Darwin, C., 31
Davis, L.E., 164, 172
Debreu, G., 54, 58, 117, 153, 219
Defoe, D., 41
demand function (consumer), 259-261
and utility function, 260-261, 266-267, 270-271
attitude properties of, 262-264, 266, 270-271
general properties of, 261
Demsetz, H., 219, 228
Descartes, R., 34
determinant, 203
Hessian (bordered), 190, 268
Jacobian, 209-212
determinate model, 65, 276
Deutsch, K.W., 6, 23
dialectical concept, 119
dialectical reasoning, 119
Diamond, P.A., 192n, 195
differential equations, 212-214
equilibrium path of, 213-214
solution (path) of, 212
director of thc firm, 132, 237
rules issued by, 134, 238, 240-242
Dirichlet, P.G.L., 35
disorder, 283
more, 285, 288, 296
Drago, R.W., 113n, 231n
Drake, S., 34n, 43
v. Duijn, J.J., 159, 173
Duncan, O.D., 78, 79
Dunlop, J.T., 132-153
Dupree, A.H., 41n, 43
Durkheim, E., 38, 39, 43
Eagle Project, 131n
Eberstadt, N., 11, 23
economics profession, 57
efficiency wage, 187-189
effort, 179-182, 221-225

measurement of, 179-180, 221
Ehrenberg, R., 154, 176, 194
Einstein, A., 31, 49, 50, 58
Ellman, M., 84, 111
embourgeoissement, 290
emergence of creative personalities, 72
Engel, J.F., 254, 258, 273
epistemological parity, 5-12
and corroboration, 8-9, 12
and measurement, 9-12
and status of laws, 7-8, 12
equilibrium, internal, 147, 225, 227-228, 240-242, 247-248, 250-251
equilibrium path, 213-214, 285. *See also* time path, stationary
globally stable, 213
locally stable, 213
equity of allocation, 283
equivalence classes, 69, 85, 86, 90, 104-105
adjacent, 88
and closeness, 101-103
between classes, 88
ordering of, 88, 90
ether, 29n
Euclidean distance, 98
and measures of closeness, 98-99
Euclidean geometry, 114-115
Euclidean space, 122
evaluations, 256-258
experimentation, 8-9
explanation, 49, 177
concrete, 177, 184
general, 177, 183-184, 198
of economy-wide behavior, 53-54
of market behavior, 53, 183
factor analysis, 203
Fair, R.C., 176, 192, 195
Feinstein, I.K., 87n, 111
Filer, R.K., 132n, 154
firm size, 244-245
Fishbein, M., 255, 256, 257, 258, 261, 273
Fisher, I., 38, 197
formalism, 113-114. *See also* formalization
in economics, 116-117
in mathematics, 114-116
formalist analysis, 120, 123-124, 148
and arithmomorphic metaphors, 151-152
and arithmomorphic similies, 151
criticisms of, 149-150
formalization, 50-53. *See also* formalism
and abstraction, 51
and accordances with reality, 50
and measurement, 51
as analogies, 51
as metaphors, 51
dissatisfaction with, 55-56
justifications for use of, 54
too much, 56-58
Fromm, E., 78, 80
function (Dirichlet definition), 35, 64, 123
administrative cost, 224
and process, 127-130
composition of, 66, 124
constant, 263
demand (consumer), 259-261. *See also* demand function
density, 73
distribution, 73
goals and premises, 138, 240
incentive, 135-136, 223, 238-239
input demand, 137

institution, 165
inverse of, 66
linear, 205
maximization of, 185-191, 199. *See also* profit maximization and utility maximiation
order preserving, 263
order reversing, 263
output supply, 137
probability, 73
production, 131, 135, 180, 222, 238
profit, 224, 239, 244. *See also* profit
Slutsky, 268
strictly concave, 205
strictly convex, 205
utility, 139, 200-201, 225, 240, 260. *See also* utility function
Gaster, T.H., 31n, 43
Galileo, 11, 31, 33, 34, 35, 36, 37, 39, 41
Georgescu-Roegen, N., 77, 79, 80, 118, 119, 125, 128, 129, 154
general equilibrium, existence of, 53, 279
general equilibrium, model of, 52-54, 279
general equilibrium, stability of, 53, 279
general equilibrium, uniqueness of, 53, 279
Gigerenzer, G., 38n, 43
Gintis, H., 79, 80, 132, 136n, 138n, 141, 143n, 146n, 154, 175n, 224, 229, 231n, 237, 239n, 246n, 250n, 251
Gödel, K., 116
Goodenough, W.H., 62n, 74, 78, 80
Goodman, G.J.W. *See* Smith, A. (pseud.)
Goodman, L.A., 31n, 44
Gordon, D.M., 158n, 159, 168, 169, 173, 180n, 195
Gorman, T., 54, 58
Gould, S.J., 28n, 40, 44
Granger, G.G., 58
Grant, E., 33n, 44
Gregson, R.A.M., 83n, 111
Guthrie, K.S., 31n, 44
Haas, P., 1n
Hagen, E., 62n, 71, 72, 74
Hahn, F.H., 68, 74
Hansen, A.H., 173
Harrod, R.F., 59
Hausman, J.H., 192n, 195
von Hayek, F.A., 175, 176, 192, 195
Heath, T.L., 31n, 44
Heathfield, D.F., 194
Heim, C.E., 27n
Heisenberg uncertainty principle, 42-43
Helliwell, J.F., 176, 195
Hessian determinant (bordered), 190, 268
Hessian matrix (bordered), 268
Hicks, J., 47, 56, 58
Hofstadter, D.R., 122, 154
Hook's Law, 36
Hoover, E.M., 84, 111
Horowitz, I., 84, 112
Huntington, S.P., 84, 111
Hurwicz, L., 215
Hutchison, T.W., 6, 23, 55, 58
ideology, 278
incentive function, 135-136, 223, 238-239
incentive motivated, 141, 246

incentives, more highly motivated by, 142
incentives, non-decreasing, 141, 247
industrialization, 291
Infeld, L., 49, 50, 58
influence, 138, 235, 240
  more highly motivated by, 142
  non-decreasing, 141, 247
  vertical, 142, 246
information, 236, 277, 284
  maximize, 288
  more and less of, 295, 296
institution, 164-165
  and change, 169
  as functional relation, 165
intentions, 256-258
internalize values of the firm, 142, 247
invisible hand, 145, 234
Janowitz, M., 235n, 251
Jessop, B., 282, 297
Jevons, W.S., 10n, 24, 38, 54, 58, 116, 154
Johnson, C., 112
Kaldor, N., 52n, 58
Kalman, P.J., 254n, 273
Kalt, J.P., 176, 195
Kamarck, A.M., 27n, 28n
Kant, I., 37, 44
Karlin, S., 215
Katouzian, H., 47n, 51n, 56, 57, 59
Katz, E., 78, 80
Katzner, D.W., 3n, 8n, 12n, 24, 28n, 30n, 37n, 42n, 44, 48n, 51n, 59, 67, 68, 71, 73, 74, 79, 80, 81, 85n, 103n, 111, 114, 117, 121n, 122, 124, 132, 136n, 138n, 139n, 141, 143n, 146n, 154, 165n, 168n, 170n, 173, 175n, 177, 178n, 179n, 183n, 194, 195, 197, 198, 200, 201, 203, 206n, 214, 220n, 221n, 224, 225, 229, 237, 239n, 246n, 250n, 251, 254, 255, 256n, 259n, 260, 261, 268, 269, 273, 282, 283, 286, 287, 297
Kaufman, C., 275n
Kelvin, (W. Thompson), 32, 46, 117, 175, 195
  dictum of, 27, 29n, 117, 155, 175
Kemeny, J.G., 18, 91, 100n, 112
Kemeny-Snell measures, 91, 100n, 101, 109
Kendall, M.G., 109n
Kepler, J., 33
Kerr, C., 84, 112
Keynes, J.M., 32, 44, 50n, 59
Kidder, T., 131n, 154
Kincaid, H., 2, 7n, 24
Kindahl, J.K., 83n
Kirman, A., 53n, 59
Klammer, A., 47n, 59
Kline, M., 31n, 32n, 34n, 35, 44, 114, 153, 154
Knight, F.H., 29n
Kollat, D.T., 254, 258, 273
Koyré, A., 34n, 44
Kristol., I., 47n, 58
Krüger, M., 157n
Kruskal, J.B., 83n, 112
Kuhn, T.S., 36, 44
Kula, W., 31n, 44
Kuznets, S., 84, 112
labor market, 139-140
Lagrange, J.L., 265, 268
Lang, K., 236n, 252
Lauterbach, A., 84, 112
laws, 7
  status of, 7-8, 12
Lazarsfeld, P.F., 78, 80

Lazear, E.P., 219, 229
Liebenstein, H., 132, 145n, 154, 252
LePlay, F., 39, 44
Lerner, D., 38n, 40n, 44
Levins, R.A., 81
Lévy-Garboua, L., 80, 154, 229, 251
Lewis, H.G., 176, 191, 194
Lewis, R., 73, 74
Liapunov, A.M., 71
Lincoln, A., 48
logic, Aristotelian (deductive), 78, 119
long-term cycles, 159, 161-162
  and institutions, 168
Lordstown plant, 131n, 133n, 152
Lundberg, G.A., 6, 24, 40, 44
Machlup, F., 53n, 59
Madden, T.J., 253n
marginal ultility, 260
market equilibrium, 53, 152, 183
  existence of, 53, 183
  interpretation of, 52-53, 183
  stability of, 53
  uniqueness of, 53
market form, 223-224, 243
  ideal, 247-248, 251
Marshall, A., 55, 59, 152, 154
Martin, M., 7n, 24
materialism, philosophical, 3
matrix, 203
  eigenvalues of, 204
  indecomposable, 204
  inverse of, 203
  positive definite, 204
maximization and changes of scale, 185-191, 199
maximization and ordinal measurement, 199-202
maximization of profit, 137, 187-189, 244, 248
maximization of utility, 139, 189-191, 200, 225, 240, 260-261
McClosky, D.N., 29n, 44, 47n, 52n, 59, 151, 154
McIntyre, L.C., 7n, 24
measurement, 9, 12, 15, 121, 178
  absence of, 9-15
  and institutions, 167-168
  cardinal, 178, 202
  changes of scale of, 179-182, 184-191, 199, 203-214
  myth of synonymity of, 39-40, 42
  necessity for explanation, 184
  nominal, 178
  ordinal, 178, 198-202
  ratio, 178-202
measures of closeness, 85-91
  and equivalence classes, 101-103
  and Euclidean distance, 98-99
  applied to Adelman-Morris data, 105-111
  Kemeny-Snell measure, 91, 100n, 101, 109
  metric characteristics of, 99-101
  properties of, 91-97
Menard, C., 231n
Mendelsohn, E., 41n, 44
Menninger, K., 33n, 45
metaphors, 51-52, 151-152
metrics, 99
  and measures of closeness, 99, 100n
Meyer, A.G., 84, 112
Meyerson, E., 118, 154
Michelson, A.A., 29n
military, 235, 236, 242-243
  ideal, 236, 247-251
Mirowski, P., 47n, 48n, 59, 113n,

120n, 124n, 154, 251
misplaced concreteness, fallacy of, 53n
model, 49, 177
arithmomorphic, 19n
as analogy, 51
as metaphor, 51
efficiency wage, 187-189
general equilibrium, 52-54
of (political) development, 283-287
of isolated market, 52-53
Morishima, M., 57, 59
Morley, E.W., 29n
Morris, C.T., 84, 103, 111
Mosteller, F., 31n, 45
multiplier analysis, 71
Mumford, L., 40n, 45
Murphy, K.H., 87n, 111
Myers, J.G., 257, 272
Myrdal, G., 39n, 45, 56, 59
myth of synonymity, 39-40, 42
Newton, I., 31
Neyman-Pearson lemma, 74
Noble, D.F., 41n, 45
nominal measurement, 178
non-Euclidean geometry, 115
non-Euclidean space, 122
North, D.C., 164-172
objects, ordering of, 69, 85, 86, 103-105, 204, 262, 288
objects, properties of, 69-85
objects, sequence of, 69, 288
objects, set of, 63, 103
objects, topology for, 69
Ordeshook, P.C., 70, 75
ordinal measurement, 178, 198-202
ordinal utility, 200-202
organization, 233
bureaucracy, 223, 226-227, 234, 236, 242-243
clan, 223, 227, 235, 236, 242-243
market form, 233, 243
military, 235, 236, 242-243
O'Toole, J., 131n, 133n, 154
Ouchi, W.G., 220, 223, 229, 233, 234n, 235n, 236n, 243n, 252
Owens, L., 27n
Oxford calculators, 33n
parameters, economic, 163
parameters, institutionally determined, 157, 170-172
parameters, non-economic, 163
Pareteo, V., 62n, 68, 75, 116, 154, 197
Pareto optimal (internal), 146-147, 226-228, 249-251
Pareto superior (internal), 226
Parsons, T., 62n, 68, 75
participation, 283
high, 288
Pavlov, I.P., 38,
Pearce, I.F., 61n
Pearl, R. 32, 45,
Pennock, J.R., 282, 297
perfectly competitive model. *See* general equilibrium, model of
periodic relation, 70-71
globally stable time path of, 71
stationary path of, 70
time path of, 70
Petty, W., 38, 39, 45
Pfanzagl, J., 69, 75, 86n, 112, 121n, 122n, 154, 262, 273
Plato, 32, 45
policy, 278
political arithmetic, 38
political elites, 292-294
political norms, 283

political system, 278-279, 284
as equilibrium point, 279
bureaucratic, 284
mobilization, 278, 284, 293-294
reconciliation, 278, 284, 293-294
theocratic, 284
political structure, 278-279
Porter, T.M., 27n, 37, 39n, 45
prediction, 8, 177-178, 193
Prest, A.R., 48, 57, 59
primary test, 276, 279
probability, 73
process, 125
and function, 127-130
arithmomorphic representation of, 125-129, 129
boundary of, 126
inputs of, 126
interval of duration of, 126, 127
outputs of, 126
profit, 136, 224, 239, 244
maximization of, 137, 187-189, 244, 248
profit-efficient, 136-137, 224-225, 239-240
proxies, 10n, 176, 191-193
pseudo-metrics, 99
and measures of closeness, 99-101
Putnam, R.D., 176, 195
quality of life, 22-23, 177
quantophrenia, 32
radicalization, 290
ratio measurement, 178, 202
reasonable agreement, 36-37
regression analysis, 203
relations, 64
arithmomorphic, 123
as objects, 90-91
" borders on" , 102
equivalence, 69, 85, 86
institution, 165
measured, 30
political structure, 278
qualitative, 30
quantitative, 30
simultaneous. *See* simultaneous relations
representation claims, 292-294
interest, 292-294
populist, 292-294
professional, 292-294
Resnick, S.A., 47n, 83, 111
Ricardo, D., 55
Ricci, D.M., 6n, 24
Richter, M.K., 215
Riker, W.H., 70, 75
Robertson, T.S., 257, 273
Robinson, W.S., 70, 75
role allocation, 283
role classification of groups, 291
bourgeous radical, 291
differentiated, 291
functional status elite, 291
functionally superfluous, 291
residual fused, 291
Rothschild, E., 131n, 154
Routh, G., 47n, 58, 59, 60
Rudin, W., 206, 209, 215
rules, 133-134, 237-238
ordering of, 141, 246n
Russell, B., 35n, 45, 119, 154
Russo, J.E., 79, 80
Sah, R.K., 231, 252
Schaffer, S., 36n, 45
schools of mathematics, 115-116
formalist, 116
intuitionist, 115
logistic, 115

set-theoretic, 115
Schor, J.B., 180n, 195
Schorer, M., 41, 45
Schotter, A., 164, 173
science, good, 2
science, interaction with society, 41-42
science, objective, 39
myth of synonymity of, 39-40, 42
science, physical and social, 2-5
secondary test, 276, 279
Selznick, P., 164, 172
semigroup, 124
Servos, J.W., 27n,
sets, 63
bounded, 204
of activities, 132-133
of human values, 63
of rules, 133-134
orderings on, 69, 85, 86, 103-105, 204
union of, 204
Shackle, G.L.S., 7, 8n, 24
Shapin, S., 36n, 45
Shapiro, C., 182, 183, 195
Shephard, W.G., 231n
Shryock, R.H., 36n, 37n, 45
Simon, H.A., 132, 138, 154
simultaneous equations, 208. *See also* simultaneous relations
and transformations of scale, 209-212
Jacobian of, 209-212
solutions of, 208-212
simultaneous relations, 65-68, 276-277. *See also* simultaneous equations
cycles of, 67-68
exactly determined, 65, 276
internally consistent, 65
model of (political) development, 283-287
overdetermined, 65, 276
political structure, 278
shifting, 277
solutions of, 65, 67, 68
underdetermined, 65, l276
skills, more of, 142
skills, receptive to new, 143
Sleigh, R.C., jr., 27n
Smith, A., 145, 154, 231, 234, 252
Smith, A. (pseud. G.J.W. Goodman), 29n, 45
Smith-Gavine, S., 180n, 194
Sneath, P.H.A., 83n, 85n, 86n, 89n, 111
Snell, J.L., 18, 91, 100n, 112
Snyder, D., 73, 74
social states, 289
industrial, 289
modernizing, 289
traditional, 289
social structure of accumulation, 158n, 159, 168-169
societal norms, 283. *See also* values of society
Socrates, 32
Socratic method, 119
Sokal, R.R., 83n, 85n, 86n, 89n, 111
Solow, R.M., 54, 59
Sonnenschein, H.F., 201, 215
Sorokin, P.A., 32, 45
Spector, B.I., 84, 112
Spengler, J.J., 37n, 38n, 45
Spulber, N., 84, 112
Standen, A.., 29n, 46
state of development, 283
more and less of, 285, 288, 289,

296
maximize, 288
state of society, 288
sequences of, 288, 290-291
Steedman, I., 176n, 179n, 188n, 195
Stiglitz, J.E., 182, 183, 187n, 195, 231, 252
Stokes, R.G., 1n
storytelling, 49
stratification, 292-294
stratification types, 289
differentiated, 289
functional, 289
fused, 289
segmentary, 289
subordinate, 132, 231-232, 237
subprocesses, 126-127
supervisor, 132, 231-232, 237
Suppes, P., 54, 60, 215
synonymity, myth of, 39-40, 42
tau test, 74, 109n
taxonomic resemblance, 83, 85
Thomson, W. *See* Kelvin
time, historical, 3
time, instant of, 125
time, logical, 3n
time path (sequence), 68, 70, 288, 290-291
cyclic, 170, 285
stability of, 71
stationary, 70, 170, 285. *See also* equilibrium path
Tinbergen, J., 32, 44, 84, 112
Tolstoy, L., 29n, 46
Toulmin, S., 6n, 24
transformations, admissible (permissible), 179-182, 202, 206-207
and derivatives, 184-185
and function properties, 205-206
and matrix properties, 203-204
and maximization, 185-191
and sets, 204
and simultaneous equations, 209-212
trend, 161
triangle inequality, 99
unanticipated circumstances, 258
unreconcilable anomalies, 36-37
utility function, 139, 200-201, 225, 240, 260
and demand functions, 260-261, 266-267, 270-271
altitude properties of, 264, 266-267, 270-271
general properties of, 260
utility maximization, 139, 189-191, 200, 225, 240, 260-261
Uzawa, H., 200, 215
values of society, 277. *See also* societal norms
variable, 63
arithmomorphic, 120-121
dependent, 64
human values, 63
independent, 64
measured, 29
non-quantified, qualitative, 30
numerical, quantified, quantitative, 29
random, 73
Vickers, D., viii, 1n, 3n, 7, 24, 27n, 47n, 83n, 113n, 157n, 175n, 197n, 203, 215, 219n, 231n, 253n
Virginia, State of, 28n
Wallace, D.L, 31n, 45
Walras, L., 38, 52n, 54, 60, 116, 154, 279, 280
Ward, B., 47n, 49n, 60

Warren, D.D., 81
Watson, J.B., 39, 46
Weber, M., 31, 46, 62n, 75
Weingart, P., 45
Weintraub, E.R., 54, 56, 60, 82
Weintraub, S., 61n
Weisskopf, T.E., 158n, 159, 168, 169, 173, 180n, 195
Wellisz, S., 148, 153, 219, 221, 229, 231, 242n, 251
Whitley, R., 45
Whyte, W.F., 133n, 154
Wiles, P., 47n, 58, 59, 60
Williamson, O.E., 148, 154, 220, 229, 231, 233n, 234n, 244n, 252
Willis, C., 175n
Wise, M.N., 36n, 46
Wish, M., 83n, 112
Wittgenstein, L., 123, 140, 150
Wolff, R.P., 27n
Woo, H.K.H., 47n, 51n, 60
Woolf, H., 44, 45
worker above, 132
worker below, 132
worker, more skilled, 142-143
worker's activities (set), 132-133
worker's rules (set), 133-134
Wright, C., 123, 154
X-inefficiency, 145n, 249n
Zartman, I.W., 84, 112
Zupan, M.A., 176, 195

GPSR Compliance

The European Union's (EU) General Product Safety Regulation (GPSR) is a set of rules that requires consumer products to be safe and our obligations to ensure this.

If you have any concerns about our products, you can contact us on ProductSafety@springernature.com

In case Publisher is established outside the EU, the EU authorized representative is:

Springer Nature Customer Service Center GmbH
Europaplatz 3
69115 Heidelberg, Germany

Batch number: 10704035

Printed by Printforce, the Netherlands